LATIN LITERATURE FROM
SENECA TO JUVENAL

LATIN LITERATURE FROM SENECA TO JUVENAL

A Critical Study

G. O. HUTCHINSON

CLARENDON PRESS · OXFORD

1993

Oxford University Press, Walton Street, Oxford OX2 6DP

Oxford   New York   Toronto
Delhi   Bombay   Calcutta   Madras   Karachi
Petaling Jaya   Singapore   Hong Kong   Tokyo
Nairobi   Dar es Salaam   Cape Town
Melbourne   Auckland

and associated companies in
Berlin   Ibadan

Oxford is a trade mark of Oxford University Press

Published in the United States
by Oxford University Press, New York

© G. O. Hutchinson 1993

British Library Cataloguing in Publication Data
Data available

Library of Congress Cataloging-in-Publication Data
Latin literature from Seneca to Juvenal: a critical study
G.O. Hutchinson.
Includes bibliographical references and index.
1. Latin literature—History and criticism.   I. Title.
PA6042.H88   1992   870.9'001—dc20   92-17935
ISBN 0-19-814690-6

Typeset by BP Integraphics Ltd, Bath, Avon
Printed in Great Britain by
Bookcraft (Bath) Ltd.,
Midsomer Norton

To my parents, with love

PREFACE

An Introduction will ensue; I can confine myself, with pleasure, to the expression of thanks. I am deeply grateful to my friend Professor Otto Zwierlein for the heartening encouragement he has given to my thoughts and my project, ever since the day when an anxious young lecturer attempted to address on Senecan tragedy both undergraduates studying it as a fifth of one paper and the world's leading expert on the tragedies of Seneca. However, he has seen none of this book, and shares no blame for anything it contains. The Oxford University Press have not only consented to publish the work, but have aided it and me by their tolerance and their skilled and meticulous labour. My greatest debt is as ever to my dear wife. She has always been ready with wise advice, and has fortified me whenever daunted (perhaps once a week) by the size of my undertaking. I cannot forbear from mentioning, on this as on most occasions, our daughter Isobel, whose sweet and sunny temper has lit up the last two years, and kept the writing of books firmly to its proper place in the scheme of things.

Exeter College, Oxford, April 1992   G. O. H.

CONTENTS

ABBREVIATIONS

Periodicals and the like are cited approximately as in *L'Année philologique*.

ANRW   *Aufstieg und Niedergang der römischen Welt*, ed. H. Temporini and W. Haase (Berlin and New York 1972–).

CIL   *Corpus Inscriptionum Latinarum* (Berlin 1863–).

CLE   F. Bücheler, *Carmina Latina Epigraphica*, 2 vols. with Supplement by E. Lommatzsch (Leipzig 1895–1926).

ILS   H. Dessau, *Inscriptiones Latinae Selectae* (Berlin 1892–1916).

LIMC   *Lexicon Iconographicum Mythologiae Classicae* (Zurich and Munich 1981–).

P. Oxy.   *The Oxyrhynchus Papyri* (London 1898–).

P. Turner   *Papyri Greek and Egyptian, Edited by Various Hands in Honour of Eric Gardner Turner* (Graeco-Roman Memoirs, 68, London 1981).

RE   *Real-Encyclopädie der classischen Altertumswissenschaft* (Stuttgart 1894–).

RIC I^2 C. H. V. Sutherland and R. A. G. Carson, *The Roman Imperial Coinage, I (2nd edn.): From 31 B.C. to A.D. 69* (London 1984).

SVF   H. von Arnim, *Stoicorum Veterum Fragmenta* (Leipzig 1903–24).

AUTHORS AND EMPERORS

The following lists a few dates, and occasionally other items, for the authors discussed and one or two earlier writers, and gives the dates of the emperors; the object is only to help those less familiar with the period to find some bearings, not to give outline biographies. The dates for authors are often the subject of dispute.

1. Authors

MANILIUS: writing *Astronomica* after (AD) 9; probably not continued into Tiberius' reign.

OVID: d. 17?

ELDER SENECA: d. *c*.39; extant work, written in old age, provides extracts from declamations and accounts of declaimers from after 38 BC to within the reign of Tiberius.

YOUNGER SENECA: son of Elder Seneca; b., on standard view, 4–1 BC;[1] exiled 41, returns prob. 49 to teach Nero; becomes Nero's adviser; begins to withdraw from public life 62; killed in aftermath of Pisonian conspiracy 65. Prose works from before 41 (*Ad Marciam*) to 65; of long works, *De Beneficiis* pub. 56–64; *Naturales Quaestiones* being written in 62; *Epistulae Morales* prob. written from 63 to 64 or 65; date of tragedies uncertain.

PERSIUS: b. 34, d. 62. Stoic, devoted to Stoic L. Annaeus Cornutus; prob. friend of Lucan; left book of *Satires* unfinished.

LUCAN: nephew of Seneca; b. 39; involved in Pisonian conspiracy, through Nero's enmity to his poetry, according to Tacitus (*Ann.* xv. 49. 3); killed 65.

PETRONIUS: *Satyricon* prob. close in date to Lucan's *De Bello Civili*; normally ascribed to Nero's friend (consul; killed 66), by no means with certainty.[2]

ELDER PLINY: b. 23–4; *Natural History* pub. 77; d. 79; also historian; procurator of Hispania Tarraconensis and adviser of Vespasian.

---

[1] If Pollio died in AD 5 (scarcely later, granted the transposition in Tac. *Dial.* 17. 6), then Sen. *Tranq.* 17. 7 might suggest that Seneca was born earlier than 4 BC.

[2] The absolute Arbiter as a posthumous sobriquet sounds curious.

QUINTILIAN: *Institutio Oratoria* pub. some time between 86 and 96, after retirement from teaching; *De Causis Corruptae Eloquentiae* (lost) written a few years before.

VALERIUS FLACCUS: prob. started *Argonautica* before Vespasian's death (June 79), and was writing after it (iv. 507–9); hence poem unrevised and presumably, as in MSS, unfinished; Quint. x. 1. 90 mentions his dying 'recently'.

SILIUS ITALICUS: b. by 29; orator, then poet; consul 68, under Vespasian proconsul of Asia; d. after 99, by *c.*104. *Punica* composed under Domitian: started *c.*83; being composed in 88, part prob. pub. by 92, some after 93, all by 96.

STATIUS: *Thebaid* pub. not long before 93, and took 12 years to write; *Silvae* i. 5 written before publication of *Thebaid*, i. *praef.* after; *Silv.* iv: 95; *Achilleid* started by 95, left unfinished at death, presumably not long after 95; *Silv.* v prob. pub. posthumously.

MARTIAL: b. *c.*40; *Spectacula*: 80; *Xenia* and *Apophoreta* (xiii–xiv): 83 or later; i: 85 or later; xi: 96, after Domitian's death; xii: 101 or 102; d. by *c.*104.

YOUNGER PLINY: nephew of Elder Pliny; b. 61–2; orator; suffect consul 100, when delivers *Panegyricus*; *Letters* i–ix (to friends), pub. from 98 to 109 or after; x (to Trajan) written during governorship of Bithynia at end of life, prob. pub. posthumously; d. before 117, prob. by 115.

TACITUS: b. *c.*56; orator; suffect consul 97; proconsul of Asia in 112–13 or 113–14; *Agricola* and *Germania* pub. 98; date of *Dialogus* uncertain, prob. written before Plin. *Ep.* ix. 10. 2; writing *Histories* 106 or 107; *Annals* iv written before 116.

JUVENAL: poem 6: 116 or later; 7 will refer to Hadrian; 13–16 between 127 and 132.

2. Emperors

Tiberius	14–37	Vespasian	69–79
Gaius	37–41	Titus	79–81
Claudius	41–54	Domitian	81–96
Nero	54–68	Nerva	96–98
Galba	68–69	Trajan	98–117
Otho	69	Hadrian	117–138
Vitellius	69		

INTRODUCTION

THIS book aspires to further a little the growing interest in a major and magnificent period of Latin literature. Of recent years, most of the texts have been splendidly edited; on individual works, and parts of them, excellent commentaries and valuable studies have been produced. There remains a place, perhaps, for criticism which seeks to take both a larger and a closer view, both exploring the similarities and differences between various kinds of literature in the period, and bringing out in detail some of the artistry and the basic aesthetic concerns that underlie it. Classicists tend to be more familiar with some authors of this time than with its literature in general; and undergraduates, and even scholars, often dwell insufficiently on the extraordinary manner of writing in many of the authors, which so crucially affects the character of their works.

No book could be more remote than this from a literary history. It makes no attempt to offer a comprehensive and justly proportioned account, or to provide the basic facts and background essential for an informed understanding. Within the period, it is brutally selective in the choice of authors and works and in the proportions of treatment, and it pursues, one must emphasize, only a very few aspects of the literature. Yet the hope is that it may give to readers little acquainted with the period a curiosity to read more of its literature for themselves, and to readers better acquainted some personal reactions, sprung from thought and study, which it might interest them to reflect on.

The work concerns itself particularly with the grander genres, especially with the 'high' poetry and the prose most closely related to it, that of Seneca: it is in these regions, I think, that a just understanding is hardest for a modern audience. The themes the book especially follows are those of greatness and reality (with their converses), and to a lesser extent form. These terms are used capaciously, to connect rather than divide. 'Greatness' denotes sublimity or elevation in style, grandeur in subject-matter, splendour in morality. 'Reality' embraces various sorts of truth, philosophical verities, historical fact, the actuality of everyday, and can relate to the world of a work or the author's detailed handling of the physical or the spiritual. 'Form' covers every scale of design, from the whole work to the paragraph, line, or sentence. In some respects the book extends and develops the lines of thought that provided the framework for an earlier book on a different period; that book, in discussing many particular poems, sought among other things to trace in them the degrees and varieties of tonal complication. The present work, however, adopts a quite different design. It concerns itself far more with genre, and hence is organized by themes rather than authors. It is also much more concerned with the detail of writing, and hence deals less with complete works and more with representative passages. The discussion of particular moments lies at the heart of the book, and provides in total a sample of the basis for my views, and material that readers can ponder themselves. Individual quotations, and indeed discussions, have been kept as brief as seemed possible; but I fear the effort of reading the Latin citations carefully cannot be dispensed with. The fine originals have much more pleasure to give the reader than my miserable renderings, which aim only to assist comprehension.

Attention is restricted almost entirely to the Latin literature of the period itself. Even earlier Latin literature receives, save in the notes, only occasional glances. It is not that I believe the links slight: on the contrary, the unity of post-Republican Latin literature is in my opinion much more important than changes after or during Augustus. But this large and difficult subject resists brief treatment. Nor has it been to the purpose to stress subdivisions of period within our period; with poetry this procedure can seem rather to obscure affinity and over-schematize difference. The book aims within its confines to allow the reader to consider divergences and similarities within a cohesive body of literature, richly interconnected.

Little attempt is made to indicate or to engage directly with the opinions of others. The reason for this is not of course arrogance or contempt, but a wish to aid clarity, avoid polemic, and concentrate attention on the primary material. The notes list on various topics some of the works I have found interesting; there is much that I should like to have seen but have not, and not a little that has reached me too late to be mentioned. On all subjects outside this literature itself references to scholarship are slight and capricious. Otherwise the notes offer a little material for more scholarly readers; for the most part, they do not simply repeat what is available in the standard commentaries. They are still more gracelessly compressed than the text itself.

The outline of the book may be briefly adumbrated. The first two chapters will look directly at genre within this period; our view will here be confined to statements and works from this period itself. We shall see how significant the notions are of reality and greatness, and begin to see what complexities attach to them. The third and fourth chapters will investigate vital aspects of the writing which relate to those themes; they will show us characteristics and differences of authors and of genres. In the fifth chapter the scope will expand to the consideration of form on various levels; the connections of structure and greatness will also occupy us. The last four chapters will use particular areas of content to display the 'higher' genres in aspects which bring them together and aspects which thrust them apart. These areas are of especial importance for the two primary themes of the book. The emphasis will be on episodes and substantial passages: we shall thus see more fully and vividly in action the art and the notions that we have pondered before. The book will touch on many topics not mentioned here; but the object of its design is not so much to present multifarious and separate features as to follow some basic conceptions into various regions, and in doing so to conjoin the regions and enrich the conceptions.

The intended omissions of the book are innumerable; the unwanted failings are sufficiently abundant. Yet readers with patience and sympathy enough to discern what it attempts to offer may, I fervently hope, find something to reward them, not from my inadequate words, but from the glorious literature for which I so desire to excite or enhance their enthusiasm.

CONCEPTIONS OF GENRE: CRITICISM IN PROSE, 'LOWER' POETRY

GENRE is an evident fact of this literature. If we contemplate the literature as from the air, we must immediately be struck by stark and primary divisions and chasms, between poetry and prose, philosophy and history, epic and epigram. What these divisions of genre entail is a more complicated question; the book as a whole will only try to illuminate some of the differences and likenesses between some of the genres. In the first two chapters we will seek some preliminary orientation in this landscape, and in doing so will introduce the book's principal themes of greatness (sublimity, grandeur) and reality (truth). (Cf. pp. 1 f.) Our attention will be devoted almost exclusively to the Latin literature of this period, in the generic scene that it displays and in the comments on genre that it offers. This path has been chosen as one of special and immediate interest for this book, not as the only valid route. It will not be possible to consider either ancient literary criticism in general or the history of the individual genres; these topics, fundamental but enormous, would not lead us to very different conclusions.

In this chapter we will consider, firstly, how genre is explicitly presented in literature of this period, and particularly, what is most revealing for us, how each author treats genres which he does not regard as his own; we shall pursue the treatment, in critical statements, of reality and greatness, which are their predominating concerns. In the second half of this chapter, which deals with poetry other than tragedy and epic, we shall also consider for ourselves the role of reality and greatness in these poets, and some related aspects; that will be our sole purpose in the second chapter, where we consider some prose, and epic and tragedy.

In considering statements about genre, we are not seeking to discover authoritative utterances, which we can then simply apply to the literature of the time. As plain literary criticism, they are very frequently one-sided, unsophisticated, and heavily indebted to critical convention from other periods. Moreover, as we shall see, they relate to their author's genre, stance, and literary intentions in such a way that it would be uncritical merely to remove them from their setting and assign them an absolute validity. And yet the statements of prose authors in particular often lie at the root of many gnarled and venerable prejudices about the period; so that the purpose will partly be the negative one of displaying their relativity through displaying their broad context. They must not be used to set limits on criticism; but their positive interest is considerable. They enable us to discern, as will gradually emerge, conventional expectations of a genre which its authors can exploit and flout. They show the felt importance of the particular topics we wish to pursue, and so stimulate us to try those conceptions for ourselves against the texts. They suggest too something of the richness of those conceptions: the interconnected areas they cover and the manifold ways in which they can be interpreted and related. Finally, they offer us a lively picture of the large and animated generic scene, of one genre conflicting with another, playing with another, or defining itself. This gives us insight both into some of the purposes actually served by conceptions of genre, and into vital aspects of the individual authors' work, which is among the book's foremost concerns.[1]

We look first at **Quintilian**, an author particularly significant for modern judgements. We shall consider first reality, then sublimity. Quintilian's attitude to literature, in his work on educating the orator, is shaped by his conviction of the supreme significance of oratory, great as any gift of Providence to man.[2] Oratory is supreme by virtue of its close relation to reality, the practical reality which matters most for Quintilian, that of Roman public life and the orator's virtuous and vital action. Hence he often deplores vehemently the unnaturalness of declamation, as

---

[1] A few works may be mentioned here as of relevance to ideas of genre in the period generally: Norden (1915), Leeman (1963); Dams (1970); Koster (1970); Häußler (1978); Russell (1981a), esp. ch. 10; id. (1989); Heldmann (1982); Steinmetz (1982); Kennedy (1989); Feeney (1991), 5–56, 250–69.

[2] This notion is placed very prominently at the end of the work, cf. also xii. 1. 2 (cf. Isocr. iii. 5 f.; Cic. *Inv.* i. 2 f.), i. 12. 18 (end of first book), i. 10. 7. On Quintilian's literary criticism and related matters cf. Rocheblave (1890); Steinmetz (1964); Gelzer (1970); Winterbottom (1983); Brink (1989); Ax (1990).

commonly practised (declamations are imaginary speeches produced by teachers of rhetoric and their pupils on fictitious or
historical and mythical themes). Declamations should prepare,
Quintilian stresses, for real oratory. In fact, he says, they aim at
pleasure alone, and involve themselves unduly in fanciful language and silly fiction. (See ii. 10, characteristic in its balance, and
especially v. 12. 17–23, where unpracticality, pleasure, and perverted use are combined in lavish images of effeminacy and castra-
tion.) Now poetry is linked with declamation in its unreality and
its concern only with pleasure (see ii. 10. 5, viii. 6. 17, x. 1. 28).
However, unreality belongs in poetry, and is connected with its
greatness; hence too its unnaturalness of language, which is also
excused by the alleged necessity of metre (x. 1. 29, viii. 6. 17; wryly
ironic i. 8. 14).[3] Yet, in spite of his respect for literary culture,
Quintilian lets us feel, not just that poetry is limited in its utility to
the orator, but that ultimately oratory is pre-eminent in value. He
does so even when introducing his great literary reading-list for
the orator. His general paragraph on poetry (x. 1. 27–30) undergoes a shift. At the start he stresses its sublimity of subject and
language; it is good relaxation for the orator with his more ordinary but more practical concerns. But he moves to contrast the
trivialities of its artificial and ornamental diction with the significance and practicality of oratorical warfare: *nos vero armatos stare in
acie et summis de rebus decernere,* 'but we, let us remember, stand in
arms in the battle-line, fighting over things of supreme importance' (x. 1. 29). Quintilian is indeed displaying balance and
deterring orators from misappropriating poetical language; but
the compelling force with which he deploys in this passage his
favourite military imagery—Roman, real, and yet glamorous—
also wins the imagination for his genre.[4]

His introduction proceeds to history, moving swiftly to stress its
difference from oratory: he uses the theme of its closeness to
poetry.[5] This closeness, its need to avert monotony, and its lack of

---

[3] Cicero is more moderate (*Or.* 67).

[4] Compare with x. 1. 30 viii. 3. 2, 5. On this (traditional) area of imagery in Quintilian,
see Aßfahl (1932), 84–98; with the present context we should see in 30 some pointed play on
the gorgeous arms of martial epic.

[5] Cf. Wiseman (1979), ch. 9. In ii. 4. 18 f. (cf. 4. 2) Quintilian in fact implies the general
difference between poets and Roman historians in relation to the reality of their subject-
matter (not in question in x. 1. 31–3), and shows an awareness of historians' critical reserve
and controversy. In iii. 8. 67–70 he uses history to assail declamation.

practical purpose, lead it to abnormal language. He sets, in effect, historical athletes against oratorical soldiers, and the many-hued robe of history against the dust in which orators fight: he thus gives us even here some sense that, while oratory may be less elevated and less gorgeous (a graceful concession), it is ultimately more serious, intense, and valorous.[6] Much more definite and important is his engagement with philosophy in Book xii. Philosophy is valuable, in itself and oratorically; but the philosophers' style of life removes them from the reality that matters. Quintilian wishes to produce in his ideal orator *Romanum quendam ... sapientem*, a 'wise man' who is a true Roman (so he strikingly reformulates the philosopher's ideal), a man who will not argue in private but act in the state (xii. 2. 7). He treats of the various philosophical schools with light mockery; the perfect orator's task (the virtuous practice of eloquence) is a *maius ... opus atque praestantius*, a greater and more splendid task (xii. 2. 27): the ringing phrase marks the sublimity with which he invests his ideal. Philosophers regard their own genre as supreme, and disapprove of rhetoric and emotion; but their approach is utterly unpractical.[7]

Sublimity is of great importance in Quintilian's handling of his catalogue in Book x. (The Greek, and to some extent the Latin, side of his catalogue draw heavily on tradition; but Quintilian's own outlook and phrasing are also important.) He expresses this rich and flexible notion in terms of largeness, height, weight, force, inspiration; yet balance and judgement are also needed to avert the descent into kindred vices.[8] The element matters to him as an orator too, above all for its emotional power. In xii. 10 we see him lauding Demosthenes as supreme through sublimity; he does so in rhetoric which itself mirrors that quality (23 f.).[9] He urges it as especially suitable for Roman orators (35–7), and deplores the

---

[6] The sharper adaptation in Tacitus brings out this point (*Dial.* 10. 5).

[7] See esp. ii. 17. 26–9; note also v. 11. 39 (imagined superiority, in relation to poetry), vi. 1. 7, xi. 1. 33 (emotion). Cf. Atherton (1988), 423 f. In xii. 2. 28 Quintilian goes on to indicate the sublimity of language merited by the sublime subjects of philosophy (note also 2. 20). For *Romanum ... sapientem* cf. the polemical *vereque sapiens* at xi. 1. 35.

[8] The term 'sublimity' is used in this book with no specific limitation to [Longinus'] outlook: when I apply it to writing (as opposed to subjects), I mean it to evoke the wide area of grand and excitingly elevated utterance. For [Longinus] see especially Russell (1964), xxx–xlii (perhaps marking too sharp a discontinuity between [Longinus] and most rhetoricians); besides [Longinus] and the Pliny discussed below, Hermog. *Id.* i. 5–11 (pp. 241–96 Rabe), esp. 6, is of particular interest; cf. Hagedorn (1964), ch. 3; Patillon (1988), 223–39.

[9] Cf. for the passage Cic. *Or.* 23, *al.* (Atticism); [Long.] 16–17 (same example), 34. 4.

false sublimity of the fantastic and extravagant manner now
popular in oratory (73–80).

In Book x, sublimity or grandeur is thought to appear more
naturally in some genres than others. It belongs particularly in
narrative epic, through subject-matter and style alike: *sublimitate
heroi carminis ... et ... magnitudine rerum*, 'the sublimity of epic
poetry' (note the possessive) 'and the greatness of [Homer and
Virgil's] matter' (i. 8. 5). Even here it is not ubiquitous or all-
important (cf. x. 1. 46, 86, i. 8. 5). Lyric by nature is less grand than
epic: Stesichorus is said, strikingly, to bear up all the weight of epic
subject-matter on his emblematic lyre (x. 1. 62).[10] Prose is by
nature less grand than poetry (cf. 81 etc.). Yet sublimity is not
simply a neutral attribute: we see further some suggestions of rank
and hierarchy connected with sublimity. Authors who in sublimity 'rise' above the limits of their genre tend to be far more
favourably regarded than authors who deliberately fall below.
This resembles a characteristic hierarchical pattern: women who
behaved like men would typically be more admired than men
who behaved like women. The transcending of limits is something
very much bound up in various ways with some aspects of sublimity itself, and enhances the positive appeal of the upward
motion. Thus we are to find the idea of Plato's frequent rises
above prose in itself sublime and thrilling; their inspiration makes
them sound no longer a human utterance but divine and oracular
(81): he transcended the cosmic hierarchy.[11] When Quintilian
discusses Greek lyric (61–4), his valuations essentially correspond
to the sublimity of each author. He praises Simonides for the
stirring of emotion in his laments; he is not much admired for
being elsewhere *tenuis*, 'slender, light'. The closely related [Dion-
ysius] on the contrary praises Simonides highly for lamenting not
magnificently but movingly (*Imit.* ii. 6). Alcaeus Quintilian avers
to be rightly extolled by Horace, because of his 'greater' elements,
maioribus; but he also wrote playfully and 'sank' to poetry of love
(*lusit et in amores descendit*). These lower elements appear to be not
only less suitable to Alcaeus, but less worthy in themselves.

Quintilian's unenthusiastic attitude to falling beneath one's

---

[10] The passage is similar to [Dion. Hal.] *De Im.* ii. 7; Quintilian's language is individual
and expressive. Note Haslam, *et al.* (1990), 2.

[11] See the passages cited by Petersen ad loc., and Cic. *Or.* 67, [Long.] 13. 4, and especially
Max. Tyr. 32. 8e.

genre has been deeply influential, despite the superficiality and unfairness which his appearance of judiciousness here masks. Even his sentence on Lucan becomes wittily negative: he is *ardens et concitatus et sententiis clarissimus et, ut dicam quod sentio, magis oratoribus quam poetis imitandus* (90), 'fiery, impassioned, splendid in his generalizations; indeed, to speak out frankly, it is orators who should imitate him more than poets'. The positive suggestions of splendour turn into the indication that Lucan is unpoetic; the chief point is probably the unglamorous world of his demythologized epic. Quintilian's opinion on this very popular poet, though actually not original, is seen to be one that many would have disagreed with.[12] More remarkable (though again not original) is his verdict on the *Metamorphoses*: 'Even in epic Ovid is frivolous (*lascivus*) and too enamoured of his own talent; but in parts he is to be praised' (88, cf. iv. 1. 77; cf. especially Sen. Rh. *Contr.* ii. 2. 12). The air of balance only highlights the coolness of this verdict on the poem most influential for the period. It is clear that Quintilian has no sympathy with deliberate play in an elevated genre; it is portrayed as a kind of moral and aesthetic failing in a poet with good points.

Obviously linked is his discussion of Seneca (125–31). Here the controversies are important to him: Seneca's vices had contributed to the alleged decadence of oratory which he, professing to follow Cicero, had attacked and remained zealous to eliminate. Defending against criticism the temperance, and correctness, of his position on Seneca, he allows that Seneca's prose has good elements, but ultimately insists on its degeneracy of style. Seneca lacks the crucial judgement, and is too enamoured of his own conceptions (130 f.); hence he enfeebles the natural weight of his philosophical subject-matter by the most trifling epigrams (130). The discussion shows that others placed a higher value on the ingenious element in Seneca, the *dulcibus vitiis*, 'alluring faults'; Quintilian acknowledges that it springs from a deliberate, but regrettable, purpose. We glimpse beyond Quintilian's inviting simplicities the possiblity of other approaches.

Tacitus' dialogue on oratory differs fundamentally in its own

---

[12] Cf. Mart. xiv. 194 (which makes clear the point of *poetis*); probably Petr. 118. 6; Suet. *Poet.*, *praef.* 55–7 Rostagni (if this part is Suetonius). *oratoribus* obviously plays with his present purpose; *sententiis clarissimus* is positive, cf. 197. Nothing in Quintilian really suggests that Lucan's involvement with his subject is likely to be unacceptable (cf. Häußler (1978), 231–8).

genre from Quintilian's treatise.[13] The literary effect and force of
the statements on genre derive above all from the openness and
resonance possible in a dialogue, from the formal withdrawal of
the author and the appearance of disputing characters with their
own lives and personalities. In the first part, which particularly
concerns us, the orator Aper debates with Maternus, who has
abandoned oratory for poetry. Maternus exalts his new pursuit of
poetry above his old one, 'narrow law-cases', with quasi-religious
language of sublimity (4. 2). Aper in 10. 4f. at first paradoxically
and provokingly allows even light genres of poetry to be sublimely
'sacred', not just epic or Maternus' genre of tragedy, because they
are all parts of 'eloquence'.[14] Then he turns the language of
sublimity against the poet: Maternus has not risen to the heights,
the citadel, of eloquence, but stopped amid lighter things (10. 5).
Practical reality and sublimity are not formally disjoined but connected; the extreme Aper sweeps on to a sharper, more dramatic
version of Quintilian's language: *nunc te ... ad vera proelia voco*, 'I
summon you now ... to real battles'. The verb takes up Aper's
preliminary speech: Maternus, he indicates, curiously spends his
time on characters from myth and history when real and present
people 'summon' him to help them in the courts (3. 4). Maternus is
evading alike moral reality and an illustrious role in society (3. 4, 9.
2). Strong and concrete language exalts the orator's fame and
power, mocks the poet's recitations, and reduces the poets' mythology of pastoral seclusion from the city to blank *solitudinem*, 'isolation' (9. 5).

Maternus in reply devalues the orator's reality, himself using
concrete language to paint its bustling ugliness; that is the foil to
the poetic lyricism with which he describes the innocence, detachment, and spiritual serenity of his 'sacred abode' (12. 1, 13. 5).
Aper's hierarchy of 'eloquence' is countered by a temporal picture: poetry is the first eloquence, part of the Golden Age, oratory
the morally degenerate development of a corrupted epoch (12).

---

[13] See on the *Dialogus* particularly Syme (1958), 100–11; Michel (1962); Cameron (1967);
Häußler (1969); Williams (1978), 26–51; Martin (1981), 58–66; Heldmann (1982), 255–86;
Barnes (1986); Merklin (1988); Brink (1989); Heilmann (1989).

[14] *eloquentia, facundia, disertus*, etc. can be used in relation to any sort of literature, without
a strong suggestion of oratory in particular; cf. e.g. Petr. 96. 6; Sen. *Ot.* 1. 4; Mart. viii. 70. 1,
ix. 26. 1; Plin. *Ep.* v. 8. 4. But here the oratorical connotations of the word are made to enjoy
a kind of primacy or hegemony within this range of sense; note also 8. 2 (where quasi-
religious language is used of *Eloquentia*).

This powerful confrontation of outlooks is complicated and enriched by the form of dialogue. When Aper plays on the idea that his attack is a prosecution of Maternus, we see even in Aper a certain detachment from his extremity; we are led to feel that his vehemence and his views are not quite unmixedly earnest (note 2, 24. 1). Maternus' own speech, though a speech, is said (with some play) to be more like poetry than oratory (14. 2); he himself shows a certain urbane self-consciousness in his use of poetry (13. 5f.; 12. 3). He shows self-consciousness too in presenting what may seem the poetic unreality of his words on the Golden Age (12. 4f., cf. 12. 3). On the other side, the reality of Maternus' moral and spiritual choice, and of his insistence on truth to himself, leads him to encounter through his tragedy political danger. Things here are made more elaborate by his bringing Roman history into tragedy, and by the complex relationship of poet with character.[15]

We must add a word on what survives of Maternus' final speech (36–41). Here the alleged decline of Roman oratory is linked with the improvement of the Roman state: oratory presupposes an immoral world, and Roman oratory reached its height, he avers, amid the social chaos of the late Republic. Sublimity in this genre, here equated with excellence, is now linked with an undesirable reality (37. 8, 39. 1f.). Language that had been used of oratory to exalt and excite now wins new and grim actuality, notably the ideas of warfare, fire, and freedom (37. 7f., 40. 1, 36. 1, 39. 2 with 40. 2; cf. also 12. 2). The perspective from which the orator's reality is condemned is no longer poetic but historical. It is unlikely that we should suppose the approach to history to be the author's; but the position of the speech and the force with which historical reality is evoked make this a still more telling indictment than the other, and a more haunting and arresting vision.[16]

[15] For what is said on poets and the Golden Age—of course an idea with a philosophical background too—it is interesting to compare Quint. i. 10. 9; Hor. *AP* 391–407 (Suet. *Poet. praef.* 2–10 Rostagni is different). On tragedy and politics, note Tac. *Ann.* vi. 29. 3. It is far from certain that we should suppose Maternus to be about to meet his death for writing his *Cato* and *Thyestes*: 8. 3 on Vespasian (cf. Suet. *Vesp.* 13) would then seem odd rather than an effective irony.

[16] Our ignorance of the date of the *Dialogus* prevents us from knowing whether history was Tacitus' special genre at the time; but that is not crucial. What matters most is that deeper understanding comes from outside oratory, and in a form contrasted with (seeming) poetic detachment from historical reality. A philosophical element also enters in:

Pliny's letters do not primarily defend the author's own chief
genre of oratory: generic rivalry plays little part in their genial
and catholic approach to literature.[17] An individual author is
writing about his own work and those of other individuals: literature means above all achievement and fame (a central theme of
the letters). Much interest hangs on the way in which critical
notions are deployed, often playfully, in relation to himself and
others. The humble status of the letters as a form allows them to
sport with genre and themselves.

In regard to history he principally uses the notions of truth and
greatness; it is not only his sense of these notions but his exploitation of them which is to please his readers. So at vii. 17. 1 he says
that histories are written 'for the sake not of display but of reliability and truth', *non ostentationi sed fidei veritatique.*[18] He is contending that his own speeches may legitimately be given a reading
before an audience (as opposed to a jury), and pointing out that
even a history can be so performed; the simplified picture of
history furthers his energetic argument. In v. 8 the subject-matter
of orators' and historians' narratives is contrasted: *huic pleraque
humilia et sordida et ex medio petita, illi omnia recondita splendida excelsa
conveniunt* (9), 'it suits oratory that most of its material should be
low, undignified, and everyday; it suits history that all its material
should be remote, glorious, and lofty.' Here Pliny is writing as an
orator; it has been suggested that he should turn to history. The
reader is to be interested by his manner as well as his connoisseur-
ship. He wishes to show a seemly modesty by stressing the low-
liness of his genre's *material*; at the same time its potential greatness
is also to appear (note 11). The stylistic force of oratory is set, not
negatively, against the grace and charm available to history. In
suggesting earlier (4) that history can succeed without style, he is
displaying modesty about himself.

The two notions of truth and greatness are made to interact,

cf. Cic. *Hortens.* fr. 110 Grilli. On the relation to Maternus' *Cato*, I think, firstly, that
Maternus is to some extent moving beyond his poetic stance (note, indeed, 39. 1), and,
secondly, that if the speech does acquire irony from his own future, that will not undermine its basic *moral* outlook.

[17] For Pliny on literature see esp. Guillemin (1929); Cova (1966); Gamberini (1983);
Armisen-Marchetti (1990).

[18] Quint. x. 1. 73 indicates the stylistic achievements and range of history. Plin. *Ep.* i. 16. 4
suggests sublimity as one significant quality; but there is more sense of variety here, and less
of a contrast with oratory. In v. 8. 4 we are surely to be charmed by a stylish echo of Aristot.
Met. i. 980[a]21. For the reference of *huic* and *illi* in v. 8. 9 see Gamberini (1983), 58–72.

particularly in regard to blame and praise. In ix. 27 he exalts lavishly the greatness of history because a certain 'exceedingly veracious' (*verissimum*) history will condemn evil contemporaries for ever; his enthusiasm is coloured by the moral firmness of the historian in the tale, who effectively resists pressure to expunge.[19] More complex is vii. 33, where he mentions a brave deed of his own for Tacitus to include in his *Histories*. Tacitus in writing of it would be a eulogist (*praedicator*), by his style and his function making Pliny's actions *notiora, clariora, maiora*, 'more famous, glorious, and great' (2f., 10). Pliny leads us to feel a tension here with the generic requirement 'not to exceed truth' (10), which he then resolves neatly and nobly: for fine deeds the truth is praise enough. The letter is to charm by its tact and address of style and thought.[20] In vi. 16 and 20 he informs Tacitus, first on his uncle's death during the eruption of Vesuvius, next on his own experiences at that time. Tacitus' account of his uncle's death will evidently unite truth and celebration (16. 1). On himself Pliny at the end of the first letter affects to break off: his own deeds are no matter for history. He lingers further on himself only in order to show the reliability of his account, and to stress that this is merely a letter, which the history will need to excerpt (16. 22). He is combining soberly and gracefully his addressee, himself, and the two genres, while displaying his awareness of the dignity, selectivity, and impersonality of history, and its critical approach to truth. The second letter, where he is prevailed on to talk about himself, at its close toys more playfully with self and genre, and in fact advertises the power of his own epistolary narratives.

[19] For the special difficulties of contemporary history and providing truth there cf. v. 8. 12; see more widely Luce (1989). The exchange in ix. 19. 5 exploits generic principles urbanely but significantly; the dependence of the mere historian on men of action for the very possibility of speaking the truth comes in the more strikingly in view of Cluvius' own career (*PIR*² C 1206).

[20] Pliny wishes to better Cic. *Fam.* v. 12. The idea of praise we may link (cf. 9) with historians' emphasis on memory and example (memory e.g. Liv. *praef.* 3; on example, an idea more descriptive and less prescriptive than we might think, cf. Ch. 2 n. 43). Note *Ann.* iv. 33. 4 (though perhaps *laetius* gives a half-objective air), and the 'objective' utterances in Livy, like xxvii. 10. 7, xxi. 46. 8, viii. 10. 7. 'Truth' in the present passage plainly means what happened, as it happened, without factual exaggeration; *actae rei modum* must mean 'the limits of what was done' (which Pliny knows and has told Tacitus). The possibility of bias leading to exaggeration does not seem to indicate that a different concept of historical truth as such is in question, here or at Cic. *Fam.* v. 12. 3. (Cf. Woodman (1988), 73 f.; even the notion of a 'hard core' of fact might seem ultimately to make difficulties for such a view— but I may misunderstand it.) See now Pelling (1990), 42 n. 65, 52.

The unreality and fabulousness of poetry (higher poetry) Pliny takes as a standard notion which he delights to play with. In ix. 33 he tells Caninius of a friendly dolphin, for Caninius to write of in verse. The tale appears fictitious, and so worthy of Caninius' inventive, lofty, and utterly poetic spirit (one notes the combinations); but in fact it is true, and the source is to be credited—*tametsi quid poetae cum fide?* (1), 'yet what has a poet to do with credit?' Generic unreality becomes the object of amiable badinage. The style of Pliny's own narrative hovers: it is sometimes mock-poetic, generally unlike prose in its richness of detail, unlike poetry in the elegant simplicity of its symmetries.[21] It ends, however, abruptly and sordidly, with the killing of the dolphin as a burdensome tourist-attraction; here Pliny hands the story to poetry to be converted into a satisfyingly emotional and tragic piece. Yet the poet will not need to invent or add; here Caninius' effort must be to prevent diminution of the truth (11). This letter charmingly lightens the themes of viii. 4, where Caninius is urged to write on Trajan's Dacian campaign. Poetry, apparent unreality, elevation, and richness are again combined; the difficulty is again to match the lofty truth. Pliny conveys the 'poetic' quality of the subject: extraordinary physical events, a character's mental greatness in failure. Later (5), a quasi-poetic exhortation to poetry is broken off with *cur enim non ego quoque poetice cum poeta?* 'Why should *I* not talk poetically, to a poet?' The letter-writer shifts amusedly to personal and generic play; but the letter has also suggested the stylistic range of its lowly genre.[22]

The significance of sublimity in high poetry is underlined by ix. 26, on its permissibility in oratory (particularly Pliny's own). Pliny turns to Homer for his supreme examples of daring, of astounding combinations and images.[23] The objection that poetry and oratory are allowed different things he sweeps away with sublime disdain, pointing to Cicero and Demosthenes. The argument becomes one about the limitations of one genre and its relation to

---

[21] One may contrast the Elder Pliny's account, *NH* ix. 26 (unlikely to be the direct but hidden source, because of *Ep.* ix. 33. 9). In § 1 of the letter the link of *simillimam fictae* and *dignam* is shown by viii. 4. 1.

[22] The reference to Trajan in 5 indicates that *proinde* etc. though with a parodic element is not simply humorous. The more intense § 2 is also Pliny's own act of praise.

[23] Whether the Homeric moments attain or miss sublimity Pliny does not decide; but he is hereby modestly avoiding decision in his own case. For the controversy on *Il.* v. 338 see Demetr. *Eloc.* 83; note [Long.] 9. 6.

another. In oratory at least, what is in question is sublime moments, not a continuously sublime manner.[24] The letter itself in its richly colourful first paragraph excites us with the idea of daring and achieves a consciously magnificent close. Self-referential sublimity is familiar from [Longinus]; but the effect is more striking in a letter, and Pliny at the end glances back in a playful and personal way to the audacities into which he had supposedly been swept.

His attitude to lower poetry is characteristically positive and open, not only because he writes it himself. Any genre in perfection can be *eloquentissimum*, 'most eloquent and excellent' (vi. 21. 4): the openness on genre, as on period (1), is to sound independent (it is hardly original). Lighter poetry is 'called' playing (*lusūs*), but can actually win as much fame as serious poetry (vii. 9. 10—he then lapses playfully into verse). Sexual impropriety, which offended some in low poetry, he defends as relaxing and human (v. 3. 2); precedent and generic 'law' separate the poet's moral life from his poetry (v. 3. 3–6, iv. 14. 5). In his own work this improper element forms merely one part in a whole range of manners, including elevation (iv. 14.3). He often stresses variety, a feature which attracts him greatly, in other people's lower poetry: lower genres, including elegy and probably lyric, can both play and rise.[25] Even in his third-person descriptions of contemporary poets we are to feel the warmth and range of his approach towards literature and people together.

Seneca's philosophical prose adopts a very different attitude to other genres from Pliny's: it approaches them as rivals. The rhetorical antagonism should not be thought necessarily to represent Seneca's full feelings on the matter: on him too, it is apparent, general literary culture exerted its power.

History concerns him in the prose more than oratory, despite his own orations; and the subject-matter of Roman history plainly interests him.[26] However, his fundamental disagreement with history concerns the type of reality which it handles and exalts:

---

[24] Cf. iii. 13. 4 for the avoidance of continuous sublimity in a speech (Pliny is keen on variety); note also vii. 12.

[25] So iv. 27 *poematia*, v. 17 elegiac *καταστερισμοί*; vi. 21. 5 is a little different, since the supposed moral force of Old Comedy had given it *granditas* as one traditional ingredient: cf. Quint. x. 1. 65, Pers. 1. 124. With v. 3. 3–6 cf. especially Mart. viii. *praef.* 11–14 Shackleton Bailey; Auson. *Cent.* p.139 Green, where Pliny himself becomes an example.

[26] On Seneca's historical reading see Schendel (1908).

from the philosopher's perspective this has little significance in comparison with the life of the spirit and the system of the universe. In the pugnacious *Naturales Quaestiones* he goes further, and assails its claims to strive for historical truth. So at vii. 16. 1 he gives his curt reason for thinking the historian Ephorus an unreliable witness: *historicus est*, 'he is a historian'. He then assaults the 'whole tribe' for the various intellectual vices which lead them to tell 'lies', deliberately or otherwise. Thus some *lectorem aliud acturum, si per cottidiana duceretur, miraculo excitant*: 'the reader would be bored if he proceeded through everyday matter, so they rouse him with a marvel.' The multiple irony embraces, not only the historians' attitude to truth, but also the famed emotional involvement of the reader in history, and even the supposed greatness of its subject-matter. Presently he uses historians' own methods against Ephorus; elsewhere too he displays a sharp understanding of his opponents' approach.[27]

The treatment of history in the *Ad Marciam* is particularly important. That work consoles the daughter of Cremutius Cordus for the death of her son; her father's histories had, under Tiberius, led to his death. The opening treats Cordus and his work with great warmth, as the situation invites. Author and work, literature and reality, are powerfully related, in a perspective above all national and moral. A long sentence moves subtly from the historical and literary interest of the work for Romans to its moral, and political, significance, embodied in the author: for it will show *quid sit vir Romanus, . . . quid sit homo ingenio animo manu liber* (1. 3), 'what kind of thing a Roman man is . . . what kind of thing a human being is who in his writing, his spirit, and his hand [in suicide] is free'. Even in these two clauses we see stark and noble patriotism passing into something more universal.

The close of the work takes up and transcends the opening, and philosophy asserts its supremacy. Cordus is imagined to address Marcia from heaven. His artistic powers (*ingenio*), like himself, have risen high above even their earlier elevation (26. 1, cf. Quint. x. 1. 104); this ascent in the type of reality belongs to philosophy,

---

[27] Cf. notably iv b 3. 1f. (probably quoting Sall. *Jug.* 17. 7), where he actually shows a shrewd understanding of a device used partly to create authority. His own adoption of the device creates a relaxed humour (cf. i. 13. 3 after the implicitly critical II. 1, cf. Liv. xli. 21. 13). Our passage actually presupposes expected claims from history to pursue and achieve factual truth. Note the standard *religiosissimae fidei* (vii. 16. 2): cf. e.g. Plin. *Ep.* v. 8. 5 *religiosissime*, Cic. *Brut.* 44 (note 42f.); Plin. *Ep.* ix. 19. 5.

not history, and Seneca's own style must match it. All these different kinds of elevation, greatness, and hierarchy, acquire in the passage a coherent continuity. Viewed from heaven, Cordus declares, life among 'you'—humans on earth—contains nothing lofty or glorious, it is all low (*nil excelsum, nil splendidum, sed humilia cuncta* 26. 3). His history had concerned deeds done in a remote spot among a tiny number of people (the Romans); now he contemplates all time and space. His vision broadens ever further into the destruction which will overtake the whole universe in its present form. In such a perspective, the content and significance of notions like truth, knowledge, and time dwarfs that which they possessed at the beginning; philosophy and the universe make history and Rome look small.[28]

Seneca objects to the untruth of poetry (mythological poetry) not only as untruth, but because the trivial and self-contained world of poetry distracts from the reality that matters.[29] Near the start of the *De Beneficiis* he attacks with independence the allegorical use of poetry made by the foremost Stoic writer Chrysippus in his own work on benefits. He mocks Chrysippus for taking the poets so seriously and, by contrast, mocks the poets for their frivolous and fabulous inventions: they are indifferent to truth and aim only at a shallow literary pleasure in sound and story.[30] The manner is robust and lively: everyday words and Roman reality deflate the pretensions of poetry. Their goddesses are 'girls' (*puellis*, i. 3. 6, *bellis puellis* 4. 4), and may be dressed in *Phryxianae* (3. 7); they themselves are like forgetful *nomenclatores*, slaves kept to remember names (3. 10). Seneca then uses Greek poets and Greek philosophers to highlight by opposition the reality and seriousness of his own work. The spiritual and social importance of the subject demands great strength (*magnis viribus*)

---

[28] So there is a pointed contrast between *vetustatem* in 1. 4 and *vetustatem* in 26. 6; and *quam diu* in 1. 3 now looks very limited. Cf. for 26. 5 Cic. *Somn.* 16. A word of knowledge ends the work; for knowledge of nature as the goal of the blessed cf. Badstübner (1901), 8–11. The passage is discussed by Rutherford (1989), 253–5. Note that Cremutius' famous speech at Tac. *Ann.* iv. 34 f. is probably unhistorical (though not therefore invented by Tacitus, cf. Dio lvii. 24. 2): see Momigliano (1990), 113.

[29] See esp. Mazzoli (1970); Dingel (1974), I; Wirth (1900).

[30] Naturally Seneca had read for himself Chrysippus' eminently relevant περὶ χαρίτων (*SVF* ii. 1081–3, iii, 725 f.): cf. Chaumartin (1985), 33 n. 25. The attack on Chrysippus' use of Homer by the non-Stoic Diogenianus (fr. 2 Gercke) thinks poetry acceptable in its own non-veridical terms. On Stoic views of poetry see De Lacy (1948), who unifies too much; add Asmis (1990). In some respects Seneca's approach looks back to Plato.

and serious utterance, not 'light, unserious, mythical writing' (*levi ac fabuloso sermone*) and 'old women's stories' (*anilibus argumentis*). Truth and literary gravity are conjoined in suggestion: unreality is not sublime. Against such a manner is set, in a weighty image of Roman political reality, the danger his work must prevent: 'a cancellation of all moral debts', *beneficiorum novas tabulas*.

In *Epistle* 88 he is attacking both philosophical and philological study of Homer as 'irrelevant' (he repeats his blunt criterion *ad rem pertinere*); he proceeds to disjoin Ulysses' physical troubles, Homer's subject, from our own spiritual ones. The link of metaphor does not here join us to Homer, by the common devices of allegorization or example: *non vacat audire*, we have no leisure to listen to discussions of Ulysses' wanderings, amid the tempests of the mind (7). Seneca's urgent elaboration of the comparison with Ulysses not only thrusts upon us something real and infinitely more important; it also invests our daily mental experience with all the extremity and strangeness of mythological poetry.

Seneca loved poetry, and wrote it; now and then a more positive picture appears. Even here the emphasis is commonly moral, and positive elements are turned to serve an imperious philosophical purpose. In these exclusive works value is scarcely seen in purely imaginative enjoyment, or in lightness and play, least of all in high poetry (despite these elements in his own). In *Ep.* 8. 8f. poetry, and even low poetry, is seen as a source of eloquent maxims; he is quoting from Publilius' mimes to justify his quoting so much from Epicurus, not from Stoics. He intends his approval to be startling; he is exploiting hierarchy, and ultimately maintaining it. The hierarchy of poetic genres is given a moral twist, and connected with a hierarchy which places philosophy above poetry and Stoicism above Epicureanism. Seneca then turns to praise and play on his correspondent's own poetry, several times in the *Letters* a focus for personal warmth and teasing, and for the exaltation of philosophy over poetry. His own poetry he does not mention, here or anywhere.

To complete the picture we must add a little on Seneca's presentation of philosophical writing. Philosophy treats of the most important reality, and the philosopher's eloquence must form a unity with his life. Great philosophical utterance has in a

sense the impact of sublime literature, but its impact springs precisely from its absorption in reality.[31] In writing on his contemporary Demetrius (*Ben.* vii. 8. 2f.) he stresses the union in him of
eloquence and virtue; his eloquence is of the kind that befits his
heroic philosophy, 'not neat, and anxious about particular words,
but discoursing with mighty spirit on the matters that truly belong
to it just as the sweep of feeling (drives it on?)', *non concinnatae nec in
verba sollicitae, sed ingenti animo prout impetus †retulit† res suas prose-
quentis.*[32] Much here, even the indifference, has links with [Longi-
nus'] depiction of the sublime writer (so 33. 4); but the emphasis is
more exclusively moral, and the moral emotion fulfils literary
values while transcending them. The writing of Q. Sextius, like
Demetrius morally a 'great' man, is not, unlike some other philosophers' writing, uninspiring and 'bloodless' (*exanguia Ep.* 64. 3, a
literary term).[33] His writing makes the reader exclaim about the
author (not about itself), in terms that mix literary and spiritual
force and transcendent elevation: *vivit, viget, liber est, supra hominem
est,* 'he is alive, vigorous, and free, he is greater than a man'. He
brings Seneca when reading him to challenge Fortune for himself
(*Ep.* 64. 4), with sublime boldness.

Epistle 100, defending the philosopher Fabianus, both urges the
literary excellence of his writing and stresses the importance of
the spiritual against the merely literary.[34] He did not concern
himself with verbal detail and sharpness; that attitude, noble in
itself, went with a calm breadth. Seneca defends his writing from
the charge of being unelevated and low (*humilia*): rather it was
tranquil, and so mirrored his mind (8). And listening to him swept
one away (3). Greatness, *magnitudo*, belongs to his subject, philosophical reality, not to petty words (10). The unimportance of
mere literary pleasure is driven home by a whole sequence of

[31] For the three philosophers treated here, see especially Oltramare (1926). The importance of Q. Sextius for Seneca's own writing has been greatly built up, without sufficient
justification. On Fabianus, note esp. Sen. Rh. *Contr.* ii *praef.*; in the Younger Seneca note
Brev. 10. 1, 13. 9, *Ep.* 40. 12, 52. 11.

[32] *retulit* N[1] (the only authoritative MS and hand): *tulit* N[2] and edd., but this tense allows
at best the unsatisfactory meaning 'has brought the matters severally to mind'. Sen. Rh.
Contr. iv *praef.* 9 if sound is different: note the verb, the tone, and the reference to declamatory *divisio*; in the present passage *tulit* in the sense 'has swept along' would not seem apt or
complimentary. We probably need something like *pellit. Ep.* 115. 2 rebuts the *cincinnatae* of
Madvig (1873), 422.

[33] Cf. Cic. *Brut.* 68, Plin. *Ep.* v. 17. 3, etc.

[34] See on the letter Leeman (1963), ch. 11.

ingenious and forceful puns, plays, and images, which in fact display the literary qualities that Fabianus lacked: *mores ille non verba composuit*, and other such untranslatable things. The letter ends with a word evoking literary sublimity, but also moral splendour: *magnificus*, 'magnificent'.[35] This is a philosophical piece, and also literature: as when Seneca discourses on his own supposedly casual epistolary style (*Ep.* 75), we learn less about his actual approach to writing from what is stressed than from what receives little stress, and from the thesis than from the manner. Had he dwelt overtly on the value of conspicuous wit, he would have undone his own complex and poised effect; and as usual, his philosophical purpose makes his powerful statements on literature drastically selective.

In the novel of **Petronius** we see statements on literature independent in pose, vigorous in expression, and conventional in approach; they undergo all the literary complications of this particular work. This work sports incessantly with its genre, other genres, and itself; its very mixture of prose and poetry is used to keep such play before us.[36] So in 132. 9f. the impotent narrator upbraids his penis with a speech of rebuke, insulting its indignity; the speech is surrounded by narrative, partly in verse which plays with epic and with a low metre. The narrator then makes a speech justifying the making of such a speech, with examples from everyday life and high literature. After all this we turn, surprisingly, to verse that suggests a defence of Petronius' impropriety in general as true to reality, and so forth.[37] The defence is significant; but the play and the bizarreness of its context are essential to its full effect. The more substantial and dignified disquisitions on literature in the opening fragment of the work and at 118 contain their own surprises; and simply by appearing they add an incongruous turn to this exuberantly unpredictable creation.

In chs. 1–5 the two speakers assail declamation: its unreality is

---

[35] Cf. Cic. *Brut.* 201, [*Opt. Gen.*] 12; *De Or.* ii. 89 with Leeman-Pinkster-Nelson's n.; Plin. *Ep.* i. 20. 19, *al.*

[36] The mixture is 'low' in its connotations and wide in its possibilities; particularly significant are P. Oxy. 3010 (cf. Parsons (1971)) and P. Turner 8. On the literary comments in Petronius and the related question of the long poems see Stube (1933); Courtney (1962); Sullivan (1968), ch. 5; Walsh (1968); Zeitlin (1971a and b); Guido (1976), ch. 5; Grimal (1977), 165–88; Kißel (1978); Beck (1979); Slater (1990).

[37] For *purus* cf. Bentley on Hor. *AP* 99.

educationally pernicious; it has destroyed the true grandeur seen
in older poetry and prose through the diseased and unnatural
substitute for that grandeur, undisciplined extravagance and
folly. Excellence and grandeur go together (note 4. 3, 2. 7), and
grandeur is associated with reality, sobriety, and nature; grand
utterance *naturali pulchritudine exurgit* (2. 6), 'rises to its elevation
with a natural loveliness', as of a beautiful woman: in its context
the image is simple, attractive, and restrained. The essential attitude to declamation is often found elsewhere; the form renders
the impact involved. The first of the speeches is referred to as if it
were a declamation itself (3. 1); it had been prompted by a real
declamation, before our text begins, from the second speaker (6.
2), a teacher of the art who now proves entertainingly cynical (3.
2–4). His speech shifts from prose into pointedly low, and then
into lofty, metre; he is presently mocked by students for the declamation he originally delivered. All this play makes the speeches
piquant, but need not invalidate their point of view, commended
to us by the rhetorician's unexpected assent (3. 1); the irony of the
students' opinion on his declamation may be turned either against
or for his present speech. Part of the literary effect of the passage is
to intrigue us as to its standing and even its relation to the views of
the silent author.

This applies still more to 118. Here a poet speaks of poetry. It is
no mere declamation, he stresses; yet crucial to its success is
remoteness from ordinary reality, in diction, manner, and content. The poem Lucan had started on the Civil War is implicitly
criticized in this regard.[38] Epic should be unlike history, with its
scrupulous truth; it should resemble the frenzied inspiration of
prophecy (*furentis* 118. 6), and employ the gods of myth. Sublimity
appears in wilder form than in 1–5, when oratory stood to the fore,
and the language is exciting: through poetic regions *praecipitandus
est liber spiritus*, 'the unfettered inspiration must be hurled along'
(the word-order increases the excitement). But there are numerous complications and surprises in the passage. The speaker, like
the other speakers, cuts a grotesque figure in the narrative; the
sudden appearance of a particular contemporary work is startling

[38] 118. 6 would read oddly without a work by another to prompt it; and the coincidence
with other judgements on Lucan would, given the subject, be implausible. There is little
difficulty with the date, given such practices as recitation, even if the author is indeed
Nero's courtier.

(*ecce* 118. 6); and much more startling is the alternative version
offered of the opening of a poem on the Civil War. For a fair
proportion of an epic book (about 300 lines) this low work ascends
into purported sublimity.[39] These surprises need hardly undermine altogether. The poetry does not seem to me parodic or
amusing; the character's modesty about its unfinished condition
rather points our thoughts to the author and his poetic creation
(to which 118 becomes a prelude). An exhilarating and bemusing
audacity and range is evinced by the whole passage on various
levels, of which the statements on literature form one; we must
enjoy it on all these levels. Taken simply as literary criticism, the
view of Lucan seems remarkably crude (though found elsewhere):
this starkness in the handling of categories can do no justice to
complexity.

We have already seen the conflict of genres, at different levels
of intensity and earnestness, and also, by contrast, the acceptance
of their harmonious coexistence; a hierarchical ordering by sublimity can be used in either context. We have seen in lighter works
how play and self-reference can amuse themselves with generic
categories. In general, we have seen how much statements on
genre are affected by the nature of the work they occur in, and the
author's polemical or artistic purposes; but we have seen too, and
shall later draw out, some underlying assumptions, such as that
epic and tragedy are in their world unreal. We shall now turn to
some of the poetry other than epic and tragedy, and shall divide
our space between the poets' treatment of genre and related
aspects, roughly sketched, of their own writing more generally.
We shall not only see the links between their explicit treatment of
genre and their wider purposes, but shall glimpse some of the
complications attaching to greatness and especially reality in their
own work. We shall give attention too to an aspect of genre the
significance of which is intimately bound up with that of reality in
particular: the treatment of the author. The presence or formal
absence of the author, and the way he is handled, receive little
mention in direct discussion of genre within this period, although
the aspect had been emphasized by Plato and Aristotle. Its actual

---

[39] Length and sublimity take up and exceed 89 (same speaker). We can hardly suppose
such a poem as 119–24. 1 to have been so common in the lost parts of the work as to undo the
surprise; the two long poems are specially associated with Eumolpus, who in 83. 7 is plainly
making his first appearance.

importance in regard to genre is obvious, and has emerged already in our consideration of prose.

The rejection and acceptance of poetic hierarchy are conspicuous in the literary remarks of the epigrammatist **Martial**.[40] Sometimes in the courtliness of social communication he will accept the idea of a hierarchy within poetry. In iv. 14 he addresses Silius Italicus, and sets Silius' grand epic against his own light epigrams. In the world of his epic Silius with 'mighty voice', *ingenti . . . ore*, forces the fickle Carthaginians (*levis*) to yield to the 'great' Scipios, *magnis*; greatness of poetry and of subject, aesthetic and moral, are fused in the strong 'action' of the poet (a conventional but here forceful turn). Martial's poems, 'drenched with racy humour', Silius should read for relaxation, at the holiday of the Saturnalia, when normal rules were suspended. Martial uses the Saturnalia (cf. e.g. v. 30) to create a real, unelevated, yet attractive environment which will match his poems; his description of it here suggests the ideas of looseness, play, naughtiness, and charm. He ends by likening his own standing in relation to Silius with the standing of his model, 'sensuous' Catullus (*tener*), in relation to Silius' model, 'mighty' Virgil (*magno*). The suggestion of Martial's own positive, though inferior, value, now reaches a new stage as modesty is combined with the dignity of a generic tradition.[41]

More fully characteristic is x. 4. The reading of mythological poetry is vigorously attacked: its subject-matter is horrid, unreal, and useless.

> quid te vana iuvant miserae ludibria chartae?
>   hoc lege, quod possit dicere vita 'meum est'.
> non hic Centauros, non Gorgonas Harpyiasque
>   invenies; hominem pagina nostra sapit.
> sed non vis, Mamurra, tuos cognoscere mores
>   nec te scire: legas Aetia Callimachi.   (7–12)

---

[40] Some works relevant to these remarks and the wider aspects: Paukstadt (1876); Pertsch (1911); Besslich (1974); Muth (1976); Salemme (1976); Classen (1985); Szelest (1986); Holzberg (1988). The bibliographical suggestions in this and some of the similar notes in the first two chapters seek also to provide some matter helpful in introducing one to the author; works on models are often mentioned here because the scope of the chapters excludes this crucial aspect.

[41] Contrast the relation of Catullus and Virgil in xiv. 195 (which uses and goes beyond Ov. *Rem.* 394 f.). Martial's chronological vagueness should interest the literary historian of our period. As to Martial and the Saturnalia cf. Citroni (1989).

What good will you get from these substanceless fictions of pitiful paper?
Read my work: Life can say of it, 'This belongs to me.' Here you'll find
no Centaurs, Gorgons, or Harpies; my pages taste of man. —But you
don't want to get to know your own behaviour, Mamurra, or learn what
you are like. Then read Callimachus' impenetrable *Aetia.*

Martial indicts the fabulous content of high poetry with scorn and
bracing rhetoric, while pungent devices and vocabulary proclaim
his own reality; the concreteness of paper is used (7, 10) to annul
poetic fancies, but to join his own work to life.[42] The moral
significance of this truthfulness is stressed in the last couplet;
Martial commonly gives this grandiose dress to his purpose of
producing comic pleasure. That couplet itself turns its sudden
personal confrontation into humour, with its pithy and particular
dismissal and mock-curse. *ludibria* (7) suggests 'play' by grand
poets as well as fiction: this ironically reverses the term 'play' often
used of epigram. The reversal is developed at more length in iv.
49, where Martial contrasts his own artistry with the crude false
sublimity of high poetry (including the *Metamorphoses*!). He there
deflates the pretentiousness of readers too, both neatly and
shrewdly: *laudant illa, sed ista legunt* (10), 'those poets' work they
praise; mine they read.'

Play and pose are obvious in these upsettings of hierarchy; but
the possibility of serious assertion about his work is also felt, and
left open. Martial can simply sport with his genre, himself, and his
reader, as in ii. 8. The reader states, 'these things are bad' (7),
referring to faults of style in Martial; Martial accepts the remark,
but turns it to refer not to his faulty writing but to the incorrigible
immorality of epigram. We are just to be amused by Martial's
seeming admission, his adroitness, and his final crossness of manner.[43] On the other hand, there is obvious earnestness in the
humour when in the preface to Book i he defends the impropriety
of his language and content, on the grounds both that it is true
and real, and also that the genre requires it; and he there indicates
both the tradition and the success of epigram. Art and reality are
almost paradoxically conjoined, and both presented in Roman
terms: his rude words are plain 'Latin', he does not mention his

[42] For *vita* cf. viii. 3. 20; for the monsters, Ov. *Trist.* iv. 7. 11–20 (Ovid is sporting with his
own work and genres). However, the name Mamurra points with teasing paradox not to
his own time but to the work of Catullus (29, 87).

[43] *tu non meliora facis* means 'your particular criticisms are not amending my epigrams,
which are "bad" (wicked) by genre'. Cf. iv. 10. 7f.

Greek models, he assimilates his work to the uninhibited festival of the Floralia.[44]

The main sphere of Martial's poetry is contemporary Rome; the reality of its life (in some aspects) is colourfully evoked.[45] The colour, the vivid lowness, is part of the appeal, and his comic exuberance will often run beyond literal verisimilitude. But the significance of reality in his work goes further than colour. Things are reduced to their alleged basics as the poet exposes fraud and pretension, or simply manifests his own supposed outlook, robustly down-to-earth. 'His' suggested personality is commonly essential to the poems: forthright, fond of pleasure, mostly sound or shrewd in its instinctive evaluations. Yet the blunt attitudes and the undignified matter appear through poetry of sparkling elegance: art and reality stand in agreeable tension.

One or two poems will illustrate some of this. Various epigrams use the notion and phrase, taken from actual society, of the *homo bellus*: the 'pretty fellow', with something of the beau and the wit.[46] In its opening couplet iii. 63 asks one such person to define the elusive term. He then takes over the poem, and for five couplets describes the activities of the *homo bellus* in terms racy with modern life and its scents, tunes, easy chairs, and circuses: he conveys with unreal obviousness the effeminacy and intrigue of his existence. The final couplet returns to Martial:

> quid narras? hoc est, hoc est homo, Cotile, bellus?
> res pertricosa est, Cotile, bellus homo.

What are you saying? Is that, *that*, what a pretty fellow is, Cotilus? A pretty fellow, Cotilus, is an utterly paltry thing.[47]

The splendid explosion of surprise and disgust demolishes the *homo bellus* in a personal confrontation of comic frankness. Yet the

---

[44] For its ethos cf. the wonderful passage Ov. *Fast.* v. 159–378; Mart. i. 35, where it occurs again, is generally relevant. The tradition of self-defence does not of course exclude the air of significant intention in the preface any more than in Pliny (or Ovid's *Remedia*).

[45] On Rome the preface to xii is of interest, though at 10f. Shackleton Bailey *illud materiarum ingenium* may be corrupt (note indeed the rhythm; Tert. *Hermag.* 17. 2 (Waszink) is of course irrelevant).

[46] For its everyday currency cf. Petr. 42. 3 (freedman), and also Cat. 24. 7; *CIL* iv. 2310b?. As to wit, cf. Plin. *Ep.* iv. 25. 3. Monteil (1964), 230–3, does not seem wholly satisfactory on this usage.

[47] This sense, which suits *tricae* well enough, fits better with line 11, *res*, and i. 9. 2, xii. 39. 2, than 'preoccupied with trifles' or 'full of difficulties' (Holford-Strevens (1988), 164f. n. 114; note also line 8).

symmetry of the couplet and the whole poem creates even here a degree of formality and distance. Another poem shows how someone practises all accomplishments *belle* 'prettily'—but not *bene* 'well'; its ending is still directer than the last: *magnus es ardalio*, 'you're a great busybody' (ii. 7. 8).[48] But here the engagement and deflating insult are preceded by a sort of lullaby of seeming praise, in which Martial endlessly repeats parts of *bellus*: he is building up to knock down, and evoking much of contemporary culture, but at the same time he is luxuriating in symmetry and the very sound of the word, and recalling Catullus (78. 3f.).

In less aggressive vein, ix. 40 reuses and combines various themes of Greek epigram to create a forceful mixture of reality and lowness.[49] A Greek from Egypt went to the Capitoline Games (a concrete and highly contemporary setting); his wife Philaenis swore to the gods that if he returned safely

> illam lingeret ut puella simplex
> quam castae quoque diligunt Sabinae.   (4f.)

she would suck, like an unsophisticated girl, that thing which even the chaste Sabine women are fond of.

The startling vow shifts us suddenly to heady indecency. The periphrasis itself turns surprisingly to look beneath a proud surface and indicate that sexual interest is not merely for Greeks with the names of famous courtesans (Philaenis). This will prepare the final twist of the poem.

The man is shipwrecked (in poetic lines)—and swims back: the vow will be fulfilled. Martial unexpectedly exclaims at the husband's sluggishness:

> hoc in litore si puella votum
> fecisset mea, protinus redissem.   (10f.)

If *my* girl had made that vow on the shore, I would have returned at once.

With amusingly unreal invention, and with brevity both neat and blunt, the poet thrusts forward his own humorously earthy and

---

[48] With the insult cf. *CIL* iv. 4765 *Aephebe, ardalio es.*

[49] Bizarre narratives of shipwreck are popular in Greek epigram, e.g. (with rescue or partial rescue) Philip xxxix Gow-Page, Flacc. iii; dedication before or after voyage Phil. vii, Diod. iv; female fellation Argent. vii, xxxiii (explicit). All these are 1st cent. BC or AD, and earlier than Martial. It is possible that Diodorus is to be thought a poet, which would add a turn to the close.

undignified priorities. This poem converts the improper and the forthright into drastic and genial play.

The satirists **Persius** and **Juvenal** we shall take together. In Persius' first satire we see literature in the light of a philosophical concern with moral reality and truth, through language rich in vivacious humour.[50] The poet, in the tradition of his genre and its Greek predecessor Old Comedy, will boldly expose unwelcome truth in his own society, 'graze poor soft ears with truth that bites' (*teneras mordaci* [purposefully juxtaposed] *radere vero / auriculas*, 107 f.). In doing so, he is also expressing his own feelings; yet the feelings are of laughter, and presented with comic play and self-reference. So in lively burlesque he sports with a myth from epic and our very reading of his poetry:

> me muttire nefas? nec clam? nec cum scrobe? nusquam?
> hic tamen infodiam. vidi, vidi ipse, libelle:
> auriculas asini quis non habet? (118–20)

Is it utterly wrong that *I* should just murmur the truth? Not even in secret? Can't I even tell the ditch [like the slave who knew that Midas had donkey's ears]? I'll dig it in here. Listen, book: I've seen it, seen it for myself ... everyone at Rome has the ears of an ass.[51]

It is a part of the present moral weakness and obsession with praise, not truth, that contemporary authors occupy themselves with artistry alone, not morality or the expression of real feeling (*verum* 90); higher poetry now escapes from reality into wild imaginings and language, colourfully evoked by Persius (92–106). Roman grandeur and sublimity have disappeared, like Roman manliness, and facile effeminacy ensues; elevation is claimed in vain (67 f., cf. 14).[52] Persius does want artistry for his own poetry, in a subordinate role; he does not aspire to grandeur (note 123–5 and 45 f. against 14). His modest and truthful words about art and praise, drawn from him by the interlocutor he has himself in-

---

[50] For 1, 5, and the choliambics, see in particular Anderson (1982*a*); Nisbet (1963); Waszink (1963); Tosi (1977); Korzeniewski (1978); Rudd (1986), 99 f., 178–82; Scholz (1986); Bellandi (1988).

[51] A Stoic truth (all except the wise are mad, *SVF* iii. 657–70) is turned into a merry absurdity. For Midas cf. Ov. *Met.* xi. 172–93. In 11 f. here Housman's punctuation should be seen to mimic uncontainable laughter.

[52] On effeminacy note Arist. *Thesm.* 130–45, and the whole scene. The various traditions behind the depiction generally should make one more cautious in using it as evidence for contemporary poetry. In 69 I prefer *videmus*.

vented (44), subserve the moral priorities of the poem—and permit further play with self-reference.

In poem 1 it is not the genres as such that are in conflict, but their present manifestations. 5. 1–29 approach genre in a more absolute fashion; but again the matter is subordinated to spiritual truth. The point fully emerges only in the last part of the passage. Persius begins by referring to the commonplace in high poetry of demanding a hundred tongues. Cornutus, his friend and philosophical teacher, interrupts in surprise: we now hear Persius' literary ideals in the form not of a vaunt but of a reminder and admonition from another voice.[53] The speech disparages the pomp of tragedy. It does so in part through self-contained humour, which graphically and fantastically develops the ideas of mouths and eating from the elevated commonplace; in part it assaults the swollen failed sublimity of the genre. But Cornutus attacks tragedy too by dwelling on its unreality (note 7): tragedy rants on mythical crimes, Persius skilfully and with ordinary words attacks actual immorality. It is tragedy that is aesthetically and morally the real *nugae* 'frivolous, worthless stuff', a term normally used of lighter poetry (19, in Persius' reply). In 17f. starkly concrete language brings to a height the grotesque outlandishness of the tragic world; low and humdrum terms present, with relaxed irony, the Roman reality that matters.

> hinc trahe quae dicas, mensasque relinque Mycenis
> cum capite et pedibus, plebeiaque prandia noris.

Draw your subject-matter from Rome; leave those feasts of Thyestes at Mycenae, along with those human heads and feet, and be familiar with mere everyday lunches.

In fact the reason Persius desires a hundred tongues is to tell of what Cornutus has done for him. Unreality turns into deeply significant reality, with solemn language of inward truth, and into personal and actual communication. Grandiose convention and even play with self-reference ('we are speaking alone', 21) Persius alters into something daringly and movingly real and earnest.

Juvenal in his first poem as elsewhere is much indebted to

---

[53] The speech obviously belongs in the tradition descending from Callimachus; its length should not obscure the positive significance of the movement in 19ff. For the hundred tongues cf. Skutsch on Enn. *Ann.* 468. The device seems less likely for the voice of tragedians: there is humour in the satirist's vagueness.

Persius; but he gives far less firm a sense of an underlying seriousness of thought.[54] In the central body of the poem (21–146) he
depicts himself as driven by passion, not to treat of myths (52–4),
but to expose the vice passing before his eyes at Rome, in the
present, an age of unsurpassed wickedness. Yet in a final section of
dialogue the reader checks this precipitate zeal, and points out the
dangers of attacking the living; Juvenal retreats, and shifts his
target to the dead. This sudden withdrawal from immediate
reality is made the more peculiar by what has preceded: Juvenal
seemed to have swept already onto forceful and particularized
assault. In fact, the names there had not come from the present.
What looked like simplicity and directness becomes teasing paradox and energetic but evasive drama.

This toying with reality and satire is elaborated by wider play
with genre. In the introduction, where he resolves to write poetry,
he gets sport from the grand unreality of epic and tragedy: in
recitation-halls it is declared 'what the winds are up to', *quid agant
venti* (9); he knows the grove of Mars better than anyone knows his
own home (7 f.); his own motives for writing are an absurd version
of grandiose violence and honour. Throughout the poem, low
language is used in relation to high poetry, grand language in
relation to satire; play with genre is the goal, more than a reversal
of hierarchy or an exaltation of his own art. When he explains
why he is deciding on satire, he describes it exaltedly as the field
'through which the great offspring of Aurunca once steered his
horses [Lucilius, who founded the genre]', *per quem magnus equos
Auruncae flexit alumnus* (19 f.). But this is undercut by the prosy
coolness of the following line (*si vacat,* 'if you've got time to listen',
etc.); and it becomes the more ironic when the close reveals that
the poet cannot follow in the steps of the quasi-heroic Lucilius.
Lucilius roared 'as it were with his brand drawn', *ense velut stricto*
(165); but war is not for Juvenal (168–70).

Tragedy is played with at the end of Satire 6, with an apparent
force rendered sportive by the detail. Juvenal alludes to a
mother's 'recent' poisoning of her children; he imagines that he

---

[54] On 1, 6. 627–61, 7 cf. Adamietz (1986*b*) and other general works; Anderson (1982*b*),
198–209; Kenney (1962); Griffith (1970); Bramble (1974), 164–73; Tosi (1977); Smith (1989);
Hartmann (1912); Wiesen (1973); Rudd (1976), ch. 4; Braund (1988), ch. 2; Jones (1989);
Hardie (1990). For the wider aspects discussed below cf. also Scott (1927); Anderson (1982*d*);
Mason (1963); Gérard (1972); Townend (1973); Bramble (1982*b*); Jenkyns (1982), ch. 3;
Classen (1988); Baumert (1989); Wiesen (1989) and even Hutchinson (1988).

may be accused of breaking the rules of the genre by departing from Roman reality into grandiose tragedy, with its mythical crimes (628–31, 634–7).[55] In fact, modern women, though subtler in their methods (poison, not weapons), match those of tragedy, and exceed them, for, still more wickedly, they do not act from passion. The play is elaborate here: although present reality excels tragedy in 'greatness' through the extremity of its crimes, yet the difference of its means and motives is used to make its 'greatness' low and amusing in impact. The mother's voice startlingly obtrudes an admission of guilt, *feci, / confiteor,* 'I did it, I confess' (638f.); but with no less startling humour she turns out to be admitting the 'guilt' of using only poison.[56] With vigorous rhetoric and paradox the poet bids us surrender our disbelief in tragedy (643f.); his argument follows, *a fortiori*:

> et illae
> grandia monstra suis fecerunt temporibus, sed
> non propter nummos. (644–7)

Medea and Procne too performed great enormities in their day, but not for money.

The magnificent enjambment links an ingenious climax of greatness in one sense, that of crime, with a bathetic anticlimax of greatness in another. The play grows only more elaborate as the passage proceeds.

Satire 7 looks with exuberant and disrespectful humour at various genres as ways of life.[57] It sets coarse and basic financial reality against the aspirations and pretensions of literature. To 'see' the lofty and unreal world of epic, the poet 'needs a mighty mind, overwhelmed, but not by the need to buy a blanket', *magnae mentis opus nec de lodice paranda / attonitae* (66f.); the prosiness of the second half of the line breaks in roughly. Without Maecenas' support,

---

[55] 632f., which lead less well into 634–7 and are worrying in their attestation, should probably be deleted. 634–7 are better as a statement (so Courtney's text, and Jahn and Clausen). It is at first formally unclear whether *scilicet* is ironic or not: either meaning is possible in Juvenal.

[56] This I think to be the force; *facinus tamen ipsa peregi* stresses that it was none the less all her own murder (note 642; 657–61 revert to the idea of means with further twists). Housman's understanding of the lines seems less pointed.

[57] The poem can be taken too seriously. Even on the surface it does not primarily commend the intellectuals, but emphasizes the lack of support for them; yet much of the humour against writers (especially dead ones) is merely playful, if impertinent. 12 seems to heighten the irony of the true poet's lot (the auctioneer).

caderent omnes a crinibus hydri (70), 'all the snakes would fall from the hair [of the Fury in Virgil]': the expression with fantastic humour metamorphoses unreality backwards. Orators claim to be immersed in civic reality, by contrast with historians (105): the more pointedly does Juvenal deflate their claims to financial success, which they deliver with all the lying grandiloquence of oratory. *magna sonant*, 'they sound forth grandly' (108), *immensa cavi spirant mendacia folles*, 'their hollow bellows breathe forth enormous lies' (111); but their 'true harvest', *veram ... messem* (112), is shown in a list of meagre presents (119–21), written with all the low particularity and colourful absurdity of satire. It is striking, however, that a long satire on universal meanness towards culture (except from Caesar) should touch on the author himself (32–5, 48 f.) only slightly and obliquely.

Reality is variously important to these writers in their own poetry. In obvious contrast to high poetry their works are mostly set in contemporary (or quasi-contemporary) Rome; they evoke this world with pungent detail, the lowness of which they relish. But further, they commonly transform the ordinary into strange and arresting poetry. To take simple examples, at Juv. 3. 90–7, in broad humorous outline, someone's voice is uglier than a cock's, and you would think someone acting a woman actually was one; but the cock is described as 'the husband that bites the hen [in intercourse]', the female genitalia as 'the parts separated only by a slender crack' (*quo mordetur gallina marito*; *tenui distantia rima*).[58] The startling, sordid kennings absorb us in themselves. In Pers. 3. 4 'at 11 o' clock' becomes the allusive and sharply picturable *quinta dum linea tangitur umbra*, 'while the line [on the sun-dial] is touched with the fifth shadow'. For the poet lying in, the sun between the shutters *angustas extendit lumine rimas* (2), 'broadens the narrow slits with light': the humdrum is made both vivid and excitingly unfamiliar.[59]

Again the idea of reality goes deeper, and the concreteness of language accompanies a severely reductive approach that takes us into truth. Very relevant to Persius' art is the tradition of low colour in some philosophical writing. In him the exposure leads us

---

[58] The comparison with the cock is slightly odd when the voice is *angusta* (Quint. xi. 3. 51 is different). Alteration along the lines of Claverius' *illa ... quum*, itself unsatisfactory, is apparently not encouraged by the behaviour of hens during mating. (Several people have kindly helped with my shy inquiries.)

[59] One may compare and contrast Ov. *Am.* i. 5. 3–6.

from the futile world that dominates the surface of his poetry into
the firm and simple truths of Stoicism. He dramatizes repeatedly
men's avoidance of this level of spiritual actuality: *ut nemo in sese
temptat descendere, nemo . . . !* (4. 23) 'How far everyone is, everyone,
from trying to descend into himself!' The reader of Persius too
must make a descent, from the extreme deviousness of expression
into the fixed and powerful belief underneath it: a strange
process, but one which renders the belief moving through contrast. The strong existence, and the separability, of the two levels
mean that we are ultimately less distanced from the message than
say with writers who revel in self-subversion and paradox.

In Juvenal matters are more complicated. He is on the surface
concerned to expose, but beneath we have little solid sense of a
coherent and spiritual outlook, or even of earnest belief. This
sensation is hardly altered by the appearance in Books 4 and 5
(10–16) of more philosophical elements; and even these poems are
much less spiritual than Persius'.[60] The form of his satires often
tantalizes. Poem 3, in which his friend attacks Rome and leaves it,
ends by hinting with gentle irony that Juvenal is different: he and
his satires may need and belong to the city this satire has
condemned (note especially 321). The main part of poem 5 depicts
a feast; it shows an air of warm engagement (note 107–13) for a
poor client and against his patron. The close shifts drastically to a
hard and humorous conception of the feast; despite the formal
continuity with the opening admonition, the superficial
earnestness and feeling of the main part seem to be startlingly and
radically infringed.[61]

The humour and the rhetoric of exposure and revelation seem
often to be enjoyed for themselves, and with no strong sense of
ultimate seriousness (Martial is an important influence on
Juvenal). So the unchaste Laronia replies to the attacks on her sex
by devotees of philosophy with an attack on their own perversion.

> fugerunt trepidi vera ac manifesta canentem
> Stoicidae: quid enim falsi Laronia?   (2. 64f.)

The sons of Stoicism fled in panic from Laronia and her oracles, which
were true and visibly true: *she* had said nothing false.

[60] For these elements see Courtney (1980), 16; significant are 13. 120–3, which dissociate
Juvenal from philosophy (taking up 19–22).

[61] The change is 'planted', but not disclosed, in 141–5. For the notion of the *parasitus* see
Nesselrath (1985), 15–121, [Quint.] *Decl. Min.* 152. 11f., 296. 7f., 298. 8–10, 379. 5.

Truth is paradoxically turned against those who lay claim to it; but Laronia had been smiling (38), the second half of the speech had been more amusing than imposing.[62] The effect here is of agreeable comedy, with touches of mock-grandeur.

Juvenal is always moving between mock-grandeur and lowness: in that sense grandeur is vital to him. Sometimes there is a barbed point, but most often the effect is primarily playful. At the feast in 5 the patron gets a luxurious kind of eel obtained in the sea adjoining Sicily:

> nam dum se continet Auster,
> dum sedet et siccat madidas in carcere pinnas,
> contemnunt mediam temeraria lina Charybdim.
> vos anguilla manet longae cognata colubrae ...   (100–3)

While the South Wind restrained himself, while he sat still and dried his wet wings in Aeolus' prison, the audacious nets scorned the midst of Charybdis. You clients an eel awaits who is relative to a long serpent ...

In the mock-grandiose fantasy the wind is treated with a humorously prosaic touch, and the nets are used half-whimsically. The portentous menace and epic resonance of the last line leads up to disgusting particulars of relished squalor. In effect, not in ostensible tone, this is all entertaining comedy, and can scarcely be taken very seriously.[63] Even Juvenal's most darkly impressive effects (as at 10. 112f.) derive from peculiar combinations and from twistings of grandeur.

Persius obtains his underlying depth with little grandeur of poetry; his text interacts principally not with epic but with Horace's hexameter works. Even at 3. 66–72, where we have some feeling of grandeur, the list of philosophy's concerns mingles solemn with concrete language, and has more philosophical weight than poetic elevation.[64] That list is purposefully contrasted with colourfully mundane concerns (73–6), and with the centurion's speech deriding philosophy (77–85). A parable follows, full of pithy conversation and ugly detail, with sinister

---

[62] Compare with 47–64 Arist. *Thesm.* 785–29.

[63] I would thus differ from Morford (1977). Courtney rather over-simplifies the style of these lines (on 100–2). 101 prosily develops Ov. *Met.* i. 264 (itself clever); for *vos ... manet* cf. Virg. *Aen.* vii. 596, x. 630 (Sen. *NQ* vi. 32. 2 has a grandiose flavour). *longus* is a common epithet of snakes in Ovid (cf. Virg. *Georg.* ii. 320), played with again at 6. 431.

[64] See the parallels in Casaubon (1647), 273–91.

and significant force. We are far away here from Juvenal's toying
exploitation of epic.

In Persius the author is felt strongly, if schematically, as the
being at the centre of the poems. Horace had formally marked out
the author's life and personality as an essential feature of the
genre. Persius, following him, tells of his own (spiritual) life in 5.
30–51; in 3. 1–67 depicts his faults and his present existence, in
44–51 recollects an aspect of his childhood; and in 6. 6–17 refers to
his own exemplary retirement in the country, in a poem that
begins with a warm and epistolary air.[65] Juvenal offers startlingly
little sense of such a person; this strengthens our feeling that his
satire is ultimately elusive. He can play with himself as a poet;
otherwise it is only in 12 and especially 11 that we find any but the
lightest adumbration. Even here there is little very distinctive
colour; even in 11 he appears as a fairly straight foil to modern
luxuriousness, and the poem closes with a twist that lightly undercuts his stance.

We are discouraged from simply assuming that the utterance of
'Juvenal' shows us the historical Juvenal in his actual beliefs. At
the same time, it would be wrong to divorce Juvenal's speaker
from a formal and notional sense of the poet, and to turn him into
a third-person figure, himself the main object of exposure. That
would lose us the zest and challenge of first-person poetry, which
give the elusiveness and play their force. To take poem 8 as an
example, it is difficult to see there any clear and wholesale undermining of a quite separated speaker's morality. Rather one should
feel uncertainty on the priorities and earnestness of the notional
author; one should savour the mixture of play with energetic
moralizing, in the floating and unfixed poem.[66]

The occasional poems of the epic poet **Statius** formally
employ firm conceptions of the higher genres of poetry as sublimer and more admirable; but the poet toys with these concep-

[65] Note in Horace's *Satires* esp. i. 4. 103–43, 6, ii. 1. 32–4, 3, 6, 7.

[66] It would also be an odd collection of features that were exposed in the speaker. For
uncertainty and play in the poem note e.g. 125 f., where the portentousness of the claim to
truth invites doubt. 215–30 play with tragedy, and then with quirky indignation and
concrete incongruity (the passages referred to by Courtney (1980), 383 f. are, I think, quite
different); 221 f. (even without 223) seem too consciously paradoxical, 220 f. too consciously
anticlimactic, for unwitting self-indictment. Lighter is the play with time at 39 f. in the
involvement with a figure who emerges as past (71 f.; cf. and contrast e.g. Plin. *NH* xxviii. 6);
complications are introduced by the whole interplay in the poem with the Neronian
period. See on 8 esp. Fredericks (1971); Braund (1988), ch. 3.

tions, not to challenge convention, but to play on other people and on himself and his own *œuvre*.[67]

Silvae i. 2 is a marriage-song for an elegist; in it Statius addresses elegists with jocular partisanship as *qui nobile gressu / extremo fraudatis epos* (250 f.), 'you who cheat the noble epic of its final foot'. He depicts the personified Elegy as being 'loftier than usual' for the wedding, and fraudulently gaining a place among the Muses (7–10): he is gaily distorting the fictions of elegy itself.[68] He delights to make the bridegroom relinquish love-elegy, and plays with its reality and deceit, its licentious and unelevated character (24–37). He delights too to cast the real bride in an ungrand and untragic version of Dido, and to bring into her falling in love, not Aeneas' heroic narrative, but the actuality of elegy (194–200, *Aen.* iv. 1–55).

In ii. 7 he marks his admiration of the dead Lucan by writing his anniversary-poem not in the metre of their shared genre epic, and of most of the *Silvae*, but in the much lighter hendecasyllables: 'I feared my own hexameter', *hexametros meos timui*, he says with charming artifice and warmth (ii *praef.* 26 Courtney). Generic hierarchy is obviously implied here. The poem itself depicts Lucan's grandeur in manner and matter: he 'thunders', he 'sings of battle and in lofty voice consoles the mighty dead' (*detonabis* 66; *arduaque voce / das solacia grandibus sepulchris* 102 f.). Only indirectly does Statius show his appreciation of the stranger elements in Lucan, such as the bizarre treatment of Pompey's corpse. He plays with Lucan's own advertisement of that bizarreness (ix. 14) and imagines Lucan perhaps laughing at his own burial (110). Lucan, he says, gave Pompey a tomb *altius*, 'loftier', than Egypt did (71 f.): the word conveys both grandeur and physical size, and so wittily evokes both the grotesqueness and the elevation of Lucan's own passage (viii. 692–872). For the main part of the poem a Muse, here made highly mythological, prophesies Lucan's career: the very device is used to play delicately on Lucan's own renunciation of Greek mythology for Roman reality (cf. 48–53). The poem avoids bringing out openly the full extent of that renunciation, which essentially includes mythological gods

---

[67] On these aspects of the *Silvae* see Friedrich (1963); Cancik (1965);, Aricò (1972), ch. 2; Szelest (1972); Newmyer (1979); Bright (1980); Hardie (1983); Vertraete (1983); Vessey (1986*a*); Coleman (1988) and van Dam (1984), introductions.

[68] Cf. esp. Ov. *Am.* iii. 1. 250 f. are stronger than v. 3. 99, itself playfully antagonistic; that whole passage is interesting for genre, as is i. 3. 99–104 (cf. ii. 2. 112–17).

and mythological Muses; but we are intended to contrast it with
the poem's own world.

At iv. 4. 46–73 Statius modestly sets his unwarlike art of poetry,
with its retired way of life, against the concerns of his younger
addressee: oratory, with its great practical ends (*magnos ... usus*
48), and active warfare. The whole poem plays with genre and
reality in the most complicated fashion. This passage itself uses,
and twists, Virgil's *Georgics*, an intriguing point of reference for the
imitator of Virgil's narrative epic. Statius' whole poem is by an
epic poet; yet it is presented as hardly a poem (93, probably 32 f.),
and models itself, with manifold play, on the *Epistles* of Horace. In
the plans he is making for epic, Statius *temptat* Troy and great
Achilles (*temptatur* 94): the verb, both 'try' and 'attack', sports with
real war.[69] At the close the warlike addressee is made to surpass
Achilles, not in warfare but in friendship. The ending strangely
joins Horace, and present and personal reality, with the terrible
world of epic, in which Achilles dragged Hector's body out of love
for his friend.

The prose prefaces confirm with apparent plainness the inferior status of the *Silvae* in comparison with Statius' epics. They
are mere preludes to the *Thebaid* (i *praef.* 9 Courtney); the *Thebaid*
cost long and intense labour, their excuse is their rapidity (i, ii;
contrast *Theb.* xii. 811 f., *Silv.* iii. 5. 35 f., iv. 7. 1 f., 26). Doubling the
image of play, he makes these poems a kind of mock-sport, a
practising in jest (*exerceri ioco*), as with wooden swords (iv *praef.*
29–31). Assuredly Statius will have regarded his epics, and rightly,
as the more important works; but so elaborately do these prefaces
themselves play with modesty and with pride that their explicit
description of the *Silvae* gives only a limited idea of what they are
like. In them present reality is lifted up, by poetry, to the level of
the full mythological genres: gods bulk large, myths are excelled.
And yet we know it is present reality. This produces a certain pull
between reality and elevation; the effects vary considerably, but
we are to feel always a certain decorous extravagance and
exquisite artifice. The crucial figure of the poet concentrates the
complications: the enthusiasm, the play, the concrete social
relations, the basic sincerity assumed, all are absorbed into a

---

[69] Note further Virg. *Aen.* xi. 436–9. On the poem see Hardie (1983), 164–71.

poetic stance which mediates the poised charm of these amphibious poems.[70]

Silv. i. 5, on the baths built by a friend, praises, but also stresses its own playfulness; it contrasts itself explicitly with the *Thebaid* and its grandiose inspiration, its effort, and its content of warfare and moral perversion. This poem is play for a well-loved friend (*dilecto volo lascivire sodali* 9). Yet the subject is approached—and made playful—through mythological beings, the water-nymphs. As in the epics, Statius revels in his picturesque aquatic deities; but their world is to be strangely combined with the realities of Roman aqueducts.

> praecelsis quarum vaga molibus unda
> crescit et innumero pendens transmittitur arcu,
> vestrum opus adgredimur, vestra est quam carmine molli
> pando domus. non umquam aliis habitastis in antris
> ditius.   (28–31)

(You nymphs) whose wandering water grows on towering structures, and is conveyed, suspended in air, on numberless arches, it is your work that I approach, your home that I lay open in my soft song. In no caves have you ever lived more richly.

The familiar is not only made unfamiliar, as in satire, but exalted; yet its unpoetic reality is allowed to show through.[71] The address accumulates mock-grandeur (marked out generically by *molli* 'soft'). The standard poetic notion of 'a home of nymphs' is used to naturalize the baths in the poetic world, but also to indicate a divergence, and to create, with the human idea of wealthy living, a degree of entertaining bathos (the enjambment in each of the last two lines here is full of purpose). There follows elegant fantasy on the god of fire.[72]

---

[70] The handling of the poet in some ways resembles Pindar's (as I conceive Pindar); but Statius smiles more often, and is polished like marble. Of course one must avoid any rigid antithesis between artifice and sincerity, particularly in a period so formal in social utterance.

[71] The effect in this context is not affected by the enthusiasm of Plin. *NH* xxxi. 31f. and Front. *Aq.* i. 16; cf. also *Silv.* i. 3. 66–9, where the effect of 67 is only confirmed by Hor. *Epist.* i. 10. 20f. and Ov. *Met.* iv. 122–4 (a simile, with Ovidian disruption). For the nymphs compare and contrast Mart. vi. 47, *al.* On the Roman aqueducts see Ashby (1935), etc.

[72] At this point even Markland applauded (on *tit.*). For *domus* cf. especially Virg. *Aen.* i. 168 *nympharum domus*, with Hom. *Od.* xii. 318, Call. fr. 66. 8f. Pfeiffer. The puns in *opus* and *pando* elaborate the play. On the poem cf. Hardie (1983), 132–6; Vessey (1986), 2792–4; Holtsmark (1972–3).

In ii. 6 Statius encourages Ursus, with warmth and stylized immediacy, to mourn for a dead slave-boy; he depicts him as surpassing the heroes of myth in beauty and valour (he is substantiating the ingenious thesis that he was no mere slave).

> non fallo aut cantus adsueta licentia ducit:
> vidi et adhuc video ... (29 f.)

This is no deceit, nor is my poetry being drawn on by its accustomed licence: I saw, and see still, (a youth who excelled both Achilles and his enemy Troilus).

The emphatic claims to truth, made by contrast with his own and other poetry, undermine themselves in their content: lavish mythological comparison, beyond the reach of autopsy. The poet is not crudely exposing his own insincerity, but investing his utterance with artifice, paradoxical and courtly.[73]

We close this chapter, and look forward to others, by drawing out further a point or two on the statements about literature. We have now glimpsed, among other things, the variety and force with which these works handle the basic ideas of sublimity and reality: what different notions may be adopted of reality, of its relation to sublimity, and of how far either gives a genre supremacy. For all this variety, we discern clearly enough that an expected pattern and hierarchy is presupposed, which authors can adopt, reverse, or distort as they choose. In this pattern, epic and tragedy concern themselves with an unreal world; their greatness or sublimity makes them as genres superior to other forms of poetry. Indeed superiority is suggested by the very terms used for the quality (hence the sublimity of higher genres is mostly presented, when attacked, as false sublimity). When the prose-writers speak simply of 'poetry' they are usually thinking of high poetry, such is its pre-eminence; that poetry is grander than prose. The patterns within prose itself are less clear. There is some sense that history, less immediate in its matter, is grander than oratory, and so hierarchically superior; to some extent the same is true of philosophy. But the rival understandings and assessments

---

[73] Similarly ii. 1. 50 *nil veris adfingo bonis* follows a very unlikely utterance. In lamenting for his own slave-boy (v. 5), Statius stresses his emotion by saying that now he cannot compose proper poetry (such as the consolatory *Silvae*); yet the poetry is as elegant as ever, and the author relishes the paradox of being pleased to sing bad verse (33 f.). (Håkanson (1969) 156 f. seems mistaken on this point; one may add that the soundness of 35 f. appears questionable.)

of truth and reality here break clamorously in, and prevent our tracing expected hierarchy much further. Reality too is relevant to the ranking of prose genres. It is relevant indeed to the ranking of poetry, for lower poets, sometimes; but they are more palpably affecting to defy an orthodoxy.

The pattern is presupposed and played on, not only by the authors we have been considering, but also, we shall see, by tragedy and epic themselves. It will be apparent how contemporary statements about tragedy and epic are liable to prove, as critical description, particularly unrevealing. High poetry itself is expected by genre to talk little about literature. Prose writers are most interested in prose, and seldom explore poetry deeply or freshly for itself; lower poetry wants from high poetry a simple foil (so for the most part Statius himself in the *Silvae*). Further, prose critics do not respond warmly to an author's deliberately falling beneath or playing with an elevated or even a serious genre. Such an attitude would prove unrewarding with the high poetry, and with Seneca's prose (and also declamation)—the works most deeply affected by the most distinctive fashions of the period. Yet the attitude is adopted, in his prose, even by Seneca (note p. 129). If we combine that fact with Quintilian's disapprobation of Seneca's own prose for its ingenious wit, we see sharply how artificial or unsympathetic this criticism can be with generically startling elements, and how plainly those elements exist and matter.

2

GENRE AND PHILOSOPHY, HISTORY, AND HIGH POETRY

In this chapter we shall look principally at the aspects of genre considered in the first: sublimity, grandeur, greatness; truth and reality. With reality and truth we shall again look at the handling of the author; emotion and intellectualism will also be drawn in. The full complexity of these questions will properly appear only with succeeding chapters; the discussion of the verse is little more than an introduction. On prose we shall say something at the start about one or two other authors, but we shall largely concentrate on **Seneca** and **Tacitus**, the two main representatives of philosophy and history and the two greatest writers of Latin prose in our (or perhaps any) period.

Both Seneca and Tacitus wish to be seen as eager, and well fitted, to give us truth. Both accordingly bring into contrast and fruitful commerce with their more emotional elements a critical manner, an air of judgement and independence. Seneca in particular engages enthusiastically in controversy and argument: philosophy has no prosecution of a narrative to limit it here. The place of reality and the author in their works is bound up with the intellectual tradition of prose, on which we shall elaborate a little. Prose had been marked out from the first by its explicitly intellectual manner. In viewing Roman prose for our particular purposes, we shall find it most profitable to consider, not how Roman intellectuals actually worked, nor how their attainments match those of Greek or modern scholarship, but the effect they seek on the reader, and the sense of the author which they create.[1]

We may illustrate the importance of displaying a critical approach from **the Elder Pliny**.[2] His *Natural History* does not

---

[1] For the intellectual element in Roman culture see esp. Wallace-Hadrill (1983); Rawson (1985); Holford-Strevens (1988).

[2] See particularly Serbat (1973); and also Lloyd (1983), 135–49; Wallace-Hadrill (1990, with further literature). One may notice that, even on the harshest view of Pliny's readiness to believe, he is not bettered by the Republican and intellectually formidable Lucretius: cf. Lucr. ii. 536–40, iv. 710–13, vi. 879–82.

achieve, or perhaps seek, a grand intellectual cohesiveness; but he is greatly concerned to show a discriminating attitude to truth. He stresses throughout that he is transmitting reports, not subscribing to them; he will often indicate probabilities. Instances of this discrimination are his firm argument against others' views on blight at xviii. 275–7 (*id manifestum fiet attendentibus*, 'this will be obvious to those who consider with attention'); or his disbelief in tales of Prometheus at xxxiii. 8 (*omnia fabulosa arbitror*, 'I think it all mythical'); or his surprise at Aristotle's credulity about signs of long life at xi. 273 f. (*miror equidem . . . vana existimo . . . frivola ut reor*. 'I myself am surprised . . . I judge them foolish . . . silly, as I think'; the usual emphasis on the first person is combined with an amiably naïve concern for the reader's peace of mind).[3] There is a complicated interplay, even on the level of style, between this critical element and his zeal for the wonders characteristic of nature. Scholarly reserve and the heightening of marvels, lowness and exaltation of language and of content, are intriguingly and consciously mingled.[4]

The importance of controversial manner and the use of the author may be seen in **Quintilian**.[5] His language, though dignified, is alive with controversial vivacity; and he creates an attractive sense of his own honesty, rationality, balance, and zest. He ranges from the forthright curtness of *quo quid stultius?* (ix. 2. 82), 'And what could be stupider than that?', to the judicious elaboration with which he presents a concession to a common view: *quod mihi (libera enim vel contra receptas persuasiones rationem sequenti sententia est) in parte verum videtur* (ii. 8. 6), 'To me (if one follows reason one can vote freely even against received opinions) this seems partly true.' (*mihi*, 'to me', and *in parte*, 'partly', are winningly placed.) A little later in ii we see him with sprightly mischief turning an apparent concession into pugnacity: *nihilo minus confitendum est*

---

[3] xi. 274 is difficult (Ernout's and Birt's conjectures do not touch the problem). I think that Aristotle is said not to discover these connections to be generally true; the turn with *frivola* is slight and acceptable. At xxxiii. 8 note the moral twist (cf. xxxvii. 2).

[4] Cf. e.g. x. 191–3 (note the lateness of *dicuntur* in 191; in 193 Aristotle (*Hist. An.* iv. 533ᵃ34–ᵇ5) with fairly little change becomes amazing, and is supported with contemporary evidence). vii. 6–8 is a significant passage for the intellectual questions concerned (of which Pliny is well aware); important for sublimity and reality are *Praef.* 12–15 (note the shift in the course of the passage), xx. *praef.* (cf. xxxvii. 59 f.).

[5] See Adamietz (1986*a*); he cites further literature.

etiam detrahere doctrinam aliquid ... sed vitia detrahit (12. 8), 'none
the less, one must admit that instruction in oratory does actually
remove something ... but what it removes is faults.' He can also
withdraw from pedantic discussion, and play on his discourse
with a fleeting smile.[6]

   Seneca outmatches both these writers in his air of mental
sparkle, sharpness, and energy.[7] This all subserves the presentation, through the author, of philosophical truth: our impression of
his intellectual address, intensity, and judgement enforces his
message. (In practice, the intellectual brilliancy also makes, and is
intended to make, a more self-contained appeal.) We may look
first at some ways in which Seneca displays his own mental individuality, his independence and life. To manifest his independence he will even stress his freedom in relation to the writers of
his own Stoic school. At *NQ* vii. 22. 1, he has elaborated what he
presents (20. 1) as the main Stoic view of comets; he has written
placet ergo nostris (21. 1), 'Our philosophers, then, hold ... '. Against
this he now sets the resounding *ego nostris non assentior*, 'I myself do
not agree with our philosophers'. The argumentation that follows
is based partly on a warm feeling, which his language expresses,
for the nature of the different parts in his hierarchical universe
and for its overall 'greatness' (24. 2): his intellectualism is not cold.
But the argument is also forceful; and he deploys his own observation in a tone of epistemological canniness: *hoc an cometae alii fecerint
nescio; duo nostra aetate fecerunt* (23. 1), 'whether other comets have
done this I do not know; in our time two have' (cf. 21. 3f., i. 1. 12).
His attitude to truth looks forward to new discovery, not merely
back to old authority (25. 7, 32. 1); still more striking and impressive
is his bleakness on the possibility of knowing or plumbing truth
(29. 3, 32. 4).[8]

   In the surviving part of Book iv b he exhibits his critical detach-

---

[6] Cf. e.g. iii. 6. 21; v. 10. 92.

[7] See Hirzel (1895), ii. 24–34; Weber (1895); Guillemin (1952–4); Hadot (1969); Michel
(1969); Russell (1974); Wright (1974); Griffin (1976), esp. 12–20; Abel (1985); Wilson (1988);
Armisen-Marchetti (1989), 37–60; Maurach (1991). Our plan prevents us from treating here
the immensely complicated background of traditions in philosophical writing, with the
attendant notions of thorny Stoics, lively 'diatribes', eloquent Romans, etc.; Rutherford
(1989), 21–3, leads one into the subject effectively.

[8] For vii, and iv b, see Gross (1989); I doubt whether *nec ... emersit* in vii. 17. 2 are
Apollonius' words. See also for vii Kidd on Posid. frr. 131–2. It is interesting, though
ultimately unimportant, that Seneca is on the right lines in his independent view of comets.

ment through a more playful manner. He happily ascribes to Stoic writers *ineptias*, 'absurdities', and possible 'lies' (6. 1, 5. 4, 4. 1), and refutes or abstains (7. 2, 5. 1–4). But he conveys his own shrewdness with a humorous affectation of casual and undemanding attitudes to truth, and with play on his own activity. So:

ut fallar, tibi <   > verum mihi quidem persuadetur, qui me usque ad mendacia haec leviora in quibus os percidi, non oculi erui solent, credulum praesto.[9]   (4. 1)

even if I am mistaken, [I shall tell] *you* [what] *I* at least am convinced true; my credulity extends as far as the slighter lies which earn a blow in the face, not the tearing out of one's eyes.

In this sentence the air of serious honesty and communication at the start yields to gentle, and then robust, comedy (the two violent actions are not expected after *leviora*, 'slighter'); and it yields to a seeming combination of professed credulity and frivolous scepticism. With less ironic humour, he declines to ascertain by his own experiment the effect of snow on the feet. He advises his addressee to make the experiment on a vile body, if he wishes to investigate the truth (*si volueris verum exquirere*, 5. 3; Seneca has not done even this).[10] All this play in fact marks his own responsibility of mind; it also delights us in itself.

Seneca accepts Stoicism in a rational, not a dogmatic, spirit; his frequent vigour and vehemence in controversy express intellectual force and engagement.[11] His abundant employment of imaginary interlocutors—other minds, not other personalities—often creates a spirited drama of the intellect; it is also often used to sharpen the personal edge in the presentation of his own thought and outlook. In *Vit. Beat.* 7–12 the debate with Epicureanism gains from its animated half-dialogue a sense of argumentative sharpness and of Seneca's own mental commitment (indeed

---

[9] So I would suggest one might read (with e.g. <*exponam quod esse*>). For the eyes cf. Suet. *Ner.* 5. 1. For different views on the passage, see Shackleton Bailey (1979), 453; at the start, his reading seems to give the relative clause rather less point.

[10] Delete *nivem* with Gertz. For the proverb alluded to in *Care* see Sch. T on Plat. *Lach.* 187 b; serious controversies are probably glanced at humorously, cf. esp. Herophil. T 63 a (and also b–c) von Staden.

[11] For the spirit in which Seneca accepts Stoicism cf. *Ot.* 3. 1, *Ep.* 33. 7 ff.; the use of the Senate as a compelling image for rational debate appears also in *Vit. Beat.* 3. 2 (more restricted) and *Ep.* 21. 9 (Seneca's whole use of Epicurus in Books i–iii displays his critical openness, cf. Freise (1989), and *Ira* i. 6. 5). For the attitude criticized cf. e.g. Quint. xii. 2. 26.

his very style of life will presently be involved).[12] Such vigorous plural phrases from Seneca as *quid est, oro vos*, 'Pray tell me, what is the reason ... ?' (7. 1) pass over to a singular adversary, who is given lively ripostes (10. 1, 9. 1), and is himself cajoled or assailed: *age, non vides ... ?* 'Come now, don't you see ... ?' (11. 1); *quid mihi voluptatem nominas? hominis bonum quaero, non ventris*, 'Why do you speak of pleasure? I am looking for a good pertaining to man, not the belly.' (9. 4). A string of contrasts confronts not simply tenets but 'you' and 'me': so *tu omnia voluptatis causa facis, ego nihil* (10. 3), 'for the sake of pleasure you do everything that you do, and I do nothing.'

Seneca can give himself, and the person to whom a work is addressed, a somewhat fuller appearance of being particular people, with a relationship. He and his addressee often move between such an appearance and the guise of more generalized and emblematic figures; these aspects and movements have a varied significance. Richest in this respect are the *Letters*: as formally belonging to a lower genre, they can affect to treat the author in more extensively personal a fashion. In 68. 6–8 Seneca has talked about the spiritual use of Lucilius' and his own retirement from Roman life.[13] Even here both men have stood to some degree as representatives of universal truth, and some air of generality has attached to the 'you' and the 'I'. But in 8 f. Seneca acquires a much more individual role, through his relationship with Lucilius. Lucilius is urged to see in Seneca's retirement no sign of spiritual elevation and to seek from him no spiritual help.

nolo nolo laudes, nolo dicas, 'o magnum virum! ...' ... malo illa cum discesseris dicas: 'ego istum beatum hominem putabam et eruditum, erexeram aures; destitutus sum, nihil vidi, nihil audivi ... ad quod reverterer.' (8 f.)

Please, please don't praise me, don't say 'What a great man! ...' ... I would rather you said, when you left [after visiting me], 'I thought the

[12] One may rewardingly compare the place and treatment of dialogue and exposition in Cic. *Fin.* ii. Seneca's formulaic *inquit* without *aliquis* derives from a tradition seen, but not exclusively, in philosophy: cf. Hirzel (1895), i. 371. 2; Schmid (1906), 274; Housman on Man. iv. 869. On the *De Beneficiis* Lavery (1987) is deliberately selective, but could give a one-sided impression.

[13] The letter is related to the *De Otio*, which is in my view probably the earlier work (cf. the discussion in Dionigi (1983), 48–54; in general see Griffin (1976), ch. 10). It gives a much more intimate sense of personality and relationship than what survives of the treatise (*Brev.* 18 f. gives more concrete detail of the addressee). The rare use of Seneca's name accordingly seems much richer in *Ep.* 68. 10 than in *Ot.* 1. 4.

man was a blessed soul and a deep philosopher; my ears were pricked up to hear him. But he disappointed me, I saw and heard nothing ... to return for.'

Any claim to greatness of soul is renounced with a suitably collo-quial animation (too Mediterranean to capture in English); Lu-cilius' disappointment is unsparingly pictured in vividly ordinary speech, which presents Seneca in the distanced third person. The spiritual relationship is in imagination almost undone as Seneca drastically displays that ability to face the truth about oneself which he had enjoined on his friend. Later (12f.) the two are brought together in their pursuit of philosophy as death draws near. In this letter the particular people give truth its most pierc-ing expression.

Ep. 56 uses individuality quite differently.[14] With mock-gran-deur, colloquialism, and racy exuberance of description, it creates a suspicious picture of Seneca the sage, loftily undisturbed by the noises of the public baths. At the close this picture is surprisingly and amusingly reversed. The first part describes his current aural and pyschological experience with almost Proustian attention; at the beginning and end Seneca evokes lively contact with Lucilius by imaginary conversation (this is here an epistolary device).[15] The final reversal has point as well as charm; but the letter reaches its greatest depth as it moves away from personal particu-larity to expound more general and inward truth (5–14). The concrete individuality recedes, and then returns playfully to disrupt.

We have seen something of Seneca's use of himself, and the intellectual manner through which he seeks our belief in the truth of what he says. We turn now from reality and the author to sublimity. Seneca's writing embraces the whole range of his hier-archical universe, from the low and sordid to the supremely high: it is magnificently inclusive. The traditions of philosophy offered Seneca many possibilities; like Plato, he makes transcendence vivid while remaining shrewdly and vigorously in touch with familiar reality. The literary grandeur or lowness of effect in a passage is related to the place of the content in his philosophical

---

[14] On the letter cf. Motto and Clark (1970).

[15] Cf. e.g. Cic. *Att.* vi. 6. 3, xv. 9. 1. The use of the addressee in 14 is more generalized in quality, but prepares for 15; *inani ... circumstrepet* echoes 4 and the mock-elevated *ecce ... circumsonat* of 1. *torqueri* in 15 marks a definite inconsistency with 1–5.

hierarchy. But he also surprises us, upsetting other hierarchies, like those of language in his use of low diction; and there are many intricacies and complexities in his lively and mercurial use of sublimity and lowness. We shall for the present mark out different levels relatively simply, and suggest some of the complications.

We begin at the bottom, with some of Seneca's numerous assaults on modern behaviour. Like the satirists, he relishes his low colour, but is less whimsically absorbed by it, and controls it more incisively in the starker rhetoric of prose. In *Helv.* 10 he indicts the importation of luxurious foods from distant regions; he sets the grandeur of geographical range against the baseness of eating.[16]

quod dissolutus deliciis stomachus vix admittat ab ultimo portatur Oceano. vomunt ut edant, edunt ut vomant, et epulas quas toto orbe conquirunt nec concoquere dignantur.   (10. 3)

What can hardly be taken by a stomach worn out by delicacies is transported from furthest Ocean. They vomit so they can eat, they eat so they can vomit; the fare they seek over the whole earth they do not see fit even to digest.

The disparity between the two halves of the first sentence is highlighted by the emphatic separation of *ultimo*, 'furthest', and *Oceano*, 'Ocean'. In the second the bizarre and futile circularity of their disgusting logic leads into a scornful opposition between *toto orbe conquirunt*, 'seek over the whole earth', and *concoquere*, 'digest', underlined by the explicit *dignantur*, 'see fit', and by the play with the sound of *conquirunt* and *concoquere*.[17]

More elaborate is *NQ* i. 16, on a man who used mirrors to produce magnified reflections of his sexual activities. Here perversion seeks in an unreal fashion to be greater than nature (a supremely exalted entity in Seneca's universe). Sordidness becomes not reality but unreality; the 'greatness', though only the crude physical greatness of enlarged obscenities, is clearly made a wild distortion of the transcendent sublime (16. 8f.). The common idea of perverting nature gains special force from the theme of the

[16] For the theme cf. Housman on Man. v. 195f.; compare too Luc. x. 155–8, Juv. 5. 92–102 (p. 33 above). On pheasants cf. Mayor on Juv. ii. 139: Seneca substitutes for the Argonauts more Roman, moral, and ingenious play with the Parthians. On luxury in general cf. Griffin (1976), ch. 9.

[17] With *vomunt ... vomant* cf. *Ben.* iii. 16. 2 *exeunt matrimonii causa, nubunt repudii.*

Naturales Quaestiones (note ch. 17); but it is hard to miss Seneca's delight in paradox, ingenuity, and the creation of grotesque colour, for their own sakes as well as for the argument's.[18] The close of the passage returns curtly to the murder of the man by his own slaves:

facinus indignum! hic fortasse cito et antequam videret occisus est; ad speculum suum immolandus fuit. (16. 9)

Perhaps he was killed swiftly and before he could see. What an appalling crime! He should have been slaughtered in sight of his mirror.

We must feel here not simply indignation but pleasure: deliberately implausible ferocity (note *fortasse*, 'perhaps') expresses itself so deviously and so cleverly.

More ordinary behaviour is vividly described by Seneca and penetratingly exposed. The *De Beneficiis* is full of significant niceties and satirical observation, as in i. 1. 5 f. on our reluctance to grant favours (the frown, the prolongation of talk with others, the grudging, halting consent). *Brev.* 11 paints with pungent animation the attitude of the old to death, dwelling on their self-deception.[19] Against their frantic indignity ample rhetoric sets the spaciousness of philosophical retirement, and elevated simplicity sets the heroism of the wise. Seneca's vision can further turn the familiar world into something frighteningly unfamiliar. So in *Ben.* vii. 27. 1 f. the true picture of human life produced by a knowledge of the passions dramatically transforms normal society into the grandiose abnormality of a city being sacked. One may contrast *NQ* ii. 59. 8; there, with an unelevated and grim obliteration of social categories, we are all made like criminals condemned to death.[20]

The most important subjects of grandeur in Seneca are the divine, the heavens, the cosmos and nature as a whole, and some aspects of the vital world of the *animus*, 'mind, spirit', in particular virtue, often as shown in great actions. These categories plainly link up both with the beliefs and values of Stoicism and with

[18] On reality, luxury, and nature cf. Sen. Rh. *Contr.* ii. 1. 13 (Fabianus); for the mirrors cf. Suet. *Vit. Hor.* 62–4 Rostagni.

[19] A common subject is treated individually; cf. Lucr. iii. 955–65; Muson. 17 p. 92 Hense; Powell (1988), 246 f. For *moriuntur* cf. Petr. 62. 8, Dem. iv. 45, etc.

[20] On the text see Hine ad loc. With *Ben.* vii. 27 cf. also the less grand *Ira* iii. 26. 4; note the tones of exposure there.

general literary tradition. At *Ep.* 8. 5 Seneca brings out with rich paradox both the importance of the *animus* and its scope for greatness: *cogitate nihil praeter animum esse mirabile, cui magno nihil magnum est,* 'Think that nothing deserves wonder save the spirit; if it is great, nothing seems great to it.'[21] He then presents the concerns of philosophy, at once human and divine, as more important and greater (*maiora*) than those of Roman life. With more imposing breadth the preface to *NQ* iii brings together the greatness of nature and god, the greatness of mind needed to consider these subjects, and the greatness of the spirit defying fortune; it demeans conventional, and historical, notions of human greatness. All this generates in the passage a sweeping sublimity which encompasses the reader's, and especially the author's, own rise in spirit as they contemplate the sublime (4, 18, 3). At 9 Seneca builds up a superbly grandiose and impressive picture of the destruction of empires, which he contrasts with mere domestic calamities. He ends *alia summittit nec molliter ponit sed ex fastigio suo nullas habitura reliquias iactat,* 'others God lowers, not laying them down gently but hurling them from their height and leaving no remains'. The grimly ironic negative clause leads up to the magnificent *iactat* 'hurls', given power by its position and its place in the clausular rhythm.[22] Yet he continues: *magna ista quia parvi sumus credimus,* 'we think these things great because we are small'. In outdoing normal human conceptions of greatness here he is also in a sense outmatching the very sublimity he has been creating. For Seneca the highest sublimity lies not in massive destruction but in unshakable virtue and the unchanging heavens.

We can see this further in *Ep.* 71. 8–16. Here Cato's unchanging virtue, never greater or less (8), is set against 'the ruin of so great an empire', *tam magni ruina imperi,* in the fall of the Republic (9). His 'greatness of spirit' (*magno animo,* 11) and his scorn for the world of change is marked by actions of unglamorous calmness: on the night of his death he reads a book, as on a slighter occasion of

---

[21] Seneca builds here on a common Stoic attitude (e.g. Epict. i. 28. 14–18; Marc. Aur. i. 15. 6; *SVF* iii. 642). For the soul in Stoicism, see Long (1982), and also Inwood (1985). In Seneca (cf. Motto (1970), 200–3) the *animus* is roughly the scene of passion and the vehicle of reason, and descends from the divine. On the sources of grandeur generally cf. Hermog. *Id.* i. 6 (pp. 219–23 Rabe).

[22] Contrast the opening ἰάπτει in the related passage Aesch. *Supp.* 95f. As to the exceeded *ponit* note Hor. *Odes* i. 34. 16.

political failure he played at dice (ii: *lusit ... legit*). More strikingly still, Cato makes a speech sonorously depicting universal destruction; this is set against his cool acceptance of death at the close (15). The whole passage ends, characteristically but significantly, with wilfully prosy language: unaltering virtue, like a military unit, 'has got all its numbers; it is at full strength', *habet numeros suos, plena est.*[23]

The range seen in Seneca's writing as a whole, and in individual paragraphs, appears no less remarkably and significantly in the course of a particular work or part of one. We may instance *Ep.* 120. A sharply intellectual element is conspicuous at the start, as Seneca purposefully distinguishes words used as synonyms by Lucilius and purposefully discusses the use of a Greek term, and as he shows critical awareness of how truth is distorted, and generally explores our acquisition of notions of virtue.[24] He then elaborates the deeds of two Roman heroes, evoking moral greatness with grandeur; the grandeur is somewhat contained by the critical indication he has just given that these stories have been exaggerated (5). In the second case, the grandeur is heightened by narrative; in both it finds expression in magnificent utterances from the heroes themselves. So in the first Fabricius, refusing to let his foe be poisoned: *Vive ... beneficio meo, Pyrrhe, et gaude quod adhuc dolebas, Fabricium non posse corrumpi* (6). 'Live, Pyrrhus, by my gift; rejoice at what hitherto had grieved you, that Fabricius cannot be seduced by bribes.' The decisive imperative, the proud use of the speaker's name, the very neatness, are grandiose and impressive. We also relish the ingenious link forged by the author between the two separate deeds of Fabricius'. That ingenuity in turn has its point: consistency is to be a theme.[25]

Returning to the reality we witness, Seneca shows a shrewd and subtle moral discrimination (even while his argument attributes such discrimination to 'us' generally). So at 9 his construction abruptly exposes apparent greatness: we observed when young *quis rem aliquam generoso animo fecisset et magno impetu, sed semel*, 'who had done some deed with noble spirit, and with a mighty urge of the mind, but only once'. Gradually Seneca builds up a

---

[23] Ov. *Her.* 10. 36 is deliberately prosaic too.

[24] Cf. Cic. *Fin.* iii. 33 f., with Madvig's note.

[25] Note the placing of the two incidents in Plut. *Pyrrh.* 20 f. With the utterance compare the soured magnanimity of Luc. ii. 512 f. On Cocles Seneca gives less physical detail than Livy (ii. 10), but elaborates extravagant moral grandeur more strongly.

sense of the sublimity and greatness of true virtue, *magnitudo super omnia efferens sese*, 'its greatness raising itself high above everything' (11). The truly virtuous man is also given a sublime utterance (12), but its nobility, superficially less heroic than that of the Roman heroes, goes deeper; he acts as 'a citizen and soldier' of the universe. We then move in a different direction, and see the divine origin of the mind in general from its discomfort at low bodily pains, concretely recalled ('now diarrhoea, now catarrh', etc., 16). A transforming and startling vision develops of life as gradual death; in contrast stands the 'great spirit', aware that it does not belong here. Its greatness appears in its very unpretentiousness: the final phrase is impressive because it is so swift and unfussy: *peregrinus et properans*, 'as an alien and in haste'. The resolution in *prŏpĕrans* is masterly.

Finally, Seneca opposes to this firm 'true greatness' (19) the inconsistency we see in ordinary people. The section is full of vigorous satire, and indeed quotes the *Satires* of Horace; but it becomes less extreme and more searching as it moves from 'some people' to 'us'. We feel the powerful mind and imagination of Seneca making the familiar world absorbingly strange (we need to forget twentieth-century thought): *praeter sapientem autem nemo unum agit, ceteri multiformes sumus* (22), 'No one but the wise man acts the part of one person; the rest of us have many forms.' The close conveys this unfamiliarity with more everyday vividness. *hic qui est?*, 'Who is this?', one could rightly say of someone seen yesterday.

In considering **Tacitus'** historical writing we shall look first at its concern with truth; this is displayed with particular prominence in his text.[26] For our special purposes we shall disregard the actual extent of Tacitus' researches and his actual historical depth; what matters to us here is the effect that he seeks on the reader. He wishes the reader to see him as (among other things) a scholar who devotes labour, erudition, and critical acumen to the ascertaining of what is true. To stress this intellectual element is

[26] From the great mass of writing on Tacitus we may mention here Boissier (1903); Syme (1958); Walker (1968); Goodyear (1970); Martin (1981); Woodman (1988), ch. 4 (note also Martin and Woodman (1989)). In what follows only slight bibliographical hints are offered on some of the subjects touched on. It should be evident that I have much sympathy with Woodman's picture of ancient historiography in his very valuable and important book; but also that I wish to complicate that picture. In general, I would wish to give less authority to Cic. *De Or.* ii. 51–64, where I would lay rather more weight on the nature of the work and the profession of its writer.

not to deny the importance to Tacitus of arousing emotion. On the contrary, it is vital to perceive how densely and significantly they are interwoven and combined. Critical procedures and language can simultaneously serve emotional ends, or contrast with overtly emotional language, without one effect or type of impact annulling the other. Strong and emotive language is commonly called forth by moral truth, which is not only intellectually compatible with factual truth and the attempt to achieve it, but is often closely or inextricably bound up with them. We shall illustrate the complex relationships in Tacitus' writing between different types of truth and between the intellectual and the emotional by considering some of Tacitus' means for exhibiting his historian's concern for the truth of fact.[27]

Tacitus sometimes advertises his diligence in employing sources other than previous histories: such is his zeal in pursuing truth. His use of these sources is also made to display his critical power, and expose moral truth. On the election of consuls under Tiberius Tacitus writes *vix quicquam firmare ausim: adeo diversa non modo apud auctores, sed in ipsius orationibus reperiuntur* (*Ann.* i. 81. 1), 'I hardly dare affirm anything, so different are the things one finds, not only in the historians, but in Tiberius' own speeches.' He is marking his own caution, and his use of the less immediate resource; at the same time he is preparing wryly and authoritatively for the account that follows of Tiberius' restless and elaborate efforts to give an appearance of liberty to the elections. He brings his paragraph to a climax in a contrasting tone of voice; piercing through the tangle, he pronounces forthrightly on Tiberius' futility or hypocrisy, and closes with strong words on slavery. In the same way *extat oratio*, 'a speech of Tiberius survives', at ii. 63. 3 nails down the deceitfulness of the emperor. When Tacitus stresses proudly at iv. 53. 2 that he has found for himself an event not in the historians, we should also feel that his labour has enhanced the dynastic confrontations of chs. 52f., which probe Tiberius' hidden mind. Tacitus, unlike the mob scorned in *Hist.*

---

[27] We may just mention the fresh and favourable light thrown on Tacitus' procedures by the Tabula Siarensis, particularly fr. 1. 18: see esp. Lebek (1987), 139f., (1988), 265–7. Our scheme again precludes discussion of the historiographical tradition; but since Curtius Rufus belongs somewhere in our period, the following passages may be cited as examples interesting to compare with Tacitus in the respects that concern us here: iv. 4. 19–21, 15. 11, vi. 2. 15, viii. 10. 35f., ix. 5. 21 (cf. Bosworth (1988), 80f.), x. 10. 14–19. See also Dosson (1887), 173–82.

iv. 49. 3, shows no *indiligentia veri*, no lack of care and concern about truth.[28]

Equally rich is his treatment of disputed truth at particular points. Such moments were a conventional opportunity for displaying professionalism; as appears from other accounts, the particular questions treated at *Hist.* i. 41 and ii. 37f. were themselves conventional. In the first, on the death of Galba, he shows awareness of the motives that produced conflicting accounts of his last words, base or noble, and makes us feel the inaccessibility of the truth; this brings to a height our uncertainties on how to evaluate Galba morally.[29] Tacitus' brusque addition *non interfuit occidentium quid diceret*, 'It did not matter to his killers what he said', powerfully twists the controversy; he affects to distance it grimly, but in doing so manifests his moral scorn for the slayers. In the second, on the question whether before the first battle of Cremona the armies might have considered ending the civil war, he marks his own opinion with an emphatic *ego*, 'I'; his unusually elaborate and balanced structure of sentence expresses his own judiciousness, force of argument, and critical sagacity. These qualities are united with strong and assured moral assessment. It is with an effect simultaneously emotional and intellectual that we receive Tacitus' insight, dark, firm, and finally oblique. At his close he tells us that most of the leaders, 'conscious of their own dissipation, poverty, and crimes', would only tolerate an emperor who was *pollutum obstrictumque meritis suis*, 'stained with guilt, and bound to them by their services'; the *pollutum*, 'stained with guilt', and the context, blackly suggest the character of *their* services. Tacitus proceeds to survey the history of civil strife, not actually to decide the argument, but to impress and stir us with his sweeping and sombre vision.

The mention of sources can give terrible authenticity to a particular moment; it can further, by suggesting that an event appears incredible, enhance at once its horror or strangeness and

---

[28] Contrast *Hist.* iv. 48. 1; Plin. *Ep.* vii. 33. 3 (and e.g. Sall. *Jug.* 95. 2). On *Ann.* ii. 63. 3 compare Goodyear's note; and for the phrase note also Plin. *NH* xi. 187. At iv. 53. 2 neither explanation of *ex re publica* in Martin and Woodman's note appears plausible; the phrase must, I think, be corrupt. Historical questions and historical bibliography, like those relating to i. 81, will normally be excluded in this book.

[29] Cf. esp. 6f., 16, 18, 31. 2, 35; certainty comes (at least in appearance) with the obituary in 49. For the question here cf. Suet. *Galb.* 20. 1; for that in ii. 37 Plut. *Otho* 9. On ii. 37f. cf. e.g. Klingner (1964).

the author's responsible approach; or it can set the horror in greater relief through contrast with an apparently detached and academic manner. At *Ann.* xi. 27 (the 'marriage' of Claudius' wife Messalina to Silius) Tacitus begins with formulaic hauteur 'I am not unaware it will be thought fantastic that ... ', *haud sum ignarus fabulosum visum iri*, and proceeds to build up rhetorically the extraordinary event. Then, with a forceful 'but', he affirms that no detail has been made up to procure amazement, *sed nihil compositum miraculi causa*: it all derives from contemporary sources.[30] The double effect is here obvious: the cautious author and the extraordinary happening are both enhanced. In *Hist.* iii mention of sources heightens the killing in civil war of father by son (25. 2 f.), brother by brother (51); in both cases the mobile voice of the historian produces multiple effects, and conveys vehement moral condemnation as well as scholarly scruple. At *Ann.* v. 9. 1 Tacitus pathetically depicts the childish innocence of Sejanus' daughter, who is being led to execution; he continues:

tradunt temporis eius auctores, quia triumvirali supplicio adfici virginem inauditum habebatur, a carnifice laqueum iuxta compressam.(2)

Contemporary writers report that, because it was thought quite unheard of for a virgin to undergo capital punishment, she was violated by the executioner, next to the noose.

Tacitus stresses that the horror is true; at the same time the superficial austerity of manner gives immense power to the statement. The force here is increased because the decision itself so perversely unites legalistic precision with a hideous absence of moral feeling. The words in the last clause are so placed as actually to bring out the monstrosity, whereas the clause before is coldly legal. *inauditum habebatur*, 'it was thought quite unheard of', points the contrast ironically.[31]

Often Tacitus indicates a possibility without affirming it. Such possibilities indeed linger and invite; but one should not so emphasize his wish to affirm in practice that one underplays the positive importance to Tacitus of exhibiting critical caution, and of intensifying through the expression of uncertainty a sinister

---

[30] Compare Wiseman (1987), 259, Levick (1990), 67.

[31] *inauditum* is a choicer word here than the *nefas* and οὐχ ὅσιον in Suet. *Tib.* 61. 5 and Dio lviii. 11. One may contrast with Tacitus the relative weakness here of Dio stylistically, and of Suetonius intellectually. For *temporis eius* cf. *Ann.* xii. 67. 1, xiii. 17.

murkiness.[32] At *Hist.* ii. 99 the 'German' army has sunk into degeneracy:

accedebat huc Caecinae ambitio vetus, torpor recens, nimia Fortunae indulgentia soluti in luxum, seu perfidiam meditanti infringere exercitus virtutem inter artis erat.

A further factor was the commander Caecina's old courting of popularity, and his recent sloth, the excessive favours of Fortune having reduced him to lax and luxurious dissipation; or else he was planning treachery to Vitellius, and undoing the valour of the army was one of his wiles.

The first half of the sentence, firm in movement, sounds damning and decisive; but the second possibility trumps the first, it seems with sombre and twisted ingenuity. Yet Caecina's treachery soon emerges plainly; the point of the form cannot be simply to assert treachery, although obliquely.[33] Tacitus shows great caution on precisely how and when Caecina's treachery came about: *credidere plerique*, 'most believed'; *nec sciri potest*, 'one cannot know' (99. 2, 100. 3, cf. *creditur*, 'it is believed', 93. 2). At the same time he exposes and rejects the bias of those earlier historians who find the treachery noble motives; he condemns it strongly, and with reasoning of emphatic independence (*nobis* 'to me' at 101. 1 begins the clause). In our passage he is combining a sober historical and a forthright moral integrity, while adding a touch of cool deviousness; he is also investing the actions of Caecina with a shady and disreputable obscurity.

Such obscurity well suits the world of Tacitus' work (most especially the *Annals*), which is filled with uncertainty both for posterity and for the people of the time. An emperor's mind must often be guessed (e.g. *Ann.* i. 12. 3, iii. 22. 2); the emperors themselves find it difficult, or disagreeable, to learn the truth (e.g. vi. 38. 3, xiii. 47. 1, xv. 67. 3, *Hist.* i. 29. 1). Events and behaviour are alarmingly unpredictable and strange (e.g. *Ann.* iv. 58. 2f., *Hist.* ii. 97. 2), the more so as the emperors are so terribly or weirdly devoid of ordinary feelings (e.g. *Ann.* iii. 15. 2, xi. 38. 2f., *Hist.* ii. 70.

---

[32] See on the subject notably Ryberg (1942); Whitehead (1979); Develin (1983). *Ann.* xiv. 2. 2 suggests that these items are at least often Tacitus' own addition. Note that the device is already used at *Agr.* 7. 3, *Germ.* 16. 1.

[33] One may compare the development of *Ann.* xiii. 19, where an appearance of great cynicism in 1 (cf. Nipperdey on xi. 9 l. 2) turns retrospectively into great caution; in part this conveys the predictable unpredictability of Tacitus' world.

4). Obscurity at that time and obscurity in Tacitus' are atmospherically, and causally, connected. And yet the historian himself stands in contrast to the dominating features of that world; to its dark deceit, concealment, pretence, and vice, he opposes his dedication to factual and moral truth. That truth he prosecutes scrupulously, vehemently, or subtly.

The modes and tones change; the scrupulousness both serves as foil to the vehemence and predisposes us to accept the vehemence as authoritative and veracious. But there is no inconsistency. Tacitus wishes us to see his moral judgements as judgements, undistorted by bias. We may find 'bias' in his treatment of Tiberius; but he accepts the estimate of that reign as a whole that was probably present both in his literary sources and in general tradition, and then penetrates the detail of his material in a manner plausible within the world of Tacitean history.[34] He wishes to display his caution even in handling Tiberius' guilt (not Tiberius' pleasure) with regard to the death of Germanicus (especially *Ann.* iii. 16. 1, contrast ii. 82). The strong language and forceful questions in which at iv. 11 he defends Tiberius from poisoning his son are intended, among other things, to manifest his fairness to a character he disapproves of. Fairness, and subtlety, are exhibited in the constant twists and complications of his writing. So in the monumental summation of an obituary even Vitellius has his merits (*Hist.* iii. 86. 2). Warm writing builds up the generalship of Vespasian (ii. 5. 1), but the climactic *antiquis ducibus par*, 'equal to the generals of old', is undercut by the phrase immediately before it, *si avaritia abesset*, 'if he had been free of greed'.[35]

Whether or not Tacitus himself faced external pressures towards distortion (he would like us to think so), we are to appreciate the difference between his account and earlier accounts: they are vitiated by bias, which Tacitus' acumen penetrates and his truthfulness discounts. The difference is conveyed in general terms at the start of *Histories* and *Annals*; we are shown it in

---

[34] On Tiberius' general reputation note particularly Sen. *Ben.* iii. 26 f., Plin. *Pan.* 11. 1. Levick (1976), 294 n. 85, is assuredly right in her view of Philo (she is alluding to *Leg.* 33, 141, 159 f., 298, 304, etc.). Sen. (?) *Apoc.* 1. 2, where literary purpose or play is at work, would be very doubtful evidence for general approval (the absence of *divum* with Tiberius, not Augustus, must in this context bring one up short); Sen. *Clem.* i. 1. 6 fits the opinion in the text. For Tacitus' presentation of Tiberius see Pippidi (1944), etc.; on the problems of cohesion note Gill (1983); Woodman (1989); Martin and Woodman (1989), 22–33.

[35] On obituaries (in the *Annals*) see Syme (1970), 79–90; note Sen. Rh. *Suas.* 6. 21.

practice at, for example, *Ann.* xvi. 6. 1. Here as on Tiberius and his son at iv. 11 Tacitus rejects the notion that Nero poisoned his wife Poppaea: *neque enim venenum crediderim, quamvis quidam scriptores tradant, odio magis quam ex fide.* 'I would not believe that poison was in question, although some authors relate this, more from hatred than with honesty.' The structure sets the judicious historian against 'some authors' (the 'some' and the anonymity are here tinged with scorn), and thrusts the motives of those authors into relief; an argument follows.[36] Tacitus, we are to feel, claims justly in his work an *incorruptam fidem*, an incorruptible honesty (*Hist.* i. 1. 3). The figure of the historian is to impress and impose by its commanding insight and authority.

Greatness is both a fundamental aspect of Tacitus, and an explicit focus of attention; in both respects the *Annals* are particularly rich. Underlying his handling are the notions that history acquires greatness both negatively, by eliminating the low and the trivial, and positively, by narrating extremes, extremes not only of virtue, but also of vice and disaster. But things become more complicated.

The literary grandeur of extremes is communicated with overwhelming power in the prologue to the *Histories*, where abruptly yet profusely Tacitus amasses in short units the remarkable features of the period. So:

pollutae caerimoniae, magna adulteria. plenum exiliis mare, infecti caedibus scopuli. atrocius in urbe saevitum ...   (i. 2. 2)

Religious institutions were polluted, there were heinous acts of adultery. The sea was full of exiles, island rocks were stained with murders. Still more dreadful was the savagery in Rome ...

magna, 'heinous' (more closely 'great'), the extravagant *plenum*, 'full', the startling *atrocius*, 'more dreadfully', mark the union of moral horror and literary grandeur; in its context *saevitum*, 'savage acts were done', by taking up the magnificent *saevum*, 'savage', in i. 2. 1, encapsulates that union in itself. Concern with impressive extremes shows itself everywhere in Tacitus, in the whole design of the *Annals*, as we shall see, and equally in the design of para-

[36] The anonymity is notable after the declaration in xiii. 20 (cf. Koestermann here), and the conspicuous increase in the naming of sources for Nero's reign. The failure to keep up to the earlier promise scarcely constitutes a problem (note Russell (1981*b*)); and the actual and alleged intensification of the device is, I suspect, designed to enhance the impact of this climactic part. (Contrast Syme (1958), 291 n. 4.)

graphs. These often begin by registering the act or event of a day or year as great, remarkable, or appalling. So at *Ann.* xiii. 45. 1 a paragraph begins *non minus insignis eo anno impudicitia magnorum rei publicae malorum initium fecit*, 'No less celebrated an act of unchastity in this year started off great evils for the state' (45. 1, opening a paragraph). The arrangement of the sentence highlights *insignis*, 'celebrated', and also *magnorum*, 'great', marks the progression from personal vice to the state, and creates the characteristic sensation of a fatefully significant moment. The year generally (AD 58) is to be contrasted with the year before, which Tacitus grandly and revealingly finds meagre in things 'worthy of mention', *memoria digna*. He dismisses trivialities like major building projects: these are material for the Roman gazette, not for Roman history, which treats of *res illustris*, outstanding events (xiii. 31. 1). His own stance here converts into loftiness undignified physicality and satirical scorn.

Despite his emphasis on greatness, Tacitus not infrequently exploits possibilities of lowness. So, most conspicuously, in *Ann.* iv. 32f., where Tacitus contrasts his own seemingly slight and trivial material with the subject-matter of Republican history. After evoking its attractions with Ciceronian grace (33. 3), he changes style:

nos saeva iussa, continuas accusationes, fallaces amicitias, perniciem innocentium, et easdem exitii causas coniungimus, obvia rerum similitudine et satietate.

But I am presenting a series of savage commands, incessant prosecutions, the deception of friends, the ruin of the innocent, the same reasons for death, with obtrusive similarity and tedium in my material.

Formally the style conveys monotony; but the heaping up of terrible and wicked events in pungent phrases, as at the start of the *Histories*, actually indicates their potential for grandeur and power.[37] And we must see the repetitiousness of the subject *(rerum)* as a challenge overcome by Tacitus' resourceful and grandiose art.

The matter extends further. We may take first, for its simplicity, the greatness of heroic courage, which is sublime with little qualification. Searching for Tacitus' views, we single out his occasional commendations of prudence; but in the major works it is

---

[37] *continuas* too also serves to heighten, cf. Coel. Antip. fr. 26 Peter.

the bold and masterful acts and utterances which are made to fire our imaginations. These moments stand apart: they contrast with the general vice or weakness of the Tacitean world; often they are performed by some anonymous or hierarchically inferior character. Even when major characters do (for all the complexities) attain greatness, it is in opposition to what surrounds them. Such solitary isolation is indeed built into the very dramas of courage. The greatness of these moments may be seen from *Hist.* ii. 13. 2, where 'a Ligurian woman' defies the tortures of Otho's soldiers. *praeclaro exemplo*, 'setting a glorious example', comes near the start of the sentence describing the event. That sentence proceeds to a matter-of-fact narrative but leads it up to a brave and pithy *mot*; it then continues: *nec ullis deinde terroribus aut morte constantiam vocis egregiae mutavit*, 'and thereafter none of their terrors, nor her death, made her alter the firm courage of that outstanding utterance'. The sudden rise into rhetoric inspires us, while the clause seems to retain the authoritative dignity of fact. Its shape sets the most dreadful physicalities against unmoved grandeur of spirit.

Still more powerful, however, is the ampler development of such a scene at *Ann.* xv. 57, where in the aftermath of Piso's conspiracy the freedwoman Epicharis defeats the torturers of Nero.[38] The rhetoric of negatives appears more magnificently here, the ingenious twist in the last negative clause only enhancing the transcendence of hierarchy:

at illam non verbera, non ignes, non ira eo acrius torquentium ne a femina spernerentur, pervicere quin obiecta denegaret.   (1)

But she could not be prevailed on to cease denying the charges, not by whipping, not by fire, not by the anger of torturers acting more fiercely to avoid being defied by a woman.

In a large sentence after this (2), *clariore exemplo*, 'setting an example the more splendid', stands in superb relief on the one side against the pitiful physicalities of her tortured body and her means of hanging herself, and on the other side against the conspirators, hierarchically far her superiors, whom she so nobly excelled.

---

[38] Tacitus significantly gives us only the plurality of torturers, and the orders of Nero; Dio lxii. 27. 3 (Xiph.) places the emphasis on Tigellinus. Polyaen. viii. 62 stresses the defeat of Nero. On the heroism of Epicharis note Tresch (1965), 171. Tacitus' narrative should be compared with Sen. Rh. *Contr.* ii. 5. 4 (Fuscus).

The sublimity which emerges from these contrasts and from Tacitus' vehemence is devastating.

Vice, however, the more dominating feature in Tacitus' work, has less secure a purchase upon greatness. Tacitus often depicts outstanding vice, not as impressive, but as sordid and disgusting; he also writes much of moral inadequacy, intrinsically less grand a theme. In both cases, greatness frequently remains, but it remains foremost in the contrasted figure of the historian. Tacitus creates an image of himself as sternly and grandly Roman and senatorial (though often also cool and witty); his moral elevation and lofty scorn produce grandeur of impact from supposedly base material. At *Hist.* i. 82. 1 Otho, in the Palatium, faces the rioting praetorians: *contra decus imperii toro insistens precibus et lacrimis aegre cohibuit*, 'flouting the majesty of his imperial office he begged and wept, standing on a couch, and with difficulty restrained them'. The moral baseness of the character supports a proudly disdainful utterance from the historian. The concrete *toro insistens*, 'standing on a couch', is at once comically undignified and grandly contemptuous. The passage as a whole is still more complicated, for the events are made to mingle sordidness, absurdity, and greatness of scope. Similarly, the account of the battle in Rome at *Hist.* iii. 83 rests for its effect on uniting the grand disaster of war with the low depravity of riotous pleasure, which is carried on simultaneously. The union is both bizarre and terrible; further grandeur is produced by the wondering contempt of the historian for the common people, who reduce war and historical catastrophe to a sport for spectators.[39]

At *Ann.* xv. 37 Tacitus describes one of Nero's orgies, and its sequel. The description actually conveys with colour the extremes of luxury, and marks with vigour the extremities of turpitude. But it gains a more stately grandeur from the distaste which the aloof historian alleges for the handling of such matter. This celebrated banquet he is describing as an example, lest he should have to tell frequently of the same extravagant luxury (*ne saepius eadem prodigentia narranda sit*, 1): his aversion is for the despised material as well as for the repetition. The grandiose pre-

[39] 1, 3, cf. i. 32. 1, Seiler (1936), 26f. Contrast Sall. *Jug.* 60. 3f. *prospectabant* (Thuc. vii. 71. 3). On *inhumana securitas* (3) Heraeus and Heubner catch the sense better than Wellesley. Tacitus' general scorn for the people is both moral and intellectual.

tensions of luxury are deflated by altitudinous contempt.[40] In the final 'wedding' of the emperor to a pervert, 'everything had spectators which even in the case of a woman is concealed by night', *cuncta denique spectata quae etiam in femina nox operit* (4). The words are informed by scorn, from a great height, for that obscene openness which they in fact disclose and yet drily conceal. This passage too uses greatness and lowness with forceful complexity.

For all Tacitus' complexities in the handling of greatness, and for all Seneca's actual selectivity, an important part of the historian's impact lies in the impression of exclusiveness, of the philosopher's in the impression of the reverse. Tacitus plainly brings before us a more limited range of reality. We may remark particularly that, although the contrast between inner and outer is so important in him, we are offered little depiction of the mental world so vividly portrayed by Seneca. Dark passions are grimly exposed or conjectured, but it would spoil the grimness to elaborate on how they feel from inside. A stunning moment divines, from a historical document, the tormented consciousness of Tiberius (*Ann.* vi. 6); but this is explicitly presented as a philosopher's vision (Plato's), and marks out Tacitus' normal and deliberate boundaries.[41] The physical side does not counterbalance this. Tacitus paints visual scenes with great force; yet their phrases, commonly potent in brevity, diction, and arrangement, have often a certain generality. They lightly and tellingly suggest particularized detail rather than plunging us into it with abundance. So in the description of Germanicus' funeral: *plena urbis itinera, conlucentes per campum Martis faces*, 'the streets of Rome were full; torches shone throughout the Campus Martius' (*Ann.* iii. 4. 1). The first phrase is general, the second is brilliant but brief, without the sharpness of its Virgilian model (*Aen.* xi. 143 f.). One may contrast with Seneca's depictions of far-fetched luxury (p. 46) *Hist.* ii. 62. 1 *ex urbe atque Italia inritamenta gulae gestabantur, strepentibus ab utroque mari itineribus*, 'from Rome and Italy were carried things to stir up appetite; the roads from the seas on either side resounded'. Tacitus does not pursue zestfully the disgusting or the de-

---

[40] For Nero's enthusiasm for greatness in luxury cf. Griffin (1984), 126–42.
[41] Tacitus has particularly in mind *Gorg.* 524e-5a; on the letter cf. Levick (1976), 201f. For the aloof mode of reference to philosophy here cf. *Hist.* iv. 5. 2, contrast iii. 81. 1 (and note that the irony there is not just against philosophy).

tailed; *strepentibus*, 'resounding', offers a bold, but not a precise and graphic touch.[42]

Also different is the relation of author and text to the reader and his world. Seneca is continually addressing someone; the reader's own mind and morality are perpetually pricked and challenged by the author's nimble intellect and unsettling insight. Tacitus sometimes stresses the moral value of his work to the reader, a value which sometimes conflicts and sometimes coincides with greatness (cf. *Ann.* iii. 65. 1 f., iv. 32. 3–33. 2, etc.); yet the text itself betrays that any such force is slight in comparison with our moral reactions simply to the narrative. Even when Tacitus refers explicitly to readers, and seems to communicate his own feelings as a writer, as at *Ann.* xiv. 64. 3 or xvi. 16, we gain little sense of intimacy or relationship.[43] In reading Tacitus we watch and are compelled by a world which he contrives to render separate from the reader's, and by himself, a distanced and magnificent figure. In Tacitus the author's presence has a weightier quality than in Seneca; his very restraint, like his historian's caution, gives his frequent vehemence and indignation a noble gravity; this imposing being stands apart from us. The style strengthens our sense that there is something remote and even assumed about the grand severity of his attitude. Certainly the Romans of our period could (unfortunately) imitate archaic austerity even in action.[44] But the *Dialogus* and Pliny's letters suggest at least the selectiveness and exclusiveness of Tacitus' historical pose, and Tacitus' world. The largest part of that world is intensely restricted. It resembles a tight, dark prison of hatred,

---

[42] Cf. also *Ann.* xv. 37. 2. The references to motions of the bowels at xii. 67. 1 and xiii. 15. 4 do not conflict, since they are needed for the account, and scarcely display relish. (Compare Goodyear (1972), 343 n. 2.)

[43] The former passage shows a complicated intermingling of the intellectual and the emotional; the question is not in form an outburst of indignation (compare e.g. Martin (1981), 178; cf. Dio lxii. 27. 4 (Xiph.)). The latter passage may be contrasted with the warmer, more emotional Sen. *Tranq.* 14. 10, and both passages may rewardingly be compared with epic; note the touch of Sallustian colour in the Seneca (see Maurenbrecher on Sall. *Hist.* ii. fr. 72 Maur.). At *Ann.* xvi. 16. 2 one should, I think, adopt the conjecture *oderint*. As to the element of value to the reader, even Tacitus' seemingly overt emphasis can sometimes itself show other purposes; thus the word *exemplum* often seems actually to place more stress on glory than on inspiring the future: so e.g. *Hist.* ii. 47. 2, iv. 67. 2, *Ann.* xv. 63. 2, and indeed *Hist.* ii. 13. 2 and *Ann.* xv. 57. 2 above.

[44] For notable aspirations to a past grimness in punishment note *Ann.* xiv. 42–5 (with Wolf (1988)); Suet. *Dom.* 8. 4 and Plin. *Ep.* iv. 11. 6 (with Vinson (1989), 432 n. 6), and e.g. Tac. *Hist.* iv. 42. 6–43. 1, *Ann.* ii. 32. 3.

anger, and fear; its narrowness and claustrophobia are part of its fascination.

With tragedy and epic we appear to reach the summit of genre; but we do not find at all the simple splendour we might have been led to expect by the ancient depictions. The unreality that ancient statements emphasize is certainly of prime importance in the genre, though there are many complexities here; but still more attach to greatness and sublimity. Particularly important here is an aspect we shall develop more later, their daring distortion, complication, or undoing not only of grandeur but of seriousness, its usual prerequisite. This effect depends for its impact on the standard notions of epic and tragedy as especially elevated and sublime. In different degrees, and with change from passage to passage, the poets are concerned to mingle in their works much grandeur of a powerful and imposing kind with not comedy but the tonal complication of grandeur. It is the mingling and the subtlety that make this aspect so difficult to find acceptable or to give weight to; it is easier to feel at home even with the *Metamorphoses*, less concerned with actual sublimity and more obvious and accessible in its play. Partly we are imprisoned by the conceptions of genre which these poets move in and out of; partly we find it hard to accept, in works with much seriousness, an element of self-contained and even frivolous unreality: even if they remove us from the familiar world, such works must constantly promote (our critical tradition still inclines us to feel) a vision of universal or political truth. At present we shall see something of their complication as we briefly glance at this and various other aspects of reality and especially greatness. The object now is to acquire some preliminary feeling for the high poetry in general, and a little for its individual authors; most of the aspects considered are mentioned or illustrated only for some of the poets. We are merely dipping our toes in the ocean.

Seneca's tragedies effectively display the impact of genre on the relationship of a work with reality.[45] They leave behind the truth of philosophy. Philosophical sensibility can shape the writing, and distinctively philosophical elements sometimes appear (notably in the excursive choruses). But only if we think that

[45] See (again a particularly stark selection) Leo (1878), 147–83; Friedrich (1933); Egermann (1972); Herington (1966); Zwierlein (1966); Dingel (1974), ch. 2; Fantham (1982) and Tarrant (1985), Introductions; Pratt (1983); Jakobi (1988).

poetry must present the author's beliefs will we wish to constrain
the world of these works into conformity or connection with an
outlook which, in my view, it neither suggests nor suits.[46] We lose
in the tragedies the sense of a benignly ordered universe fundamental to the Stoic world of the prose. Instead, we find such
things as grim mythological deities destroying the virtuous (so the
HF); the virtuous annihilated in death that appears as a calamity
(so *Phaedra*); wicked characters at last joyfully triumphant, and,
what is worse, exhilarating in their energy (so especially *Medea*
and *Thyestes*). The detached relish we feel for these wicked characters is quite different from, and hard to square intelligibly with,
the disgust created in the prose for monsters of vice. At the very
least, there is a large difference in the superficial appearance of
this world, which is most naturally explained by the promptings of
the genre of tragedy towards unreality, disaster, and greatness of
crime.[47]

Physical events in Seneca's plays are often wildly unreal; on the
other hand, the physical concentration of imagined drama limits
visual exuberance, and allows forceful contrast between what is
seen and not seen on the imaginary stage.[48] The tragedies are at
once fantastic and darkly claustrophobic. Formally the physical
unreality conduces to greatness. Greatness is also pursued in virtue, vice, and emotion: emotion is characteristically lavish and
fierce, even when we might have looked for gentleness.[49] Yet
greatness of effect is insistently modified and complicated (least

[46] This opinion is particularly controversial. For passages with a distinctively philosophical air cf. the choruses *Tro.* 371–408, esp. 397–408, *Ag.* 589–658 (but note 605), *Oed.*
980–94 (note that fate is disastrous in this play; cf. the chorus *Phaedr.* 959–88, where a
philosophical contrast—cf. e.g. Man. i. 483–531—is given a grim turn); and esp. the
chorus *Thy.* 336–403 (cf. *SVF* iii. 332, 617, 620; Plut. *Stoic. Abs.* 1058c–e; Varr. *Men.* 245
Astbury; Hor. *Sat.* i. 3. 124–33; it is interesting that this play is the most daring in anachron-
ism). The speech *Thy.* 446–70 has links with philosophy (470 takes up the chorus), but also
with Latin literature more generally (see Tarrant), as does say *Phaedr.* 483–564. The *HO* I
think spurious.

[47] For the association of tragedy with extremes of crime, and so with grandeur, cf.
pp. 28, 29f., and further e.g. Man. v. 458–67; Hor. *AP* 89–91; Liv. i. 46. 3. For the *HF*
and the *Phaedra* cf. pp. 208f. and 163f. below.

[48] The plays, I take it, were not staged: see especially Zwierlein (1966). *Oed.* 371–80 seem
sufficient to decide the matter: contrast Zwierlein, 24–6, with Sutton (1986), 22f.—and
Sutton does not mention 379f. The visual imagination of the reader (or listener) can be too
little regarded even by opponents of staging. For palpable instances of contrast, note *Tro.*
678–735, *Pho.* 38–44 ('visible' action is vital to the whole scene).

[49] So Antigone's speech at *Pho.* 51–79 turns the tenderness and restraint of the start of
Sophocles' *OC* (cf. Hirschberg (1989), 9) into consciously extravagant heroism.

drastically in the case of virtue), and its relationship with unreality is far from straightforward. The absence of the author's voice produces a large difference from the prose; but the forcefulness with which he diverts straightforward responses makes his mind, like Ovid's in the *Metamorphoses*, a distinct and dissonant element in our experience.

One or two passages will offer some preliminary illustration. At *Med.* 893–977 a monologue by Medea leads up to the killing of her children. Her sudden revulsion at 926–32 is powerful, and in this play startling; when at 945–7 she calls her children to her embrace, we have forceful imaginary drama, and a sad sonority in the address *unicum afflictae domus / solamen*, 'only consolation of this stricken house' (944 f.).[50] But there is much more to the speech than this straightforward emotional impact. At the start Medea urges herself to devise a truly great crime, disparaging her dreadful past crimes as 'slight', 'of common quality', mere practice, mere girlishness (*levia, vulgaris notae, prolusit, puellaris*, 905–9): the language, in this context prosy, adds to the somewhat entertaining air of this dismissal. Her contrasting *Medea nunc sum* (910), 'now I am Medea' (now she can realize her full potential for wickedness), rings out with commanding force. Even so, we are not merely awed, we relish and savour the inverted greatness of character and the extreme expansion of ordinary language.

Later Medea affirms her decision to kill the children, with extravagant and yet ingenious elaboration; but her passion is overtaken by mythological unreality. She sees the Furies, and then, in a bizarre conception, the ghost of the brother whose body she cut up and cast into the sea by pieces: *cuius umbra dispersis venit / incerta membris?*, 'Whose ghost is this that is coming, an unfixed image, with body scattered?' (963 f.).[51] Apparent grandeur had risen with the unreal and the imagined unseen; but now these are turned to weirdness. With a fresh rise, the brother is told to bid the Furies depart: Medea will perform the task without such aid. She then sacrifices a seen child to the unseen ghost: this

[50] The complexity of Medea's feeling for her children has been prepared at 809 f., 847 f. Comparison with Euripides' own intentions is of course complicated by the textual problems of Eur. *Med.* 1056–80 (not all spurious, in my view).

[51] Furies and ghost are probably to be thought realities, not hallucinations. Such beings are of course perfectly at home in Seneca (*Thy.* 1–121, *Oed.* 530–658, *Tro.* 169–202, *HF* 86–112), so that we have no positive reason to disbelieve, and the question at 963 f. makes reality the more likely. Edgeworth (1990), 153, leaves the question open.

interweaving, strangely handled, presents the crucial action with grandiose but consciously disconcerting mannerism. Medea ends by looking forward to a public audience for her act of *virtus*, 'heroism', her killing of the other child: here the inversion of values achieves a spectacular and artificial ostentation.[52]

The *Thyestes* goes still further in its distortions of greatness. Atreus' crime of making his brother eat his children is presented as an extreme in its greatness; and yet its possibilities for lowness and bizarreness are seized on, in a fashion that is piquant for this genre. The extremity appears, for example, at 742–53. The messenger passes on from Atreus' killing of his nephews; the chorus ask in horror if nature permits any 'greater or more dreadful' crime (*maius aut atrocius*, 745); he replies:

> sceleris hunc finem putas?
> gradus est.   (746 f.)

Do you think this the end and limit of his crime? It is only a step upwards.

The curtness of dialogue, the enjambment, the boldly prosaic effect of the metaphor in verse, somewhat distance our emotion at this trumping. Play with credibility increases the formal greatness, and the distance (753 f., no future age will believe the crime). Gross lowness and perverted loftiness are conjoined to deliberately startling effect in 911: *eructat—o me caelitum excelsissimum*, 'He is belching: oh, I am the highest of the gods'. The combination unfolds into a sharp point: Thyestes has not only eaten his children but is sated (913).[53] With a fantastic unreality that precludes grandeur or involvement, Seneca has the children (unheard to the reader) break in on Thyestes' call to them, from within his stomach. *unde obloquuntur?*, 'Where are they objecting from?' (1004), he asks in ignorance: the question produces a sudden and bathetic deflation in style, in content a surprise of almost amusing cleverness.[54]

---

[52] The heroic note itself derives from Euripides, where it is mixed more incalculably with womanly gentleness and womanly cunning (as 389–409, 1242–50). The killing of the first child may rewardingly be contrasted with the end of the *Aeneid* (*omnes* in 965 is surely nominative, *pace* Costa).

[53] I would punctuate the passage with 911 as above, a colon after *mea* 912, a full stop after *est* 913.

[54] Since Thyestes does not yet know what has happened to the children (note 1032 f.), he cannot merely be interpreting the rumblings. Tarrant's note catches some of the effect here, but implausibly holds that Seneca (in a spirit of honesty?) is making Thyestes' situation seem mundane.

Lucan, though turning a historical account or accounts of the Civil War into epic, daringly declines to invest them with the unrealities of myth. Yet everywhere he pushes far beyond the limits of historical reality.[55] His poem sombrely excludes the luxuriant charm of mythology; but within its limits, his ingenuity and fancy riot darkly. He builds up the greatness of his events, as historians do, but in an unhistorical manner, and with far more radical complications in view. Richness of physical detail, which so distinguishes epic from history, in Lucan works more typically against greatness and involvement than for them. In these epics the handling of the author lends special complexities to the reality and the closeness to the reader of the poem and its world; but quite peculiarly so in Lucan. The narrator's voice had normally been in epic restrained, and contrasted with the characters'; it now partakes of their passion, with a sublime or seemingly sublime intensity and elevation. The actual chasm between characters and narrator in time and knowledge is felt; it enhances both the strangeness and the pathos of the narrator's interventions.[56] Many features suggest, with deliberate artifice, a controlling author behind the narrator's impulsiveness. Yet the formal identity of author and narrator is essential to the excitement and danger of the text; in particular the underlying political vision, though not merely Neronian in scope, should not be insulated from contact with present reality. The poem should not, however, be resolved and reduced, in my view, so that all is basically subsumed into a serious purpose and an earnest statement of belief, which the abnormalities and the avoidances of grandeur essentially serve only to enhance. The distancing is too obtrusive, the political outlook too often appears as the fixed starting-point for the brilliant inventions of Lucan's mind. The perversity, the play, and the bold modification of sublimity and seriousness should be allowed in the poem not only an expressive role but also a larger autonomy. The full complexity of the poem is hard for us to accept.

[55] See especially Syndikus (1958); Seitz (1965); von Albrecht (1970); Marti (1975); Ahl (1976); Lebek (1976); Bramble (1982a); Conte (1985), 75–108; Johnson (1987). For works on more than one of the epic poets see Lorenz (1968); Juhnke (1972); Häußler (1978); Burck (1979); Vessey (1982).

[56] In expanding the part of the narrator the Silver poets build not so much on Virgil's normal practice, which is more reserved than is often realized, but on exceptional passages, above all *Aen.* ix. 446–9. See also Endt (1905).

Complications of tone will only be touched on very lightly for the present; we shall rather be concerned with other aspects. The first book shows the poet building his world for the reader, and moving increasingly beyond the historical manner he had appeared to espouse. It starts, after the prelude, with an account of causes (67–182), and closes with the speech of a woman swept in a vision from Apollo through the scenes of the future war (673–95). The account of causes in broad outline resembles history, the vision takes us beyond reality almost into the world of mythological poetry. At 234f. Lucan expresses what sounds a historian's reserve on the divine origin of a phenomenon; at 524f. the gods are said to fill the world with omens of the war, and at 540–4 the sudden darkness of the sun is linked with the famed marvel in the myth of Thyestes.[57] Elevating greatness formally increases with unreality, and is formally pursued throughout. So Caesar's words at the Rubicon (195–203, 225–7) become not measured, foreboding, or throwaway but assertively grandiose; yet their underlying immorality is exposed (at 202 even stylistically).[58] The account of causes from the start strongly emphasizes the greatness of the events. Near the start it does so by introducing the end of the universe according to Stoicism (72–80): through philosophy the range of reality is magnified beyond that of history. Presently in the passage the greatness of Caesar is painted, with colours from epic and philosophy; at the same time the epic and historical idea of greatness in violence is morally assailed by the language. So *gaudensque viam fecisse ruina*, 'rejoicing to forge a path by ruin' (150), both evokes and criticizes.[59] Deflations of language add further complexity to the treatment of greatness, as in the wryly and purposefully

---

[57] The fabulousness of that event is much exploited in Seneca's *Thyestes*; cf. e.g. Ov. *Pont.* iv. 6. 47f., Eur. *El.* 737–46. Note too i. 550–2. i. 234f. is not of course unique in the work: cf. e.g. vii. 192, 19–24. For the exposition of causes note Liv. *Epit.* cix, cf. Quint. iv. 2. 2 and e.g. Thuc. i, contrast Virg. *Aen.* vii.

[58] Cf. App. *BC* ii. 140, Plut. *Caes.* 32. 3 (mentioning Pollio), Suet. *Jul.* 31 f.; for the die, Otto (1890), 12 f., Kassel–Austin on Arist. fr. 929; for the perverted prayer in Lucan cf. Virg. *Georg.* i. 497–501, Tac. *Hist.* iv. 58. 6. On the scene cf. Grimal (1970), 55–69, Görler (1976). The apparition of the personified Rome comes teasingly close to the epic world, but in a fashion not impossible to history (note Tac. *Ann.* xi. 21. 1, cf. Plin. *Ep.* vii. 27. 2). Cf. now Feeney (1991), 270 f. (and 270–3 on the first book).

[59] It is a more paradoxical version of a grandiose turn common in epic and history: cf. Ogilvie on Liv. iv. 28. 5, adding e.g. Virg. *Aen.* ii. 494 *fit via vi*, Sil. v. 392f. On the imagery of lightning cf. Rosner-Siegel (1983); on the cosmic imagery earlier, Lapidge (1979).

unelevated close to the passage. Lucan ends it *multis utile bellum*, 'war's (financial) usefulness to many' (182).

At iv. 169–205 Lucan tells how the soldiers on opposite sides achieved a fleeting reconciliation.[60] It is for Lucan a passage particularly direct in emotional impact. The abundance of descriptive detail, exceeding historical narrative, both stirs and poignantly charms; yet even here a certain sense of distance is created. So on first recognition of their friends the soldiers, alarmed,

> tantum nutu motoque salutant
> ense suos.   (174 f.)

greet their own only by nodding and moving their swords.

A transitional moment (they soon embrace) is here devised with Ovidian cleverness. The use of the swords is significant and is enhanced by the enjambment and the conjunction with *suos*, 'their own'; it is also odd and amusing.[61]

Lucan's own impassioned comments give the moment significance and greatness, though strangely. He leaps into the action and harangues the individual Caesarean soldier, as if from outside that time he could persuade him to abandon war, as within it Petreius' harangue will persuade the Pompeians to abandon peace (211–36). And yet his vehemence (*quid, vesane, gemis?*, 'why do you groan, you madman?', 183), and his rationality, create pathos through their conscious impotence. The emotional impact is modified a little at the close: if his soldiers cease to fight, *Caesar generum privatus amabit*, 'Caesar, then without office, will love Pompey his son-in-law' (188). The address does not culminate, as we expect, in forceful but unrealizable truth: if we grant the condition, the belief (couched in the double paradox of normality that astonishes) must in this poem strike us as of extreme and alienating unlikelihood.

The poet then expands in seeming rapture, with the grandeur of invocation and of philosophy:

---

[60] Cf. Caes. *BC* i. 72–7, App. *BC* ii. 170 f.; and also Tac. *Hist.* ii. 45. 2 f. Caesar's role in the whole episode is probably devised by Lucan (although some modern historians are too trusting about Caesar's motives). The reconciliation and what follows are treated by Metger (1957), 138–46.

[61] At 209 f. the sword again divides; it is used bizarrely at 295. The present moment is taken up at Stat. *Theb.* xii. 401.

nunc ades, aeterno complectens omnia nexu,
o rerum mixtique salus Concordia mundi
et sacer orbis Amor.[62]   (189–91)

Now you are here, Harmony who enfold all things in your everlasting embrace, salvation of the world and of the universe in its combined elements, and you are here, the salvation of the earth, sacred Love.

Yet the poet turns out to be expressing not momentary joy but dismay: for the recognition among the soldiers establishes and increases the guilt of civil war. The drastic turn is powerful; but even here the effect is slightly complicated by a sense of the author's cunning and devious strategy. The following episode, we may add, stands in contrast to this one. It depicts the extreme thirst of Caesar's army with a blackly exuberant series of extreme and grotesque physicalities (292–318); these formally enhance, but remove us much further both from the credible and from the serious and the grand.

Valerius Flaccus' epic on the Argonauts, though Rome has in it some small presence, to my mind essentially immerses itself in a mythological world.[63] This author is scarcely distinguished from his colleagues by a 'classical' restraint, and he strives no less for a lavish grandeur (seasoned with ingenuity); yet his large and forceful strength has a certain straightness. He gives more sense of clear day than his fellows—less of weird darkness than Lucan, less than Statius of subtly shifting light.

It accords with this that the narrator fairly seldom obtrudes his emotion; but the few instances are forceful, and of significance for the epic of the period. So when coming, in a digression, to the Lemnian women's killing of their menfolk, he exclaims, *o qui me vera canentem / sistat et hac nostras exsolvat imagine noctes!*, 'Oh for someone to stop me as I sing this true tale, and to release my nights from this scene' (ii. 219 f.). The dramatic gesture and the intrusion of supposed experience have considerable power. Yet we are intrigued by the discordant resonances of *noctes*, 'nights' (nightmares, the time when the diligent poet is at work, that time in

---

[62] *ades* is at first to appear an imperative, and is usually taken to be one, but it turns out to be indicative, as 191–4 show. *Amor* corresponds to Empedocles' Φιλότης (e.g. frr. 8. 7, 47 Wright), as *Concordia* to his Ἁρμονίη (fr. 48. 4), but to fit the context cannot be only cosmic, and have *orbis* depending on it.

[63] See Summers (1894); Mehmel (1934); Kurfess (1955); Lüthje (1971); Adamietz (1976). For Rome cf. esp., beside i. 7–21, vi. 402–6, i. 555–60, ii. 571–3, vi. 55 f.; vii. 83–6, iv. 507–9.

contrast with the night of the killing). The reference to truth, with an epic poet and this myth, must be intended to tinge and modify our response.

Valerius' zeal for grandeur can be seen in Jason's speech when the Argonauts are to pass through the Clashing Rocks. The whole scene has been made wildly grandiose by Valerius; now, after a sign from Minerva,

> 'sequor, o quicumque deorum'
> Aesonides 'vel fallis' ait.   (iv. 674 f.)

'I follow you, whoever of the gods you are,' said Jason, 'even if you are deceiving us.'

The magnanimity of attitude is superb. The masterful brevity, surprise, and twist in syntax (uncapturable in English), and the outdoing of Virgil, enhance that magnanimity and yet also lightly complicate our reaction: so consciously does the author display and savour both nobility and wit.[64]

Very different is a passage where Medea is sending to sleep for Jason the dragon that guards the Golden Fleece. Medea's grim future is the subject of emphatic and repeated irony in the poem; her eventual crimes were famed for their greatness. Here Medea, charmingly lamenting her tricked and sleeping pet, deplores what she has so far done for Jason, and declares, *iamque omne nefas, iam, spero, peregi*, 'and I have now already carried out, I hope, every wickedness I must' (viii. 108). The 'wickednesses' she lists, in particular her sending the snake to sleep, seem in comparison with the future crimes so slight, and the perspective so unlooked-for and ingenious, that we are more amused and touched than stirred with horror. Greatness has been more radically modified even than in Sen. *Med.* 905–10 (above). The moment itself is distanced by what follows: Jason, on Medea's advice, mounts the tree by climbing up the snake. The action evinces the hugeness of the snake; the symbolic scorn and harshness of treading on it carries implications for Medea. But so cleverly and oddly does the poet

---

[64] Cf. Virg. *Aen.* iv. 576–9. The sign does not appear in Valerius' source Apollonius (the whole episode, AR ii. 549–649, well illustrates the difference between Apollonius' grandeur and Valerius'). Compare here the celebrated sublimity of Hom. *Il.* xvii. 645–7, with Sch. T and A and [Long.] 9. 10 f. (cf. Bühler (1964), 37–41). One is at first to think that *o . . . deorum* is a complete clause (cf. Nisbet and Hubbard on Hor. *Odes* ii. 13. 2), but *quicumque* turns out to govern *fallis* (cf. Stat. *Theb.* x. 680). On the scene to be discussed next, the romanticized comments of 'R. M.' (1829) make fascinating reading.

handle the fabulous physicalities that we find the moment chiefly entertaining and unserious—until the writing changes again to beauty and magnificence.

Silius Italicus' epic on the Second Punic War in its fierce grandeur and its unreality both evokes and makes remote a world variously distant from the poet's own.[65] Mythological deities are prominent; but for other aspects of his unreality Silius is much indebted to Lucan. His grandeur is often more straightforward than the other poets'; but this vigorous poem also pursues physical bizarreness with black enthusiasm.

The poet's interventions are frequent and emotional, but swift and formalized. Silius exploits the poet's position in time, like Lucan, but less strangely. As the disastrous battle of Lake Trasimene is to begin, and trumpets sound, the poet excitingly calls out:

> heu dolor, heu lacrimae, nec post tot saecula serae!
> horresco ut pendente malo ...   (v. 190–2)

Oh my grief, oh my tears, not too late in time even after so many ages! I shudder as if the disaster were still about to happen ...

The poet's emotion bridges the gulf of time, and then places him on the far side of it, before the event. The immersion of the reader in history, which Lucan's epic had appropriated in drastic and yet distancing form (vii. 212 f.), is here transferred to the poet, with startling but essentially strengthening effect.[66] The touch of metaphor in *pendente* (literally 'hanging') enhances the contagious sensation of present reality. By contrast, at the end of Book x, the poet dwells on Rome's moral strength in her darkest hour, placing that strength in the vanished past with a simple 'was' ('such was Rome then', *haec tum Roma fuit*, 656). Grimly asserting the morality of that time and spurning Roman triumph, he wishes in effect that Carthage still stood, since the decline of Roman morality ensued on its fall. The grandiose paradox is driven home by his addressing not his own city but

---

[65] See Bruère (1958, 1959); von Albrecht (1964); Kißel (1979); Burck (1984*b*); Ahl–Davis–Pomeroy (1986); Nesselrath (1986); Laudizi (1989).

[66] Lucan distances us precisely by referring to us and our involvement as in the present. For related notions in regard to history, cf. e.g. Sen. *Ira* ii. 2. 5; Lucian, *Hist. Conscr.* 51 (where the text needs some change: note Nesselrath (1984), 603). On the trumpets here see Spaltenstein's note; with the exclamation contrast the historian's manner, Liv. xxii. 7. 1.

Carthage, and in doing so recalling Aeneas' address to his lamented Troy.[67]

Various kinds of greatness are contrasted and evaluated within the framework of the poem's severe morality. Greatness in adversity, an important concern, achieves strong expression a little later than the end of x, when a speaker refers to the Romans' *pectora magnis / numquam angusta malis; capiunt, mihi credite, Cannas . . .*, 'hearts never little in great troubles; be assured, they can contain and endure the disasters of Cannae, . . .' (xi. 171f.). Greatness of calamity and greatness of spirit are forcefully matched, with an expressive suggestion of spatial metaphor, and with stark and significant assonance (ma*gnis* ma*lis*, ca*piunt* Ca*nnas*); the second part of the quotation effectively particularizes the first. That Roman greatness Silius opposes to the *ingentia facta*, the 'mighty deeds', of Hannibal (134; denigrated by this speaker, 184); not least of these is his crossing of the Alps (135–7), a deed sublime in a quite different and less moral fashion. The greatness of that act resounds through the poem, with altering significance. So in the phrase of Venus at the time, *Alpibus imposuit Libyam*, 'he has set Africa on top of the Alps' (iii. 562), the language, though hostile, evokes above all the magnificent confounding of categories by transcendent heroism. At the end of the poem we are shown the reversal and punishment of the Carthaginians' impious vaunt that they have transgressed the limits set by gods for men (xvii. 500–2)—an impious vaunt, but still sublime.[68]

During the battle of Lake Trasimene itself, some hide in a tree, which the enemy then fell (v. 475–509). The grotesque episode, grown from a comic moment in Ovid (*Met.* viii. 365–8), mingles physical largeness, physical indignity, and moral lowness. The first indication of the subject, *ramorum*, 'branches' (477), appears with conscious bathos, bizarreness, and contempt, after enjambment and an address of grandiose appearance. The motif of hiding in trees reappears, as if obsessively, in both the following books (vi. 189–99, vii. 667–79); the last version takes grotesqueness furthest. In it the victim while he pleads is *mutantem saltu ramos* (672), leaping from branch to branch.

---

[67] Virg. *Aen.* ii. 56 is evoked, although the subjunctive in *maneres* has a different force in the two passages. *si stabat fatis* denotes strictly an inevitable link (cf. Hom. *Il.* xviii. 96). For the fall of Carthage and Roman decline cf. Vretska on Sall. *Cat.* 10. 1.

[68] Cf. Albin. Ped. fr. 1. 20–3 Büchner, with the Elder Seneca's comment. For the paradoxical suggestion of iii. 562 (*Libyam* actually denoting men) cf. Man. iv. 661; *imposuit* recalls and surpasses Virg. *Georg.* i. 281f., Hom. *Od.* xi. 315f., cf. [Long.] 8. 2.

Statius' *Thebaid* and unfinished *Achilleid* form, with Lucan's poem, the finest high poetry of the period.[69] Greatness and reality are handled here with extraordinary richness and range. The *Thebaid* concerns the expedition against Thebes that arose from the strife between the two sons of Oedipus. It both opens up to us a spacious and delectable mythological world and engulfs us in impressive darkness. Greatness of crime, and especially greatness of valour, are grandly evoked; but Statius also goes particularly far not only in introducing gentler elements but also in subverting seriousness with Ovidian resilience. His physical imagination is quite unlike Ovid's; with sudden intensity it bestows both strangeness and a vivid air of reality on his unreal material. A related intensity permits the creation of piercing but transient pathos. The epics are (in my view) essentially removed from the Roman world save when it is glimpsed in the poet's interventions. These are for the most part more tightly restricted than Lucan's in passion and length; but they are often very striking, and often distance us from the narrative, not least through suggesting Statius' own poetic activity.

Greatness is conveyed with magnificent force at *Theb.* xi. 437 f. Adrastus' words can no more prevent the duel of the two inflamed brothers

> quam Scytha curvatis erectus fluctibus umquam
> pontus Cyaneos vetuit concurrere montes.

than the Black Sea raised up with its curved waves could ever prohibit the Cyanean mountains [the Clashing Rocks] from rushing together.

The power of the fearsome Euxine is dramatically exceeded, and not simply by an immovable rock, as we might expect, but by rocks, magnified and mythological, in swift and irresistible action. The image confers tremendous and inhuman power on the appalling passion and crime. That greatness of sin is also treated in the book more entertainingly, as when the Furies, now redundant and outmatched, look on with both admiration and envy (537 f.). One may contrast the version of the motif seen in Seneca above (*Med.* 967–9), not amusing and not vigorously

---

[69] See Deipser (1881); Legras (1905); Micheler (1914); Krumbholz (1955); Schetter (1960); Dilke (1963); von Moisy (1971); Vessey (1973 and 1986*b*); Koster (1979); Ahl (1986); Aricò (1986).

personifying.[70] Sublime courage is at vii. 819 depicted with simple physicality which the negative rhetoric makes superbly extreme. The earth opens to swallow Amphiaraus in his chariot, and *non arma manu, non frena remisit*, 'not arms, not reins did he let drop from his hand'. In what follows the pointed physical precision slightly modifies the sublimity: *sicut erat, rectos defert in Tartara currus*, 'remaining just as he was, he brought his chariot down upright into Tartarus' (820). The physical grandeur of the engulfment has already been greatly complicated, particularly by the poet's surprising enumeration (809–16) of possible scientific or supernatural causes.[71]

Play between the great and the less great stands to the fore in the completed portion of the *Achilleid*, in which the young Achilles accepts and then throws off disguise as a girl. It is promoted by rich play, physical and psychological, with gender, age, and other things. *plurima vultu / mater inest*, 'there is very much of his mother in his face' (i. 164 f.); but he resists his mother's plan through the idea of his father (275), and through the *cruda exordia magnae / indolis*, 'the raw beginnings of his mighty nature' (*magnae*, 'mighty', is stressed). Statius' audacity with unserious physical grotesqueness is well shown when an Argive boy grasps a tree and has his arms cut off: *truncus in excelsis spectat sua bracchia ramis*, 'amputated, he looks at his own arms in the lofty branches' (*Theb.* ix. 269). The cool *spectat*, 'looks at', is startlingly surreal; Silius is left far behind.[72]

More evocative physicality appears when the shields and crests of men in ambush in a grim forest are seen *rutilare*, 'to glow redly'; beneath the shade *flammeus aeratis lunae tremor errat in armis*, 'the quivering brilliance of the moon flickers over their bronze armour' (ii. 532). Intensifying Virgil (*Aen.* ix. 373 f.), Statius gives this moment uncanny presence, with a sharp contrast of

---

[70] On this moment in Statius see Venini's note; it also gains force from 100 (where Venini is somewhat too restrictive on *grande opus*), and much else in the poem. Cf. also i. 87. In xi. 436 *Scytha* (cf. Ov. *Trist.* iv. 1. 45) conjures up the grimness of the sea and the whole region, cf. e.g. Ov. ibid. 4. 55–64; Tert. *Adv. Marc.* i. 1. 3; and for the description VF iv. 725–8. For the image of an immovable rock cf. e.g. Virg. *Aen.* vii. 586–90, Sen. *Ira* iii. 25. 3 (and note *Ben.* vii. 23. 1). On *concurrere* cf. Luipold (1970), 26, 85–7.

[71] Cf. also xii. 420–2; iii. 482–8. The enumeration simultaneously builds up tension. For *rectos* cf. also *inclinat* 799.

[72] *spectat* is also made pointed by *nondum conamine adempto* (268). In *truncus* the poet toys with a word apt to trees; cf. Nisbet (1987). On Achilles' age, Tertullian's pungent comment brings out Statius' fluidity (*Pall.* 4. 2).

brightness and darkness and a strange delicacy of unfixed light.
(One must savour the grouping of words in this line; *umbra*,
'shade', ends the line before to heighten the opposition with this
one). Stranger again is the development at ix. 592, where with the
abundance of weapons set against a tree *viridem ferri nitor impedit
umbram*, 'the gleam of steel obstructs the green shade'. The
strenuous *impedit*, 'obstructs', is essential to the effect, which is to
be surprising, not relaxing. Vividness and remoteness, reality and
unreality, are absorbingly combined.

We come to Statius' interventions. Reminiscent of Lucan are
for example those at i. 144–68 and iii. 551–65. In the former,
Statius, expostulating with his characters (less insistently than
Lucan), contrasts the wealth of his own time with the poverty of
that of the narrative.[73] The sudden expansion presses in an irony
about the action (the kingdom over which the brothers dispute is
paltry), and mixes lowness about the heroic age itself with extremity of vice. The second intervention denounces the forecast-
ing of the future; the two ages are now linked, and Statius
trespasses on philosophical and almost on satirical territory (*hinc
pallor et irae ... et nulla modestia voti*, 'hence spring paleness and
anger ... and the absence of all restraint in desires', 564f.).[74]
More Virgilian is the promise of immortality to the dead pair at
x. 445–8 (cf. *Aen.* ix. 446–9); but it is made quite different from
Virgil precisely by the manner in which it refers to him. Epic is
the most intertextual of genres, but it is particularly severe over
explicit reference to models and sources. Statius' reference to his
own *inferiore lyra*, 'lower-sounding lyre', openly indicates comparison with Virgil; his suggestion that Nisus and Euryalus perhaps will not spurn the company of his pair in Hades intriguingly
mingles fiction and literary reality and displays his touching
modesty.[75] The reality of writing literature is here so obtruded as

[73] Luc. i. 96f. has been remarked as the seed of i. 144–64. For *a miseri* 156 see Heuvel's
note, and observe the absence of *a* from the *Aeneid* and Silius; cf. *a miser* (narrator) in Luc. vi.
724, ἆ δειλώ etc. (speeches) in Homer.

[74] For divination in heroic times note Cic. *Div.* i. 1; ibid. ii. 22f., Diogenianus fr. 4. 45–64
Gercke, for simpler psychological objections. As to satire, note Juv. 14. 125, 1. 168 (!), etc. As
to *scrutari*, an exclamation does not lead well into what follows, nor is the perfect *scrutati*
suitable here; the old conjecture *scrutamur* attracts.

[75] It is an intriguing comment on this modesty that Ariosto bases *Orl. Fur.* xviii. 165–xix.
16 on Statius' episode rather than Virgil's. Statius openly refers to Homer and Virgil, in the
frames of his poems (*cantu Maeonio, Ach.* i. 3f., *Aeneida, Theb.* xii. 816); cf. Luc. ix. 984, Sil. iv.
525 (Homer). Silius' reference to Virgil at viii. 591–3 is something different: it forms

to modify and distance the impact of the poet's warm engagement with his characters.

Some of the salient differences between the highest genres of poetry and of prose the reader has already been enabled to sample. For instance, in the handling of the author we have seen the overtly intellectual element which is far more conspicuous in prose than in poetry, and the lavish and aggrandizing ardour, and the air of strangeness and paradox, which are more characteristic of poetry; and we have seen the larger context and rationale of these divergences (which are sometimes blurred). But we shall have much more opportunity later to set this poetry against this prose. For the present we have gained some idea of the importance and complexity of genre; and still more we have seen in some measure the importance and complexity of the notions of reality and greatness. Perhaps that importance might induce the enduring reader to follow as the investigation proceeds inwards, and we explore a central area of style.

---

part of a series of places which celebrate literary figures (so Cicero viii. 406–11; Homer at xiii. 778–97). Ennius' dream at the start of the *Annals* comes from a period of Latin literature much freer in such respects.

3

WIT

VERBAL ingenuity and paradox are central to the literature of this period, and particularly to the high poetry.[1] If we largely ignored this element, we would make the works more accessible and straightforward, but we would be false to the whole texture and feel of the writing. If we treated it with amused contempt, we would merely create an obstacle to enjoying properly this unusual and brilliant literature. It will become apparent that often wit, even in high genres, plainly modifies or disrupts seriousness and elevation. When this happens regularly in an author obviously in command of his technique, we cannot plausibly suppose him oblivious to the effect; nor can we ascribe that effect to a lower order of intention, as if his real purpose to write straightforwardly moving literature were constantly thwarted by the obtrusion of a base but unresisted urge to be clever. If we suppose in him a unitary intention to produce a complicated sort of writing, we could still deplore it, and indict the perversity of the age; but it would be humbler and more interesting to discover whether we might not ourselves widen our literary experience and pleasure by attempting (however provisionally) a more sympathetic understanding. This chapter will attempt to give the reader the flavour of this ingredient of wit, and perhaps a taste for it; it will also suggest how much more there is to the subject than is frequently supposed.

We must begin with a word on the background. Often scholars might seem to write as if declamatory education were the single fountain-head from which the unified liquid of epigram flowed through the literature: as if each writer had been indoctrinated, or inebriated, at a tender age, and wrote like a declaimer ever

[1] Long experience suggests that I should explain 'wit' in this chapter to have no necessary connection with humour, but to denote the handling of language (and concepts) with a self-conscious smartness and surprise. The actual effects of wit indeed often bear a relation to humour, as will become apparent; but we must beware of applying familiar categories of the comic too simply for this literature.

after. Various points may be made here. Different sorts of epigram were expected in different genres. Those genres had their
own traditions, and authors would be influenced by these, not
simply by their own education; this is indicated by the innumerable examples of poets' adapting the *sententiae*, the epigrammatic
utterances, of Ovid, and then of Lucan. Declamation was one
genre in a generally rhetorical literature, and one subjected to
more criticism than most, not least for cultivating ingenuity without restraint: we have scarcely to do, then, with universal and
unquestioned indoctrination. One could conceivably take contemporary depiction of youths studying oratory as smitten with
an unrestrained passion for wit, and on this and other questionable bases assign a parallel condition to the poets. But one should
do so, if at all, only in a positive sense: that is, we should ourselves
learn to respond with excitement to the epigrammatic moment,
but we should not suppose poetry of such obvious control and
organization to be merely an undisciplined chaos of cleverness. It
should be noted, further, that declamation itself has suffered from
a certain bias against it in prose critics; this bias has generally been
taken over by modern scholarship. As we have seen, declamation
was particularly suspected because it was a prose genre, and one
with a practical purpose, and yet set little store by reality. Linked
with this offence was the abundant and unserious ingenuity with
which it treats its far-fetched situations. This does actually give it a
real affinity with high poetry—something very different from a
predominating influence. That affinity helps to explain how in
modern times the trangression of genre in declamation has aug-
mented by confused connection suspicion of the poets. They were
suspected for generic transgressions of their own, and were also
thought to be profoundly indebted to a genre both frivolous and
degenerate.

We shall be prepared for seeing the affinity of the genres in
their wit, and for pursuing later themes, if we now consider one or
two of the declamatory *sententiae* which the Elder Seneca pre-
serves from an earlier period. We shall then support other points
by some references to prose critics (including the Elder Seneca).
Lastly, we shall mention a few *sententiae* from earlier poets to
illustrate the tradition in poetry.

In one imaginary case in Seneca a father has disowned his
daughter for trying to kill herself; she did so in order to keep an

oath to her husband, who pretended he had died. One speech warns that disownment would itself lead to suicide: *scitis quemadmodum suos amet: non magis sine patre vivere potest quam sine viro,* 'you know the manner in which she loves her dear ones: she can no more live without her father than without her husband' (*Contr.* ii. 2. 2). The elements of the fanciful situation are ingeniously related and bound into a generalization; persuasiveness is purely formal (the crucial oath to the husband is ignored). Simple words take on a new force: the assured *scitis,* 'you know', marks the audacity; *suos,* 'her dear ones', boldly conjoins the two situations; *amet,* 'loves', acquires sinister connotations. In *Contr.* i. 6 a young man insists on remaining married to the daughter of a pirate chief (and is of course to be disowned by his father). Speaking on the father's side, one declaimer is vividly depicted by Seneca as building up a terrifying picture of a raid, only to turn it abruptly: *quid exhorruisti, adulescens? socer tuus venit,* 'Why that shudder, young man? It is your father-in-law arriving' (12).[2] The incongruous ordinariness of language and of content (a visit from relatives) curtly deflates the grandeur. The effect is on the surface persuasive; but the suddenness, extremity, and cleverness of the shift show such theatrical bravado that we are scarcely to take it seriously. In all these respects we shall see connections especially with high poetry.

The two Senecas throw light on the relation of genre and types of wit. The Elder Seneca speaks of an epigram that displays a shrewd sense of reality as capable of pleasing not just in a declamation but in some more solid genre (*solidiore aliquo scripti genere, Contr.* i. 8. 16), and of another such as fitting oratory or history (*Suas.* 5. 8). This accords with his whole stance. Cultivating an old man's charm, he claims to be indulging, though with nostalgia and evident interest, the enthusiasm of his youthful sons for declamation and especially for *sententiae* (e.g. *Contr.* i *praef.* 22). He himself affects to weary of the genre (*Contr.* x *praef.* 1), and to prefer the solidity and truth of history and its *sententiae* (*Suas.* 6.

---

[2] For the effect of the first part cf. iv *praef.* 6–11, on this speaker. In verbal detail, however, one cannot be confident that Seneca's reports are accurate, especially if he is indeed quoting from memory (compare with the original the quotation of Cic. *Fam.* xv. 19. 4 at *Suas.* 1. 5). Differences in rhythmical practice among those quoted would not guarantee verbal precision if Seneca was conscious of those differences. In general see Fairweather (1981), 37–49; her provisional hypothesis (49) seems to me rather too sanguine.

16).[3] As to verse, the Younger Seneca considers that in their moral force epigrams in Publilius' mimes rise above their genre and even above tragedy (*Tranq.* 11. 8, cf. *Marc.* 9. 5, *Ep.* 8. 8f.).[4] He also notes how moral epigrams hit the mind (*feriuntur animi*) more forcefully in the tightness of poetry (*Ep.* 108. 9–12): genre affects impact.

Other critics illustrate not only the lively discussions of this element, but the strength and quality of its appeal for many. Quintilian shows characteristic balance, but also characteristic warmth, in discussing *sententiae* (especially viii. 5). His outlook leads him to eschew in them artificiality and supposedly excessive frequency, but he also makes clear their attractiveness and force. So, with vigorous polysyndeton and a suitably pithy close, at xii. 10. 48: *feriunt animum et uno ictu frequenter impellunt et ipsa brevitate magis haerent et delectatione persuadent*, 'They hit the mind [compare Seneca above], they often drive one at a single blow, they are fixed the firmer for their very brevity, by giving pleasure they persuade.' He also emphasizes the importance of placing, and indeed implies its importance even for those he lavishly censures (viii. 5. 13 f.): the significant point is not the negative condemnation of contemporaries, which we cannot assess, but the lead offered to us by his positive sensibility. In Tacitus' *Dialogus* Aper, defending modern oratory, gives a vivid sense of the enthusiasm of the young for wit: they write home if a sentence 'has shone forth with a clever and curt epigram', *arguta et brevi sententia effulsit* (20. 4). Aper's opponent depicts modern oratory as narrowly obsessed with epigram (32. 4), while Aper himself gives a richer impression (as at 21. 8). We see again the air of controversy surrounding *sententiae*, and the prevalence of a sensibility to which they give powerful pleasure.[5]

Even amid the sustained elevation of the *Aeneid* we sometimes glimpse germs of the later ingenuity. The widowed Andromache,

[3] He was a historian himself (Peter (1906–14), ii. pp. cxviii f., 98). The text at *Suas.* 6. 16 is very uncertain: see Håkanson's apparatus; even *his* may not be right (conceivably *horum*, cf. *Contr.* ii. *praef.* 5). In Petr. 1. 2 (on declamation) we should see as connected *rerum tumore* and *sententiarum vanissimo strepitu*. On Seneca's terms and categories see Sussmann (1978), 127–9; Fairweather (1981), ch. 3, esp. 202–7. Cf. generally Norden (1918), i. 280–5.

[4] Seneca's emphasis is more explicitly moral than Cassius Severus' (Sen. Rh. *Contr.* vii. 3. 8; there is of course unconscious irony at Petr. 55. 5). His aesthetic sensibility is indicated not only by *Ep.* 8. 10, but also by his probable sharpening of Publilius in memory at *Tranq.* 11. 8. (*cunctis ... cuivis* in the MSS of Publilius, cf. Giancotti (1963), 31.)

[5] *effulsit* in 20. 4 intensifies the use of *lumen* in relation to *sententiae* (cf. e.g. 22. 3); for other exploitations cf. Quint. ii. 12. 7, viii. 5. 34 (cf. there Sch. Pind. *Ol.* 2. 18b Drachmann). In relation to Quintilian, we should beware of too readily supposing his influence to have vastly reduced audacity with *sententiae*, even temporarily; note e.g. vii. 1. 44, iv. 2. 121f.

sighting Aeneas, wonders if she is in Hades, and, if so, / *Hector ubi est?*, 'where is Hector?' (iii. 312). We are brought here to the edge of the later manner by the bold handling of reality, the manifestation of extreme feeling through a surprise for the reader, and the enhancement of that surprise through the simplicity of language and the enjambment. In Ovid wit pervades, obtrudes, disrupts; his *sententiae* influenced declamation as well as being influenced by it, and are very important for our poets.[6] Yet his wit tends not to be so dark and dramatic as theirs, to be more limpid, cool, and light. Narcissus, enamoured of himself, wishes he could leave his body and become two: *votum in amante novum, vellem quod amamus abesset*, 'I could wish—a novel desire for a lover—that what I love were absent' (*Met.* iii. 468). Ovid marks out his paradox in advance, delightfully defying what would be apt for the speaker; he savours the opposition between the mythological unreality of his poem and his special and familiar sphere of love. These areas are audaciously related by plain language. At *Fast.* vi. 97–100 Ovid declines to adjudicate the claims of three goddesses: *plus laedunt quam iuvat una duae*, 'two do more harm than one does good'. Shrewdness of attitude is here appealingly combined with a charming simplicity and dexterity of arithmetic and verse. The unelevated moment effectively follows a portentous reference to the fall of Troy.[7] At *Pont.* i. 7. 69f. Ovid tells Messalinus, if he does not grieve for Ovid's misfortunes since Ovid appears to deserve them, to grieve that he deserves them: *quoniam meruisse videtur / si non ferre doles, at meruisse dole*. The extreme elegance here sets off, lightly but poignantly, a probing subtlety of thought, and a winning humility and humanity. Particularly close to the later poets is the speech of Hecuba at *Met.* xiii. 494–532 (and the whole episode): so the audacious, imaginative, and terrible treatment of reality in *soli mihi Pergama restant*, 'Troy remains for me alone' (507: Hecuba's losses are not ended). Some of that speech receives criticism from the Elder Seneca for restless ingenuity on a single idea (*Contr.* ix. 5. 17): a vital aspect of Ovid's ill-comprehended art. In Ovid's contemporary the astrological poet Manilius we see

[6] Ovid and declamation: Sen. Rh. *Contr.* ii. 2. 8–12 (but note 8 *iam tum . . . solutum carmen*); x. 4. 5, iii. 7 (where the text may need change, since *amatoriis* could hardly be used metaphorically).

[7] The text of the couplet is not certainly sound (*laedant* Bentley, *iuvet* some later MSS); if there is corruption in the hexameter, one might soonest alter *formae*. For 100, cf. Call. fr. 194. 72 Pfeiffer.

ubiquitous and Ovidian wit growing still bolder, and often weightier: so it is in his *nascentes morimur*, 'we die at our birth (our time of birth determines our death)' (iv. 16), a resounding and disturbing audacity.[8]

We shall now consider examples of wit and paradox from authors of our period; we shall look first at high poetry, and then at lower poetry and at prose. The reader will have to put up with: detailed discussion of the quotations, necessary to bring out some portion of their art; unepigrammatic translation of epigrams, occasioned partly by the need to elucidate; and often some detail on the context. The epigrams form part of rich structures, and cannot adequately be considered as if they were isolated gems or blots.

Ingenious wit is densely strewn throughout **Seneca's tragedies**.[9] We start with what is all but the final moment of its play, *Thy.* 1110. We must look first at the section and the speech which this moment ends. In the last act Atreus exults over his brother: he has caused him to eat his own children. The scene is removed from straightforward seriousness, not only by grotesque unreality (cf. p. 65), but by the copious ingenuities with which the monstrosities are garishly combined. Atreus triumphs at the extreme of wicked vengeance he has invented; but his last main speech, boldly defying dramatic coherence, undermines some of the basis of that triumph. He affects to claim that Thyestes is really grieved, not at eating his children, but at failing to execute a plan of his own to make Atreus do the same. This idea, within its fancy, momentarily undoes central aspects of the scene and the play. It is assuredly intended to startle. Seneca likes to close with abrupt surprises; and the passage balances the close of the preceding section: there Atreus had unexpectedly demeaned his achievement, but because he then conceived, too late, a still greater turn he could have given to the revenge (1052–68). The claim about Thyestes here appears starkly, after enjambment (*quod non pararis*, 'because you did not prepare (such a feast

---

[8] Contrast Quint. vi. 3. 67. *CIL* ii. 4426. 3 robs the line of the force imparted by its context. On Manilius' date see Bowersock (1990), 385–7 (against extending his career into the reign of Tiberius).

[9] See Rolland (1906), 54–7; Canter (1925), 85–99; Wanke (1964), 126–32; Seidensticker (1969); Lefèvre (1970), 69–74. In the spurious *Octavia* wit plays a far less conspicuous part; the probably spurious *HO* comes much nearer Seneca's manner.

yourself)', 1106); Thyestes' supposed plan is then fluently elaborated. Thyestes had wanted

> instruere similes inscio fratri cibos
> et adiuvante liberos matre aggredi
> similique leto sternere. hoc unum obstitit:
> tuos putasti. (1107-10)

to contrive like food for an unwitting brother, to attack his children with the aid of their mother, and destroy them by a like death. One thing hindered you: you thought they were your own [by adultery].

The repeated *similis*, 'like', presses home the startling parallelism of the fantasy; in between the shocking paradox 'with the aid of their mother' ingeniously deploys Thyestes' adultery with Atreus' wife to add a fantastic plausibility. *hoc unum obstitit*, 'one thing hindered you', with its monosyllable and elided disyllable, forcefully dams the flow; it heightens our expectation for the stunning ingenuity at the start of the next line. This final phrase, brief and simple in the extreme, brusquely knocks down the elaboration of the plan with a new bold imagining and twist to the myth. It simultaneously turns in a new direction the theme of adultery and legitimacy which has informed this section.[10] We see, then, how the final stunning moment belongs in and gains its force from a highly organized structure of verse. Realism is cast aside, even in the logic of the speech (a coherent sequence would need 'feared' not 'thought'); a grandiose climax is eschewed. This audacity spices our pleasure in the triumphant culmination of the author's cleverness.

The narrative of Oedipus' blinding himself (*Oed.* 915-79) reaches its height in the brief speech he is reported as delivering after the deed. The deed has been built up to as a half-heroic but perverted act of greatness, which Oedipus has been seeking in order to match the greatness of his destined crime (925f., 936f., 879). It has also been built up to as the solution to a puzzle (936-57, especially 947). In describing the act, the narrative has lingered, like Oedipus in performing it; it has dwelt on the physical horrors

---

[10] The theme itself is natural (cf. Accius 206-8 Ribb., with Cicero's comment, *ND* iii. 68); but Seneca's treatment of it is at once ingenious and somewhat low. (I suspect the second half of 1103.) Tarrant's remark on 1110 in his excellent commentary does not to my mind suit structure or spirit. The role of 'wit' in the scene (with a slightly different sense) is discussed by Meltzer (1988). 314-16, a related but less striking moment, does not undo the effect of Atreus' assertion here; still less does 918.

so long as to pass into a certain grotesqueness, despite the bizarre heroism (note 961–4). The account, though complicated in impact, has been formally working to its climax:

> victor deos
> conclamat omnis: 'parcite en patriae, precor!
> iam iusta feci, debitas poenas lui;
> inventa thalamis digna nox tandem meis.'[11]   (974–7)

In victory he cried to all the gods: 'Spare my country now, I pray! Now I have done what justice required and paid the penalty I owed; at last I have hit on a night worthy of my marriage.'

The sudden *victor*, 'in victory', creates a surprising but exciting sense of valorous achievement; the invocation and the concern for his city, afflicted through his crime, convey a magnificent nobility. But the formal climax in the final line would on a straightforward reading have to appear as a weak anticlimax. It will be apparent how *inventa, digna, tandem, meis*, 'I have hit on, worthy, at last, *my*', fulfil both the grand and the less grand aspects of the preparation. *nox*, 'night', takes up the blinding (cf. 973), but with astounding and weirdly imaginative ingenuity it conjoins the night of blindness with the bridal night. Given such placing and presentation the effect must be, not to move, but boldly to distance; we are turned aside in delighted contemplation of the author's wit.[12]

In the first speech of the *Troades*, Hecuba depicts her woes, and Troy's; she marks extremes, though with often distancing ingenuity. The climax of her woes, and of the speech, is that she is to be allotted as a slave to a Greek leader, and an unwanted slave at that. The rhetoric mounts up, as she lists the various Trojan women desired by Greeks; with them she is contrasted:

> mea sors timetur; sola sum Danais metus.   (62)

Me they are afraid of being allotted; I am the only thing the Greeks fear.

Rhetorically the line brings out her humiliation; but the first half creates for the reader an almost amusing bathos. The unattractiveness of an old woman, thus expressed, comes oddly as the

---

[11] 975 *lui* Heinsius: *tuli* MSS (too passive, I think).

[12] On *inventa* see Häuptli; in view of *tandem* in particular the sense of discovery must at the very least be present in addition to that of encountering, and is more likely to be primary. For the air of heroism to the earlier search cf. Soph. *Aj.* 470–3; for the solution through chance (951–6) cf. Sen. *Med.* 549f.

culmination of woes that have superseded the fall of Troy. The
second half brings in a fresh audacity. It makes a bold link with a
passage earlier in the speech; that passage had described with
superb grimness, wit, and subtlety the Greeks' feelings on ending
their war and their lingering fear (22–6). Now they have nothing
left to fear save getting Hecuba.[13] The effect borders on humour,
though the daring and compression exclude actual comedy; the
grandeur in the superficial meaning of the clause enhances the
author's wryness. The emphasis has shifted from the dramatically
convincing expression of feeling; indeed the decisiveness of movement in the line would scarcely accord with such expression.

In these three passages our involvement, or our intense involvement, with great evil, heroism, and grief has been halted by
epigram. Continually in the tragedies moments of wit make a
fissure between the extreme emotion of the characters and the
distancing unseriousness of the author's ingenuity. Dramatic
credibility is then defied: then the merest surface affects to sustain
the appearance of serious and internally convincing drama. Wit
in general need not have such functions in plays, and does not
always in Seneca; but careful analysis shows that it is a fundamental aspect of Seneca's poetic art regularly to distance and
contain emotion by obtrusive wit, to arrest abruptly with it the
violent flow of impassioned utterance. The procedure is generically startling, but no less present, or effective, for that.

Lucan equals Seneca in the pervasiveness and obtrusiveness of
his wit; but its roles are more complex in a long epic with a
meditative and engaged narrator.[14] We may start with a relatively
light moment. At x. 107–71, Lucan describes at length a feast given
by Cleopatra to Caesar. Its luxury is opulently elaborated, and the
poet dwells on the contrast and corrupting contact of Rome and
the East, and on Caesar's past and present experience. The moral
force is modified throughout by the poet's delight in paradox.
Even austere Romans of old would have been tempted to win
such wealth by arms, but win it for higher motives (149–54); the
luxury of the East, in an implied reversal of Rome's present prac-

---

[13] Fantham thinks the Greeks fear her because evil fate accompanies and uses her. But
this would need to be explained, and 59–62 are elaborating 56–8. The passage is brilliantly
trumped at the end of the play, where *me solam times* is addressed by Hecuba to Death (1173).

[14] See Wanke (1964), 126–32; Bonner (1966), 267–9; Lefèvre (1970), 74–6; Hübner (1975);
Martindale (1976).

tice, imports from far-flung Italy (161–3).[15] At the climax of the passage

> discit opes Caesar spoliati perdere mundi,
> et gessisse pudet genero cum paupere bellum
> et causas Martis Phariis cum gentibus optat.   (169–71)

Caesar learns to plunder the world and squander its wealth. He is ashamed to have waged war with an impecunious son-in-law (Pompey), and desires grounds for war with the peoples of Egypt.

Caesar's corruption at last takes place, and the danger that he would wish to fight for these riches (146–54) is now realized. But after the portentous first line, the second entertains us even as it staggers us. The Civil War, centre of the horror (and wit) of the whole poem, Caesar discards with embarrassment as superfluous. He uncharacteristically feels shame, and shame at fighting with his son-in-law, but because that son-in-law is poor. The order and emphasis in *genero cum paupere*, 'with an impecunious son-in-law', is exquisite, as is the placing of the opponents Caesar swiftly substitutes, in a parallel phrase at the same point in the next line.[16] The extreme perversion of a moral reaction does not actually appal us morally so much as it delights us intellectually. All subserves our pleasure in the author's audacious and ingenious mind.

We see a very different effect when Pompey leaves the field of Pharsalus. In the last part of a substantial passage (vii. 647–711) which principally conveys Pompey's nobility in failure, the narrator asks him:

> nonne iuvat pulsum bellis cessisse nec istud
> perspectasse nefas? spumantes caede catervas
> respice turbatosque incursu sanguinis amnes,
> et soceri miserere tui.   (699–701)

Is it not pleasing to retreat from the war beaten and not to be a spectator of that wicked destruction to the end? Look back on the hordes foaming with gore and the rivers stained by the inrush of blood, and pity your father-in-law.

---

[15] The effect is modified too by paradox less related to morality, as in 159f. (on Lucan and Egyptian religion cf. Nisbet (1982–4)). I take it that 167, where I would read with Håkanson and Shackleton Bailey *externa ... terrā*, has a paradoxical surface; *aura* (with *cui*) prepares, and the context dispenses with the need for a genitive. Note on Book x the commentary of Holmes (1990).

[16] With *pudet* contrast esp. i. 145 and x. 77.

The form of the question conveys the warmth and impossible intimacy of narrator towards past character; it also highlights the paradox of retreat as a gain. This leads into a subtle justification of retreat (not of loss); *perspectasse*, 'be a spectator to the end', is expressively drawn-out in rhythm and prosaic in register.[17] Lucan drives home his point in the swifter action and rhythm of *respice*, 'look back' (from the same stem): with dramatic animation he bids his character confirm his judgement about a long look by a short one. The gesture is also grandiose, in its very artifice; the horrors of the battle are forcefully conveyed in language mixing up the human and the fluvial. All this is essentially a cohesive and powerful development; but it receives a startling twist with the last line. The superiority and gentleness of pity appear very unexpectedly (*et*, 'and', enhances the effect); and for pity the triumphant and impervious Caesar seems a very unlikely object.[18] And yet the underlying paradox takes up the first line, and Lucan goes on to justify it in forceful rhetoric; this he ends with the paradox and plainness of *vincere peius erat*, 'it would have been worse to win' (706). The design, the brooding narrator, the very surprise bring out the moral profundity of *miserere*, 'pity'; yet that surprise is so drastic and so flamboyantly self-conscious that our reaction is somewhat modified by the shock of pleasure. The effect is both subtle and daring; and we see in how rich and dense a texture of poetry the epigrams have their place and point.

Two passages from speeches may be briefly mentioned. Cato's men, marching through the desert, wish rather for the battle of Pharsalus:

> 'reddite, di,' clamant 'miseris quae fugimus arma,
> reddite Thessaliam.' (ix. 848 f.)

They cry out, 'You gods, give back to us poor wretches the warfare we fled; give us back Thessaly [a synonym for the battle]!'

The first line establishes the idea clearly and with little epigram; this enables the second part to fall with all the impact of anaphora, preparation, and immediate clarity. The effect of those

---

[17] One should compare Caesar's eager gazing at 789–95, 797 (delete 796?): 791 *spectat*, 797 *spectacula* (and note *par* 695). *iuvat* in 794 is also significant. The poets like to exploit that uncolourful word; with 699 cf. e.g. iv. 570.

[18] The verb is used elsewhere by Lucan only to twist the mercy which Caesar was himself famed for exercising: ix. 1061.

two words is made overwhelming by the poem. The extreme and passionate account of the battle in vii, and the extreme and mostly unserious account of the Libyan desert in ix, are here fused in a phrase of the utmost brevity and in an extraordinary theatrical gesture. It becomes particularly extraordinary through the weight of meaning which the poem and its language have given to synonyms for Pharsalia. Events are combined in an unexpected way, as they are in declamations, but the effect in this large epic is utterly unlike: the poet's audacity, while hindering involvement, wins for itself a grand magnificence.[19]

Our second example is agreeably ungrand and devious; it comes at the close of the first in the series, which ends Book i, of contrasting prescient or visionary speeches produced by heavenly signs of the Civil War. The greatest expert on haruspicy is so appalled by the entrails (which Lucan has much enjoyed describing) that he is prepared to wish:

> aut fibris sit nulla fides, sed conditor artis
> finxerit ista Tages.[20]   (636f.)

or may there be no truth in entrails, and may the founder of the art Tages have made all this up!

Notionally this surprise and this extremity enhance the horror of the coming war; but the basic paradox, itself a startling end to the section, is colourfully elaborated and draws our interest away from the plot. The bizarre legend of Tages' apparition to reveal haruspicy Cicero thought so absurd as itself to undermine the practice; the seer keeps the legend, but imagines Tages' revelations as lies: a pleasantly bathetic twist.[21] The short and peculiar name, prepared by the end of the first line, makes a nicely off-beat ending to the alarming speech; horror is far distanced by the conjunction of outlandishness and wit.

In **Valerius** and Silius epigrams are somewhat less frequent

[19] With the use of *reddere* cf. VF ii. 379 f.; for the weight of *Thessaliam* cf. e.g. the paradox at viii. 108. After the opening we proceed to a geographical fantasia with various, mostly less grandiose, flavours of paradox; 851f. already give a different quality to the combination (I think Housman mistaken on *pro*).

[20] I print with a little hesitation Shackleton Bailey's (1982) *aut* for *et*. His objection is perhaps over-sharp; but it is attractive to set this development against the standard language of 635 (cf. Williams on Virg. *Aen.* iii. 36). In 637f. the double epithet is weak, and *sic* is curious, since it suggests a summing-up.

[21] Cic. *Div.* ii. 50, cf. 80; see Wood (1980). The Cicero makes against supposing any rationalization here.

than in Seneca and Lucan, but are none the less fundamental to
their style and impact.[22] If their wit tends to be less devastating and
devious than Lucan's, it is plainly indebted to his. Valerius' is also
less insistently sombre. He shows here his easy forcefulness, and
sometimes a certain dry elegance: as when he adapts Lucan's
warning that Cornelia would become *coniunx millesima*, 'the
thousandth wife', of the Parthian king (viii. 411) into a warning that
Medea might become *coniunx non una*, 'the wife, and not the only
one', of a Scythian (vii. 235). When the Argonauts are beginning the
first ever voyage on the sea a storm breaks out. The poet's vigorous
description culminates in a vivid and drastic sentence of exclamation: how terrified were the Argonauts as *picei fulsere poli*, 'the pitch-
black heavens flashed' (i. 622)—and so forth. He goes on:

> non hiemem missosque putant consurgere ventos
> ignari, sed tale fretum.   (625 f.)

In their ignorance they did not think that the winds, let forth, were
rising in a storm, but that such was the nature of the sea.

Valerius exploits his myth and the perspective of time with excitingly imaginative ingenuity; our response to the narrative is now
complicated by absorption in the author's cleverness. There is
also something just slightly entertaining in the characters' mis-
take. After the forceful rhetoric of what precedes, this sentence
builds to its surprise, delivered with words of remarkable brevity
and simplicity (not placed at the start of the line). Our sense of
climax is not deflated so much as diverted. The moment sets off
in the ensuing passage (to 692) a whole sequence in which the
poet's wit and imagination explore the event and the ignorance.[23]

At iv. 450–9 Phineus describes how the Harpies rob him of his
food; an elaborate passing-over of other topics (444–50)
heightens the impact of this one. The description reaches its peak
with:

> diripiunt verruntque dapes foedataque turbant
> pocula; saevit odor, surgitque miserrima pugna,
> parque mihi monstrisque fames.   (454–6)

---

[22] Summers (1894), 62 f., is using *sententia* in its other sense.
[23] The scene is discussed by Shelton (1974–5); Burck (1981*b*), 493–8. There is nothing to
correspond to it in Apollonius. Valerius of course draws on the thought that the Argonauts'
voyage was disastrous for men (cf. Nisbet and Hubbard on Hor. *Odes* i. 3. 12).

They snatch and sweep hence the food, and pollute and sully the wine. A foul stench rages, and a most pitiable battle arises: the monsters' hunger and mine are equal.

The elements of the subject-matter include much that is potentially unelevated; but Valerius contrives to lift it into something terrible with the throng of forceful verbs in the first line, the violent *saevit*, 'rages', and the pathetic *miserrima*, 'most pitiable', and the sense he has created of hideous mythical creatures and pitiful old man. The final phrase, however, starting but not filling a line, brings the description momentarily down to something half-amusing, while it ostensibly justifies the phrase before. In the linking of these two utterly different beings (note *monstris*, 'monsters', and the joining alliteration), and in the matching of hungers, we perceive a brilliant simplicity of inventive combination, and a certain lack of dignity amid the character's pathos.[24] The turn is prepared at the start of the description (450), and is later taken up and trumped, with enjoyable humour: 'hunger rages on both sides', but the direst of the Harpies keeps off not only Phineus but her own 'pitiable' sisters (499f.). The adjective, *miseras*, is transferred (451, cf. 455) from Phineus himself.

Silius' wit, though generally dark in quality, often displays humour of a black species. In ii. 636–49 he tells of how two twins kill each other as part of the perverted but magnificent self-slaughter of the besieged Saguntines.[25] It is inspired by a brief passage of Virgil where in ordinary warfare Pallas 'harshly makes distinct' two indistinguishable twins, 'a delightful source of perplexity to their parents', *gratusque parentibus error* (*Aen.* x. 392).[26] Silius dramatizes this idea in a weird and amusing passage, where the mother's misidentification of her children produces a sequence of bizarre symmetry and perverse half-comedy; it ends with her falling dead on her sons' bodies, still not knowing which was which: even then they could not be distinguished, *tunc etiam ambiguos cecidit super inscia natos*. (In the order of words the event is pleasingly enclosed by the continued play on confusion). The situation is established with

---

[24] The idea of the Harpies' hunger, like that of Phineus', is itself traditional, cf. AR ii. 269; Virg. *Aen.* iii. 218. Virgil's account is particularly important for Valerius'.

[25] In Liv. xxi. 14. 1 we have merely a mass suicide from the *primores*, not mutual killing. On the episode cf. Vessey (1974).

[26] Silius is influenced too by Luc. iii. 603ff. (first subtle, then ghastly). Cf. also Stat. *Theb.* ix. 292–5; Winterbottom on [Quint.] *Decl. Min.* 270. 27.

> Eurymedon fratrem et fratrem mentite Lycorma;
> cuncta pares, dulcisque labor sua nomina natis
> reddere et in vultu genetrici stare suorum.   (637–9)

(You fell,) Eurymedon, counterfeit of your brother, and Lycormas, counterfeit of yours; you were alike in all things, and it was a sweet toil to your mother to give her sons their own names and to linger in uncertainty as she looked at the faces of her children.

The first line shows an extreme neatness which brings out the elegant geometry of the situation. The next two dwell on the simple opening *cuncta pares*, 'you were alike in all things', with charming paradox. Here the first part, on names, gives a special meaning to what sounds like absurd forgetfulness; the second, on faces, elaborates in a sweetly particular image (*stare*, literally 'to remain at a stand', is a simple verb transfigured).[27] The content and tone serve for preparation and contrast; but the whole passage defies reading as failed straightforwardness, and illustrates how the ingenuity of later epic transmutes Virgil into something very unlike him.

In other places wit approaches sublimity of effect with relatively small modification. So when the Roman general Marcellus is slain, Hannibal buries his foe with proud magnanimity; a vast pyre is erected:

> convectant silvis ingentia robora: credas
> Sidonium cecidisse ducem.   (xv. 389f.)

They amass huge oaks from the woods: you would think it was the Carthaginian leader that had fallen.

The situation is turned about with spectacular nobility, prepared for in Hannibal's own words ('a right hand so like my own', 385f.); enmity is astoundingly transcended by greatness on both sides.[28] *Sidonium*, 'Carthaginian', is in the context stressed and significant. The magnificence within the story is distanced by ingenuity much less than at Luc. ix. 849 (pp. 87f.); but the strong pause before the fifth foot, very rare in Silius, and the enjambment after *credas*, 'you

---

[27] With 637 cf. Cat. 4. 27; with *dulcisque labor* Eur. *Bacch.* 66. Spaltenstein's rendering of *stare* as 'être sûr' is implausible.

[28] One should compare the less grandiose treatment at App. *Hann.* 216f. (whether or not there is a common source). Livy says simply *ibi inventum Marcelli corpus sepelit* (xxvii. 28. 1). On the episode cf. Burck (1981a), 464. It is intended to rise still higher than the longer treatment of Paullus' funeral (x. 513–77).

would think', enhance not only the surprise but the author's self-conscious cleverness in paradox. Yet we are also to be impressed by the patriotic poet's own ability to rise beyond the normal boundaries within which he depicts the enemy of Rome.

In **Statius** epigram is as dominant and as brilliant as in Seneca's tragedies and Lucan; but in his less obsessive work it embraces a range of tone and effect larger than in either. So when he imitates Seneca's treatment of the dead Niobe, still proud of her fertility (*Oed.* 613–15, *Theb.* iv. 575–8), he modulates Seneca's incisive sharpness, well within his own powers, to a greater richness of paradox and exuberance of fancy. We may glimpse his range from three passages. Antigone closes thus the speech she makes to Polynices to dissuade him from fighting their brother:

> quid crimine solvis
> germanum? nempe ille fidem et stata foedera rupit,
> ille nocens saevusque suis; tamen ecce vocatus
> non venit. (xi. 379–82)

Why are you freeing your brother from guilt? Assuredly he has broken his promise and the fixed compact, he has behaved criminally and is savage to his own people; but yet, you can see, though you have called him, he does not come.

With ingenious obliqueness, she seeks to avert the act of hate by appealing to hate; the enjambment of *germanum*, 'brother', brings out the paradox. The devious play with guilt is highly reminiscent of Lucan. The next sentence defends and brings out the conceptual paradox of Eteocles' innocence (his relative innocence becoming absolute). Eteocles' wickedness is conveyed with strong moral language; the action or inaction of his which outweighs that wickedness is communicated in language that of itself sounds exceedingly ordinary and indeed suggests a social impropriety. The weight that the words acquire in their context shows a self-advertising virtuosity, which must in part help to distance us from a direct involvement, as must the play with bathos. The virtuosity is heightened by the enjambment and shortness of *non venit*, 'he does not come'. The web of wry ironies created by the larger context is too thickly woven to unravel here; we may note only that Eteocles will shortly appear, saying, 'I come, and envy you only that you called me first' (389 f.). Statius is coming to the climax of the whole poem; the drama of the situation, though not without pathos, gains full force, and abrogates full seriousness, in the power of the verbal moment.

At viii. 727–32 the hero Tydeus, mortally wounded, is carried off by his friends; Statius sets their sadness and his physical proximity to death against his furious determination to live and fight. The sentence ends:

> saevi rediturum ad proelia Martis
> promittunt flentes.

They promise, but with tears, that he will return to the battles of savage War.

Here paradox creates, amid the fierce violence that dominates the context, a gentle pathos, lightened by the warm but knowing charm of the wit. *saevi*, 'savage', shows this as a surprising thing to promise, and promotes the contrast of mood with the next line. Here the two words *promittunt flentes*, literally 'they promise weeping', are isolated and interact. *flentes*, 'weeping', implicitly and delicately marks their loving perjury. Tenderness takes the form of wrong inverted; in the strangest context appears familiar behaviour at deathbeds, indulgently observed. This is poetry of great richness and complexity.[29] In fresh contrast Tydeus realizes in the next sentence that he is to die, and the writing grows ever wilder and more horrible until Tydeus, despite his friends' resistance, starts to devour his slayer's head. Then, in new contrast, and with comic wit and invention, the snakes on Minerva's aegis stand erect (762f.) and veil the goddess's sight.[30]

We hear in the catalogue at the start of the horse-race in Book vi that Chromis is driving the horses of Diomedes (348), which had eaten men until tamed by Chromis' father Hercules. Later Hippodamus, who has been paired with Chromis throughout, falls to the ground:

> Thraces equi ut videre iacentem
> Hippodamum, redit illa fames, iam iamque trementem
> partiti furiis ...   (486–8)

[29] For the observation cf. *Silv.* v. 1. 159f. (which by contrast plays on epic expression, cf. Virg. *Aen.* i. 209). For the formulation cf. Quint. xii. 1. 38: with sick children *multa non facturi promittimus* (an illustration of legitimate lying). That is elegant, but less oblique or subtle than Statius, and less cleverly warm. On the scene generally cf. Zwierlein (1988).

[30] The basic story is of course traditional, cf. *Thebais* fr. 5 Davies, Beazley (1947). The hideous action would presumably have seemed in some degree credible to Curtius Montanus, though not to Tacitus (*Hist.* iv. 42. 2); obviously it stood far beyond accustomed horrors of that time. For the snakes contrast viii. 518f.; note also Luc. ix. 681–3 (Medusa).

When the Thracian horses [Diomedes'] saw Hippodamus lying on the
ground, there returned their famous hunger for men [lit.: that hunger],
and the trembling man was on the very point of being divided up by
them in their frenzy ...

Fulfilled preparation and surprise come together felicitously (one
is reminded of Boiardo). The ghastliness of horses eating men
turns into grotesquerie and humour; the effect is the more bizarre
in the unexpected context of a race.[31] The first line suggests with
startling speed the grisly psychology of renascent blood-lust; the
next opens with the name Hippodamus ('tamer of horses', but
potentially 'slain by horses'), and the decisive point comes quietly
in with simple words ('that hunger returned') that deftly allude
and connect. Statius then colours in, with mock-suspense, the
unactualized horror (*partior*, 'divide up', is grimly cool); but he
will turn the sentence back to Chromis' noble action in forgetting
victory and rescuing his rival.[32] Wit now glorifies morality:
Chromis paradoxically retires 'defeated and praised', *victusque et
collaudatus* (490). The macabre comedy of the situation tinges our
response even to Chromis' (surely rather modest?) nobility; but
the epigram retains a distanced yet pleasing moral strength.

   We have now seen something of the multiplicity of effects
which epigram possesses in high poetry, and how it acquires
different flavours in different authors. We have also seen how the
epigrams achieve their specific impact only through the form, and
in the texture, of poetry; and how these poets pursue, regularly
and with recurring patterns, related ends in the use of wit. We
have observed especially how wit complicates and modifies
emotion, seriousness, elevation, not of necessity, but in the particular ways in which the poets handle it. It is one of their prime
means towards that persistent elusion of simple categories which
forms a basic part of their whole nature and appeal. Especially
characteristic of their wit is the verbal tightness and command
and the conceptual ingenuity and boldness which with the slight-
est material alter the course of the poetry in a breathtaking

[31] The standard breathing of Chromis' horses on Hippodamus' shoulders (438f.,
Lloyd-Jones and Wilson (1990), 56) is given a special twist at the time, and produces in
retrospect both contrast and ominous connection. On the episode cf. von Stosch (1968),
144.
   [32] The effect of *partiti* may be brought out by comparison and contrast with Pind. fr. 129.
20–32 Maehler (cf. Lloyd-Jones (1990a), 160f.); Eur. *HF* 382–6, *Alc.* 494 ἀρταμοῦσι; Virg.
Georg. iii. 268 *absumpsere*; cf. also VF vi. 425.

moment. The pleasure their wit offers is intellectual, and in varying degrees detaches us; but we should also be exhilarated and excited. If the poetry is very far from straightforward and continuous sublimity, it requires a sensibility in some ways akin to [Longinus']: wit too creates the moment that amazes, overwhelms, and fills with exultation.

Now we pass to lower genres of poetry. Firstly we must resummon **Statius** to glance briefly at his intermediary *Silvae*. Wit is again a constant presence, though somewhat less dense and astounding than in his other works. It is in the *Silvae* one of the means of converting reality into poetic discourse; at the same time, that reality gives it a very different effect to wit in his epics. Yet even in the gravest real situations epigram can rein in and lightly modify the lavish emotion which formally it communicates.[33] In v. 1 Statius describes Abascantus' grief at his wife's funeral, powerfully using concrete values and imaginative expression: Abascantus seemed to the watching city as if he were burying his young sons, so much night was there in his hair and eyes (*tantum crinesque genaeque / noctis habent*, 219 f.). The paragraph ends:

> illam tranquillo fine solutam
> felicemque vocant; lacrimas fudere marito.   (220 f.)

Her they called fortunate, passed away in a calm decease; it was for the husband that they poured forth their tears.

Even in the speech of an impassioned husband, such a contrast would in the ancient world contain an element of surprise; here narrative gives it to bystanders, and the shaping makes evident the concern for ingenious paradox.[34] *felicem*, 'fortunate', placed second in the Latin and at the start of a line, seems on the surface a heartless reaction (contrast the wife's own utterance at 193, cf. 195); the pithiness of the second part, and the ring *illam ... marito*, 'her ... the husband', pursue a slight obtrusion of cleverness. The poet is exalting his recipient's devotion, and with warmth; but the wit delicately complicates the emotion, discreetly adding to

---

[33] For examples of wit in the *Silvae* with quite different flavours cf. e.g. i. 5. 46, iv. 3. 152; again the reality of the primary topic is crucial to the impact, even when there is play with higher poetry. (A striking illustration of this is i. 4. 1 f., where the use of Hom. *Od.* [24.] 351f. must be borne in mind.) On wit in the *Silvae* cf. Vessey (1986*a*), 2757–9.

[34] Cf. Admetus' speech at Eur. *Alc.* 935–61 (καίπερ οὐ δοκοῦνθ' ὅμως, 936). The husbands' wishes at *CIL* vi. 12652a 1–8; *Laud. Tur.* I. 28f., II. 61–3, etc., are meant to seem striking.

tragedy the air of urbane and graceful praise, from real person to real person.

In **Martial** the moment of wit is the goal of the poem, and the movement towards it is more institutionalized than in grander poetry; the effect is also as a rule more straightforwardly comic. But if the wit is somewhat simpler in impact, it is also imaginative and demanding, and depends for its character on the poetry.[35] ix. 70 begins, as can only be done in a lower genre, with an explicit quotation from something loftier: Martial cites (in an elegantly inverted order) Cicero's famous phrase *o tempora, o mores!*, 'This age! These ways!'. The first quatrain rapidly sketches the tempestuous times of the heroic orator, with a grandeur of language and content that seem out of place in epigram; the second more coolly asks a (fictitious) contemporary why he affects the phrase, in the present times of security and peace.[36] The final couplet brings the expected ingenuity:

> non nostri faciunt tibi quod tua tempora sordent,
>   sed faciunt mores, Caeciliane, tui.

What makes your age bad in your eyes is not our ways, Caecilianus, but yours.

The inseparable 'age' and 'ways' are separated (1 and 5 have led up to this). The second person acquires an insistent and developing force, which culminates in the final disyllable *tui*, 'yours'; there blunt insult and sly insinuation are arrestingly united. (The contrast and the ring *nostri ... tui* particularly emphasize a sort of word more commonly unemphatic in this position.) Caecilianus' high-minded contempt has changed to a desire for times of discord and crime, where he will feel more at home: he dislikes the present precisely because it is peaceful.[37] *sordent* comes to have the shade not 'seem ignoble' but 'seem dull'. Higher genres draw ingenuity out of an existing situation, but Martial creates an ingenious situation with masterful economy.

---

[35] See Barwick (1959); Citroni (1969); Siedschlag (1977); Burnikel (1981); Holzberg (1988), 24–34.

[36] A few of Martial's epigrams are indeed grandiose; but that does not alter the effect of ll. 1–4. Cicero used the phrase often and at different periods (*Verr.* iv. 56, *Cat.* i. 2, *Dom.* 137, *Deiot.* 31); it, like other phrases, is toyed with in *suasoriae* on Cicero (Sen. Rh. *Suas.* vi. 3).

[37] *sordent* comes to have the shade not 'seem ignoble' but 'be little valued', cf. e.g. Plin. *NH* xxxv. 88 (of a painter) *sordebat suis*. The variant order *tua quod tibi* (β) gives the wrong emphasis and spoils *tui*.

In v. 10 Martial explains to a patron how people always prefer poets of a previous age. He elaborates this standard theme with facility, listing great poets despised in their day. We feel still more strongly than in high poetry that such elaboration will be turned round by wit; the turn is liable to be more drastic. The weightiness of the elaboration is not much lightened by the remark that Ovid was known only to Corinna (10); the wit there is purely orna-mental, and our general suspicion is increased by the im-plausibility even of the underlying proposition (Ovid, like Martial, was far from little read in his day). However, the nature of the twist when it appears is still startling:

> vos tamen, o nostri, ne festinate, libelli:
> si post fata venit gloria, non propero.

But you, O my books, make no haste: if fame comes after death, I am in no hurry for it.

With brisk and lively fantasy, Martial addresses his books, and creates a whimsically unreal connection: if fame arrives only after death, and his books are likely to win fame once read, then their publication is likely to be fatal. One may contrast the grander use of succession and consequence in Sil. x. 657f. (pp. 71f.). Together with the humorous unreality goes a humorous realism of attitude; this is brought out in the contrast between the mock-grandeur and mock-intensity of the hexameter, and the shrewd and relaxed pentameter.[38] Combined with that ethos is the dominion of wit over words. We might expect in the words *si post fata venit gloria*, 'if fame comes after death', an emphasis on *gloria*; but the wit stresses *post fata* and points *venit* ('actually comes, appears for the first time'). The understatement of *non propero* ('I am in no hurry') appeals in style and outlook together.[39] Much is involved in these comic moments when wit erupts.

Wit plays a rather different part in satire. It is relatively unim-portant in **Persius**; it may sometimes flash out amid the rich

---

[38] *ne festinate* and *non propero* are of course set against each other. One should compare the canny attitude to literary immortality in relation to a friend at i. 25. 8 (where *sera* is used in a pointedly practical fashion, contrast Ov. *Pont.* iii. 2. 35f., Prop. iii. 1. 35f.).

[39] It is interesting to compare Stat. *Theb.* viii. 326 *ne propera* (addressed to the Earth in relation to death). The first-person reality in the Martial and the mythical unreality in the Statius contribute to the difference in effect; but if the Statius is less humorous, its wit is still related to the Martial's, and this brings out how its impact cannot be simply serious. Cf. also Sen. *HF* 867, 873.

colour and colloquial vehemence, but it is a subordinate part of
the energetic exposition rather than a prime destination of the
passage. The elegance of ingenious epigram would not really
comport with his art. In 2. 68 he has been rebuking his contemporaries passionately for attributing to the gods the desire for
wealth of the wicked human 'flesh'. Fervent rhetoric then depicts
the flesh's pursuit of luxury. With a sudden change of manner he
proceeds *peccat et haec, peccat; vitio tamen utitur,* 'these deeds of the
flesh's too are wrong, indeed they are; but it *is* getting use from its
vice'.[40] We are struck by the plainness of vocabulary. The emphatic asseveration in the first clause surprises us; the second
delights us by its sudden rhetorical concession and by its com-
pactness and the weight it thrusts on a simple verb (literally 'uses').
The poet now comes back to the absurdity of bringing wealth into
religion, with a vigorous question to Roman chief priests. The
direction of the argument becomes clear; the wit and the dryness
had served as a foil and a springboard. Poem 4 ends: *tecum habita:
noris quam sit tibi curta supellex,* 'live with yourself: you will then
know how broken your things are'. The first phrase is brief,
paradoxical, and charged with significance by the context (one
should not trust even the good opinion of others); but the wit
prepares and serves as foil to the phrase that follows and its vivid
colour and homely lowness.[41]

In **Juvenal's** style, wider in its compass, verbal sharpness is
important; but his wit, though related to that of high poetry,
moves into different regions of effect.[42] Quite close is 4. 55f. A
fisherman decides to give to Domitian the enormous fish he has
found; Juvenal elaborates the cause with exuberant imagination:
informers who would claim that the fish was the emperor's
(46–55). If we believe informers,

---

[40] Despite 64–7, *haec* must, I think, be neuter plural: a contrast between the sins of the
flesh and of the *pontifices* would hardly work or suit the argument; nor would even a
disjunction from the flesh. *et* is not postponed in Persius; at 6. 13 it means *etiam*. The
repetition is characteristic of the colloquial vigour of satire: cf., with different roles, e.g. 5.
132f., 6. 22, Hor. *Sat.* ii. 7. 92. Flintoff (1982), 351f., while rightly drawing attention to the
imagery of food, to my mind divagates too far in interpreting *pulpa* and the passage; and
ultimately the imagery can in my view be detached from the meaning. In 61 we must read
terras: even if the ablative were possible in this far from standard phrase, it would not bring
out the image sharply enough.

[41] *noris* looks back particularly to *sic novimus*, 43 (often misunderstood). In 48 *amarum*
must if sound be adverbial; *cautus* in 49 is probably corrupt.

[42] See de Decker (1913), 154–72; Martyn (1979).

> quidquid conspicuum pulchrumque est aequore toto
> res fisci est, ubicumque natat. donabitur ergo
> ne pereat. (53–5)

anything remarkable and fine in the whole sea is the property of the emperor's treasury, wherever it swims. The man will give the fish then, so that he does not lose it [i.e. is not simply left without it].

The curt closing epigram gains its force from its setting; it contrasts splendidly with the abundance of all that precedes. It drily draws the obvious conclusion, but does not exactly deflate. The preceding sentence contains its own jolts in style, with the legal bleakness and gruff rhythm of *res fisci est*, 'is the property of the emperor's treasury', after the lavishness of the preceding line, and the absurd and colourful *natat*, 'swims', after the grandiose *ubicumque*, 'wherever'.[43] The form of the second sentence is firmly epigrammatic, with the enjambment and the wry contrast between giving and merely losing. Yet that contrast does not take us into strange paradoxes or challenging ingenuities; it cynically presents what is obvious to the sensible. The effect is more sour than audacious.

We gain a verbal shock from the last word of 3. 230f., famed as a maxim; but the author is being enjoyably whimsical. One should buy a house in the country, not rent in Rome:

> est aliquid quocumque loco, quocumque recessu,
> unius sese dominum fecisse lacertae.

It is something, in whatever place, whatever nook, to make oneself the owner of one lizard.

Peculiar turns have been taken by the description of the life in the country contrasted to that in Rome; the 'excellent' house (223) has yielded to, the attractions of rusticity are mingled with, elements of poverty and oddness. The poet has humorously and frivolously been colouring his material in ways that appear to smudge the expected argument; he had ended the couplet before 230f. with an open joke.[44] He now feigns to be making a moderate and

---

[43] To see in *ubicumque natat* itself a parody of law (Griffith (1969), 149f.) would rather spoil the effect, I feel; for the phrasing *res fisci* note *Inst.* ii. 6. 9. As to the mock-grandeur of *cumbae linique magister* in 45 add to Courtney's citations Ov. *Met.* viii. 856 *moderator harundinis*.

[44] *Pythagoreis* of course undercuts the impressive suggestion of *centum. bidentis amans* (228) perhaps offers, among other things, an amusingly bizarre version of φιλογέωργος: compare the discussion at Xen. *Oec.* 20. 26–8.

sensible assertion. Our expectation is heightened and drawn out by
the change from 'place' to 'nook', and the ponderous repetition of
'whatever'. In the second line *sese fecisse*, 'to make oneself', suggests
a definite achievement. The line begins with *unius*, 'one'; it ends
with the awaited noun. This is so crazily small, and so comically
vivid, that the argument and the air of gravity are undone in the
anarchic humour with which the poetry particularizes. The effect
is tonally purposeful, and produces the climax of the play in the
passage; but we have something different from the tight combina-
tory ingenuity of high poetry—and equally pleasurable.

Wit infringes somewhat differently when Juvenal dwells on the
penalties for future crimes awaiting someone who has wronged his
addressee:

> nigri patietur carceris uncum
> aut maris Aegaei rupem scopulosque frequentes
> exulibus magnis.   (13. 245–7)

He will experience the hook of the black prison, or a crag in the Aegean
and those rocks crowded with famous exiles.

Juvenal appears to depict imprisonment and deportation to an
island with lavish enthusiasm; but after depicting the islands as
mere desolate rocks, he surprisingly makes them crowded, yet
(after enjambment) crowded with exiles. The particular combination of common ideas creates a suggestion of paradoxical and
incongruous play, which deflects the air of simple emotion. Partly
this is to seem spontaneous whimsy; partly it marks the ironic
unseriousness of the ending to the poem (239–49). For exultation
in future punishments clashes with Juvenal's previous arguments
against desiring revenge (174–92), and suggests a related clash in
the seemingly earnest passage on the pains of conscience (192–239).
The triumph of the ending becomes scornful irony, and the
seriousness of the second part of the poem as well as the first begins
to dissolve. The gusto here is tinged with absurdity by the language; but the unpredictability of the language accords with a
larger unpredictability.[45]

---

[45] *nominis invisi* (247), 'explaining' the forceful collocation *gaudebis amara* (247), is too
specific to fit a merely abstract delight in divine justice (Courtney on 248–9). It will be
apparent that on the second part of the poem I broadly agree with Edmunds (1972);
Morford (1973); Romano (1979), 179–88, and others, against Courtney, though I see its
ample developments as teasing us mischievously with the appearance of having abandoned irony.

In the apparent gravity of the passage before the ending Juvenal uses moral statements that are to seem sharp and subtle, but are less abrupt and spectacular in phrasing than we would expect in high poetry. So: *continuo sic collige quod vindicta / nemo magis gaudet quam femina*, 'you may draw the conclusion at once [that revenge is for little minds] from the fact that no one gains more pleasure from vengeance than a woman' (191 f.). Explicit argument leads slowly up to the burst of *femina*, strong and paradoxical; the spirited writing deliberately stands closer to prose than to epic. In general Juvenal's wit avoids the high poets' degree of devastating cleverness and chiselled austerity and shapeliness; often ampler, often more colourful, often directer, often more frivolous, his handling of wit is freer, looser, quirkier.

Of our prose authors we shall concentrate on those in whom wit is especially important. In **Seneca** it abounds throughout, and is crucial to his impact.[46] It is much less liable than in high poetry to draw us aside from seriousness. It drives in the thought, and its intellectual vitality partly subserves startling truth; yet also, in a degree that varies greatly from passage to passage, it produces a certain detached relish in the author's ingenuity. This does not, even in the epigram itself, place the seriousness in the background: the two levels coexist, and cannot be straightforwardly and blandly united. We can feel bitter, healing drops falling onto our spiritual wounds, and can simultaneously exult in sparkling cleverness and self-admiring wit. Such paradoxical experience is central to the fascination of reading Seneca. We may certainly say that most often the expressive purpose prevails over the self-contained display, but it prevails with an ostentatious effort. The exciting tension and the complexity of impact must be felt, or we lose the whole flavour of the writing. The epigrams belong intrinsically to his art; they belong too to their passages. Their relation to their setting is vital, in meaning, force, and texture, and nowhere is more injury done by considering *sententiae* without their context than in the large and close cohesion of Seneca's prose.

At *Ira* iii. 12. 7 Seneca ends a passage (4–7) that urges delay so as to let anger cool:

[46] See Rolland (1906), 54–7; Summers (1910), pp. xv–xli; Traina (1974), 34–6; Setaioli (1985), 815–17. Cf. also p. 9 above (on Quintilian's judgement); we may note that Tac. *Ann.* xiii. 11 *iactandi ingenii* shows both understanding and malice, like the philosopher's comments on history.

nihil tibi liceat dum irasceris. quare? quia vis omnia licere.

While you are angry, may nothing be allowed you [to do to the object of your anger]. Why? Because you want to be allowed everything.

This epigram, though set apart even in its context, only acquires from that context its true power. Most of the passage has been devoted to the stories of how Plato did not beat a slave himself precisely because he was angry.[47] Plato's own statement of this, paradoxical but plain, Seneca adorns and elaborates with his own more elegant and ingenious epigrams. When Plato stands still with hand upraised, this is turned into an intense and paradoxical moment of self-scrutiny, which Seneca again elaborates with epigram. To this involved treatment the close forms a climax. In particular, 'be allowed' takes up the theme of power that runs through the account; and the last words render more graphically the sober and searching *plus faciam quam oportet, libentius faciam*, '(because I am angry) I will do more than I should, and do it more gladly than I should'.[48] The suggestion in our epigram of a present drama makes an energetic contrast with the narrative; and, as the preceding sentence indicates, the 'you' is seen and condemned in the light of Plato's self-condemnation and greatness. This epigram does not only offer a strong summation; as is shown by the harsh and unlooked-for *quare*, 'why', it contains its own absorbing paradox. What seems a puzzle of quantities (why *nothing* because of *everything*?) turns partly on idiom: 'everything' means 'anything, however bad'.[49] It turns partly too on the whole attitude which the phrase deftly evokes. We should sense both the force of the moment and the advertised ingenuity which to some degree draws us into itself; the moment fits the passage in both respects.

The less climactic *sententia* at *Ben.* iii. 17. 3 again lives in its habitat. Seneca is ending a discussion (iii. 6–17) of whether there should be a law against ingratitude by passing inward to the mental penal-

[47] Malchow ad loc. is probably right that Seneca sees here two anecdotes not one. Of the various ancient accounts the following are particularly interesting for Seneca: Plut. *Ser. Num.* 551a–b, Procl. *Dec. Dub.* 8. 54 (the standing still); Themist. περὶ ἀρετῆς pp. 69f. Mach (the abstracted presentation of the self); Val. Max. iv. 1. *Ext.* 2 (links between slave and Plato, *deforme, Platonis*).

[48] On power, note the paradox in *sibi ipse imperium abrogaverit*: abrogation would naturally be inflicted from outside (see Mommsen (1887), i. 628–30).

[49] With *omnia* cf. e.g. Prop. iv. 8. 30 *cum bibit omne decet*. The power of emperors (cf. Suet. *Calig.* 29. 1; [Sen.] *Oct.* 450), if present at all, stands far in the background.

ties for the ungrateful, and particularly the very absence of gratitude.

at quem iuvat accepisse, aequali perpetuaque voluptate fruitur, et animum eius a quo accepit, non rem, intuens gaudet. gratum hominem semper beneficium delectat, ingratum semel.

The man who is pleased to have received a benefit enjoys a uniform and unending pleasure; he gains joy from considering the mind of the benefactor, not the benefit. A benefit delights the grateful man always, the ungrateful man once [i.e. only when he receives it].

The short second sentence contrasts patently with the prolonged and colourful sentence that will follow; it contrasts too with the richer first sentence. In its own first half it takes up with its radiantly simple *semper ... delectat*, 'delights ... always', the flowing and attractive picture in the first sentence of grateful pleasure and the short and forceful *gaudet*, 'gains joy'. The latter half of the second sentence with grim brevity of phrase and meaning returns the emphasis to the ungrateful. The subtle spiritual argument is driven home by a seemingly stark, evident, and authoritative utterance. There is also an element of self-contemplating cleverness, created by the allusiveness of thought, the spareness of the linguistic material, and the abstracted quantitative neatness, and assonance, of *semper* and *semel*. We feel these elements together, but we feel them also as separate; this particular tonality of cleverness is not simply harmonized into expression.

In *NQ* v. 15 Seneca expatiates on the exploration of old mines under Philip II of Macedon.[50] He dwells with superb rhetoric, imagination, and symbolism on the extraordinary activity of mining for wealth, and the terrifying world discovered beneath the earth. After reaching in ample sentences a magnificent climax he adds, with abrupt brevity, *cum ista fecerunt, inferos metuunt!*, 'when they have done this, they [still] fear the world of the dead!' (4).[51]

[50] On Seneca's relation to Asclepiodotus, the writer on natural philosophy from whom he takes the story (1), see Hine on ii. 26. 6. Relevant too are Posid. frr. 239–40b Edelstein–Kidd, and perhaps Plat. *Rep.* vii. 514a1–518b5. For the historical background cf. Hammond and Griffith (1979), 69–73.

[51] δ's omission of *deinde* is attractive. In what precedes one should perhaps read *habitum*, and suppose missing a participle to go with *per caecum*; *inanes* gives the Virgilian epithet new force with the sense 'pointlessly', and balances *nulli fluentium* (so, e.g., *per caecum inanes <furentis>* or (with Z's order) *inanes per caecam <solitudinem ruentes>*). *inanes per caecum* alone (Z) is too weak, and anticipates *noctem* too much. If we simply adopt Gercke's *immanes* (cf.

The link with death has been increasingly prepared: the phrase before is *alteram perpetuamque noctem*, '(they tasted) a new and ever-lasting night', the earth above the miners has ingeniously trumped the earth above the dead, *Aeneid* vi has been pointedly echoed (3). But the target has hitherto been avarice, which has finally turned into a grim' agent, digging the men into the earth; now the target suddenly changes to the fear of death. Preparation and suddenness together achieve, after the long description, a spectacular stroke of wit. Human irrationality is freshly and forcefully indicted; but still more we delight in the author's engrossing cleverness. The simplicity of the language partly exposes disproportion and expresses contempt. We see contempt in the scornful third person of *metuunt*, 'they fear', which now encompasses all mankind, and in *inferos*, 'the underworld', which presents with offhand disdain the weary old fables. But also the plainness of the summing-up in the first clause and of the verb *metuo*, 'fear' (no 'tremble', no elaboration), create a deliberate fall in style which helps in partially detaching us.

In *Ep.* 10 Seneca justifies his urging of isolation on Lucilius; an epigram forms the starting-point for most of the letter: *et vide quod iudicium meum habeas: audeo te tibi credere* (1). 'Consider how high a judgement it is you have received from me: I dare to entrust you to yourself.' The paradox is marked out with an ostentatious air of significance and drama. Entrusting a person to someone else might be risky; entrusting someone to himself sounds not only para-doxical but harmless.[52] The strangeness of language marks the strangeness of the spiritual world, where significance and danger look different, and the self multiplies into tension and complexity. The epigram challenges us with the novel vision that it presupposes and asserts. Seneca characteristically proceeds, not to explain at once, but to present the same paradox in an amusing anecdote.[53]

In **Tacitus**, more than in most writers of the period, wit harmoni-ously enhances emotion.[54] His epigrams, dry and reserved,

Axelson (1939), 232), the idea of strangeness remains undeveloped, and *per caecum* has no real function; nor does *Ep.* 91. 12 fully justify the status of *per caecum* in the phrase (*flatus* has more verbal potential, and *per clusa* explains *violenti*).

[52] Cf. Prop. ii. 34a. 1 (read *amori*, i.e. *amanti*); Cat. 15; Sen. Rh. *Contr.* ix. 5. 8; Caes. *BC* ii. 32. 2; Virg. *Aen.* xi. 153; VF ii. 292. Note in context *NQ* iv a. *praef.* 20.

[53] *PPF* 10 A 15 Diels; Crates was famed for his sayings (e.g. A 19).

[54] See esp. Voss (1963); Plass (1988). One can form no adequate impression of the historiographical background to Tacitus' use of wit, nor does space permit a discussion. Sallust, Tacitus' overt exemplar, is not a very important model for his wit as such: he rarely shows quite the air of cleverness that we would look for. The intervening period was

strengthen feeling through understatement and contrast. They also provide a mode for giving the writer authority, and for elevating him intellectually and morally above the world that dominates his narrative: so coolly and unanswerably do they probe and assert, and with such control and detachment does the wit organize historical reality. In much of this we see relations with aspects of his writing discussed earlier; the entertainment and the refined pleasure which this aspect provides create no conflict with seriousness of impact, but colour and enrich the whole.

Tacitus ends thus his account of Vitellius' poisoning of Junius Blaesus; Blaesus, Vitellius had been falsely persuaded, meant to be emperor himself:

sanctus, inturbidus, nullius repentini honoris, adeo non principatus, adpetens, parum effugerat ne dignus crederetur.   (*Hist.* iii. 39. 3)

Upright, unturbulent, eager for no sudden position of honour, let alone that of emperor, he had failed to escape being thought worthy of it.

The praise of Blaesus in 38–9 serves the wider and negative purpose of contrast with Vitellius, with those who did betray him, and with Vitellius' brother, who persuaded him to the murder. In this sentence the author at first both praises Blaesus and establishes his innocence; the warm accumulation of adjectives, moving and authoritative in an author so remote from facile panegyric, is expanded with the third of the group into more elaborate argument. The sentence then twists: although it was so unlikely he intended to win power, Blaesus had fatally appeared to Vitellius worthy to do so. The irony of the supposed reason for murder, and the oblique praise, are less important than the biting contrast with Vitellius.[55] His unworthiness to rule has been shown again in

plainly significant. Relevant items are: Pollio fr. 5 Peter; Crem. Cord. test. 6, fr. 1; Brutted. Nig. fr. 2; Auf. Bass. fr. 2; Servil. Non. test. 3. Curtius Rufus, despite his debt to Livy, is more concerned than Livy with verbal sharpness: cf. e.g. iv. 7. 29, viii. 2. 1, 5. 18. The potential significance of the background is brought out by the well-known passages where Tacitus' epigrams draw on his source or sources, notably *Hist.* i. 81. 1, ii. 48. 2 (compare Plut. *Oth.* 3. 5, 16. 1). Remarks on Tacitus' 'development' in reducing the element of wit can suggest a somewhat misleading impression of his later work (so Goodyear (1968), 26 f.).

[55] The contrast is prepared at ii. 59. 2; note also 59. 1 *impar curis gravioribus*. On Blaesus' splendid lineage (cf. iii. 38. 3, and 39. 2) note the hypothesis of Syme (1986), 163; it is in any case important that the first consulship in Blaesus' family, unlike that in Vitellius', goes back to the reign of Augustus.

the first part of the paragraph, where his treachery has been
drawn out by paradox, and a hideous utterance cited with emphasis. A weighty *Blaeso* starting a sentence has suggested Blaesus'
unlikeness not only to Vitellius' conceptions of him but to Vitellius. Here *dignus*, 'worthy', common in the wit of high poetry for a
perverted greatness, scornfully but implicitly opposes worth and
squalor. The pluperfect, the passive, the negative *parum* not *non*,
the brevity and plainness of the final words, all create dryness,
distance, and reserve; these enhance in exciting contrast the
strength of the moral judgement, and by suggesting the author's
emotional and intellectual control confer on that judgement both
authority and aesthetic appeal.[56]

In *Ann.* xi. 10. 3 Tacitus tells how the Parthian monarch Vardanes, having triumphed abroad, was slain by Parthians. After
the decisive *interfecere*, 'they slew him', the sentence extends in
retrospection:

... primam intra iuventam, sed claritudine paucos inter senum regum,
si perinde amorem inter popularis quam metum apud hostis
quaesivisset.

... at the beginning of manhood, but with few kings that have attained
old age to match his renown—had he sought love from his people as he
sought fear from his foes.

The content of this extension has been prepared, both in the less
epigrammatic *ingens gloria atque eo ferocior et subiectis intolerantior*,
'great in glory, and for that very reason fiercer and more insup-
portable to his subjects', and in the design of the whole sentence.
The sentence begins with Vardanes' marking his glory in very
Roman vein, and shifts sombrely to the murder, ascribed as if to
the people in general. The author's resounding praise defies the
event, and itself evinces the freedom of his mind: the Roman
historian appreciates the achievement of foreigners and the
greatness of Parthia.[57] Yet he complicates generosity of vision in

---

[56] With *crederetur* one may probably compare *credebantur* in the neat and piercing epigram at *Ann.* xvi. 17. 6 *quae composita credebantur de Crispino quia interfectus erat, de Ceriale ut
interficeretur*: here the belief is in my view Nero's, and the impersonality heightens the force
(Nero 'believes' out of guilt and a wish to destroy). The passage looks back significantly to
xv. 71. 4 and 74. 3.

[57] Cf. *Ann.* ii. 88. 2f. (and e.g. *Hist.* v. 26. 1); *Ann.* ii. 56. 1, 60. 4, xv. 13. 2 (a phrase often
used of Carthage: Sall. *Cat.* 10. 1; Vell. i. 12. 25; Sen. Rh. *Hist.* fr. 1 Peter). *ingens gloria*
enhances the splendour with poetic magnificence (as *Germ.* 37. 1 confirms, cf. Virg. *Aen.* vii.

turn as he characteristically converts a statement into an unfulfilled condition. Now he strikingly manifests the humanity and the exacting breadth of his criteria for greatness, by contrast with the narrow intensity of his character Vardanes. He does so in joining the two strands of his sentence into an elegant symmetry of conception, underlined by the symmetry of form (in Tacitus notable). The effect is not spectacular but neat and subtle: depth of mind is presented through coolness of expression. The aloofness, the withdrawal, the poise, attractively and compellingly unite with weight.

It is noteworthy that in the different style of the *Dialogus* epigram is very much less prominent than in the historical or essentially historical works; there are various reasons for this (the Ciceronianism of the work should not be exaggerated). It is also noteworthy that despite these reasons verbal wit continues to appear there, often in an 'un-Tacitean' form. So we feel closer to Seneca in *prope abest ab infirmitate in quo sola sanitas laudatur*, 'he is not far from sickness who is praised only for health' (23. 4—wrily and pointedly related to its context).[58] Tacitus drew on ample resources of wit in himself; but the nature of his wit is vitally affected by genre.

Pliny the Younger in his *Panegyricus* treats political matters, and with an air of political insight; but the orator's wit is far removed from the historian's in its luxuriance and its engagement, and genre will here be the largest factor.[59] In 33. 3f. he assails Domitian for putting men to death as impious because they had spoken ill of the gladiators at his games. In Pliny's first sentence (3) the language is rich in incongruity and paradox; in his second, mounting lavishness leads purposefully towards the final epigram.

411–13). For the style of self-glorification cf. Aug. *Res Gest.* 26. 4, 30, 31. 1, 32. 3, *ILS* 8995. 5f. Naturally Tacitus does not have Vardanes murdered because of plans against Rome, as does Josephus, characteristically (*Ant.* xx. 73).

[58] Contrast [Cic.] *Opt. Gen.* 8, and also Quint. xii. 10. 15. It does not matter that the speaker is Aper: Tacitus does not mimic different schools of style, but essentially devises a stylistic medium in which all his characters can move. This is relevant to the constraints placed on *sententiae*: too ostentatiously epigrammatic a manner would obviously not have suited all the characters and their views.

[59] Tacitus' own speeches, for all their σεμνότης, must have expatiated more freely and ardently than his history in their praise and attack (cf. Plin. *Ep.* ii. 1. 6, ii. 17; i. 20 certainly does not conflict). As to the manner on politics, it is interesting too to compare with Tacitus e.g. *Ep.* i. 5. 1. On wit in Pliny cf. Peter (1901), 119–21; Sherwin-White (1969), 83f.

... se despici ac contemni nisi etiam gladiatores eius veneraremur, sibi male dici in illis, suam divinitatem, suum numen violari interpretabatur, cumque se idem quod deos, idem gladiatores quod se putabat.

... he judged that *he* was being scorned and depised if we did not worship even his gladiators; that *he* was being insulted in them, *his* deity, *his* godhead were being profaned; while he thought himself the same as the gods, he thought the gladiators the same as himself.

The elements of the final combination are carefully prepared; it comes both as a fine surprise and as a conclusion triumphantly 'proved' by ingenuity. The hierarchical monstrosities that have been stressed strongly or sarcastically now fall into simple words and a diagrammatic elegance (with a little prestidigitation on *idem*, 'the same thing as'): Domitian was levelling himself at once arrogantly with gods and basely with gladiators. The chiasmus assists the elegance and the contrast, and marks the drastic rise and descent undergone by the pronoun *se*, 'himself', which the preceding clauses had so relentlessly emphasized. The orator gains a victory of wit over the tyrant.[60]

In the letters of Pliny not written to the emperor, wit abounds. It mingles artistic and social grace; it evokes (and idealizes) a milieu courteous, relaxed, and literary. The brief letter ix. 31 begins *postquam a te recessi, non minus tecum quam cum ad te fui*, 'After I departed from you, I was no less with you than when I was at your house.' The intimately resumptive start opens into obvious paradox and elegance (English fails with the prepositions). We have here no Senecan profundity, but warm play with friendship and literature: Pliny has been reading a work by his addressee, and especially the parts on himself.[61] Both warmth and play assist the nimble skating of the letter upon its potentially invidious subject-matter. The mingling of praise, indirect self-praise, and a relationship is turned throughout by elegance into something dancing, glittering, and attractive. The final epigram of the letter characteristically shows an extreme of

[60] Compare 48. 1, where heaven itself at last annihilates Domitian's claims to divinity. Pliny presumably builds on a supposed superscription with something like *impie locutus* (cf. Suet. *Dom.* 10. 1); but he gives a different point to his stories (or story) from Suetonius', where the imputation of bias is what matters.

[61] On the addressee Sardus cf. Syme (1988a), 380, (1988b), 461. Probably he was less famous an author than Pliny.

symmetry which actually highlights Pliny's subtle handling of himself and his addressee: *unum illud addam, omnia mihi tanto laudabiliora visa quanto iucundiora, tanto iucundiora quanto laudabiliora erant*, 'I will just add this: it all seemed to me the more laudable the more pleasurable it was, and the more pleasurable the more laudable it truly was.' He mocks his own partiality for praise; he affects to infringe and then asserts the praise of his friend: *visa*, 'seemed', and *erant*, 'truly were', are delicately contrasted. The striking union of ingenuity and personality is achieved with easy lightness.

A few words may be of interest on some prose authors here excluded, with regret, from detailed consideration. The Elder Pliny rises not seldom into epigram, notably in his more elevated passages. His combinations are often forceful, but he lacks the sureness of Seneca's ingenuity and the finesse of his expression. As a splendid example of his vigour (of course to be read in its context) we may cite xxx. 15, on Nero's abandonment of magic: *saevius sic nos replevit umbris*, 'what he actually did [his reaction to Piso's conspiracy] filled us with ghosts in a crueller fashion'. The word-order, and the personal 'us' for 'Rome', give the cleverness grim power. Quintilian's manner is often informed by an elegance, precision, and pungency which sometimes flower as if naturally into a sober wit, relished but tightly controlled by good sense. At xi. 1. 93, Cicero is said to excel in his relaxed and his grand styles; the inexperienced will think they can imitate one of these (the former), those with understanding, neither, *alterum imperiti se posse consequi credent, neutrum qui intellegunt*. Quintilian is in 92–3 purposefully reconciling two remarks of Cicero's own; but here the pointed turn he gives to his combination, the shapeliness of the whole, the incisive brevity of the last clause, all create a light suggestion of austere wit. More sharply and amusingly he talks of the fashion for obscurity in oratory: *tum demum ingeniosi scilicet si ad intellegendos nos opus sit ingenio*, 'we are of course brilliant only if it would need brilliance to understand us' (viii. *praef.* 25). The cleverness and elegance (note the effective ring of the order) hint in themselves a pointed rebuke to these misplaced claims to brilliance. Still more pointed is the restrained and judicious wit that Quintilian uses of those who cultivate *sententiae* to excess (viii. 5. 31), or of the undisciplined Seneca (x. 1. 131). But one suspects from his remarks that epigram would have been somewhat more conspicuous in his speeches and his declamations.[62] It is generically notable that Petronius' low novel gives little place to verbal ingenuity, save in parody of declamation (e.g. 115. 19), or in poetry, particularly in the grandest pieces, where it is very prominent.[63] Conversely, the inept and leaden wit of Trimalchio is held up for our cultured entertainment.

If we take as our point of reference high poetry, itself very varied in its handling of wit, we can see what different relations exist in other genres and authors between wit and seriousness or elevation. Wit has in this period as it were a predisposition to modify, and to move suddenly downwards; but such tendencies are exploited, contained, or transformed, in greatly differing ways. Various features have recurred insistently, such as the fondness for creating ingenuity from the plainest of words, and, most particularly, the crucial connection between the epigram and its context. But those contexts themselves differ, and wit in an author is also fundamentally related to his style and his work in general. Not only the frequency of wit but its flavour alter with writer as well as with genre. The treatment of wit is bound up with an author's whole art, not only his handling of language, but his tone, manner, world, imagination, depth. Our tasks as readers are to become ardently responsive to this whole aspect of the literature; after that, to savour the differences of genres and then of individuals (just as one soon comes to differentiate in related aspects of a common language Haydn and Mozart, say, or Gainsborough and Reynolds). One must then place wit in its larger artistic setting. But 'tasks' is too daunting a word for activities that lay open so much delight.

[62] For the evidence on these see Meyer (1842), 594–8. I would myself be reluctant to see Quintilian as creator of even the shorter declamations ascribed to him (otherwise Winterbottom (1984), xii–xvii.

[63] Unfortunately *sententiarum* in the pronouncement at 118. 6 might perfectly well be part of the corruption.

4

EXTRAVAGANCE

EXTRAVAGANCE is a vital aspect of the high poetry in our period which readers are particularly unwilling to enjoy or accept; it is important for an appreciation of the whole literature. It is also centrally related to our special themes of greatness and reality. It well merits its own chapter. We shall again spend the first half of the chapter on high poetry, where the matter is of special importance, and then turn to consider some other writers: again the matter illuminates both genre and individuality. In looking at the high poetry, and at Seneca's prose, we shall concentrate on extravagance in physical description; it is a type that readers seem to find particularly disconcerting, and the concentration will enable us to see differences among the authors more clearly. On other writers we shall broaden our scope. We shall begin, however, with a word on ancient critics, who have greatly affected modern responses to lavishness and hyperbole in this literature; we shall for once allow ourselves some mention of Greeks.

From the surviving critics' viewpoint, which is essentially rhetorical, hyperbole looks somewhat awkward.[1] It seems perilous to exceed reality palpably if one is concerned with persuasion, emotional involvement, and the maturity and discrimination of speakers. Even Aristotle thinks hyperboles, in their vehemence, apt only for young men (*Rhet.* iii. 1413^a28-^b2). Demetrius censures them as 'frigid', as attempting greatness unsuccessfully and inappropriately, because they are impossible (*Eloc.* 125, cf. 114–27).[2] [Longinus'] approach is more complicated. For him hyperbole

---

[1] On hyperbole in the critics cf. Hunziker (1896), 4–24; Schenkeveld (1964), 80–7; Manzo (1988), esp. ch. 6; the last two point to further discussions. The matter has been considered particularly in relation to Virgil: see Hunziker (1896); Hardie (1986), ch. 6; Calboli (1987). On the high poetry of our period see Burck (1971), and also (on Seneca's tragedies and Lucan) Wanke (1964), 135–40; some more particular treatments are mentioned below.

[2] The passage of Aristotle must be read in Kassel's text.

should not go too far, should not destroy persuasiveness, and should ideally seem true, as can happen through the overwhelming greatness of emotion and event (38). It is characteristic of [Longinus] to emphasize judgement and control, to depreciate falsity and immature excess; it is also characteristic of him to value the transcendence of ordinary limits, in accordance with the truth of man's real greatness. Even in mythical poetry, for [Longinus], the reader appears to accept as if true the extreme surpassing of normal physical reality; he does so through the 'surpassing greatness' achieved in the poetry (9. 5).[3] [Longinus] values inspired extremes of grandeur; he could have no sympathy with a wilful and entertaining extravagance.

The Elder Seneca, paraphrasing Maecenas, attempts to show Virgil avoiding overdone and 'swollen' extravagance even in unbelievable description, through cultivating a manner of cautious truthfulness (*Suas.* 1. 12). In Quintilian we see plainly a controversial background (cf. Demetr. 120). Unrestrained excess in extravagance he saw as a prime fault of the decadent oratory he deplored (cf. xii. 10. 73, *al.*); hyperbole had been treated at length in his work attacking the fashion for that oratory (viii. 6. 76). A quite different approach to his was therefore favoured by many in practice. His own views are like a domesticated version of [Longinus']. He appreciates the potential of hyperbole for magnificence (viii. 6. 67–72); if the subject has surpassed the limits of nature (not a frequent occurrence, his placing suggests), hyperbole is eminently in place (76). But hyperbole is never believed, and this creates problems; there is also a great danger aesthetically in carrying it too far (73). We are to savour his own balance, neatness, and wit in urging restraint and propriety even in the use of hyperbole. He notes (like others) the comic potential of hyperbole; in between sublimity and comedy there is only a chasm of absurdity, into which the unwary will tumble.

The views of the critics belong with the larger outlook of individuals and a tradition; this has its own character and its own limitations, and should not be taken as uniquely and self-evidently

---

[3] Russell rightly sees the phrase (τὴν ὑπερβολὴν τοῦ μεγέθους) as positive; cf. 16. 2 ὑπερβάλλον ὕψος, 'a surpassing sublimity', Demetr. 120, and further e.g. App. *Samn.* fr. 4. 6 Viereck-Roos. For the two strands in [Longinus'] thought, note esp. 2–5 and 35 f. respectively (observe the movement in 36. 4). The childishness of Isocrates in 38. 2 relates partly perhaps to manner (cf. 4. 1) but more particularly to the slip in argument which results.

true. It would be precipitate to accept without question Quintilian's judgement on the type of oratory he detested. It would be worse to accept without question the values of ancient critics when we are reading the high poetry, which is extant and which so plainly presupposes different values. In the first place, we should at least consider whether in poetry there could be something exciting in conscious wildness, lavish unreality, and even youthfulness. Secondly, when high poetry is extravagant, it will turn out that we are not being expected to admire extremity simply because it is extreme. On the one hand, the extravagance is characteristically set against elements which contain and control it in arresting complication or contrast. On the other hand, the extravagance is so visibly conscious as itself to possess a degree of the unserious and entertaining: hence our total response to it cannot be one of simple awe at sublimity or simple laughter at comedy. The complexity is increased by the standard notions of the high genres which the poets exploit. This kind of extravagance is an audaciously metamorphosed version of the greatness which was theoretically expected of them. More straightforward greatness is also important, and shades into such extravagance. The proximity varies from passage to passage, and from poet to poet; but extravagance with some touch of play is of fundamental significance in this poetry, and most of all in its greatest authors.

Extravagance forms a basic part of **Lucan's** narrative, and of his conversion of history into poetry; but astringent elements are always at hand to modify its impact. At vi. 29–63, Caesar surrounds Pompey at Dyrrachium with fortifications. Prose history describes the operation as one of glorious audacity; and many of Lucan's own details exploit or distort historical data.[4] But Lucan creates an effect both wilder and more particular. First he narrates (29–47). His lavish magnification mixes extremes of grandeur with bizarre, half-prosaic, or ingenious elements in a way that obviously calls for a complicated reaction. Caesar uses, not the turf most common for such works, but *ingentes cautes avulsaque saxa metallis*, 'mighty rocks, and boulders wrenched from quarries' (34). The line moves excitingly from greatness of size to energy and particularity; but in the particularity of the next

---

[4] Prose: App. *BC* ii. 254. For Caesar's plan cf. Caes. *BC* iii. 43 f., and Veith (1920), *Beilage* II (*b*). On hyperbole in Lucan see Martindale (1976).

phrase, *Graiorumque domos*, 'and homes of the Greeks' (i.e. stones from local houses), the sudden strangeness of perspective adds oddity to the grandeur.[5] The building materials are then used conceptually to mark an extreme, but fantastically and with elegant and modifying neatness underneath: these works were not only more imposing than common siege-works, but could not themselves be destroyed in a siege (36f.).

The next sentence starts with the stunning *franguntur montes*, 'the mountains are broken'. The two words confront the greatness of the physical object, enhanced by the context, and the power of Caesar's will; the passive presents us first with the sheer act, before Lucan elaborates on Caesar. The sentence finally describes the range of wooded country embraced by the fortifications; but it ends with the beasts in those woods, which Caesar's fortifications incidentally enclose in a gigantic, and metaphorical, *indago*, the surrounding of an area with nets by hunters (*vastaque feras indagine claudit*, 42). Formally, *vasta*, 'gigantic', magnifies; but the amplitude and angle of the description are here so whimsically and ingeniously reduced and altered that its splendour is drastically contained.

Lucan enjoys creating from history the paradox of vastness that while besieged by Caesar Pompey could change camp (44). Both the paradox and the uneliminated prosiness make us more entertained than awed. He proceeds:

> flumina tot cursus illic exorta fatigant,
> illic mersa suos; operumque ut summa revisat
> defessus Caesar mediis intermanet agris. (43–7)

So many were the rivers that exhausted their full course there, both arising and plunging back within that space. To revisit the extremities of his construction, Caesar had to pass the night, wearied, in the fields midway.

The subject-matter is at first loftier, but the extravagance is so great that we must relish its self-consciousness; this effect is strengthened by the neatness of the phrasing. Then, with a sudden fall, hugeness is expressed in prosaic language and content. *defessus*, 'wearied', both produces a paradox in relation to the indefatigable Caesar and contrasts with the imaginative *cursus* ...

---

[5] One should contrast the pathos of *domos* at Virg. *Georg.* ii. 209. On turf cf. Lepper and Frere (1988), 261–6; [Caes.] *Bell. Hisp.* 32. 2.

fatigant, 'exhausted their course', which is used of the rivers.[6] The whole description is no mere wallow or welter, but is both organized and unpredictable, and full of life; paradox, detail, phrasing incessantly arrest and divert.

But Lucan does not stop there: the 'narrative' makes the springboard for a great leap into authorial exclamation. With a gesture of magnificent scorn he dismisses the glories of myth and foreign history: *nunc vetus Iliacos attollat fabula muros / ascribatque deis*, etc., 'now let old legend exalt the walls of Troy and assign them to gods', etc.

> en, quantum Tigris, quantum celer ambit Orontes,
> Assyriis quantum populis telluris Eoae
> sufficit in regnum, subitum bellique tumultu
> raptum clausit opus. (51–4)

See, all the land in the East encompassed by the Tigris, by the swift Orontes, all the land that suffices the peoples of Assyria for a kingdom, has been enclosed by a work rushed suddenly through in the turmoil of war.

The swing and power of the rhetoric is thrilling; but we enjoy it most (almost as with Sterne) in its sense of game. A simple response is precluded by the air of reckless exaggeration, which is only intensified by the implications about truth in regard to Troy; a simple response is precluded too by all the play in the poet's own earlier description.[7] One must also savour the last part of the sentence: it ingeniously sharpens the rhetoric on size with a point about time, and it leads the discourse down into matter less grand, yet pointedly so. Lucan's mind sweeps on next to an unguessable subject: all the improvements to the physical world which such activity could more profitably have effected—to fill up some of the Hellespont (56), and so forth. The greatness is too wild, and too oblique, to be taken gravely; and yet it undermines the patriotic exaltation of what precedes. The end of the sentence

---

[6] The notion of the time required is not in itself preposterous, though it is made to sound wild: the distance in question was about 15½ miles, Caes. *BC* iii. 63. 4 (and note 44. 3; at Florus ii. 13. 39 the text is dubious, at App. *BC* ii. 254 corrupt). On *intermanet* see Shackleton Bailey (1982), 95.

[7] It is instructive to see how Dante, using this type of Lucanian rhetoric to trump Lucan, reads and deploys it with little sense of play and so alters its character, *Inf.* xxiv. 85–90, xxv. 94–102. *attollat* is naturally ambiguous ('laud, make higher'); it and *ascribatque deis* together correspond to *mirentur* 50. Lemaire's view that 51–3 refer to cities does not at all fit the Latin, and gives a very poor point.

descends: *aut aliquem mundi, quamvis natura negasset, / in melius mutare locum*, 'or, though Nature refused, to change *some* place in the world for the better' (59 f.). The descent has point in the argument; but we are none the less to be entertained by the wan and despairing generality which now follows the robust particulars, and by the deliberate weakness of the final phrase. This weakness the grandiosity of the clause on Nature actually heightens.

The final lines of the passage continue the poet's movement to dissatisfaction with a physical greatness that is achieved in an immoral cause. But they are much more intense. With an astounding reversal they turn hugeness into littleness:

> coit area belli:
> hic alitur sanguis terras fluxurus in omnis,
> hic et Thessalicae clades Libycaeque tenentur;
> aestuat angusta rabies civilis harena.   (60–3)

The arena of the war contracts. Here is nursed blood that will flow into all the earth, here are contained the massacres both in Thessaly and in Africa; the madness of civil war seethes on a thin strip of sand.

The physical shrinking accompanies a ghastly vision of future expansion, half-physical in its lavish imagery, but moral in its force.[8] The last line superbly thrusts together smallness and greatness, physicality and morality, to reduce the mighty war to a grim lowness and to rob the physical setting of its grandeur. *aestuat*, 'seethes', denoting frenzy but suggesting the sea, initiates the dark fusion of language; the words conflict and contrast, but issue in scorn, vividness, and finality. The commanding brevity and decisive reduction dams with powerful contrast the apparent flow of extravagance; but that extravagance itself had been no straightforward affair. If we view the passage as a whole, opulence and wryness, ingenuity and detail, grandeur, lightness, and darkness, all find their centre and significance in the spectacle, the theatre, of the poet's discourse, in his actual brilliance, his depicted passion, and his moral thought. The passage is very far from showing Lucan's extravagance at its extreme: the wildness and

---

[8] Håkanson's *capitur* is highly attractive ((1979), 42 f.); I am not quite sure that *alitur* is unacceptable. It would suggest both natural life and fate's sinister purposes; in the former aspect particularly, it would be used with more emphasis on having than on feeding, as τρέφω sometimes is (cf. e.g. Lucr. i. 883, where *aliquid* means 'some other of those things').

playfulness of, say, the storm in v (597–677) make it appear re-strained indeed.[9]

Valerius also cultivates extravagance persistently, but with somewhat less theatrical an air: he is not transforming history, and his play is more restricted in range. In Book iv he paints the ferocious boxing king Amycus in lavish colours; the lavishness is given point and tightness by the firm morality and the intercon-nections of language. But he also modifies it with wit and play, though less drastically and drily than Lucan; and he savours the extravagance with a certain detachment.[10]

Valerius is concerned to trump not only Apollonius' Amycus but even Homer's Cyclops (his Amycus is not a crude or amusing person). He takes up the most grandiose moments of each when his Amycus makes his impressive and long-awaited first appear-ance. He calls him a Giant (*gigans*, 200, at the end of the clause); he presses home the idea with the bold directness of *mortalia nus-quam / signa manent*, 'no signs remain of his being mortal' (201f.), and with the comparison of Amycus to a peak which rises above other mountains. That Homeric comparison now suggests not only resemblance but general supremacy (202f., cf. Hom. *Od.* ix. 190–2).[11] The grandeur of impact is only lightly qualified by the description of Amycus' followers: even they, when they look at him, are not 'free of a silent fear', *taciti secura metus* (200f.). The ingenuity pleases, and *taciti*, 'silent', lingers agreeably on the inglorious emotion. The reference to mortality (201f.) contains an irony which sharpens in retrospect: not only will he be killed, but he hoped (319) to be immortal.

Valerius takes up at 236–8 the connection with the Giants, and with AR ii. 38–40, where Amycus is said to be like a monstrous son of Typhoeus or like an actual Giant. He compares Amycus' scorn for Pollux, his youthful opponent in boxing, to the scorn of the confident Typhoeus (to Valerius a Giant) for his seemingly unmanly opponents Bacchus and Minerva, who stood in the front

---

[9] See on the storm Friedrich (1956); Morford (1967a), 37–44; Martindale (1976), 48–50.

[10] On the episode with Amycus see, besides Korn's recent commentary, Mehmel (1934), 30, 41–54; Kröner (1968); Lüthje (1971), 147–53; Adamietz (1976), 54–8.

[11] Cf. Korn ad loc. on the sense of *gigans*; it would seem difficult to exclude metaphorical suggestion of the Giants in view of the history of the word, the sequence 199–203, and also AR ii. 38–40. *scopuli* probably represents something fairly large, cf. e.g. Stat. *Theb.* vii. 345f., with Bölte (1914), 19f.; it will answer to Homer's ῥίῳ, for which see Heubeck on *Od.* ix. 191–2.

of the gods at their battle with the Giants. Not without bearing
here is Amycus' impiety, magnificently expressed in a grandiloquent speech (219f., *aliis rex Iuppiter oris*, 'it is on other shores that
Jupiter is king').[12] The amazing assurance of Typhoeus is excitingly conveyed, and the irony of the future is palpable; but by its
close the simile is seen to mingle irony, wild valour, and amusing
ingenuity:

> primamque deorum
> Pallada et oppositos doluit sibi virginis angues.

He grieved that the first of the gods was Pallas, and that he was ranged
against the snakes of a [mere] maiden.

We would expect Typhoeus to grieve, but from fear of the
formidable Minerva. The stress falls surprisingly on *virginis*,
'maiden', which turns delightfully into a word of contempt (not
'the virgin goddess'). The snakes on Minerva's aegis become no
terror but an insult to the overweening and semi-serpentine Typhoeus.

The connection with mountains is taken up when Amycus is
slain.

> tenditur ille ingens hominum pavor arvaque late
> occupat, annosi veluti si decidat olim
> pars Erycis vel totus Athos; qua mole iacentis
> ipse etiam expleri victor nequit oraque longo
> comminus obtutu mirans tenet.   (320–4)

That mighty dread of men is stretched out on the land, and covers a
wide space of it; it was as if some day part of aged Mount Eryx should fall,
or the whole of Mount Athos. The victor himself cannot have his fill of
looking at the man's bulk, and he holds his face close in a long and
wondering gaze.

The poet at first drives home the fall of pride, and his imagination
dwells with relish on Amycus' physical immensity. The image of
the fallen mountain gains ironic force from the earlier connection; and here the particularity and the jump forward in time give
the image lavish power. Yet by pressing time and particularity the
poet partly diverts us from his narrative, in his ingenious and

---

[12] One may contrast Polyphemus' style, *Od.* ix. 275f. The relation of Amycus' impiety to
the Giants' is only slightly complicated by his being the son of Neptune. On Bacchus in the
Gigantomachy cf. Carpenter (1986), ch. 4.

elegant contrast of 'part' and 'whole' (some of Athos had already supposedly been destroyed by Xerxes).[13] The behaviour of the victor is that expected rather of the onlookers; *ipse*, 'himself', underlines this. Formally, the unexpectedness enhances the amazing sight (as with the followers above). But there is something undignified and entertaining in Pollux's action which holds back and modifies the impact of the extravagance through the detached cleverness of the poet's invention. The amassing of words in *longo / comminus obtutu mirans*, 'close in a long and wondering gaze', only strengthens this effect.[14] Its force is increased, and the poet's intention confirmed, by the contrast with the greatness of Pollux's words just before (312–14). These words undo, and are to be set against, Amycus' overweening pride (243, *tune Amyci moriere manu?*, 'Are *you* to die [have the honour of dying] by Amycus' hand?'; 314, *sic et memori noscere sepulchro*, 'in this way [through the name of Pollux] you will also be known from a grave that brings lasting remembrance'). Valerius is not now undercutting Pollux but complicating his own poetry. He enjoys the extravagance of Amycus; but he also exposes it morally, and he prevents it from sprawling emotionally or stylistically by his attractive wit, and by the tightness and cohesion with which he organizes his writing.

Silius' constant lavishness has a harsh quality, often mixed with the bizarre; he is greatly indebted to Lucan here, but rather less exuberant. In xiv. 353–579 he narrates extravagantly a sea-battle at Syracuse; he here owes almost nothing to Livy, and much to Lucan iii. In 516–38 we see Silius too beguiled by the Cyclops. Eager to join, not separate, myth and history, he creates one Polyphemus, who 'loved this name of ancient savagery', *antiquae nomen feritatis amabat* (528). *antiquae*, 'ancient', stresses the link with myth and its monster, who has already been referred to in the book (222–6, 475, cf. 33). The light paradox that Polyphemus should revel in the association is underlined by the juxtaposition of *feritatis*, 'savagery', and *amabat*, 'loved'; it suggests a certain pleasure in Silius at the extremity of his character. He continues:

[13] Xerxes was conceived of as cutting, and sailing, through the mountain, not simply the isthmus: so e.g. Call. fr. 110. 45–8 (Cat. 66. 45 f.), and even Dio Chr. iii. 31. We cannot explain the language by saying that Eryx is larger or higher: it is not. The remarkable character of the passage is made clearer by less elaborate comparisons with falling mountains, as at vi. 383, and by Valerius' starting point Virg. *Aen.* xii. 701.

[14] For onlookers cf., besides Virg. *Aen.* viii. 265–7, Stat. *Theb.* i. 616–20; Hom. *Il.* xxii. 369–71.

ubera praebuerat parvo lupa. corporis alti
terribilis moles, mens aspera; vultus in ira
semper, et ad caedes Cyclopia corde libido.   (529–31)

When he was little, a she-wolf had given him her udders. The mass of his
lofty body was dreadful, his mind fierce. His face bore the look of wrath
perpetually; his heart possessed the desire of a Cyclops for slaughter.

Roman legend is ingeniously applied to an enemy of Rome, and
made to express ferocity (*lupa*, 'she-wolf', is forcefully placed).[15]
The contrast between the small baby and the huge adult is intended to be not only vigorous but agreeable. Yet these features
do not lessen the strength of the lavish description here. The idea
of the Cyclops runs through it, and raises its elements in grandeur,
until the last line brings in that idea explicitly, climactically, and
elegantly. The connection wildly turns martial fierceness into
something monstrous; but the particular link with the anthropo-
phagous Cyclops' desire to kill suggests the differences too, and
the poet's self-conscious enjoyment of his extravagance.
Enjambment adds force in the second line, force and cleverness in
the third (one expects the face to change and anger to pass); in the
second sentence the content and length of clauses is arranged
with conscious neatness and symmetry.

Polyphemus executes with extraordinary strength a designedly
intriguing manœuvre. A Roman and a Carthaginian ship
are joined by chains, and begin a paradoxical land-battle, as in
Lucan (cf. Luc. iii. 553–75). Developing the situation almost amusingly, Silius makes the Carthaginians seek to break the chains and
row off with those Romans who have boarded them. The
breaking of the chains *vasta mole*, 'with huge weight', is intended to
be a communal activity (523 f.), as one would expect the rowing to
be; but both are accomplished by Polyphemus alone.[16] The first
he performs *membrorum pondere*, 'with the weight of his body' (532);
the impact of phrase and action is increased by the earlier *vasta*

[15] Silius will not have been aware that the myth may have had an anti-Roman origin
(Strasburger (1982), 1039f.; Jocelyn (1971), 52f.).

[16] Our understanding of the episode is affected by the textual problem in 523–8. The
absence of a subject in 523–6 is surprising, and one prefers Ker's unwillingness to accept it
to Delz's willingness, here as in other passages (Ker (1967), 22f.). However, *Aetnaeo* is much
more satisfactory than Ker's *Aetnaeus* in 527f. This difficulty increases the likelihood that
something is amiss earlier: for it is much more probably the captain, not Polyphemus (so
Delz, Ker, and Spaltenstein), who *hortatur socios*; and Polyphemus would just act. For *socii*
thus cf. xii. 110, 192, 628, etc. Various solutions are possible (such as a lacuna after 524).

mole, and by *terribilis moles*, 'the mass ... was dreadful', in the description. It is increased too by the ironically quiet verb *relaxatis*, 'undone' (contrast *abrumpere*, 'break off', in 524).[17] The verbs used of his rowing away the ship, *impulerat* 'he had driven on', *duxisset*, 'he would have led off' (533 f.), surprise in reference to a single sailor; this sharpens the extravagance. But the plot ends his grandiose plan: he is killed. The close, while affecting to enhance, halts and contains the impressiveness of figure and action in an image of bizarre futility. After the imposing *vix morte incepta remittit*, 'he scarcely abandons his plan in death', we learn that his hand, continuing to row in death, *ignavum summo traxit super aequore remum*, 'moved the oar uselessly above the surface of the sea' (537).[18] The devious oddity of incident has provided a setting and a limit which have given the lavishness a certain distance: the passage is both lavish and controlled; it is grim, grotesque, and entertaining.

Statius handles extravagance with all the freedom and vivacity of his inexhaustible imagination and fancy. His use of language, searchingly vivid and refined, gives a constant sense of subtlety in the midst of extremity; his brilliant wit removes us from any simple immersion in narrative with a singular audacity and sharpness. In *Theb.* v. 505–33 he describes the snake that killed the child Opheltes. He draws largely on Ovid (*Met.* iii. 31–98), as does Silius (vi. 146–293); Statius may be making some use of Silius too, as he is of other authors.[19] Ovid and Silius are here both highly extravagant, and Silius gives prominence to the element of ghastliness; Statius is richer and subtler, and his fancy plays absorbingly. Comparison of detail brings out further Statius' special qualities.

The extravagance is given point throughout by the opposition Statius creates between the gigantic snake and the little child, and between wild grandeur and pathetic charm. After a short description of Opheltes' falling asleep, the ominously long description of

[17] The verb is apt to *vinclis*; not utterly dissimilar in its effect is *laxavit* at Luc. iv. 632.

[18] One might possibly ask whether *insurgere* could be preferable in 535. *ex-* as a variation for the normal *in-* or *con-* appears uninviting, particularly when the idea of the oar is not expressed. For the confusion cf. e.g. Stat. *Theb.* iv. 90.

[19] Cf. esp. Virg. *Aen.* ii. 199–227, *Georg.* iii. 414–29; Eur. *Hyps.* fr. 18 Bond (Cockle (1987), 84 f.). Cf. also Kroll (1924), 286–8; for fearsome depictions of Opheltes' snake in art see *LIMC* ii. 2. 355–7. On Statius' episode see Vessey (1973), 187–90; in respect of extravagance, one should not, I think, seek to make the world of Nemea different from that of the poem in general. The scene in Silius is discussed by Basset (1955). On extravagance in Statius' epic see Vessey (1986*b*), esp. 3003–7.

the snake begins. The first sentence ends *immanem sese vehit ac post terga relinquit*, 'it bears its vast length along, and leaves itself behind its back' (507). The first part of the line conveys immensity; the second plays with that immensity, with the locomotion of snakes, and with a phrase used of humans leaving something behind them: behind what seemed its back or backs still remains itself.[20] Grandeur here changes to a particularly obtrusive ingenuity. Statius' language then gives vivid presence and tonality to the horrid magnificence of the creature. So one may contrast with Ovid's *cristis praesignis et auro;* / *igne micant oculi*, 'conspicuous with its crests of gold; its eyes flicker with fire' (*Met.* iii. 32 f.), Statius' *livida fax oculis*, 'a livid flame burns in its eyes' (508), and *auratae crudelis gloria frontis*, '[its crests] the cruel splendour of its golden brow' (510).[21]

Statius describes its usual activities:

> miserae nunc robora silvae
> atterit et vastas tenuat complexibus ornos.
> saepe super fluvios geminae iacet aggere ripae
> continuus, squamisque incisus adaestuat amnis.   (514-17)

Sometimes it wears away the oaks of the unhappy forest, and with its embrace makes the huge mountain-ashes thin. Often it lies above rivers, on the elevation of both banks, stretching the entire length across, while the river, interrupted by the scaly body, boils up against it.

The destructive effect of the snake's climbing trees is actually very lavishly conceived (*vastas*, 'huge', is set against *tenuat*, 'makes thin'); but the verbs chosen are deliberately and teasingly undramatic in appearance.[22] Ovid's serpent more dramatically bends a tree with its weight (93), and Silius' uproots one (vi. 194-6). The seeming conflict of Statius' language and his extravagance shows

---

[20] Ov. *Met.* x. 670 *iuvenem post terga relinquit*, ii. 187. Statius is presumably imagining vertical curves, as in a lavish form of rectilinear motion (if I understand: cf. McFarland, *et al.* (1985), 328).

[21] Compare too the phrasing of Eur. *Hyps.* fr. 18. 3 γοργωπὰ λεύσσω/ν; Virg. *Georg.* iii. 433 *flammantia lumina torquens, Aen.* ii. 210 *ardentisque oculos suffecti sanguine et igne* (unlike Statius in its powerful directness); Sil. ii. 586 *ignea sanguinea radiabant lumina flamma*, vi. 220 *terribilis gemino de lumine fulgurat ignis*; for other passages see Mynors on Virg. *Georg.* iii. 433. For the second phrase cf. also Ov. *Met.* vii. 150, xv. 669. *frontis* should be preferred to *fronti*, since it is needed by *gloria*; it includes the crests, just as *frons* often includes horns. With regard to 509 f., the three rows of teeth are not Ovid's invention (Bömer on *Met.* iii. 34): cf. Nic. *Ther.* 442 (Hom. *Od.* xii. 91).

[22] Cf. *Ach.* i. 434 f., *Theb.* i. 564 f.

him savouring both language and extravagance detachedly; his *miserae*, 'unhappy', only increases the detachment. Silius has the extreme and intriguing image of the snake with head and tail on opposite banks of a river: 'not yet plunged into the river with its whole body, it was already placing its head on the edge of the opposite bank', *nondum etiam toto demersus corpore in amnem / iam caput adversae ponebat margine ripae* (vi. 164f., cf. Sen. *Oed.* 727–30). Statius' stranger language makes the image seem stranger too; the effect of the adjective *continuus*, with the significant enjambment, is impossible to render in prose. He also creates a weird and imaginative picture of the river, interrupted and in tumult, to contrast with the snake, 'continuous' and simply 'lying'. The breath of great snakes is commonly disastrous, and Silius deploys the most lavish imagery of wind and the underworld (174–8).[23] Statius describes visually the grass falling before his snake's hot breath (made hotter by drought); he then extends this into a drastic and paradoxical phrase: *moriturque ad sibila campus*, 'the plain dies at his hisses [from the breath that comes with them]' (528). Statius closes his description with two extreme similes of size, taken from a snake among the stars, and from the snake Python slain by Apollo. He is inspired by Ovid (44f.) and perhaps Silius (181–4); he develops the similes with wild and graphic images of his own, and the second makes both contrasts and links within his own poem.[24]

Statius at last comes back to Opheltes, and addressing him as *parve*, 'little one', asks with pathos and indignation what god assigned him *tam magni pondera fati*, 'the weight of so large a doom' (534f.). The words are physical, but not only physical: the whole description is now powerfully and sharply concentrated onto a single point. Yet the actual death brings the hyperbole to the finality of action in a moment astoundingly casual:

> occidis extremae destrictus verbere caudae
> ignaro serpente, puer.   (538f.)

---

[23] Note Sen. *Clem.* i. 25. 4.

[24] Note also Sil. iii. 191f. It is hard to think the similes spurious; I suppose we must accept the conflation of celestial serpents. The comparison with Pytho plainly recalls and develops i. 562–9; cf. Ov. *Met.* i. 443; Virg. *Aen.* x. 886f. (*silvam* in Statius is more pointed). The contrast between the snakes destroyed by and sacred to divinity leads us into disturbing connections with the whole story of Coroebus in i. (On links with Linus see Vessey (1973), 104f.)

You perished, child, on being brushed by a blow from the edge of his tail;
the serpent knew nothing of it.

The hugeness is formally enhanced, but by the absence of brutal
horror. Only the clash between *destrictus*, 'brushed', and *verbere*,
'blow', suggests the actual force; the hideous physical consequences are left for later (596–8).[25] The surprise and ingenuity
wryly and entertainingly distance and contain both extravagance
and emotion. The second-person form only furthers the complication. The poignant *puer*, 'child', also contrasts with *serpente*, which
is placed next to it, and is the subject of a particularly ingenious and
distancing development at the beginning of the new line. A fuller
poignancy will return as the narrative progresses; we will only
remark the new twist by which the snake, killed in return for the
child, is himself made the object of pathos (579–82).[26]

Seneca's tragedies show a drastic and often relatively simple
opposition between lavishness and tightness. His art is built from
the interaction of extravagance and ingenuity, and not from the
two features separately. Places where extravagance seems
accumulated profusely must be seen in the context of the pithy
epigrams which generally contain and twist it, or of adjacent passages in a contrasted tone and tempo. The actual expression in
these places will usually prove on inspection less straightforward
than it appears. To continue the line of our discussion, we shall look
at a passage of narrative rather than of impassioned speech; but the
same principles apply in both areas of his work. In *Phaedr.* 1007–34 a
messenger describes the perturbation of the sea which preceded
the emergence of the monstrous bull that was to cause Hippolytus'
death.[27] Almost at once (1008) the sea has risen to the stars, as it is so
often inclined to in the storms of Latin poetry. But a surprise
promptly supervenes: there is no wind or storm to stir the sea.[28]

[25] One may compare and contrast with 596–8 Eur. *Tro.* 1176f. and Sen. *Tro.* 1110–17; note
in 598 the subtle alteration of Lucan's *totum est pro vulnere corpus* (ix. 814) to *totumque in vulnere
corpus* (cf. Ov. *Ib.* 344).

[26] Cf. x. 503–7 (death of a warrior), with Williams's note. *reptatus* in 581 makes a half-
whimsical link with the child in a point that has contrasted him (note iv. 793–803). At 578
exsibilat crosses the mind.

[27] On the speech see Liebermann (1974), 14–45; Segal (1984). The parts corresponding to
our passage in Euripides and Ovid are *Hipp.* 1201–14, *Met.* xv. 508–11. On extravagance in
the tragedies cf. Friedrich (1972), 142–8.

[28] Cf. Coffey and Mayer's note. On storms and stars see Tarrant on *Ag.* 471. In 1007 I
somewhat prefer the conjecture *tumuit: crevitque in astra* seems otherwise too unsupported.
But see Zwierlein's commentary ad loc.

The poet strengthens the surprise by introducing it with asyndeton; repetition of *nullus*, 'no', produces wonder and a sort of negative extravagance. But this condenses into an epigram, which partly draws us into its imaginative ingenuity and the strange relationships that it fashions from ordinary language: *placidumque pelagus propria tempestas agit*, 'the sea had been calm and yet was driven by a tempest of its own' (1010). The poet goes on to make this disturbance trump actual storms, which themselves are lavishly described (1011–14): extravagance as well as paradox is being relished, but self-consciously, as the strangeness makes apparent.

Seneca proceeds:

> consurgit ingens pontus in vastum aggerem;
> nec ista ratibus tanta construitur lues:
> terris minatur. fluctus haud cursu levi
> provolvitur: nescioquid onerato sinu
> gravis unda portat. quae novum tellus caput
> ostendet astris? Cyclas exoritur nova?   (1015–21, without [1016])

A vast quantity of sea rises into an immense pile. So great a massed-up heap is not a disaster to mere ships: it threatens the earth. The waves roll forward with no swift motion; something is being carried by the water which makes it heavy and weights its bosom. What new land will display itself to the sky? Is a new island arising to join the Cyclades?

In the first sentence ('A ... earth') words of size lead into an epigrammatic explosion of extravagance at the start of a line (1018). This makes the climax of the contrast with storms; yet its advertised neatness and its conscious wildness of expression distance us from simple involvement. The moment also has ominous point for the plot (Hippolytus is on land); but our chief sensation is of pleasure. Having brought his mixture of elements to this culmination, Seneca moves purposefully on.[29] A new but slighter surprise, the slowness of the waves, leads into a fresh terror. The deduction from the slowness, and its alarm, are graphically conveyed through the placing of *nescioquid*, 'something', and the placing and connection of *levi*, 'swift, *lit.* light' and *gravis*, 'heavy', and *onerato*, 'weighted'. The sight and the thoughts are evoked in a very concrete manner; Seneca then leaps abruptly to evoking the

---

[29] I punctuate 1018–20 a little differently from Zwierlein.

dread of the moment with the most imposing extravagance. The form of the question makes the messenger plunge into the past as if it were the present; the content is lavishly bold and magnificent. In this context, where the existing Cyclades are to be thought of as in the region, the particularization in the second question adds a slight touch of complicating cleverness.[30]

The actual arrival of the bull is built up to both by yet greater lavishness and by more definite suggestion of the creature. The 'whole' sea is now made to 'bellow' (1025f.); a type of whale is introduced in a simile, and suggests the monster (cf. 1049f.) in a weird mixture of the bizarrely concrete and the wildly extravagant.[31] At last the bull appears on land; it is denoted only by *malum / maius timore*, 'an ill that exceeded our fears': the phrase both teases by its indefiniteness and trumps even the extraordinary fears of 1020f. The theme of the sea is also brought to a new height by the language: *pontus in terras ruit*, 'the sea rushes onto the earth' (1033). The expression is made to suggest the violation of the division between portions of the world, and so to take up and fulfil the suggestion of *terris minatur*, 'threatens the earth' (1018).

The start of the next line turns the idea to a more whimsical ingenuity: *suumque monstrum sequitur*, 'and follows its own monster' (1034). The language half-suggests, as motive for the violation of order, loyalty in the inanimate to a monster; that fancy lightly detaches us before we proceed at last to description of the beast. The poet has attacked his extravagant narrative with immense and exhilarating gusto; but strangeness, wit, and organization have complicated the extremity and made the passage as a whole not facile bombast but alert, lively, and imaginative poetry.

Much ancient poetry is interested in extremes, much Roman poetry, especially, in lavishness; such interest is turned by these poets in a very particular direction. The response they seek here is never one of simple seriousness; and, much as they enjoy playing with the appearance of unrestrained excess, the actual complexity and control of their effects and their art are always

---

[30] On the geography of the passage cf. Leo (1878), 201–5. For the conception in 1020f. cf. Pind. *Ol.* 7. 61–3. In considering Seneca's exploitation of Ov. *Met.* ii. 264, one should bear in mind his use of it in *NQ* iii. 27. 13 (the actual quotation is *et ... augent*, as rhythm confirms); it may be that he has misremembered the context there. (He quotes Tibullus as Ovid, emphatically, at iv a. 2. 2: a sobering thought for the student of poets' allusions.)

[31] The *physeter* obviously suggests an extreme of size: cf. Plin. *NH* ix. 8, and note Sen. Rh. *Suas.* 1. 13. See also Thompson (1947), 280f.

apparent. The passages from epic have also shown the moral distance the narrators so often mark from the lavishness they depict, and the pointed relations between the extravagance and the events or the larger context. This betrays again the complication and the order with which the feature is handled. The poetry excitingly conjoins and confronts in its style the wild and sweeping with the constrained and obstructing; but all is organized and mastered by a commanding discipline.

Now we come to prose and to other kinds of poetry. The concern of most prose with reality tends to diminish or alter the role of lavishness, by comparison with poetry; but it is especially important in the prose of **Seneca**. What it there depicts or drives home is not fantasy but startling truth. The difference from poetry in impact is not absolute: such lavishness may be employed in Seneca with a certain consciousness of extravagance and audacity; it is generally mixed with and contained by more sober, intellectual, and ingenious elements; and, apart from the philosophy, it makes its own independent and ostentatious appeal. But it has an intimate connection with philosophical reality, with influencing and challenging us, far beyond anything in poetry. Playfulness and frivolity largely retire, but not exuberance.

An interesting treatment of the topic occurs at *Ben.* vii. 22 f. Here Seneca modifies an earlier pronouncement (ii. 10. 4). He sometimes, he explains, makes excessive demands (*ultra modum*); the aim is to make people actually keep the true degree of obligation (22. 1).[32] So hyperbole in general exaggerates, or 'lies', incredibly in order to attain belief (or assent) for the true or credible degree of something large (23. 1 f.). He gives examples from epic, one from Virgil's narrative. In seeing poets as anxious to be believed, and relating hyberbole to persuasion, he is following a rhetorical tradition, one that underplays differences of genre; he is also ignoring his own poetry. More important, however, is his explicit dilution of his own utterance and his explicit discussion of his own procedure. As so often, Seneca wishes us to oppose the lavish element in his writing to the shrewd, practical, and self-

---

[32] This and other passages where Seneca touches on style must not of course be turned into authoritative guidelines for the critic. With regard to Seneca's moral strategy here cf., in a different context, Quint. iv. 5. 16, and Machiavelli, *Princ.* 6 (compare his more definite images with Seneca's *redeant* and *veniat*, 22. 1, 23. 1).

aware; he is both surprising us and displaying the richness of his art and his thought. To these ends, he commonly adjusts his own statements; uncommonly, he seems here nearly to be talking about his own manner of writing. But the emphasis falls, characteristically, on his moral purpose.

The last quarter of *NQ* iii (27–30, 11 pages) Seneca devotes to describing the flood which periodically destroys the world, alternately with the more famous conflagration.[33] It is a passage of overwhelming power; the description of future events is lavish to the last extreme, but it is no myth. The form subserves both descriptive momentum and intellectual argument. Seneca is contending, typically, for a plurality of causes to the flood; but while developing the causes in the order of their occurrence he generates a terrifying narrative sequence. From the interaction and contrast of intellectual and emotional elements the lavishness gains a weighty and scholarly foundation in truth; the description is also marked out as the thrilling construction, erected on that foundation, of Seneca's imagination and art.

Only a few moments can be touched on here. In portraying the effect of the rains (27. 4–15), Seneca mounts upward from plain and unglamorous detail to immense destruction: he seeks to obtain through this pattern both excitement and conviction.[34] So, in one part of one sweeping sequence:

abluit villas et intermixtos dominis greges devehit, vulsisque minoribus tectis quae in transitu abduxit, tandem in maiora violentus aberrat: urbes et implicitos trahit moenibus suis populos, ruinam an naufragium querantur incertos.　　　　　　　　　　　　　　　　(27. 7)

---

[33] For the conception cf. 28. 7; on the tradition cf. Theiler (1982), ii. 198–200, adding *SVF* ii. 1174, *al.* On the passage cf. Levy (1927/8); Waiblinger (1977), 44–53; Caduff (1986), 142–53; Gross (1989), 113 f., 142–4. It is especially important here to be aware of the readings of Z: see Hine (1980), 191–5. At 29. 4 he sees Z's *non concussione* for *motu*[2] as an addition to it, and suggests *motu; non <mundi sed mundi quoque concussione>*. But 27. 3 and the context indicate that the phrase *concussione mundi* would denote universal destruction, so that *quoque* would be out of place; and the tricolon leading into *omnia* gives much better rhetoric. Perhaps *concussione* is rather a variant for *motu*, and should replace it both times; it would improve the rhythm.

[34] Axelson (1933), 56, cannot be right in starting a new sentence with *ut quidam* in 27. 3, thus attributing all that follows to Fabianus and others. The pattern of exposition would be most peculiar. Rather, Seneca is opposing a less drastic view of the flood. At 27. 1 *ita est* should be followed by a colon and referred forward, as by Vottero; cf. ii. 59. 6, *Brev.* 1. 4, *Polyb.* 1. 1, *Ep.* 110. 20, *Phaedr.* 646, etc. (a colon should be printed too at *Ep.* 97. 13). The other view makes the phrase much too abrupt. In 27. 7 Z's *passim plana* should naturally be adopted.

(a torrent from the mountains) washes villas away, and brings down flocks mingled with their masters. It rips away these lesser buildings that it carries off as it passes, and then diverts its violence to greater things: it drags off cities, and peoples caught up in their own walls, unsure whether they have the collapse of buildings or a shipwreck to lament.

Here *villas*, 'villas', though extravagant enough, sounds an alarmingly ordinary word.[35] *minoribus*, 'lesser', *maiora*, 'greater', and the fine gesture of *in transitu*, 'as it passes', explicitly mark and enhance the rise. None the less, *urbes*, 'cities', and *populos*, 'peoples', startle in their lavishness. The shape and content of the clause *urbes ... populos*, 'it ... walls', pointedly echoes that of *abluit ... devehit*, 'washes ... masters'; its word-order is more involved, as suits its more dreadful confusion. The wit of the final clause presents a feeling strange in its situation and its content (two such disasters are not commonly confounded). The ingenuity, softened by a further clause, slightly detaches even as formally it enhances; it prevents the writing from seeming too abandoned.

This section ends not in climax but in contrasting and limiting controversy. Seneca, who both cites and imitates Ovid's flood (*Met.* i. 253–323), here criticizes the poet; he criticizes him not for exaggerating or lying but for failing to sustain the magnificence due to so great a subject. Ovid, playing elegantly with various common themes, tells of the wolf swimming among the sheep, *nat lupus inter oves* (304); Seneca rebukes him for spoiling his mighty description with such trivial and unlikely matter and such absurd and childish play (*pueriles ineptias*, 27. 13).[36] It was rather the whole world that was 'swimming' (i.e. was inundated), *orbem terrarum natare* (27. 15): Seneca closes with his own ostentatious wit. He is using criticism of Ovid to bring out his own seriousness, and the greatness of his subject and his conception of it; this ending boldly sets the lightness of Ovid's wit against the weightiness and, in his prose, the purposefulness of Seneca's. Naturally Seneca is distorting, or affecting to distort, the intentions of Ovid, along familiar lines.

An earlier moment describes the dark storm and the lightning: *quod olim fuerat nubilum nox est, et quidem horrida ac terribilis intercursu*

---

[35] *villa* is not of course confined in application to the present: cf. e.g. *Ben.* iv. 37. 1; Ov. *Met.* i. 295. The end of the extract I translate as above, not 'whether they should lament' one or the other, because the following clause would not suit the other sense at all well.

[36] There are some uncertainties in the text of *Met.* i. 304 f.

luminis diri (27. 10). 'What had once been cloudy weather is
now night, and indeed a dreadful night, made more fearful by the
appalling light interrupting the darkness in flashes.' The dire
progression is marked out by the alliteration of *nubilum*, 'cloudy
weather', and *nox*, 'night'; the stark monosyllables *nox est*, 'is
night', strengthen the force of the simple word, *nox*, given figurative power. Seneca goes on to a further extreme, extending the
grammar after the rhythmical clausula (*nūbĭlūm nōx ēst*); the paradox that light makes things worse here grimly intensifies the
description. In this sentence the actual lavishness and ingenuity
are handled with a discretion and strength that permit little distance. It is fascinating to compare declamation, epic, or tragedy
on the same material; so in Seneca's own *Agamemnon* the stark *nox
est* becomes *dirae Stygis / inferna nox est*, 'there is a hellish night of
dreadful Styx' (494 f.), and the paradox of terrible light turns into
the more disruptive and entertaining paradox of men wanting
even this light, *hoc lumen optant* (497).[37]

The supreme climax is formed by the last part of the penul-
timate section. The passage, which itself moves as in successive
waves, has gathered and surged to a point where the utmost
extremes, for all the ingenuity of the treatment, win an elemental
inevitability.

... unus humanum genus condet dies. quicquid tam longa Fortunae
indulgentia excoluit, quicquid supra ceteros extulit, nobilia pariter
atque adornata magnarumque gentium regna pessum dabit.   (29. 9)

A single day will bury the human race. Whatever Fortune with such
lengthy favour has perfected, whatever has raised men above their
fellows, things of rare distinction and splendour and no less the realms of
huge peoples, that day will destroy.

The first sentence presents its extremity with swiftness and a
stunning contrast, assisted by the placing of *unus*, 'a single'. Conversely, the second sentence (despite twists) accumulates with
devastating power and pathos what the simple verb (*pessum dabit*,
'destroy') will bleakly and brusquely undo.[38]

Seneca does not stop with this climax; what comes after it

---

[37] For the construction of *Ag.* 496f. see Zwierlein. One should note the play there with
Virg. *Aen.* vi. 721 *quae lucis miseris tam dira cupido?*. For other treatments of the theme see esp.
Sen. Rh. *Contr.* viii. 6, Luc. v. 627–31; note also Plin. *Ep.* vi. 16. 17.

[38] One may compare and contrast Sall. *Jug.* 42. 4.

produces various surprises, and modifies the whole effect. Immediately after the climax Seneca goes on, and back, with a prosaic *ut dixi*, 'as I have said' (30. 1). There follows an argument that makes the catastrophe seem alarmingly near; then, with a wonderful sense of relief and regeneration, Seneca tells how after the catastrophe order and innocence will be restored. We seem to have a stirring though unexpected close; this is in turn prevented. Seneca remarks that sin will soon return, and ends abruptly with dry and sombre generalization on the ease of learning vices. The style, and the sense of a futile cycle (contrast 29. 5), hold in all the lavishness and extremity of the finale with shrewd sobriety and unexalted gloom.

Other prose writers may now be more briefly considered (Petronius we defer). **Pliny the Elder** in his more grandiose passages can offer an unfettered extravagance of language and presentation; although affecting gravity, he exults uninhibitedly and delightfully in the extremes his words create.[39] At the start of Book xxxvi he presents the quarrying of marble as the assault of mountains. *caedimus hos trahimusque nulla alia quam deliciarum causa quos transcendisse quoque mirum fuit* (1). 'We hew and drag off, simply for luxury, the mountains which it was once a wonder even to have crossed.' The long preceding sentence has piled up nature's grand purposes in creating mountains, and ended *durissima sui materia*, 'with her own hardest substance'. The main verbs here clash sharply against that close, and mark not only the desecration but the physical greatness; the last clause, with an ingenious trumping, takes the greatness to a lavish extreme. The Alps and Hannibal promptly follow.

The combination of physical extremity and moral censure recalls what we have seen in the poets, not least in the passage of Lucan. Even the poets could scarcely go further in extravagance on such a theme than *rerum natura agitur in planum*, 'the world is pushed into flatness', or *per fluctus, saevissimam rerum naturae partem, huc illuc portantur iuga*, 'through the waves, the fiercest part of nature, peaks are carried hither and yon' (2). In the first phrase the incongruity swells both the greatness and the impiety, but is also enjoyed for itself; in the second Pliny even more obviously relishes the wild and bizarre conjunction of extremes. The force and vividness is increased by the placing of *fluctus*, 'waves', and

---

[39] For the variations in Pliny's style cf. Önnerfors (1956), ch. 1.

iuga, 'peaks', and by the choice of those more graphic terms instead of 'sea' and 'mountains'. The sentence continues, however, and closes with drastic and significant bathos. The whole paragraph ends contemptuously and ingeniously deflating human folly.

Tacitus and Quintilian keep a far tighter rein; it is a significant negative aspect of their manner that audacious extravagance plays in it so limited a part. We might very crudely relate the styles of Seneca, Tacitus, and Quintilian by stressing the prominence and conspicuousness of wit and extravagance in Seneca, of wit but not extravagance in Tacitus, of neither (relatively speaking) in Quintilian. The combination in Tacitus is particularly notable. But of course so simple a formulation blurs the varied forms of either feature, and might suggest too uniform a view of each writer. So Tacitus, while scarcely indulging himself in any great extremity of utterance, can deploy a lavishness of content or expression which from him surprises and is intended to surprise. We remarked on the reference to sources in *Hist.* iii. 25. 2, where Tacitus tells how a son unknowingly slew his father in war (p. 53); we seem remote from Lucan, where such slaughter of kin in civil war is extravagantly presented as ubiquitous. Yet Tacitus, after describing the amazement and horror at this prodigy, goes on: *nec eo segnius propinquos adfinis fratres trucidant spoliant*, 'that made them no slower to slaughter and despoil their relations, kinsmen, and brothers' (3). The abrupt reversal and the sudden burst of rhetorical extremity startle and impress; Tacitus then somewhat reconciles and contains with a more detached epigram, *factum esse scelus loquuntur faciuntque*, 'they said an enormity had been committed and they committed them'. At *Ann.* xii. 43. 2 he suddenly inveighs, on the basis of his scholarly knowledge, against the importing of grain from abroad: *navibusque et casibus vita populi Romani permissa est*, 'the life of the Roman people has been abandoned to ships and chance calamities'. Here the lavishness and the audacity of language look slighter, not only than in the Elder Pliny, but than in the expression of the same point in a speech by Tiberius: *vita populi Romani per incerta maris et tempestatum cotidie volvitur*, 'the life of the Roman people daily rolls amid the uncertainty of sea and storm' (iii. 54. 4). Yet from the author the boldness surprises and excites.

Sometimes Tacitus plays with our surprise. In a portent at *Hist.*

iii. 56. 1 a vast flock of birds 'hides the daylight with a black cloud', *ut nube atra diem obtenderent*; the choice of words heightens the extremity (however far Tacitus believed it). 'But the most extraordinary prodigy', he shortly avers, 'was Vitellius himself', so palpably incompetent was he: *sed praecipuum ipse Vitellius ostentum erat* (3). The gesture of trumping is used extravagantly, but in sardonic and entertaining scorn.

Pliny the Younger in his letters seldom offers an arresting extravagance which goes beyond charming compliment or play. His one surviving oration, on the special theme of the emperor, takes praise to a much higher pitch. The contemporary reality of the subject, and the tones of laudation, give the extravagance a distinctive quality, as part of a personal and formal act of communication. But the particular quality of the extravagance comes also from the various factors which hold it within bounds: Pliny's genre, his type of wit, and his special desire to sound dignified and sincere, a consul praising Trajan (not Domitian).[40]

In 35. 4f. he dwells on Trajan's provisions against delators. Titus had been made a god by the senate for his own provisions against them, says Pliny; how much worthier of heaven will be Trajan, who has added so many (*sed quanto tu quandoque dignior caelo qui tot res illis adiecisti ...*). Trajan is made to excel not only a predecessor but the extreme of merited deification itself. One might have thought the resemblance of action argued only an equality of merit; but Pliny cleverly stresses the difficulties of discovery when great discoverers have been before one. The artifice of this thought (more familiar and appropriate in the deification of textual critics) Pliny carries through with bold and elaborate extremes: before Trajan Nerva, making his own additions, *nihil ... reliquisse nisi tibi videbatur, qui tam multa excogitasti ut si ante te nihil esset inventum*, 'appeared to have left nothing to be added, except by you; you devised as many fresh ideas as if nothing had been hit on before you'.[41] The second *nihil*, 'nothing', stands in lavish opposition to the first; the word-order increases the great force and weight of *tibi*, 'you, so great a person as you'.

The number of Trajan's devices leads into a new and unlooked-for point, their being introduced together. Had they been passed separately, how much favour would each have won!

---

[40] Note *Ep.* iii. 18. 1f., 7.
[41] It is more natural to make *tibi* depend on *reliquisse* than on *videbatur*.

at tu simul omnia profudisti, ut sol et dies non parte aliqua sed statim totus, nec uni aut alteri sed omnibus in commune profertur.

But you poured forth all your benefits together, just as it is not some part of the sun, light of the day, that comes forth, but the whole at once, and not for one or two individuals but for the common good of all.

The image and the beautiful phrasing exalt a slight aspect of the deed into supreme glory. The sun represents Trajan's benefits, but more himself.[42] The comparison gains new sharpness from the vigour and physicality of the imagined moment. The simultaneity of the legal measures is made to show the same vast and easy generosity as the heavenly body, which so acts from its very nature. Yet, extravagant and inventive as the passage is, its extravagance has nothing playful about it; the invention is handled discreetly enough for us not to feel that the ingenuity is partly separated from the decorous praise and absorbed in itself. The lavishness is to seem stately, flowing, in a sense almost natural.

In his *Silvae* **Statius** too devotes extravagance chiefly to present reality and praise; this gives the extravagance in general a quite different flavour from that in the epics, for all the similarity in artistic treatment. However, Statius is so extreme, so imaginative, and often so playful that his extravagance also feels quite different from Pliny's. Statius' play is naturally constrained by his social purposes; but by complicating his extravagance, even on the most solemn occasions, he keeps it poetically alive: poetry which so lavishly and continuously praised contemporaries would without seasoning lose its relish.

Silv. iv. 2 thanks Domitian for dinner. The emperor forms a theme that crosses literary boundaries: central here, he enjoys a glorious marginality in epic. But the overlap with epic does not eliminate differences; and the link with Pliny brings out the remoteness of the *Panegyricus* from this poem.[43] In this poem the standard themes of the emperor's deity, and his connection with

[42] For the comparison see e.g. Sen. *Clem.* i. 8. 4; Housman on Man. iv. 765. Cf. also Plin. *Pan.* 80. 3.

[43] A pleasing example of difference from epic occurs at 22, where the request to Caesar to delay climbing heaven (cf. *Theb.* i. 30f.) is justified by the splendours of his palace. (For the theme generally see Nisbet and Hubbard on Hor. *Odes* i. 2. 45; note here the play with the familiar warning, Alcm. fr. 1. 16 Davies, etc.) On this poem cf. Cancik (1965), 65–89; Vessey (1983); on extravagance in the *Silvae*, Friedrich (1963).

Jupiter, are treated with freshened extravagance and delightful play. On that occasion Statius thought himself 'reclining to feast in the midst of the stars with Jupiter', *mediis videor discumbere in astris / cum Iove* (10 f.). The drastic and pointed use of an epic conception (feasting in heaven) is made more striking by the expression. The relaxed action, the stars, and the company of Jupiter (note the enjambment) make a startling combination as the experience of an ordinary mortal. The combination is taken up shortly:

> tene ego, regnator terrarum orbisque subacti
> magne parens, te, spes hominum, te, cura deorum,
> cerno iacens? (14–16)

You, ruler of the earth, great father to the world you have vanquished, you, the hope of men, you the beloved of the gods, was I able to behold you and yet lie recumbent?

The lavish praise formally serves to enhance the astounding experience: the experience proves to be, not merely seeing this supreme being, but doing so in a physical attitude of friendly equality, not worshipful respect.[44] The short final word *iacens*, 'lying' (expanded above), brings the air of extremity to a new pitch. Yet the ingenious surprise, the relished incongruity, the flirtation with bathos, detach us into enjoyment of the poet's witty extravagance; they do so without subverting the praise. The exploitation both of physical detail apparently trivial and of the poet as a concrete person together create something different in colour from the extravagance of Pliny or of epic.

Much of our attention is focused in the poem on the aspiration for extremity itself, and on its elaborate and intriguing movements, as in the sequence 38–56. Statius first states that he had no leisure to observe the feast, for which the poem is giving thanks, or the palace, which he has just described: his attention was engrossed by Domitian. He then portrays Domitian amicably but ineffectively hiding his divine glory (note 43–5). The lavishness here pursues an oblique tack, and the contemporary is clothed in vivid but fantastic dress: so *maiestate serena / mulcentem radios*, 'with calm majesty softening his rays' (41 f.). With graceful insistence Statius continues pushing in the opposite direction to Domitian's

---

[44] One should bear in mind also the rising of the gods when Zeus enters, Hom. *Il.* i. 533–5; Stat. *Theb.* i. 203 f. On 6 I agree with Coleman against Courtney.

attempted concealment by likening him to numerous deities at rest; but he abandons even these comparisons as slight and inadequate (52): only the resting Jupiter will do. Thus the standard connection with Jupiter becomes in this work the summit attained by the poet's arduous ascent. The ascent is actually handled with confident and often smiling elegance; we are charmed as throughout the poem by the artificiality in the poet's courtly gestures. Throughout, extravagance is elaborately entangled with play on genre, with Statius' adequacy or inadequacy, and with his supposed experience; an important part of its interest is involved with Statius as poet and person. The extravagant expression is not facile. It arrests, it affects to strive, it contemplates itself. The poem praises lavishly, but in doing so it also in part absorbs us in its own ingenious and vivacious handling of extremity.

Extravagance is a basic ingredient of **Juvenal's** manner. It creates an exciting energy; but it also tends perpetually in a comic direction, and works against our accepting Juvenal's utterance as a communication of belief, either directly or through irony that demolishes. At 9. 93–101 Juvenal is asked by the frightened Naevolus to keep quiet the secrets of Naevolus' rich patron: Naevolus has told how he himself satisfies and (by sleeping with the patron's wife) disguises the patron's shameful passive homosexuality.[45] Juvenal replies:

> o Corydon, Corydon, secretum divitis ullum
> esse putas? servi ut taceant, iumenta loquentur
> et canis et postes et marmora.   (102–4)

O Corydon, Corydon, do you actually think there exists a rich man's secret? Even if the slaves keep silent, the mules will speak, and the dog, and the door, and the marble walls.

The opening sentence seems to offer shrewd sense; the quotation from Virgil (*a Corydon, Corydon, Ecl.* 2. 69) indicates Naevolus' folly, though whimsically.[46] Yet in what follows the extravagant expression of that sense surprises and modifies. We do not simply

---

[45] See on the poem Braund (1988), ch. 4, and, on 102–15, Romano (1979), 155f. On extravagance in Juvenal see Streifinger (1892), 11–13; De Decker (1913), 138–54; Fredericks (1979).

[46] Part of the effect lies in the transference of the vehement self-address (ironical enough after *Ecl.* 2. 68) to another speaker, who addresses, with a quotation, a man far from infatuated by passion. So not even the first sentence is straightforward in its impact.

have colloquial exaggeration: the real danger, from slaves, is kept apart in a concessive clause, and the unspeaking, and then the voiceless, are paradoxically endowed with language. The effect is enhanced by the polysyndetic series which accumulates in a new line after the elegance and apparent completeness of *servi ut taceant, iumenta loquentur*, 'even ... speak'. The extravagance infringes upon the appearance of conveying grim truth to the reader.

Juvenal proceeds to heap up imperatives in vigorous asyndeton: *claude fenestras, / vela tegant rimas*, etc., 'close the windows, let curtains cover up the chinks', etc. (104–6). We expect all this anxious activity to be curtly undone (cf. e.g. 15. 147–59); but Juvenal goes on exuberantly:

> quod tamen ad cantum galli facit ille secundi
> proximus ante diem caupo sciet, audiet et quae
> finxerunt pariter libarius, archimagiri,
> carptores. (107–9)

What he does at the call of the second cock [i.e. at the very border of day], the nearest shopkeeper will know of before daybreak; he will hear then too the related fictions of baker, chefs, and servers.

The precision of time heightens the fantastic brevity of the interval which is required for the dissemination of rumour and the inventions that rumour inspires. The second part of the quotation, from *audiet*, 'will hear', and the very contrast of *sciet*, 'will know', and *audiet*, 'will *hear*', show the author's sharpness and insight. But the abrupt succession with *audiet* of a new main clause, and the series at the end, flowing over into a fresh line, display also the extravagance and gusto of the treatment. The next sentence affects to support the alarming extravagance with insight and argument; the next reaches an extreme conclusion: a drunkard seeks out Naevolus himself in the street and talks to him of his own doings.[47]

In the whole account one can scarcely miss the comic vitality of the extravagant rhetoric; this unsettles and distances a simple

---

[47] *te* in 112 could refer to the rich man; but this seems somewhat less probable. One may contrast with 112 f. the plot of *Middlemarch*; and the appearance in 108 of the effect without the cause (slaves, it transpires) makes a particularly interesting point of comparison. *inebriet* in 113 playfully suggests the transmission of drunkenness to the ear; it is unlikely that the word will in itself suggest distress or fear. At Lucr. iii. 1051 mental confusion is involved; at Nonn. *Dion.* xxxvi. 79 φόβωι is needed, and *miseram* and *aurem* make the notion less inviting here.

response to the underlying point. Canny point and wild expression stand in pleasing tension. The presence of a self-contained humour is confirmed by the dramatic situation. Naevolus, fearful for his life, naturally expects Juvenal to answer by assenting to his request; in fact Juvenal's reply stands at a wild extreme from the reassurance he seeks. We are meant to imagine, and be entertained by, the effect on poor Naevolus; this is indicated by the following lines, where Juvenal bids Naevolus ask the slaves, not him, to keep silence. The fact of the published poem itself throws a further and amusing light on the (ungranted) request for secrecy. Readers are actually learning of Naevolus' deeds, and his interlocutor and the author are formally one.[48]

The complications of extravagance run through most of Juvenal's work; they do so not least in the harangue against wives of poem 6, extravagant in its very length. So at the beginning Juvenal asks how Postumus can endure the servitude of marriage when suicide is so easy (30–2). There are various strands of humour here; but the fantastically extreme attitude, the eminently reasonable manner, and the colour and zest with which the opportunities for suicide are elaborated, together disincline us to accept the lines straightforwardly. We are not simply to react to the underlying antipathy, accepting it or censuring it; and our response even to that antipathy must at least be complicated by the language. The following lines advance the argument with an incoherence and an amusing bathos that undermine the pretensions of what precedes them: if none of all these many deaths will do (*si de multis nullus placet exitus*, 33), why not at least persevere with your boy-lover instead? The ensuing description (in negative form) of quarrelsome and demanding females is calculated more to entertain than to appal.[49]

We have concentrated on Juvenal; the importance of extravagance in Juvenal differentiates him from **Persius**. In Persius the

---

[48] Cf. Pers. i. 119–24 (above, p. 27). Housman's approach to the textual problem of 118–21 is in essence attractive, and Courtney adopts it. But the plural *his ... causis* is not really suitable in itself (contrast [Quint.] *Decl. Min.* 260. 3), and rhetorically *plurima* cries out for a singular. Conceivably one might consider something like *tum est hac / pr. causa, linguas ut*, with *causa* referring forward. (For the metre cf. 10. 325).

[49] The idea that the advice of 34 is ironical scarcely suits the context; poem 2 is irrelevant. For the notion of death as liberation from enslavement cf. e.g. Sen. *Ira* iii. 15. 3f. The more heroic sword is omitted from the means of suicide; cf. Fraenkel (1964). On this passage cf. Romano (1979), 117; on the whole poem see especially Winkler (1983), chs. 5 and 6.

wild imagery often creates a colourful extravagance of phrase; but he is much less inclined to accumulate extravagance, his underlying earnestness is plainer, and often what seems at first sight extravagance is actually disturbing truth.

In **Martial** extravagance is the servant, and one of the chief servants, of an overtly comic technique. In him expansive lavishness is typically followed by wit that crisply twists or deflates. That pattern is significantly related to patterns characteristic of high poetry, but is much more straightforwardly humorous, much simpler in its effect (simpler to feel, not to analyse). None the less, the roles and types of extravagance are much more varied than one might suppose; and the poetic impact of extravagance should not be confined to the structural purpose of 'waiting' for the conclusion.

The variety of Martial's extravagance and lavishness may most sharply be seen in poems placed near each other. vi. 33 speaks in its first couplet, with ordinary colloquial lavishness, of the homosexual Sabellus' extreme fall from joy to woe.[50] The next couplet ends the poem:

> furta, fugae, mortes servorum, incendia, luctus
> afligunt hominem; iam miser et futuit.   (3 f.)

The thefts, flights, and deaths of his slaves, and fires and griefs all prostrate the fellow; and now, poor wretch, he has even fucked.

Martial piles into one line a stream of calamities (all plural), which increase in gravity. It appears a wild succession of misfortunes; but it is trumped and deflated by a single word. That word denotes something normally thought pleasurable, and something done, not inflicted (the change of Sabellus from object to subject is significant). The comic climax and anticlimax is strengthened by the relished impropriety of *futuit*, 'fucked'; but the word also makes us regard the earlier misfortunes in a more prosaic light: Sabellus has been driven to lie with a woman by impoverishment (cf. xi. 87). Even comic extravagance turns into slyness.

The following poem, with a cheerful shift in sexual stance, responds to the question of a lovely boy. He asks how many kisses he should bestow on Martial; Martial answers that he is being told

---

[50] *nil miserabilius ... vidisti*; the turn is very common in Cicero's letters, e.g. *Att.* i. 12. 1. On extravagance in Martial see Siedschlag (1977), 39–55, Citroni, introduction to i. 41, etc.

to number infinity.[51] The passionate moment is created in a line; thereafter Martial uses the elegiac couplet in a quite different fashion from the poem before. Decorous images of the innumerable accumulate with stately grace, three drawn from nature and occupying a line each, the last occupying a couplet and elegantly praising Caesar. So: *et maris Aegaei sparsas per litora conchas / et quae Cecropio monte vagantur apes*, (you might as well bid me count) 'the shells scattered over the shores of the Aegean Sea, or the bees that wander over the Attic mountain' (3 f.). Here the rich extravagance acquires a poetic autonomy that distances us from the drama. This distance is increased by the pressing invitation to the reader to compare Catullus 7; that poem treats this theme not in smooth and graceful elegiacs but in weird and startling hendecasyllables. Martial's close takes the evocation further by explicitly and paradoxically refusing the vast number of kisses which Catullus demands in the intenser poem 5: for *pauca cupit qui numerare potest*, 'he desires few kisses who can count them'. The poet is not deflating his extravagance but bringing it to a new height and a sharper point. Yet we are also to be amused by his extravagant and ingenious ascription of a slight desire to the extreme Catullus. We are distanced anew from the passion which the lines profess to exhibit. In these consecutive epigrams extravagance is quite differently handled and serves quite different ends.[52]

A much more stunning example of extravagance is xi. 18. We have often seen extravagant content enhanced by the opulence of length accorded it. Martial loves, especially in metres which repeat a single line, to take the length of his accumulations to remarkable and humorous extremes. As he does so his comic imagination riots exuberantly. In this poem Martial has been given a farming-estate, but a tiny one. He thrusts back the gift with forthright rudeness, and indignantly embarks on a prolonged sequence of hyperboles; these are of the type noted by rhetoricians that 'makes small' rather than 'enlarges'.[53] He achieves a constant

---

[51] Cf. on the poem Salemme (1976), 80 n. 27.

[52] Or again, one may compare the extravagance of vi. 70 and 77. (As to 77 cf. iv. 51, Lamer (1924), 1089 f.; Timpanaro (1978), though in 7 f. the idea of absurd similarity seems too abstruse to be the main point.) At vi. 34. 7 f. Martial is simplifying the intricate mixture in Cat. 5. 6–13 of the passionate, the frantic, and the playful: cf. xii. 59.

[53] Cf. *Ad Her.* iii. 44; Cic. *Top.* 45. Virg. *Georg.* i. 181–6 provide only a distant inspiration. With the treatment of *rus* in 1–3 contrast iii. 58. 51, iv. 64. 25. On the poem cf. Burnikel (1980), 105–10.

freshness and absurdity; the fantastic series dances with life and flickers with strange perspectives. We may contrast the dry wit of *nec serpens habitare tota possit*, 'a serpent could not live there in its entire length', with the drastic oppositions and whimsical drama of *consumpto moritur culix salicto*, 'a midge eats the thicket of osiers and dies [from hunger]' (II, 13). Later the fantasy wears bolder colours:

> finis mus populatur et colono
> tamquam sus Calydonius timetur;
> et sublata volantis ungue Procnes
> in nido seges est hirundinino. (17–20)

The lands are devastated by a mouse, which the farmer fears as if it were the Calydonian Boar. The crop, which Procne [the swallow] in flight has taken up in her claw, is now located in a swallow's nest.

The first phrase is sufficiently parodic, with its strident juxtapositions, but the parody is magnified and brightened by the introduction of epic myth; the monosyllable *sus*, 'boar', starkly takes up and contrasts with the monosyllable *mus*, 'mouse', and is then extended with its own glorious epithet. The third line ('which ... claw') sets up the situation for the superb statement 'the crop is in a swallow's nest'. Breathtaking and bathetic, surreal and matter-of-fact (one cannot capture the flatness of *est*, 'is'), that statement gives the extravagance of absurdity brilliantly ridiculous expression.

All this burgeoning abundance is finally curtailed and contained by a dry joke. Lupus has erred only in one letter: he has given a *praedium*, 'estate', when Martial would rather he had given a *prandium*, 'lunch'. The humour is now tight and verbal, not expansive and imaginative: Martial stresses the single letter.[54] The tone is wry, and the matter returns us from fantasy to humdrum necessities. We are also made to look back on the sequence, and note the increasing prominence in it of food and profitable growth. Martial's practicality has now taken command, and is no longer subservient to the profusion of Martial's comic fancy.

Petronius too employs extravagance principally for humour; but his use is less central and uncommonly diverse. Parody of poetry and declamation plays some part in it; indeed the grander poems show how far Petronius feels extravagance, of a certain

---

[54] For the form of the joke cf. *Priap.* 7. 1, Plaut. *Rud.* 1305f.

flavour, to be essential to modern high poetry.[55] But there is much more to the question; we shall touch only on some aspects here.

The main narrative, delivered by a character, tends to an uncommitted plainness which offsets the comic extremes of its events. The expression, however, often swells into lavishness; much less often does the style expand with it into sweeping rhetorical development. The darkness in a storm is so thick *ut ne proram quidem totam gubernator videret* (114. 3), 'that the helmsman could not see even the prow entire' (at which he stood). The conception is neat and lavish, and strengthened by the precise *totam*, 'entire'; but the emphasis is on the practical danger, and the author does not indulge himself with the range or wildness of the poetic storms which he suggests.[56] Much freer is the description of the beautiful Circe in 126. 13–17. The beauty is conveyed partly through hyperbole: so at the close in the strong brevity of *Parium marmor extinxerat*, in her whiteness 'she would have quenched the brilliance of Parian marble'. But the beauty is conveyed also by medieval precision of description, and by lyrical and imaginative expression. The extremity of the subject is announced at the start: *nulla vox est quae formam eius possit comprehendere, nam quicquid dixero minus erit*, 'there is no voice that could describe her beauty: whatever I say will be too slight'. The basic device is a common one for heightening. Here it conveys the rapture of experience; the second half, lower in diction than the first and less lyrical, marks more plainly the distinction between author and narrator. Subjective passion and objective depiction are both important to the passage: its object is to build towards the comic, low, and ignominious anticlimax of the narrator's impotence.[57]

The narrator often describes extravagantly emotions that he felt. He typically appears powerless, the emotions ignoble, the extremes comic; the expression is varied, but has frequently a racy vivacity which generates an undignified energy. The first-person form, and the form of narrative, are crucial to the particular

---

[55] So e.g. 119. 36–8, where the extravagant handling of luxury is obviously very different from that in the *Cena*. On extravagance and related matters in Petronius cf. particularly Schönberger (1951), esp. 23–7; Sullivan (1968), 215; George (1966).

[56] Petronius probably has poetry especially in mind, as *Italici ... possessor* confirms; cf. also Juv. 12. 21–3. Note also Sen. Rh. *Contr.* vii. 1. 4, etc. Arat. 428f. uses a similar closeness, lavishly but with grim irony.

[57] Cf. esp. Ov. *Am.* iii. 7; see Tränkle (1990), 345–8. For *extinxerat* cf. Plaut. *Men.* 181 *occaecatust*. On the passage cf. Courtney (1962), 99.

effect. In 19–21 (fragmentary) the narrator and others are bizarrely and shamefully set upon by women. He, unlike Ascyltos his companion, grew in fear *frigidior hieme Gallica*, 'colder than a Gallic winter' (19. 3); the phrase has a robust and humorous earthiness. One may contrast the dramatic and mock-poetic description soon after of fainting with fear: *mors non dubia miserorum oculos coepit obducere*, 'the death that seemed certain began to cover our wretched eyes in darkness' (19. 6). With both phrases one may compare the unelevated and drastic mock-pathos used of the narrator's private organs, chill partly with fear: *mille iam mortibus frigida*, 'now cold with a thousand deaths' (20. 2).[58] The whole passage characteristically combines vigour of language with feebleness of personality.

Quite different is the gigantic extravagance, in boast as well as in deed, of Petronius' large and loud creation, the ignorant millionaire Trimalchio. The boasts are not simply empty: Petronius creates a preposterous world of riches which often supports Trimalchio's wild and tasteless words as true or permits them to float headily. At 48. 2f. Trimalchio's claims ascend. So extensive are his estates that he does not buy wine, *non emo* (stark simplicity); with one of his new estates he as yet has no acquaintance, *non novi* (a would-be sublime aloofness); the estate 'is said' to border two places 200 miles apart (fantastic lavishness, delivered in a manner intended to sound casual); *nunc coniungere agellis Siciliam volo, ut cum Africam libuerit ire, per meos fines navigem*, 'now I wish to join Sicily to my little properties, so that when I desire to go to Africa, I may sail entirely through my own territory'. In this last sentence *Siciliam*, 'Sicily', falls stunningly after the false modesty of *agellis*, 'my little properties'; *Africam*, 'Africa', extends the range; and the lordly and emphatic *meos*, 'my (own)', stamps with pride the ludicrous extreme of size and independence. He passes to another topic with calculated abruptness. Quite where we separate fantasy and fictional reality here scarcely matters; we are to enjoy the wild mixture of extravagant conception, absurd ambition, general unreality, and alert mockery.[59]

[58] A colloquial basis seems not improbable in the light of the play at Mart. vi. 73. 7 (cf. xiii. 34. 1, Ov. *Am.* iii. 7. 65).

[59] Cf. for the passage D'Arms (1981), 117f. I would take a somewhat less naturalistic view. Note that *fabulae* of the speech in 37–8 does not indicate falsehood, any more than *efflaverat* in 49. 1; 38. 2–4 do not show an *inability* to be self-sufficient. As to *non novi* cf. 37. 9.

Our consideration of prose and of lower genres of poetry has shown what different colours extravagance can put on, and how varied and important are its relations to genre and author, to reality, imagination, and greatness, to seriousness, playfulness, and comedy. It will also be apparent that, for all their variety, most of these types of extravagance are significantly interconnected: as with wit, we see a cohesive phenomenon, not a series of disparate features. So the desire to hold in and contain extravagance, especially by wit, has emerged in various genres. The tension between lavishness and control is something that characterizes much of the literature; when other writers reject or greatly modify it they are doing so consciously and with purpose. Extravagance too is an aspect of the literature that we must come to terms with; once we have done so, it can afford us abundant pleasure.

5

STRUCTURE AND COHESION

WE turn now to explore directly and on a larger scale the question of form which has already concerned us on a smaller. The audacity, and the cohesion, which we have seen there also appear here. In the past this literature has often been accused of devoting its attention chiefly to the individual episode, or even the individual sentence, and of disregarding wider entities. This view continues to find very distinguished adherents. More positive judgements are now often delivered on particular authors, frequently on the basis of detailed and rewarding study. Yet in justly stressing how works cohere, scholars perhaps fail to stress sufficiently how bold and strange these works can be. It is not enough to attack disunity or defend unity: unity of one kind (say in theme) can effectively be combined with disunity of another (say in plot), and rupture and excursion can be positively valued, for their daring or their expressive force or both. The very treatment of such combinations can contribute to the manner which binds the work together. We must seek to grasp the complexity of what (as I shall argue) the texts present.

Structure is something that itself operates on many scales: both a limited digression and the shape of a whole work affect our sense of cohesion and design. A diagrammatic outline of a work tells us little, because it does not evoke the actuality and the density of the literary experience through which we encounter overall structure. The closer detail gives the large design much of its force, and much of the significance of that design lies in the weight it confers on particular moments. It would be futile to discuss the structure of all these works in a single chapter, even had Fortune preserved in a more accommodating manner the lives of authors and the manuscripts of their productions. We shall concentrate on the most challenging and difficult works, and mostly on some of the high poetry; we shall consider in that poetry different scales of structure, in order to suggest what this subject involves and to illustrate some ways of approach to it which appear to me plausible. The course of the discussion will also develop the book's broader lines of thought in areas besides form. In particular we shall consider the relation of structure and greatness.

We must first touch on some aspects of cultural history. Practical causes are often alleged for the indifference to structure that is supposedly found in the literature. Clearly these cannot themselves establish that indifference, but their very practicality seems to make it plausible, and to discourage more searching consideration. To begin with, the practice of reciting literature before an audience is said to have disposed writers to fix their attention on the impressive episode (or instant) at the expense of the whole. The supposition we are concerned with is not simply that recitation encouraged the production of effective and well-defined episodes, but that it also caused the neglect of the larger work. There is no intrinsic reason why the first should necessarily entail the second: it would be difficult to maintain that firm divisions and brilliant scenes, however anthologizable, must prevent the work from cohering or from bearing significance beyond the borders of the episode. (Few novels would survive such a contention.)[1] Authors, as we shall illustrate, wrote their works not only to recite, in extracts or as a whole, but to publish. It follows that they were catering not only for an audience but for readers. Only if they were considering the audience alone would it be possible to urge that they neglected matters which would supposedly be of no interest to an audience, only to readers. Nor does the evidence suggest that writers would have no interest in the final, lasting, and widely-circulated medium of publication. When Tacitus' Aper shows the poet's glory to be inferior to the orator's, he of course dwells satirically on poetic recitation, which differentiates poet and orator, not on the publication which unites them (*Dial.* 9–10. 2). The more practical conversation at 3. 2f. shows publication to be an essential and expected part of literary production. The satirists give their attention to recitation, a much more promising theme for them than reading (see especially Juv. 1. 1–13, 7. 36–49, Pers. 1); yet both the poets' first satires presuppose for their own work readers and not an audience. Juvenal may picture the wild success of Statius' recitations (7. 82–6); but Statius' own

---

[1] I skirt the serializing of novels before publication, though it ultimately favours my case. For the evidence on recitation see esp. Mayor on Juv. 3. 9; Friedländer (1920), ii. 223–8; Funaioli (1914); Dalzell (1955).

references to publication reveal clearly how important and decisive a stage it was for him. Those references indicate how unlikely it would be that through all Statius' long labours the supposed blandishments of applause should seduce him into ignoring the reader of the whole.[2]

The clearest and fullest evidence comes, predictably, from the Younger Pliny and from Martial. From Martial it is apparent that poets are expected to recite and expected to publish (cf. e.g. ii. 88; iv. 33). He himself did both (cf. e.g. ix. 81. 1); but it is the medium of reading, the form of the book, and the figure of the reader which dominate in regard to his own published works. At the least the published version is no mere appendage to recitation: his works as published not only presuppose but make extensive play with reading and the reader and use them as an important theme. In Pliny it is plainly expected that works recited will presently be published, if of merit; indeed publication seems the more momentous and important occasion, to which the recitation is a preliminary.[3] With regard to his own recitations he places heavy emphasis on his wish to improve works before publishing them (especially v. 3. 6–11, v. 12, vii. 17). In placing little emphasis on the wish to be applauded, he is furthering the delicate treatment of his own desire for fame (note iv. 19. 3); but it is plain enough that not only he but others regard publication and recitation as at the very least of equal importance.

One or two points may be added. Firstly, we may observe how diverse are the works whose shortcomings recitation is held to explain. Recitation is to account for inattention to the whole not only in lengthy epics, from which extracts might be read, but in the satires of Juvenal. The difference in scale, structure, and tradition seems in itself suspicious; and yet so wide-ranging a cause has not affected the histories of Tacitus, to which few would deny a concern with large structures. But the recitation of history

---

[2] Cf. *Theb.* xii. 810–18, *Silv.* iv. *praef.* 16, 4. 87–92, 7. 26. Persius 1 is especially interesting in the light of *Vita* 21 Clausen.

[3] Cf. e.g. iii. 15, and even ix. 27 (cf. Sen. Rh. *Contr.* x *praef.* 8). In ii. 10. 6 (cf. Mart. iv. 33) he concentrates on the first stage for the benefit of a shy author, but clearly the two are assumed to belong typically together. Note the importance ascribed to the reader in Martial (not without play) at v. 16, vii. 12. 11f. (cf. Ov. *Trist.* iv. 10. 131f.); *aures* (vii. 12. 11) has of course no bearing on our inquiry, since its implications would extend to any ancient work. Burnikel (1990) to my mind rather exaggerates the special significance of recitation for Martial's poetry.

was no less firmly established than that of poetry.[4] Secondly,
scholars often appear to be prejudiced against recitations, partly
through a direct acceptance of the satirical and comic depictions
in various Latin authors, and partly through a modern distaste for
such disagreeable things as applause for fine moments, cries of
enthusiasm, and the vanity of the Younger Pliny. The circumstances of recitation (which were actually varied) add little solidity
to the argument.

It may be argued that indifference to design was deeply inbred
in all literate men, whether listening or reading. We lose the
practical support of recitation, but declamation can try to take its
place. One would have to suppose that the experience of belonging and performing to the frivolous audiences of declamation
had inculcated indifference to the whole in impressionable youth.
Unfortunately declamation itself was intensely concerned with
structure. What declamation suggests rather, like much other
evidence, is that members of this culture cannot have been oblivious to the demands of design. Rhetorical theorists and teachers
debated vigorously on the handling of the basic set structure of
speeches, and on the handling of particular cases, which related
to structure on a smaller scale. The Elder Seneca marks out as
abnormal the voluble Q. Haterius: he ignored not in theory but in
practice the requirement to organize the argumentative part of
his speech, and simply followed his impulse (*Contr.* iv *praef.* 9).[5]
Declaimers were often keen to treat structure audaciously, but
very consciously so. Quintilian condemns the blurring of a structural division with a *sententia* not as artless but as an affected and
self-advertising piece of legerdemain reminiscent of Ovid (iv. 1.
77); the Elder Seneca admires it (*Contr.* i. 1. 25). One should likewise
assign to paraded art the enthusiasm of declamation for

[4] See, among other passages, Sen. Rh. *Contr.* iv *praef.* 2 (probably); Suet. *Aug.* 89. 3; Sen.
Ep. 95. 2; Plin. *Ep.* vii. 17. 3, ix. 27 (possibly Tacitus himself); see also Cichorius (1922), 262 f.
As to the reading of extracts and the brevity of recitations note, probably, Plin. *Ep.* iii. 15. 3,
viii. 21. 4; Durry (1938), 8. I find it hard to apply to the texts Williams's contention, in a not
unsympathetic discussion, that recitation produced epics composed of episodes normally
about 180 lines long ((1978), 246–53). And surely not every passage would have been written
for possible selection. One should not exaggerate either the need for independence before
a passage can be anthologized.

[5] Cf. Tac. *Ann.* iv. 61. It is unclear whether in Seneca *declamatoriam legem* refers backwards
(Winterbottom) or forwards (Håkanson); probably both. The general discussion at the
time on the structure of speeches emerges clearly from Quint. iv–vi. Cf. esp. [Quint.] *Decl.
Min.* 338 *sermo.* On structure in the *Decl. Min.* see Dingel (1988). See also Innes and
Winterbottom (1988), 4 f.

expatiating in description or generalized argument which was hardly demanded by the case. Quintilian ascribes the penchant for sporting with descriptions remote from the subject to the imitation of poetic freedom (ii. 4. 3): a comment significant for poetry. The tendency for such digression to acquire a fixed structural position (Quint. iv. 3. 14) suggests again that we have to do with no unskilled indifference to form as such. Examples preserved by the Elder Seneca show clearly enough with what conscious ostentation such excursive passages are brought back to the matter in hand (e.g. *Suas.* 3. 1). Declamatory practice shows not only the fundamental significance of form in the literary culture but the attractions of formal audacity.

We turn to the texts of our period, and come first to prose. Here we shall consider a few aspects only, and look chiefly at Seneca; he is in this respect as in others the most audacious writer, and also the one nearest the poets. Some mention will be made of Tacitus and Quintilian.[6] Intellectual prose tends to seek an appearance of firm and lucid organization. It promotes this appearance particularly by overt announcements of the next topic, or the sequence of topics, or by comments on the author's procedure. Here the manner characteristically suggests, on the surface, mental clarity and purpose. The treatment of digressions is especially interesting in this regard. It is part of a tradition in prose often to signal openly movements away from the main exposition, commonly in dry and standard phrases that justify at the opening or proclaim a return at the close: 'this topic urges me', 'it will be apt', 'briefly', 'to return to my subject'.[7] Such phrases show a strong consciousness of relevance in this culture, of the theme delimited for discourse;

---

[6] On structure in Seneca see Uhl (1899), 31; Albertini (1923); Grimal (1949–50, 1960); Abel (1965, 1967); Currie (1966); López-Kindler (1966) Büchner (1978); Maurach (1970); and, for *Tranq.*, id. (1991), 128–30; Morturaux (1973); Wright (1974); Schiroli (1981), 12–16; on Quintilian, esp. xii, Börner (1911); Austin (1948), pp. xxvii–xxxi; Classen (1965); Schneider (1983); Adamietz (1986a); on Tacitus, mainly *Annals*, Graf (1929); Halm (1933); Fuhrmann (1960); Ginsburg (1981) (note also Verbrugghe (1989)); Wille (1983; with further literature); Martin (1990); Morford (1990), and more general works. On the earlier history of structure in Roman prose, see Rawson (1991).

[7] Some examples are given below; cf. also e.g. Tac. *Ann.* iii. 25. 2 *ea res admonet ut* (cf. Sen. *NQ* iii. 27. 1 *sed monet me locus ut*), *Hist.* v. 2. 1 *congruens videtur* (cf. e.g. *Ann.* xii. 24. 1 *haud absurdum reor*); Sen. *Ben.* iv. 27. 4 *ut ad propositum revertar*, *Ep.* 59. 4 *sed ut* etc. Such phrases are very common in Cicero's treatises (not only dialogues), e.g. *Off.* ii. 77, *Div.* i. 109, *ND* iii. 60, *Brut.* 300 and often, *Or.* 148, and in Sallust, who (though himself more exuberant) gives Tacitus much of his vocabulary here, e.g. *Cat.* 5. 9, *Jug.* 4. 9, 17. 1, 19. 8, 42. 5, 79. 1, 95. 2; cf. also e.g. Vell. ii. 38. 1, 68. 5. Livy does not care for them.

their chief function is to emphasize and display that consciousness. However, authors can achieve with them more complicated
effects. With them they may suggest, and highlight through tonal
contrast, the depth of passion or wealth of thought that notionally
disrupts or threatens the orderly design; or they may charm us by
their self-awareness, or arrest us by their daring.

At Quint. ii. 4. 15 the phrase *sed ut eo revertar unde sum egressus*, 'but
to return to the point from which I digressed', enhances the
appeal of the preceding close, where the old man fondly remem-
bers his practice as a teacher. A few pages later we see rather his
pugnacity and zeal, when he declares, 'I cannot bear to put off
pronouncing a verdict on this practice', *neque enim eius rei iudicium
differre sustineo* (4. 28). He presently contains the polemic with 'but
let that be wandering enough', *verum hactenus evagari satis fuerit* (4.
32). The passage which sweeps through centuries at *Hist.* ii. 38
(above p. 52) Tacitus ends *sed me veterum novorumque morum reputatio
longius tulit: nunc ad rerum ordinem venio*, 'I have been carried too far
by reflecting on ancient and recent ways; now I come to the
sequence of events'.[8] He is accustomed, when he comments on
digressions, to justify austerely rather than excuse; now he gives a
dramatic sense of absorption in his brooding, as if he had momentarily forgotten his narrative (a sufficiently improbable notion in
this author!). Similarly at *Ann.* vi. 22. 1 we seem to witness his actual
musings on tremendous questions, which he holds in and breaks
off curtly at the close (22. 4). The sense of artifice is heightened by
the language: the intimate opening *sed mihi haec ac talia audienti*, 'as
for me, when I hear this and similar things', obviously echoes
Sallust's introduction to a digression of his own (*Cat.* 53. 2). Seneca
can show a self-conscious jauntiness, as at *NQ* v. 14. 4–15. 1: 'but I
shall follow the topic through more thoroughly when I come to
earthquakes; for now allow me to tell you a story', *nunc mihi permitte
narrare fabulam*. By contrast, at iii. 18 it is passion that supposedly
impels him. He mentions how modern diners like to watch the
fish they are to eat expiring; he presently bursts out *permitte mihi
quaestione seposita castigare luxuriam*, 'allow me to lay aside the investigation and attack luxury' (18. 1). A digression assailing the
practice ensues. Seneca's resumptive *sed ut ad propositum revertar*, 'to

---

[8] C. Heraeus's *redeo* retains attractions; but note Quint. v. 12. 23. In Quint. ii note also 17.
1 (cf. i. 12. 19 and v. 10. 92); these turns are often neatly self-referential. After ii they occur
more rarely.

return to my subject', follows a climax that is said by Seneca to violate the limits of language through ungovernable feeling (18. 7); the resumption holds in and brings out the emotion. To think the author actually so beyond discipline would be no less naïve than in the case of Tacitus, and would ignore the flagrant elegance and artifice of language and form.[9]

We already see complexities. Authors can exploit structure and the starkest structural ossature to emphasize effects which professedly run contrary to that of tight control. Assuredly, digression is a recognized device, actually accommodated into the standard organization of prose even as formally it is excluded from it. But we have seen how the reader is often to be delighted by the appearance of transgressing, from various appealing impulses, the rigorous confines of intellectual form. It is not inconsistent with this, but a part of the literary complexity, that digressions often help to enrich a work by placing in a larger context its tautly constructed discourse and so extending our view of the author's mental world. Thus in Tacitus digressions help to draw out the wide historical vision which is actually essential to the viewpoint of the tightly limited narration by year. In Seneca's *Naturales Quaestiones* the carefully placed digressions on vice help to bring out by contrast the true nobility and order of nature, and the spiritual significance of man's moral departure from that order. Cohesion and apparent looseness intermingle richly, and neither must be ignored.[10]

The topic of signals may be pursued further. We shall now concentrate on **Seneca**, whose robustness stands out even in the examples above. He presents us often with firm structural demarcations, often with an ostentatious blurring of divisions, sometimes with a flaunted appearance of improvisation. The manner and proportions vary from work to work: his approach to structure is extremely diverse. A brilliant example of blurring appears in a passage whose intricacy of detail we have already noticed: *Ben.* iii. 17 (pp. 102f.). Seneca is finishing, it may be recalled, his consideration of whether a law should exist against ingratitude.

[9] The very close, *oculis quoque gulosi sunt*, deftly takes up the phrase before the introduction, *oculos ante quam gulam pavit* (17. 3), and pointedly combines what it had kept separate. It will be seen that I should prefer a semi-colon at the end of v. 14.

[10] The play with relevance at *NQ* iv b. 13. 1–3 variously brings out the relevance of the digression. For a small and rhetorically forceful example of the bearing in Tacitus of historical range see *Ann.* xi. 22. 2–6; subtler is xii. 23. 2–24. 2.

The long climactic sentence that compares the grateful and the ungrateful reaches a climax itself with the generosity of the grateful even to persons of lowly status (*humilioribus ... personis*). The final sentence of the section goes further still. 'Even if he receives a favour from his own slave, he considers what he has received, not from whom he has received it [from how humble a source]', *nam etiam si a servo suo beneficium accepit, aestimat non a quo sed quid acceperit* (17. 4). 'Yet some ask', Seneca continues, 'if a slave can confer a favour on his master', *quamquam quaeritur a quibusdam ... an beneficium dare servus domino possit* (18. 1). This sentence gives us the subject of the new section (chs. 18–28). The craft of the dovetailing is meant to be seen. The mention of slaves in the preceding sentence (quoted) forms the culmination of the whole section of the book; the closing epigram of that sentence is to appear to reverse, elegantly and provokingly, a phrase used of the grateful man a moment before (*animum eius a quo accepit, non rem, intuens*, 'he considers the mind of the man from whom he has received the favour, not the thing'). The *quamquam* in 18. 1, a particle slightly less independent than 'yet', parades a particularly gliding and mock-casual transition. The next transition in the book (29. 1) reinforces the self-conscious obliquity here. Yet there is also here an expressive purpose: the truth of Seneca's answer seems obvious in advance.

When Seneca presents himself as developing a theme on the inspiration of the moment, we are to enjoy his fertility and address, to be struck by the range of his philosophy, and to relish the adventurous surprise. It is neither possible nor important to determine precisely what part was actually played by happy thoughts in Seneca's process of composition. What must be stressed is, firstly, that he is well aware of the effect he is making, and, secondly, that he does not in fact lose sight of his design in the intoxication of the moment. He keeps large units in view at these points and he intends his handling of structure to please and startle.[11] It is significant that such passages are most numerous and most notable in the *Letters*, which profess spontaneity and cultivate structural surprises. One conspicuous instance occurs at

[11] Quintilian acknowledges the charm of seeming to happen on a new topic (ix. 2. 60f.), and soon deploys a related device himself, not unplayfully (2. 81 *incidimus*, cf. 60 *incidi*; he does not use the verb to this purpose elsewhere). Even the pretence of accident does not seem very strong in these places. Cf. also e.g. Plin. *Pan*. 18. 1. Interesting too is Quint. vii. 10. 17, where Quintilian affects to have blurred a transition inadvertently.

Ep. 108. 17–23, where the elderly Seneca, not actually prone to indiscriminate reminiscence, seems charmingly drawn on to recollect wryly an episode which illustrates his own youthful zeal. *quoniam coepi,* he says, ... *non pudebit fateri* ... , 'since I have begun ... , I shall not blush to confess ...' (17). The first phrase is a standard one in Seneca, and the passage actually fits into the elaborate argument and themes of the letter; the delay appears still more calculated, and provoking, when we consider the letter as a whole. In it Seneca never reaches the question Lucilius has put to him, despite his opening *statim expediam,* 'I will settle it at once'; he finally puts it off for a separate letter. The strategy is palpably intended to tease and to scrutinize.[12]

Seneca, it is now apparent, means often to be unexpected and irregular in his form. This is artistry, but not only artistry. Through lively unpredictability he seeks to invigorate and challenge the reader's thought. His construction even at its strangest exhibits both art and purpose. Serpentine lines of discourse can often communicate the breadth and richness of his philosophy more effectively than would straight ones. To follow his thought and themes, we must frequently look beyond the advertised structure, and we must ponder closely his very particles. We must approach him, that is to say, with the same respect as difficult poetry; we will be well rewarded if we do so.

We may touch on some aspects of the *De Tranquillitate Animi,* structurally to my mind the most difficult of his works. It may seem at first an ill-organized miscellany, which in the very detail of its paragraphs meanders inconsequentially. Yet such a view would be dubious. It can hardly be a coincidence, for example, that the closing passage on sublimity, unexpected as it is, appears to look back so definitely to a passage on sublimity which is prominently placed in the opening speech (1. 14). The cohesion and firm progress of some paragraphs and sections make unlikely the somnambulism that might be supposed in others. Seneca clearly purposes two unexpected broadening movements near the start. The work begins, uniquely in Seneca, with dramatic form, and a self-revelatory speech by another character (Serenus); but it soon

---

[12] *quoniam coepi:* cf. 70. 22, 114. 24, *VB* 5. 1, and also *Clem.* i. 7. 1; for different instances of the device cf. *Ep.* 67. 14, 113. 21 (< *me* > *t.?*; cf. *Ben.* vii. 1. 2 for the combination with *mehercules*); 80. 2; also *Brev.* 10. 1, 20. 3. On the *Letters* note the contrast of *sermo* with *disputationes praeparatae* at 38. 1; for surprises cf. e.g. 57. 7, 58. 25, 77. 14, and note the play with closes in the early letters, e.g. 17. 11, 18. 14. Note in *Clem.* the handling of relevance at i. 5. 1.

expands into general and impersonal exposition by Seneca. That is the first movement; the second takes our attention beyond the problems of ennui alone to embrace misfortune too, and its more dramatic threats to tranquillity. The first movement is explicitly signalled; the second is strongly prepared at the same time (2. 3f.), though it is realized more gradually. Seneca positively desires the effect of proceeding from intense evocation of one person's state of mind to that of a malady wider and graver in scope (2. 5–15), and then to a more expansive vision of life and action. Serenus matters, and engages our interest in the work; but his personal experience is significantly subsumed into the universalizing wisdom of philosophy.[13]

We shall discuss one important element in this breadth of vision: it governs much of the detailed movement in the work, and throws light on various passages that puzzle. Seneca depicts different levels of tranquillity, and forcefully juxtaposes the heroic tranquillity attained by the great sages with the prudential tranquillity of the lower man.[14] Hence we should not at all view as actually tangential the powerful and parallel accounts of Diogenes' abjuration of wealth long ago and Julius Canus' acceptance of death under Caligula (8. 4–9, 14. 4–9). The sublime tranquillity of both is the prime point of emphasis, and Canus' actions invest the very word with fresh strength: *ecce in media tempestate tranquillitas*, 'see there tranquillity in the midst of the storm!' (14. 10, cf. 14. 6). Diogenes' renunciation of possessions is explicitly set against the lesser mortal's sensible limitation of his wealth (8. 9). The part including Canus (14. 2–10) plainly dwells on this highest tranquillity. After it Seneca, who has lingered on Canus in an elevated and enraptured conclusion, returns with deliberate abruptness to more common experience and the cen-

---

[13] It is significant that Seneca offers no grand return to his addressee, as in *Brev.* 18 f., only a brief *envoi* (17. 12). With 2. 4 cf. esp. 14. 2. 2. 6–15 generalize not on all dangers to tranquillity but on Serenus' predicament (note *interim* in 5). Democritus' work, spoken of in 2. 3, displayed the larger conception, as Seneca obviously knew (note *egregium*); that conception appeared in the opening (B3 DK; cf. 13. 1 f. (and 10. 6, etc.), *Ira* iii. 6. 3; and note Diog. Oen. fr. 102 Casanova). It also informed the general tradition which constitutes the basis for Seneca's piece; Seneca must have intended from the first to adopt it. Revealing for that tradition is Plutarch's essay on the subject (464e–477f), which, like Seneca's, bears the strong impress of its author's mind. Seneca leaves only small traces of the pattern of headings relating to tranquillity which is prominent in Plutarch (see Broecker (1954), 23–5).

[14] Interesting for this division, and for other aspects of the structure, is Cic. *Tusc.* iv (see 59 f.).

tral line of argument: *sed nihil prodest*, 'but it is no good', to have cast away reasons for a personal gloom (15. 1). The drastic movement from the close on Canus, which is grandiose and formally excursive, reinforces the spaciousness of that ending, and creates a beautiful and significant sense of wide-ranging utterance.[15]

In II Seneca exploits levels of tranquillity in more complicated fashion. At II. 1 he stresses vigorously that his circumspect advice for ordinary men does not apply to the superb confidence of the wise; this gives us the same contrast that we have seen. Very shortly, however, he glides, and assimilates to the wise man's response to fortune and death the response 'we' should have ourselves. This cannot be an accident: Seneca must have intended us to see as parallel, and as divergent, consecutive sentences which give matching impassive speeches, one introduced by *dicet*, 'he [the wise man] will say', one by *dicemus*, 'we will say'. In raising us with inspired exhortation to so high a level Seneca is reaping the fruits of his indirectness. He gradually climbs downwards, and begins the next part announcing a further descent (12. 1).

The construction of the work is intricate and variously fruitful; we must avoid turning it either into a geometrical parterre (curiously overgrown) or into an anarchic jungle. When, say, the section on wealth ends by abandoning tranquillity and discoursing on the purchase of huge collections of books (9. 4–7), we must begin by relishing the fecund rhetoric which can so suddenly grow this thought into a little structure of its own, till it is cut back with a dialectical 'but' (10. 1). Next, we must appreciate the actual place of this passage in the larger shape of the work; on that shape we shall now say a word. The earlier part of Seneca's prescriptions (chs. 3–9) takes up, though not explicitly, the divisions of Serenus' opening speech: these were wealth, political activity, and, more briefly, literary pursuits (1. 4–14). Wealth and political activity generate the principal divisions in 3–9; the second part, on wealth, echoes Serenus' 'heading' with particular clarity (cf. 9. 1 with 1. 5). The following chapter, 10, considers an objection to

---

[15] The idea of imitation in 15. 2 does not impede the immediate effect at 15. 1; that idea introduces a more striking complication at 16. 2f. after 16. 1. *utique* in 14. 2 marks a definite break; the appearance of the *sapiens* in 13. 3 strengthens the force of 14. 2–10. Plut. fr. 211 Sandbach brings out the pointedness of Seneca's treatment in 14. 9f. At 8. 7 Seneca chooses the harsh *turpe*: compare Ael. *Var. Hist.* xiii. 28 (αἰσχρόν), as against Stob. iv. 19. 47 (δεινόν), Diog. Laert. vi. 55 (γελοῖον).

this whole portion (3–9) on the general choice of life: one cannot always choose. The rest of the work considers not such general practical choices but, with elaborate intermingling, both attitudes of mind and the closer practical detail of existence. In 3–9, the topic of *studia*, intellectual and literary pursuits, is not given a separate section, although it has been touched on (3. 6, 5. 5, 7. 2); but the present passage on amassing books, placed where it is, and beginning *studiorum*, clearly serves to take up Serenus' third area, from an indirect and unexpected angle, linking it surprisingly with wealth and the important theme of display.[16] That theme itself belongs to the larger concern with the relations between oneself and others, between looking inward and outward. That concern is again a vital principle of form in the work, which is only partly acknowledged in the overt articulation. It takes many unlooked-for and thought-provoking turns.

Seneca's approach to structure is highly complex. He often thwarts the expectation, of which he is well aware, that prose should be lucidly organized. Yet design and interconnection are palpably important to him; his deviousness does not preclude a manifold cohesion. He treats prose structure with great expressiveness and with sovereign liberty, commanding rather than commanded.

The structure of whole works of prose is of course often intended to make an emotional as well as an intellectual impact. A vital illustration of this is the common pattern whereby the later or the last part of a work rises above the rest in grandeur of style or greatness of matter. Simple as it is, this pattern exercises immense potency over the literature of our period; it is treated as variously as greatness is conceived.

Quintilian tends to see the peroration, the last part in the standard form of the speech, as characteristically excelling the rest in grandeur of language and, correspondingly, in power of emotion.[17] His own work is clearly intended to rise with its final book, which turns to consider directly the perfect orator, now fully educated. This structure matters to Quintilian both artistically and morally: his lofty conception of the man himself

---

[16] For 9. 6 cf. Meiggs (1982), 286–91.

[17] Cf. xi. 1. 6, vi. 1. 51; iv. 1. 28 (cf. viii. *praef.* 7), vi. 1. 29, cf. (for the association of grandeur and emotion) xii. 10. 36, vi. 2. 20. Both the grand manner and the arousing of passion Quintilian thinks supreme in worth for oratory: cf. xii. 10. 61–5, vi. 2. 7.

must impress and inspire us supremely. Even at the start of his work, where he outlines very roughly the design of the rest, he dwells far longer on the last book. The outline of its topics becomes an exciting anaphorical sequence, and ends by implying the greatness of the theme and of Quintilian's undertaking: *quantum nostra valebit infirmitas disseremus*, 'on this I shall discourse with all the strength in my inadequate power' (i. *praef.* 22). The superb preface to Book xii itself makes us vividly conscious that we have reached the summit of the work in greatness. In conveying this, Quintilian begins from the metaphor of weight but moves to the more dynamic metaphor of sailing, and describes his supposedly unwitting progress to the large and lonely perils of mid-sea. The image is a common one for grandeur, but it is striking to find it used at the last part of a work, when the voyage might be expected to be reaching its end.[18] For all the lightness of tone we are made to perceive not only the theme but the undertaking itself as something excitingly sublime.

The book itself is so shaped as to strengthen its impact. Quintilian spends little time on the perfect orator's oratory (xii. 10), notionally the third part of the whole work (ii. 14. 5, xii. 10. 1): he wants to emphasize the man, who appears conspicuously at the end of this very section (10. 77 f.). The section itself gives a forceful emphasis to the scope for sublimity within oratory; in doing so it aims to inspire by its own sublimity of writing. The practical detail of the book inevitably brings us down from elevation of style and matter. Yet through their position, the last chapter of the book, in its grandiose and exhilarating protreptic, and the first two chapters, in the moral and intellectual depth of their concerns, give the book as a whole a strong impression of heightened nobility and intensity.

It seems to me reasonably likely that, in broad design, **Tacitus'** *Annals* were intended to achieve, with their final part on the reign of Nero (Book xiii on), their extreme of greatness: greatness in evil, in virtue, and probably also in the massed power

---

[18] Contrast the placing of the model, Liv. xxxi. 1. 2–5 (on size); and contrast conversely Ariosto, *Orl. Fur.* xlvi. 1f. (1–19). Quintilian is looking back to the start of his voyage, *Ep.* 3. For the image cf. Bömer on Ov. *Fast.* i. 4; Fedeli on Prop. iii. 3. 22, 9. 3–4. On the preface to xii cf. Ahlheid (1983), 37–42. For other prospective references to xii see esp. ii. 21. 24, iii. 8. 42 (*altior quaestio*).

and horror of violent and significant deaths.[19] There are complications here, characteristic of Tacitus, particularly in relation to evil. Nero presents an extreme of cruelty and crime, but also of sordidness and absurdity; Tacitus' account of him often depicts degradation and displays humour—though with the loftiness of supreme contempt. Yet it seems apparent that the Neronian books were meant also to possess a terrible and climactic extremity. The incompleteness of the text precludes assurance; but the point looks clear enough from the surviving part on Tiberius, and on Claudius (immediately before Book xiii). We are lamentably deprived of the books on Caligula; but most likely there were only two of these, against at least four and most likely six for Nero: the part on Nero would inevitably fall at the least with heavier weight. One might say that the pattern was simply dictated by Tacitus' conceptions of imperial history and by his earlier decision to begin the *Histories* after Nero. But Tacitus is still acutely sensitive to the structure and aesthetic impact of his work; and one of his tasks as a historian is to give substance through the force of his writing to the perceived shape of history.[20]

Various moments point the contrasts sharply. Right at the start of his account of Nero, Tacitus registers very meaningfully the decline from the oratorical talents, or abilities, of earlier emperors to Nero, who is too frivolous for this great public art, and needs to have his speeches written for him (xiii. 3. 2f.). Nero's exile of his wife Octavia, no less emphatically placed, is shown by argument to have been crueller than Tiberius' and Claudius' exiling of members of their own families, Agrippina the Elder and Julia Livilla (xiv. 63. 2). We are plainly to compare too the sinister and distasteful passage on that Agrippina's end (vi. 25) with the

---

[19] The text of M^2 itself, which numbers the books of the *Histories* as if part of a single work with the *Annals*, contains Tacitus' preface to the *Histories* as a separate entity, and much that would be out of place had the *Annals* preceded (e.g. v. 10 and the whole passage). Hence Tacitus is unlikely himself to have produced a merged edition. On virtue note esp. the climactic xvi. 21. 1; contrast with *virtutem ipsam excindere concupivit* the phrasing at Dio lxii. 26. 1 (Xiph.). Sen. *Helv.* 13. 7 is less boldly put, though by a more lavish author.

[20] Intriguing is the picture of decline given by Montanus at *Hist.* iv. 42. 5: Tiberius and Gaius were each followed by a worse tyrant. On Tacitus' account of Nero cf. Heinz (1948); he somewhat exaggerates its positive elements through overplaying comparison with other sources and underplaying language and irony. Note *Agr.* 45. 2, where Nero seems to provide the extreme of crime before Domitian; cf. also e.g. *Hist.* i. 78. 2 (Plut. *Oth.* 3. 1f., Suet. *Oth.* 7. I do not have anything like the biting *tamquam* phrase). It is noteworthy for Nero's reputation that he is much more prominent in Epictetus than any other past emperor, including Domitian; cf. e.g. Marc. Aur. iii. 16.

ghastlier horrors and the intenser writing of the passage on Octavia's murder (xiv. 64).[21] It is hard not to link with each other the passages in iv and xvi where Tacitus affects to remark how his subject-matter must weary the reader (iv. 32f., p. 57, xvi. 16); but the accumulation of deaths under Nero is made to seem much more dreadful than under Tiberius, and the underlying tonality of the later passage is much more deeply tragic. Besides all this, the language which Tacitus uses of Nero and of Tiberius relates them indeed, but marks Nero as the more wicked and repulsive.[22]

These ascending structures **Seneca** uses, declines, and turns. How conscious he is of them, we see plainly enough when he uses a speech by an august being (God, the glorified soul of Marcia's father, and Socrates) to end the *De Providentia*, the *Ad Marciam*, and probably the *De Vita Beata*. We see it still more openly at the start of the last book of the *De Beneficiis*; there Seneca says that he would best have kept his reader had the work grown gradually (*paulatim ... crescere*), that is increased in gravity and greatness (vii. 1. 2). He is defiantly calling attention to his own more devious procedure in this work.[23] Even with the speeches that we have mentioned, the grandeur can twist unexpectedly. The speech of God in the *De Providentia* closes with pithy drama and a humiliating address ('Do you not perhaps blush a little? ... ', *ecquid erubescitis? ...*). In the speech of the sainted father in the *Ad Marciam* (cf. pp. 16f.) the grandeur of universal ruin undoes the magnificence of the beatified dead and ends that heavenly life which had consoled the grieving mother. Even the beatified dead become a *parva ruinae ingentis accessio*, 'a little addition to the mighty destruction'. In the one work the twist is pungent, in the other disquietingly profound.

---

[21] One should note that both at xiii. 3. 2f. and at xiv. 63. 2 Tacitus uses the perspective and memories of spectators (cf. esp. *Hist.* iii. 68. 1f.). He wishes in general to avoid on the surface too open and broad a comparison of his four emperors, preferring subtlety and formal restraint.

[22] For characteristic language on Nero, which differentiates him markedly from Tiberius, see e.g. xiv. 56. 3 *velare odium fallacibus blanditiis* (cf. Vitellius, *Hist.* ii. 59. 2); xv. 42. 1 *usus est patriae ruinis extruxitque domum* (contrast vi. 45. 1, iv. 64. 1f.; *patria* is never used against Tiberius); xvi. 21. 1 *concupivit* (see n. 19), cf. e.g. xiii. 20. 3 *interficiendae matris avidus* (*cupio* etc. are not used of Tiberius in a bad sense). xiv. 11. 2, xv. 35. 1, xvi. 18. 3 illustrate further the extreme phrases Tiberius escapes.

[23] For *cresco* used in relation to greatness of various kinds cf. *Ep.* 86. 2; iii. 4 (there with play); Quint. vi. 1. 29, viii. 4. 8, 27. On speeches note the less lofty but more searching form of ending with a speech to deliver to oneself (*De Ira, De Beneficiis*); the two are powerfully combined in the last part of Lucr. iii.

The *De Tranquillitate Animi* too exploits such structures. It closes, but for its last sentence of address, with a self-contemplating virtuosity. The last main section (17. 4–11) pointedly descends, to the theme of relaxation and even drink; but it contrives to end discoursing on and in the language of sublime inspiration. (Wine can inspire.) The passage has purpose; but it flourishes before us Seneca's structural bravado.[24]

We shall begin our consideration of poetry on a relatively small scale, with Hippolytus' speech at Sen. *Phaedr.* 483–564. **Seneca's tragedies** are unlikely to have been performed on a stage; they were doubtless recited by the poet and then published.[25] Often they appear to abandon dramatic tension, to move away from the specific situation, to leave unclarities and awkwardnesses which would appear strange if narrative through drama were the central concern. Yet no less plainly, forceful conceptions of action and characters are carried through, with effect, from scene to scene: one cannot view Seneca as being interested solely in the individual episode. It may prove more rewarding to think of the tragedies as poems: poems in which dramatic elements play an important part, but which also proceed with conscious freedom and boldness. In Seneca excursive and concentrating impulses stand not in contradiction but in effective opposition, and each play stamps itself on the mind as an individual and memorable whole.

The nurse of Phaedra, Hippolytus' stepmother, has made a speech in which she urges Hippolytus to relax his regime of hunting and chastity. She means to move him towards accepting the love of her mistress. Hippolytus speaks in reply on the in-

[24] This inspiration will be part of Seneca's regime of deliberate variety, not Serenus' state of uncontrolled oscillation (1. 14). But the artistry is ultimately more important here. In the final sentence of the *Ad Marciam*, the accent falls on knowledge, so that *felicem* has a considerable and demanding twist.

[25] Cf. Ch. 2 n. 48. Quint. viii. 3. 31 most likely provides evidence for Seneca reciting himself; the practice is well-attested for tragedy. There would be no difficulties in Seneca for a single reader not equalled in plays read out in homes by single readers in 17th–19th-cent. France and England. On structure in Seneca's tragedies see, among much else, Friedrich (1933); Zwierlein (1966), 88–126; Schetter (1972); Tarrant (1976), 3–6; Hine (1981). On the passage of *Phaedra* see Henry and Walker (1966), 234 f.; Bauzà (1981); Petrone (1981); 365 f.; Boyle (1985), 1284–347; and, most closely and fully, Segal (1986), chs. 3 and 4. For a recent discussion of structure in the poets more generally, see Galinsky (1989), 69–88; cf. also Williams (1978), 246–55. On ancient critics, and on wider issues, see Heath (1989).

nocent pleasures of the pastoral life, on the Golden Age and its dissolution, and lastly and briefly on the badness of women. The formal generality pushes further something already notable in Euripides; it is seen conspicuously in Hippolytus' reaction to the direct proposal in Euripides' second *Hippolytus*, 616–68. But in our passage the dramatic goal of the proposition of love stands further off, and the section on the Golden Age increases the distance; the topics possess, and are meant to possess, the air of standard poetic and philosophical themes. The first thing to notice is the contrast which Seneca intends between the two halves of his whole scene, and between two kinds of writing. After this half, which is deliberately immobile, generalizing, and relatively undramatic, there comes a second half strongly and vivaciously dramatic, where Phaedra appears and makes her own declaration. There we have drastic imagined action, drastic passions, and vigorous tension and momentum; ingenious and then explosive language gives animation and force to the situations created by Phaedra's love, which there stands fixed in the forefront of our attention. The contrast with this half is exceedingly effective, and the shift is clearly marked: the Nurse acknowledges the futility of her efforts and then Phaedra comes to speak to Hippolytus *praeceps* ..., *impatiens morae*, 'rushing, unable to bear the delay' (583); a rush of action succeeds as she faints and is raised by Hippolytus. The appearance of both Phaedra and the Nurse at the start of the scene enhances the whole design.[26]

Even within Hippolytus' speech, Seneca is highly conscious of his formal movement away from the subject in hand. With an ingenious, and paraded, sleight of hand, he returns to it through ingenious dramatic irony. Near the close the speech presents the familiar catalogue of internecine crimes that pollute the present age. This ends:

> perimuntque fetus impiae matres suos;
> taceo novercas. (557f.)

---

[26] Seneca has probably created his long scene by reworking and combining situations from at least two originals (cf. Zwierlein (1987), 18–33); there has been some cost, at least to the scholar, in dramatic logic. The details of his procedure must, I think, remain obscure; but it is probable that in Euripides' lost first *Hippolytus*, unlike the second, Phaedra made a proposition in person, and it is perhaps improbable that the Nurse there attempted to make one for her unsuccessfully.

Unnatural mothers destroy their own offspring; I say nothing of stepmothers.[27]

The famed malice of stepmothers is made to form a climax; in fact
the stepmother is paradoxically in love. The device of 'passing
over' (*praeteritio*) sharpens the wit. The point is taken up in the
second half of the scene (638, 684), and has made a brilliant close
to the preceding choral ode on love; that ode returns to the
immediate situation with the brief *quid plura canam? vincit saevas /
cura novercas*, 'Why should I sing on longer? Passion overcomes
[even] savage stepmothers' (356 f.). The link (cf. also 1199 f.) both
confirms that Seneca here plays on relevance and shows how
cohesive his creation is poetically.

The short and final section on women which ensues brings us
nearer to the plot, with the obvious implications, for the proposal,
of Hippolytus' extreme misogyny. This misogyny reaches its
height after the formal end of the long speech; the Nurse has been
made to interject a line (565) to provide a step to the climax, to
underline Hippolytus' sudden irrationality, and to highlight the
reference to Medea which closes the speech proper. That reference is to be taken up at the close of Hippolytus' next long speech,
his speech of reaction to Phaedra's declaration and appeal
(671–97); that ends (694–8) with another stunning variation on
stepmothers (Medea was the stepmother of Hippolytus' father).
The movement towards the dramatic subject in this section of our
speech is made the more startling and effective by the shift in
Hippolytus from serene wisdom in the earlier sections to irra-
tional vehemence now. *detestor omnis*, he will say, *horreo, fugio, exe-
cror*, 'I loathe all women, I detest, flee, and abhor them' (566). It is
evident how vigorously and how purposefully Seneca is exploiting
proximity to his plot and remoteness from it, and different sorts of
poetry.[28] Other treatments of these themes show a related exploit-

---

[27] *fetus* may heighten the wickedness by stressing parturition; a reference to abortion
would be a sad anticlimax. There is a problem in the rest of 558, *mitior nil est feris* (cf.
Zwierlein, and Coffey and Mayer, ad loc.). Anything to the effect that stepmothers are not
gentler than beasts would here fall very feebly, and lead ill into *sed dux malorum femina* (559).
But *nil* of parts or even deeds of the human race appears difficult, and the transition to 559
(a new paragraph in Zwierlein) remains a little awkward. I should prefer to end a sentence
with *novercas*, and not to begin one with *sed*, perhaps supposing a lacuna after 558. (I also
think the break at 525 greater than at 540.) For the telling curtness and pause cf. e.g. Ov.
Met. viii. 522.

[28] I doubt that Seneca is simply ignoring the cohesive presentation of dramatic
character: note 230–43; and he likes to jolt our evaluations of characters too.

ation. The long excursus on wealth in a declamation by Fabianus
(Sen. Rh. *Contr.* ii. 1. 10–13) comes back to the immediate situation
with calculated panache; even the handling at Tib. i. 3. 35–50 is
meant to surprise and intrigue. Such play with excursion is
nothing new to Latin poetry; what is distinctive in Seneca is the
way he uses it in this genre.[29]

None of this removes at all the positive contribution of the
speech to the dramatic poem. We may dwell on one particularly
important part of the speech, and a particularly important aspect.
Seneca's Hippolytus is a creation of his poetry; different poetic
elements accumulate and coalesce to constitute this vivid figure.
His rough beauty, his vigorous and innocent pastoral life, his
moral austerity and fierceness, are powerfully evoked by the language. They interact, and they combine into a predominantly
attractive conception; this is distorted morally by his father's mistaken speech of condemnation (903–58), and destroyed physically
in the catastrophe (e.g. 1094–6, 1265–70). This speech uses the
resources of poetry to create, especially in its first section, a fresh
and radiant image, morally and physically, of Hippolytus' life.[30]

The Nurse, urging licence or *vegeta libertas*, 'vigorous freedom'
(460), had repeatedly used the language of loosening: *mentem re-
laxa*, 'loosen your mind' (443), *tristem iuventam solve*, 'undo
the austerity of your youth' (449), *quid te coerces?*, 'why do you restrict
yourself?' (453). Hippolytus' reply depicts a truer and more lovely
liberty; the effect loses none of its significance because Hippolytus'
speech, wider in moral scope and less immediate, does not until
the end give much attention to the theme of licence as such (the
end of the Nurse's speech supplies Hippolytus' lead). Life in the
country is called at the start of his speech supremely 'free' and
innocent (483); it avoids servitude to rulers and to passions

---

[29] Criticism, unsympathetic to declaimers, sees in the Fabianus only an absurd anticlimax: Norden (1915), 276f.; Bonner (1949), 58f. The *sententia* is of course only the formal
point of connection: the whole digression is relevant to the case. With the Tibullus cf. also i.
10. 1–10, ii. 3. 67–70; naturally one would not deny these passages relevance to the personal
situation (cf. Murgatroyd on i. 3. 35–48; Whitaker (1983), ch. 3).

[30] Its themes form part of the stock common to poetry and philosophy, but it is poetic
models which are most in evidence here (see the commentators and Jakobi (1988), 75–7).
Critics mostly assess Hippolytus, and less plausibly all this speech, much more negatively,
in my view with insufficient reason. The approach is sometimes perhaps too narrowly
moral, sometimes too psychologizing. The matter cannot be discussed here; but I would
myself lay considerable weight on the impact of the last three acts, and precisely on
Hippolytus' heroism in failure at 1064–7.

(490–2). Instead of oppressive luxury the man who gives himself to this life *rure vacuo potitur et aperto aethere / innocuus errat*, 'possesses the empty country and wanders guiltless in the unconfined air' (501f.). *vacuo*, 'empty', is enhanced by the paradox that it is desirable to possess something 'empty'; the easy *errat*, 'wanders', beautifully negates the idea of moral wandering through the suggested paradox of erring innocently.

The first section ends significantly and penetratingly presenting royal adultery not as opening out but as confining and dark:

> non in recessu furta et obscuro improbus
> quaerit cubili seque multiplici timens
> domo recondit; aethera ac lucem petit
> et teste caelo vivit. (522–5)

He does not shamelessly seek for amorous thefts in a recess or the darkness of a bed, or hide himself in fear in a labyrinthine dwelling. It is the air and the light that he seeks; he lives with the heavens as his witness.

The moral is superbly fused with the physical; in the two incisive clauses of the second part the openness of the sky now takes on a more commanding moral firmness. The whole section deepens and enriches the atmosphere that hangs about Hippolytus' life. The following section increases first the weight and significance of that atmosphere and then its precariousness: crime will occur within this family too, because of a woman. The example of this speech shows us something of the range in approach we need to appreciate Seneca's highly deliberate and effective handling of cohesion, excursion, and form. We can see here too, in the relation of wit to structure and the interaction of abundance and arrest, the continuity and kinship of larger and smaller elements in Seneca's audacious art.

In considering **Lucan** we shall concentrate on aspects of the main part of Book ix (1–949). This illustrates characteristic features in an extreme form, and, still more importantly, shows Lucan handling and exploiting the form of his whole poem in a particularly daring and challenging way.[31] It is in general obvious enough that Lucan gives his poem cohesion and shape. Scenes

---

[31] On structure in Lucan see Eckardt (1936); Rutz (1970); Syndikus (1958); Due (1962), esp. 106–32; Schrempp (1964); Marti (1968); Lebek (1976); on ix, and Cato: Wuensch (1930), ch. 2; Morford (1967*b*); Vögler (1968); Narducci (1979), 130–44; Thomas (1982), 108–19; Zwierlein (1986); Johnson (1987), ch. 2; Pecchiura (1965); and Goar (1987).

look forward and back. So the poignant close to Book v, where Pompey's wife parts from him, explicitly refers us back (802f.) to the close of Book ii, where Pompey leaves Italy with her, and presents that scene in an altered perspective; and it explicitly refers forward (814f.) to the reunion in Book viii (cf. vii. 675–7).[32] Prospective devices abound in the poem: the tension of narrative time, of the awaited future, is felt insistently even when conventional narration is left furthest behind. The narrator's discourse, in its themes, outlook, and forms, constitutes the most powerful and ubiquitous force for cohesion, as for excursion. The poem, then, does not in the least fall apart into unconnected episodes. The firm demarcations and abrupt transitions do not at all hide the larger designs and manifold connections; indeed, they articulate the patterns and divisions which organize the poetry and which provide strongly defined units for the reader to relate. We should not see indifference to structure even in the detail of handling transition, in the recurrent leap, for example, from the narrator's eloquent expatiation at the end of a portion of narrative to a dry 'meanwhile', or 'now', at the beginning of the next. These moments are one of the beauties of the poem: form and apparent caprice, lavishness and tightness, wonderfully intermingle.[33] One must give full weight to the surprise and often the playfulness of Lucan's excursive elaborations in description or unpredictable thought: he treats narrative even more drastically than Seneca treats drama, and is determined to be wayward. But although excursive and unifying elements stand in elaborate relations and even effective contrast, excursion in no sense injures the powerful structure of the poem; it helps to create the poem's complex aesthetic cohesion.

In Book ix the dead Pompey receives a kind of mock-funeral, and from Cato a searching reassessment; Cato, in a sense Pompey's successor as Republican leader, takes men through Libya and its desert; Caesar visits Troy, then reaches Egypt and learns of Pompey's murder. The book is of particular interest structur-

---

[32] Shackleton Bailey rightly rejects Housman's corrigendum to v. 804f.; but his punctuation seems to give *fida comes Magni* much less force and point (especially *fida*). The more personal *Pompeium* in 805 is pointedly juxtaposed with *fugit*; *duce* gives all 804 a military suggestion.

[33] One should obviously contrast the phrases of return in prose (p. 149). As to the attractions of suddenness and void in place of transition, note, on a quite different effect, Proust, *Flaub.* p. 595 (in *Contre Saint-Beuve*, etc., éd. Pléiade).

ally. Firstly, it takes the poem beyond what had been made to seem the essential resolution of its action; secondly, the section which dominates it, the account of Cato's journey, is itself filled with excursuses to a degree and to a distance uncommon even in Lucan. These features are deliberate, significant, and related.

Our expectations had been principally directed towards the battle of Pharsalia (vii), emphatically and repeatedly presented as deciding the war, and towards the death of one of the two contending leaders (viii). At the start of ix, even as Lucan presents the continuation of Pompey's effort by others, it is made clear that the issue of the war has been decided (19f.). The question of the unwilling soldier at 232f. brings out the sense of conclusion pungently: *quis erit finis si nec Pharsalia pugnae / nec Pompeius erit?*, 'What end will there be to the fighting if neither Pharsalia nor Pompey's death is such?' (The word-order gives emphasis to *finis*, 'end'.) Lucan exploits both morally and aesthetically the feeling that the main action of the poem is or should be finished; he means to surprise us. Morally, it is Cato's action, in defeat and without hope or concern for practical success, that marks the greatest achievement in the poem to this point. The structure thus displays virtue's victory in failure. The values of the poem reach a new profundity; the political intensity remains, but is deepened by the supremacy of spiritual greatness. At 593–604 the poet, stressing virtue not success as the proper criterion of fame, presents Cato's as the only rightful glory, unlike the glory of Rome's supposed great men (least of all like the emperors'). He declares that Cato's figurative triumphal procession excels Pompey's three real ones.

> hunc ego per Syrtes Libyaeque extrema triumphum
> ducere maluerim quam ter Capitolia curru
> scandere Pompei. (598–600)

I had rather lead this triumph through the Syrtes and the edge of Libya than mount the Capitol three times in Pompey's chariot.

As often, metaphor is used to mark the supremacy of spiritual reality; but even the metaphorical triumph of Cato, and the imagined action of the poet, are drastically physical.[34] Lucan's

---

[34] For the procedures of the triumph alluded to cf. Ehlers (1948), 501f., 510. Pompey's triumphs are a prominent motif in the poem; note esp. viii. 553f., spoken by the poet, and significantly echoed here. The reference to Marius' Libyan triumph (cf. ii. 69) is also pertinent. Note how Lucan springs into the whole passage from *lixa* (593), low though transformed.

ardour takes him almost outside the narrator's realm of words; he is not only setting this part of his poem against what precedes it but shifting from his 'own' zealous praise of Pompey at the end of Book viii. There he dwells on Pompey's great deeds (806–22) and passionately wishes he could himself perform the physical action of bringing Pompey's body back to Rome (842–5).[35] His own eager substitute for a funerary inscription then is actually corrected by Cato's substitute for a funeral oration now (viii. 806–15; ix. 190–214 (and note viii. 797–9)). Cato here judiciously registers the extent and limitations of Pompey's patriotism; his words are accepted as true by the poet and by Pompey's own shade (188 f.). The poem is using the figure of the poet in the boldest fashion to exhibit the movement in its outlook. In fact, the movement has long been prepared, not only by Lucan's treatment of Pompey's own failure, and his original attitude to him (i. 84–157), but by Cato's sublimely patriotic speech, dubious of Pompey, at ii. 286–323. The change in the poem is very much designed, but is executed in a startling and dizzying fashion.

The sense of wandering into strange regions, literally and poetically, connects in no trivial fashion with the amazing action of virtue; and the very digressions have more bearing than might appear. So the lengthy mythological excursus on the origin of Libya's snakes (619–99) presents, though with much play, a false world of myth where evil is defeated, with the aid of the gods. Such a world Lucan's poem has rejected, and the episode stands in significant opposition to the poem, to the concerns of this book, and even to Cato's own outlook on the divine (563–86).[36] The excursus on Libya (411–44) has an obvious general relevance, and draws the locale into relation with the other significant areas in the poem: the poem spans the world, and its geographical digressions serve an important purpose in marking, colouring, contrasting. Yet even the weightiest effect of the passage depends on excursion; its sections (411–20, 420–30, 431–44) grow successively

---

[35] It is interesting to compare Lucan's physicality here with Hardy's epigraph to *Tess*, where in Hardy's context the physicality, though engaged and poignant, is a metaphor for action through words.

[36] The other large mythical digression, iv. 594–655 on Antaeus, shows good vanquishing evil, with a related purpose of contrast. There divine support does not appear for the self-sufficient Hercules; but evil is linked with Earth and the Giants. One should not try to demythologize that passage too far; cf. Piacentini (1963), 32–9. Martindale (1981) well brings out the play and the mythological status of the episode, but not what I think its larger point.

grimmer and it is with a climactic movement that we return to the narrative: *hac ire Catonem / dura iubet virtus*, 'this is the way Cato's hard virtue bids him take'. The emphatic *dura*, 'hard', is a crucial and recurring word.

Still less must we hide the vitality and mischief of Lucan's divagation. Why Libya is so plagued with snakes, he begins at 619–23, *non cura laborque / noster scire valet, nisi quod ... fabula pro vera decepit saecula causa*, 'my own effort does not enable me to know, save that [i.e. he can say only that] a false tale has deceived the ages of the world instead of the true cause'. This tale, stressed to be false, he then recounts for 76 lines. The procedure is bizarre, and is made more so by the larger opposition of mythical narrative and intellectual introduction. The form of the sentence here displays, with humour, the contours of intellectual prose, but its movements of content surprise (especially with the almost parenthetical *nisi quod*).[37] The play on truth is enhanced by the blasé introduction to an earlier mythological digression: there he avers it unsporting to insist on truth from poets (359 f.). When the long account of the myth here is over, we expect at least to return to the main narrative; but Lucan, teasing indefatigably, glides into 34 lines which ennumerate the species of snakes. The digression on Libya begins abruptly, unlike such digressions in prose: *tertia pars rerum Libye*, 'Libya is the third portion of the world [continent]'. It then immediately undermines this standard notion: Libya is more part of Europe. We are drawn disconcertingly into academic debate on the topic (411–20). Both the likeness and the unlikeness to prose are used to startle us defiantly, almost impudently.[38]

The wilfulness is characteristic of Lucan's digressions; but their number, and the unusual character of in particular the long mythological narrative from Lucan himself, make the whole section appear especially peculiar: it seems to float unanchored. The narrative has for its most memorable action a particularly

---

[37] Cf. and contrast Tac. *Germ.* 9. 1 (*unde causa et origo ... parum comperi nisi quod ...*); on *advectam* there cf. *Hist.* iv. 84. 4: one should not understand and stress 'by sea'. For the story cf. Ov. *Met.* iv. 617–20, Bömer on 614–20; Apollonius' parallel digression on it lasts five lines (iv. 513–17). On truth compare Nicander's more reserved εἰ ἐτεόν περ, 'if Hesiod said truly' (*Ther.* 10 f., Hes. fr. spur. 367 Merk.–West).

[38] Contrast the manner of introduction at Sall. *Jug.* 17. 1 and e.g. Tac. *Agr.* 10. 1. The type *Zela est oppidum in Ponto positum* (*Bell. Alex.* 72. 1, cf. Thuc. i. 24. 1, etc.) is both different and a special case. On such excursuses generally cf. Thomas (1982). On the catalogue of snakes see Lausberg (1990).

grotesque and unserious sequence of assaults by snakes. Lucan writes as if he were striving for greatness in extremes of suffering and marvel; but the physical and conceptual play go well beyond even Lucan's norms. It must suffice here to mention the *prester*. With unlimited physical grotesquerie, Lucan makes its victim swell out in an *informis globus*, a 'shapeless ball' (801); with his bizarrest wit he makes the man himself (that is, the original form of him) remain deeply hidden in his vastly expanded body, *ipse latet penitus* (796). At the end he refuses finality and close: the corpse is still growing as the man's companions flee from it, *crescens fugere cadaver* (804).[39]

It is hard to explain by reference to Cato the manner in which the sequence is developed: tone apart, he fades from the foreground soon after the scene has begun, and is mentioned only once (807) until its end (881-9). We are meant to feel that the narrative has entered territory not only particularly strange but bewilderingly unfamiliar; other series of deaths, however odd, have not been caused by snakes in the desert. Our sense of disorientation is articulated and sharpened in the only speech of the section (848-80), where the soldiers comment at length on the terrible strangeness of the place, and contrast the present with their previous experiences. It is eminently characteristic that this book and the earlier part of the poem should be brought explicitly and pointedly together in the explosion of an epigram (848 f.); this epigram we have discussed from the other end above (pp. 87 f.). Diffusion and sharpness, excursion and point, interact in truly Lucanian fashion.

In this book we see Lucan deploying in two different ways the form of his poem and the appearance of moving beyond its obvious and decisive climax. On the one hand, he uses the structure to attain a deeper meaning and a higher sublimity; on the other, he gains from it a still further degree of strangeness and unpredictability, and a provoking and exhilarating sense of disorientation. The two aims are pursued principally in different parts; but the parts are interwoven and connected, and the combination shows Lucan taking to a new extreme the conjunction of weirdness and greatness that he loves. The remainder of what

---

[39] The mention of the snake at Ael. *Var. Hist.* xvii. 4 should be contrasted. Lucan's account is inspired by the name, as from πρήθω (cf. πίμπρημι as used at Nic. *Ther.* 403, etc.).

Lucan completed confirms this sort of approach. Book x presents a quite remarkable movement away from the story in a speech of 138 lines on the source of the Nile (194–331). The movement from the poem is marked by Caesar's breathtaking declaration that if he can see the sources of the Nile he will forget the Civil War (191 f.). On the other hand, the last part of Book ix significantly opposes to Cato's truth and virtue Caesar's hypocrisy, spurious patriotism, and concern with success before all. We see in Book x significant changes from i–viii. Fortune, which had so conspicuously supported Caesar's evil cause, will turn against him (339, 525–9); Caesar himself is affected and humiliated by real fear at danger (443–70).[40] Incomplete though the poem is, we discern the largeness of Lucan's purposes.

We come now to **Statius'** *Thebaid*: here we shall consider principally some aspects of the entire structure.[41] But first we must say something on the notion that Statius, unlike Virgil, concentrates his attention on the episode or even moments within the episode; since Statius' narrative art is less distant from Virgil's than Lucan's is, the question becomes more pressing. The notion contains an element of positive truth, but in its negative implications is difficult to establish. Emphatic interconnections and sustained conceptions are apparent throughout the poem (we shall see some instances). One could hardly assert that the poet is interested only in the individual episode or paragraph; to assert that this was his real or main interest seems arbitrary. As was remarked earlier, the existence of strong divisions in itself proves nothing; and in any case there is less large an interval here between Statius and Virgil than is often imagined. The *Aeneid* abounds in episodes, and even paragraphs, which are strongly divided from what adjoins them. Even in the last books Nisus and Euryalus form an obvious instance. More intriguing structurally is the last of the three distinct parts of Book xi; that part Virgil goes out of his way to focus on Camilla. She has a significant role in the action of the poem in this last section only; a long narrative speech

---

[40] The passage becomes more demeaning as it proceeds; even with 444 f. one should not compare v. 241 f. (note the infinitive, and 300), iv. 121, or the sensations at vii. 242–8 and i. 192–4.

[41] See Krumbholz (1955), 247–55; Schetter (1960, cf. 1978, 87–90); Venini (1961); Götting (1969); Aricò (1972), ch. 1; Vessey (1973), esp. 55–67, 317–28; Burck (1971), 60–3, (1979), 300–51, esp. 311–26; see the last for further literature, adding Bonds (1985); Carrara (1986); Kytzler (1986); Heath (1989), 69 f.

about her (535–94)—intrusive and absorbing in itself—directs us to see the following account as above all the last and greatest scene of Camilla's life.[42] It would (as we shall see) be palpably and intolerably false and crude to say negatively that Virgil's real interest is in the section for itself. But similar conclusions have sometimes been reached about the less respected Statius, on the basis of preconceived opinion. There are indeed differences between Virgil and Statius here; but we can appreciate them only if we give full attention to Statius' technique.

Thus it would be mistaken to accuse Statius of incoherence for describing at disproportionate length the Fury (i. 88–122) who fulfils Oedipus' curse on his sons: disproportionate, it would be held, because the actual action of the Fury is not narrated in detail. Statius positively desires to achieve a startling and impressive effect by avoiding a detailed account of possession (such as Virgil's of Allecto and her victims in *Aen.* vii). 'As soon as' the Fury stands on the roof of the palace and so affects it, 'immediately' the brothers feel the wild urges of evil (*ubi ... primum ... protinus*, 123–5). The large relation of Oedipus' curse, the Fury, and the brothers' emotion is entirely clear; and the description of the Fury is by no means out of place at the start of the poem in which she is so important. We can say that Statius also enjoys and dwells on his description in itself, but that is a different matter.[43]

We often find Statius developing his situations in unexpected and fanciful directions, so that we savour and relish the fertility of his wit and his imagination. In this sense, we see a forceful impulse to deflect and for the moment to absorb our vision in the brilliance before our eyes. The impulse and the effects detach us more than in Virgil, and are primarily related to Statius' divergent approach towards greatness of impact. On the other hand, the force of these conscious surprises itself depends on the larger context; to see the poem as a string of separable moments would destroy that force. And the discursive impulse once again combines fruitfully with the strong and powerful impulse towards cohesion.

One example may illustrate some aspects of this: the first part of

[42] On xi generally see Gransden (1984), 154–92; note 155. On Camilla cf. Bremmer and Horsfall (1987), 9, 11.

[43] Cf. Williams (1978), 251. His objection concerning the following episode seems rather slight; and the pre-eminence of Jupiter is in any case very relevant to the scene. Williams's wider view of Statius' structure is more complex.

Book viii. Book vii has ended with the superb engulfment of the prophet Amphiaraus (see p. 74); viii begins with Amphiaraus' appearance in a startled Underworld, Pluto's resultant indignation against Jupiter, and Amphiaraus' aversion of Pluto's anger against himself (1–126). There is obvious effect in the contrast of tone with the end of vii; it intensifies our pleasure in Statius' playfully imaginative treatment here of the situation and the poem's mythological world. Play on death and the Fates, and the scene in the Underworld, are germane enough in topic to the concerns of the poem, and there are many links of theme; but we must relish, in particular, the rich mythological excursiveness in Pluto's aggrieved oration against Jupiter. Our return from this excursiveness to the central story is abrupt, exciting, and momentous. With a dismissive *sed quid ego haec?*, 'But why do I dwell on these things?' (65), Pluto in vengeance on Jupiter bids the Fury Tisiphone cause most of the major events in the succeeding books: the crimes of Tydeus, Capaneus, the brothers, and Creon. We are here given not merely prediction but renewed causation, from the Jupiter of Hell (80–3); the cause is repeatedly referred to hereafter. The relation between the scene and its wider setting is exploited with masterly vigour.[44]

We turn to some aspects of the whole design. Virgil's *Aeneid* is intended to rise in grandeur as it proceeds. For this reason above all, it becomes more Iliadic and less Odyssean as it goes on: the *Iliad* was the grander poem, the war, and death, that preoccupied it the sublimer themes. Virgil stresses that the second half of his epic is 'greater' (vii. 44 f.). Books ix–xii are dominated by war, and by death, and death not simply as a terrible moment but as the close to lives or careers which have been given narrative dimension and shape (Mezentius, Camilla, Turnus). In the first half even the fighting at Troy gives little detail of war or death, aside from the symbolic death of the king; the death of Dido stands above the rest of that half as a death intensely experienced by the reader, and as the end of a life with a tragic pattern. Dido stands apart too because the reader sees the action sympathetically from her perspective, as well as Aeneas'. Such double perspective is

[44] For references to Pluto's design cf. viii. 757, ix. 148 f., xi. 57, 76 f. On the Homeric background to his speech see Juhnke (1972), 123 f., and contrast with 47 Hom. *Od.* xii. 382 f.; note too Virg. *Aen.* vi. 392–410, which also bring in other descents to Hades (cf. Lloyd-Jones (1990*b*)). Such descents, employed excursively in Pluto's speech, are made neatly pertinent in Amphiaraus': he uses them to show by contrast (95–8) the innocence of his own arrival.

vital to the second half of the poem and to the *Iliad*, of little
importance in most of the first half or in the *Odyssey*. Aeneas
himself grows (or is perceived as) grander and less accessible in the
second half, where he is able to do rather than be done to. As the
poem grows greater and grimmer, so it becomes more disquieting;
the two movements are most intimately connected.[45]

Statius takes over this basic form. Narrative of war dominates
the second half of his poem, but not the first: the war against
Thebes begins in vii. Vivid deaths in war, closing an existence
with dimension, are basic to the second half as they are not to the
first, and are prominently placed in the structure, as in Virgil.
Yet within this basic resemblance the differences are large and
significant. Some difference was bound to proceed from the
difference in myth, although all dissimilarity of effect remains a
literary fact; but much pointed difference springs from the poet's
handling in detail and from primary differences in aim.

Remote from Statius is the sense of challenge to the moral
imagination which I think that Virgil's structure offers. Statius
need not himself have read Virgil in this way, but the causes of the
remoteness extend further. Statius' complication of greatness
does not lie primarily in the distribution of moral sympathy.
Rather, while the moral presentation of characters and issues is
relatively firm and unambiguous (not unsubtle), the complexity
resides particularly in the very elaborate interactions of emotion,
greatness, extravagance, and play. Certainly Statius may alter
our responses to his figures, with gradual, abrupt, or fluctuating
turns, particularly through characters' reactions to the deaths of
others in the second half. We may instance his depiction of the
better of the two immoral brothers Polynices, or of the fall of the
successor Creon to tyranny, or of the sudden change from the
Oedipus who cursed his sons (i. 56–87) and rejoiced in the war and
the coming fratricide (viii. 240–58) to the Oedipus who fears and

---

[45] It is revealing to compare the ending of the *Aeneid* with that of the *Orlando Furioso*. For
the particular grandeur, and value, of the *Iliad* see [Long.] 9 and the passages cited by
Bühler (1964), 47f., Prop. ii. 34b. 66; also interesting are Plin. *Ep.* ix. 26. 6f.; *Priap.* 68. 17f. (in
context); Ov. *AA* iii. 413f.; Varr. *Men.* 398 Astbury; and indeed the mode of reference at
Quint. x. 1. 46. How much the *Odyssey* is imitated by poets in lesser genres shows little. One
must not divide the *Aeneid* too starkly into Odyssean and Iliadic halves (cf. Cairns (1989),
177f.); but it would be wrong so to press a somewhat vague resemblance of plot with the
Odyssey as to obscure the immensely greater significance of the *Iliad* by the time we reach
Book xii, or the fundamental importance of war. On the matter of perspective cf. de Jong
(1987), Fowler (1990).

laments the fratricide when it occurs (xi. 105–8, 580–634). The change in Oedipus, which spans the poem, certainly possesses power, and there is psychological subtlety in its paradox (along with a considerable emphasis on ingenuity); but it scarcely disquiets or unsettles our moral judgement.

We see even in Oedipus' moving lament that poetic complication of greatness which Statius takes particularly far. Such complication affects radically the impact of a structure that formally presents a growth in greatness. Still more is this so when the greatness that most concerns the poem is greatness of evil, a kind particularly prone to modification in this poetry. The very climax of the poem, the brothers' slaying of each other in a duel, neither awes nor disturbs like the slaying of Turnus in the duel that ends the *Aeneid*. Characters and passage are driven by a compelling energy of hatred; yet much of the wickedness appears at this climax through a twisted ingenuity in the brothers and in the author. At the last, Eteocles, while dying, falls prematurely in pretence so as to be able to kill his brother in trickery. He accomplishes this while Polynices despoils him; Polynices is doing so as part of his own blithely and perversely immoral triumph and to pain his still conscious rival (xi. 552–67). The author's phrasing makes us savour his cunningly achieved extremes. Eteocles *sponte ruit*, 'falls of his own will'—the oxymoron is relished; *fraudemque supremam / in media iam morte parat*, 'and he contrives his last deceit in the midst of his death'—the enjambment gives elegance to this ultimate consistency and to the physical trick.[46] A line is also begun by the gloating *dum videt*, 'while he can see', that ends Polynices' speech of 557–60: the enjambment makes us enjoy the poet's cleverness in devising this devilish obliquity. The poet's writing and treatment of his theme deeply modify and complicate the shape of his structure, and give the poem its most fundamental unity.[47]

The most intriguing and distinctive part of the structure is the

[46] *sponte ruit* turns round Virgil's *ad terram non sponte fluit* (*Aen.* xi. 828), and converts to quite different purpose Lucan's paradoxical *sponte cadit* (iv. 642, of Antaeus; note also *Theb.* vi. 803). *in media iam morte* also gives a fresh tang to Virgil, cf. Venini's note. With both brothers Statius' narrative greatly sharpens Euripides', itself far from simple (*Phoen.* 1407–22); note Mueller-Goldingen (1985), 216 f.

[47] It is significant that at the close of the poem, narrative fades into presentation of the exhausted but hopeful writer; the tone should be contrasted with that at the end of the *Metamorphoses*. *Praeteritio* has set tragedy at a certain distance (xii. 797–809, cf. Ov. *Met.* viii. 533–5), and it has somewhat diverted the satisfying and noble ending we looked for.

first half of the poem. Statius shows various concerns: to make the two halves cohere tightly, to exploit, play on, and sometimes almost to transgress the interval between them, and to move sometimes startlingly far from his theme. The interaction of these impulses is often elaborate, and none must be obscured.

The main part of the first half Statius' design relates still more basically to the second half than is done in the *Aeneid* itself. That main part presents the happenings that lead up to the war; these happenings are obviously part of the same single action as the war itself, while Aeneas' arrival, and his war, in Italy are potentially distinct. Much of the first half is concerned with why, whether, and when the war will occur, while Virgil keeps that principally for the beginning of his second half. We are introduced by Statius to the characters who will act and die in the second half long before that half itself, while the principal figures of Virgil's second half, Aeneas apart, make little appearance before it; the very sequence of deaths in Statius' second half wins a particular neatness from this preparation.

Even the funeral games of Book vi are more tightly related than are, on the surface of story, the games of *Aeneid* v. Of the competitors in *Aeneid* v only Nisus and Euryalus will be important in the second half (Mnestheus has little substance), and the relation of the games themselves to the rest is not made for the most part palpable. In Statius we see the chief Argive heroes in extended action, and we are often pointed explicitly forward, and the resemblance and especially the contrast with the coming war is repeatedly dwelt on.[48] Particularly significant here is death, dominant in the second half, often close in the games but averted. Both the cohesion of the poem and its ascending shape are emphatically established in moments themselves pointed and effective. A striking instance of such a moment occurs when Polynices almost perishes in the chariot-race. The poet exclaims:

> quis mortis, Thebane, locus, nisi dura negasset
> Tisiphone! quantum poteras dimittere bellum!
> te Thebe, fraterque palam, te plangeret Argos ...   (513–15)

What a place for death was that, Theban, had not the stern Fury refused! How great a war could you have dispersed! You would have

---

[48] Cf. e.g. vi. 457f. (where read *credas: / is*: Statius is turning round Virg. *Georg.* iii. 112), 730, 735–7, 828–33, 905–23; and cf. also 379–82, 934–6.

been mourned by Thebes and, in public, your brother, and mourned by
Argos ...

The poet delights in separating and almost conjoining the parts of
his poem, as he celebrates, paradoxically, the imagined death,
and builds up in an unfulfilled condition the standard forms of
pathos at death.[49] Place is emphasized in the lines, not least in the
pointed *Thebane*, 'Theban', and its juxtaposition with *locus*, 'place';
the different spheres of the poem are related. The thought also
drives in how separate is Nemea, where the Argives are delayed,
from the poem's prime spheres of action.

Statius toys with bringing his two halves close, in matter and in
the course of events, when in Book ii Tydeus massacres a Theban
ambush of fifty (482–743). Particularized and accumulated death
springs to the fore, and we are plunged into the conventions of
martial narrative in epic. The fighting is insistently presented in
relation to the war to come, both as a foretaste of it, and as falling
short of its extremes of grandeur.[50] We seem to be rising towards
the prime matter of the poem; but there are to be two 'surprises'.
Firstly, despite the urge of the poem and of Tydeus towards war,
the shape of the poem keeps that outcome a long way off, above all
through the extended part where the Argive army is kept at
Nemea (iv. 646–vi (vii. 104)). The impetus is teasingly frustrated,
and the reader's sensations are articulated by characters in the
poem.[51] Secondly, the result of the war will be utterly different
from the extension of the present fighting that Tydeus imagines.
Tydeus' side will be vanquished, for all his mighty feats; the Fury
and his own zeal for war (note ix. 6) will carry him beyond
heroism to horrific wickedness and to the alienation of the goddess who has so ardently favoured him (cf. p. 93). Her words to
him here are full of irony, conscious and unconscious: *iam pone
modum, nimiumque secundis / parce deis*, 'now set a limit and spare the
gods who are all too favourable to you' (ii. 688f.). The various

---

[49] Cf. vii. 695–7, x. 503–7 with Williams's note.

[50] See esp. ii. 699–703 (cf. 659), 732–5, iii. 160f., 206–13, 237, iv. 601 f.; cf. viii. 664–9,
677–9. *bello* at iii. 355 (in a magnificent period) should not necessarily be thought exaggerated, cf. 395, ii. 546; iii. 356 remains significant.

[51] This occurs in prominent places structurally: see esp. the start of vii, the end of v
(740–5), and the end of iii, where resolution, delay, and irony are mingled as if casually. In
vii. 1 Damsté's *ita* is attractive, since a notion of the games as *primordia belli* would suit ill with
Jupiter's perspective. Either an internal or external object would be possible with *cunctantes*
(Smolenaars's note does not distinguish).

extremities of the second half stand out all too clearly from this perspective. The poet in this passage exploits and turns proximity and contrast, intently conscious of his design, yet treating it with complexity and daring.[52]

Questions of excursion and cohesion arise particularly in relation to the part of the first half spent at Nemea. This part, marked out by an invocation (iv. 649–51), brings in Opheltes, the child who is killed by a snake and honoured in the funeral games, and his nurse Hypsipyle, once queen of Lemnos, who for the greater part of Book v (49–498) narrates her history and the colourful story of the Lemnian women. Not only Opheltes but Hypsipyle had long been connected with the Argive expedition, most notably in Euripides' *Hypsipyle*; but it is none the less striking that Statius should allot the episode so much space. Little obstacle is posed to unity by the Argives' initial search for water, which Hypsipyle ends, by the events that follow the death of Opheltes and entangle Hypsipyle and the Argives, by the funeral games themselves, or indeed by the notion of delay as such, which is a standard aspect of epic narrative (stressed in the introduction, iv. 646–51, and at the end, vii. 1ff.). We must consider rather Opheltes' death and Hypsipyle's tale.

Myth gave Opheltes his alternative name Archemorus ('beginning death') because his death was the sign and start of those fated for the Argives.[53] Statius dwells on the significance of the name (v. 738f.), and more widely on the connection of the deaths. Pointed contrasts and links are openly displayed. So the passage quoted above on Polynices finishes *Archemori maior colerere sepulcro*, 'you would have been worshipped as a greater divinity than Archemorus at his tomb' (vi. 517). The glorious outcome of Opheltes' death is contrasted with Polynices' dreadful end. Yet we feel

---

[52] In 688f. *nimium* on the surface means a strengthened 'very', cf. xii. 684, *Silv.* iii. 3. 25, the paradoxical *parce* 'do not press too hard' (ix. 813f. is somewhat different). On *modum* note both i. 41 *immodicum irae* and viii. 757 *plus*. One should observe the spelling-out of Hom. *Il.* [x]. 509–11 by Sch. x. 509 (bT). The whole point of the speech is spoiled if we make Minerva a mere personification of Tydeus' mind; *Tydeus'* mind would be very unlikely to work so, the difference of narrative technique from Homer's does not in any case suffice to impose this understanding, and one should observe 686 *dignata* and 687f. Cf. Lewis (1936), 52; Mulder on 687f.; Vessey (1973), 147; Feeney (1991), 365f. On the intervention one may notice Sch. Hom. *Il.* iv. 398 (bT). For reference forward to Tydeus' cannibalism, see, besides i. 41f. and viii. 71f., iii. 544f.

[53] Cf. Bacch. 9. 10–94; Eur. *Hyps.* fr. 60. ii. 15f. Bond, Cockle. On delay in epic cf. Reichel (1990).

the striking ingenuity that combines them. The bitter lament of
Opheltes' mother (one in a series of such laments in the poem)
explicitly connects itself with the future lamentations of Theban
mothers (vi. 172f.), and marks her lament and his death as the
primitias ... lacrimarum et caedis, 'the first-fruits of tears and
slaughter' (vi. 146f.). Yet at the same time it stresses the surprise
of the connection. Statius both joins his material firmly and
makes us feel its drastic diversity. The space, pathos, and tenderness which the poet devotes to the little child make his
oustanding death in the first half; it makes a forceful contrast to
the deaths in war, and suits the opposition of the two halves. But
the death goes further than one should expect in the direction of
its difference. One may think of Dido's death, different from
most deaths in *Aen.* vii–xii as a suicide and for love, but noble
and magnificent as this death is not: the very pathos of the death
springs from Opheltes' littleness. We are shown here the
boldness of Statius' range.

Much more challenging structurally is the narrative of Hypsipyle. Given Statius' eagerness generally to join in story the first
half of his poem to the second, it must be thought notable that this
long digression has in plot no connection with Thebes. The digression on the Argive Linus and Coroebus in i. 557–668 is also
separate in plot, but it is shorter, and its appearance is modelled
on that of Virgil's digression on Cacus (*Aen.* viii. 185–275), which is
equally separate in plot: in theme both those digressions are to
be compared and also contrasted with aspects of the main story
in their poems—but that is another question. The model for
Hypsipyle's narrative, often alluded to by Statius, is Aeneas'
description of the fall of Troy (and of his wanderings): in that
description, as in Odysseus' account of his travels, the relation to
the main story in plot is fundamental. Furthermore, Statius
openly declines to connect the narration causally with the principal story and make it add in itself to the Argives' delay. Hypsipyle
suggests that the Argives, who are preparing to depart for their
war, will have no time to listen to her; but their leader explains
that it will take a long time to organize their troops in such terrain,
and urges her to speak while they do so (v. 36–47). The poet here
emphasizes the separateness of the story, and pleasingly combines
practicality with a highly artificial setting for the telling of a tale.
What the length of the narration is connected with causally is the

secondary story of Opheltes: as Hypsipyle talks, her abandoned charge is killed (500f., 626–8). The Chinese boxes of story, and the entry of unrelated myth through a character's narration, must recall the procedures of Ovid in the *Metamorphoses*, a work where connection by story is treated with supreme mannerism.[54] Statius must wish us to be conscious of the audacity of his excursion on the level of story.

On the level of theme and subject-matter we see connection, contrast, and difference. The graphic descriptions of slaughter in 200–64 (cf. 159–63), and the concern with frenzied perversion and with piety, create evident connections with the rest of the poem, and particularly with its second half.[55] Even if we denied the significance of thematic links in ancient poetry, we would still have to concede that the episode felt at home in the world of the poem; that concession ultimately opens an adequate path for the investigation of unity in other areas than those of plot. But the killings, of fathers, husbands, and children, are executed, most abnormally for this poem, by women. Again this goes beyond the simple differentiation of the two halves; Statius gives the heaviest weight to the paradox, and extracts from it the fullest colour. So he conjoins murder and a confused conjugal embrace (206–16); or he creates a probing opposition between a fierce mother, who enjoins on her daughter the killing of the mother's son, and the daughter herself, who is overcome by feminine tenderness but obeys (226–36); or he produces appalling and distinctive paradox from the placing of words, as in *barbara ludentem fodiebat Epopea mater*, 'in her brutality Epopeus' mother was stabbing her child as he played' (225). The whole account explores, though in very Statian manner, areas remote from the rest of the poem: it both coheres with the rest of the poem and moves boldly away from it.

In **Juvenal** too we see disunity and cohesion designedly interwoven, but the satirist's treatment is, on the surface, more

---

[54] For narrations connected with the narrators themselves cf. e.g. *Met.* v. 269–678, xi. 291–345, xiii. 738–897, xiv. 130–53, 167–440.

[55] The descriptions of killing are quite unlike Valerius' account (in ii. 82–310; see ii. 216–41). At v. 37 *et* must I think link *arma* (not *arma vocant*) with *arma* in 31 (despite Götting (1969), 110 n. 64): the Argives like the Lemnians are concerned with fighting, and the war robs them of time to listen. *et* is unlikely to join on to the question, and the second half of the line is insufficiently different for an *et . . . -que*. The link also makes a contrast for the reader in the type of fighting.

defiant, and more complicated in regard to genre.[56] It also extends further. Epic and tragedy on the largest scale follow a shape defined by a narrative pattern. Juvenal's satires, far shorter than epics, and for the most part bound to no story, delight in disconcerting shifts of concern. They do so on every level from the immediate flow of individual or consecutive sentences to the poem as a whole. So, for example, in the sentence 12. 98–110 the poet talks of the extravagant sacrifices that are promised by those who desire a place in a rich person's will; they regret that they can procure no elephants. The sentence then expatiates on the keeping of elephants by the great alone, now and in history; it runs on unpredictably, colourfully and interminably. Later its rhetorical point emerges: the elephants, like the hunters of legacies, will be slaves only to the great (or those supposedly great).[57] But the reader should also enjoy the appearance of quirky development, and the eventual union of surprise and integration. On the scale of whole poems, Juvenal is often eager to startle, and to end in a decidedly different area from that which had seemed to constitute the subject. This is in itself an inheritance from the genre, and advertises its vivacity; it is enhanced by the perspicuity with which Juvenal often seems to divide and head his material. Such effects, precisely by puzzling, are to draw us in Juvenal into obtrusive awareness of the strange genre, and into reflection on his meaning.[58]

No poem can simply be taken as a pattern for the rest; but poem 4 is a particularly blatant example of Juvenal's techniques. It appears to devote itself to the purchase of a huge fish by Crispinus, a luxurious upstart (allegedly), who rose under Domitian. But after 27 lines it turns noisily and devotes itself to Domitian's own response to the gift of an enormous turbot. (37–71, the fisherman

[56] On structure in Juvenal, and 4 in particular, see Stegemann (1913); Helmbold (1951); Helmbold and O'Neil (1956, 1959); O'Neil (1960); Kenney (1962), 30 f.; Heilmann (1967); McDevitt (1968); Griffith (1969); Stein (1970); Adamietz (1972); Kilpatrick (1973); Townend (1973), 153–8; Anderson (1982*b* and *c*); Adamietz (1986*b*), 299–301; Flintoff (1990); Adamietz (1986*b*) gives further literature on particular poems.

[57] This point is, I think, needed to give proper sharpness to the second half of 114. *siquidem* in 107 naturally justifies the assertion *nulli . . . servire paratum / privato*. 103–10 concern indeed the unavailability of elephants, but even as imitation of the *captatores* would still seem strangely protracted. The essential procedures are nothing rare in Juvenal: cf. e.g. the unexpected turns in 2. 149–57.

[58] On the satiric tradition cf. Griffith (1969). Hor. *Sat.* i. 2 and 3 form obvious examples; note that there the decisive shifts of direction spring formally from interruption (i. 2. 35 f., 3. 19 f.).

finds the turbot and brings it to Domitian; 72–119, there being no plate large enough for it, Domitian summons his advisers, whom Juvenal describes; 119–49, the advisers flatter, a decision is reached, they are dismissed.) The surprise is ostentatious, and is set up energetically from the start of the poem; though distinct in its effect, it belongs with other surprises and delays and changes of direction in Juvenal. Particularly notable is the change of focus at 2. 65 ff. There Juvenal marks, in one sense, a rise in subject, from the combination of perversity and allegiance to philosophy to the combination of perversity and lofty birth: *sed quid / non facient alii, cum tu multicia sumas, / Cretice ... ?*, 'what will others not do when *you*, Creticus, put on effeminate transparent clothing?'.[59] On another level, the satire now becomes particularly comic. In 4, Juvenal likewise ascends in social scale, and also in vice:

> qualis tunc epulas ipsum gluttisse putamus
> induperatorem ... ? (28 f.)

What feasts must we think were gobbled down at that time by the emperor himself?

The portentous archaism *induperatorem*, 'emperor', engrossing the whole first half of the line, marks the ostensible rise in grandeur, but with obvious comedy and bathos. The same applies to the invocation of the Muses which follows. This moves from a grandiose *incipe, Calliope*, 'Calliope, begin' (34), to an entertaining and impudent bathos; the bathos appears in the manner towards the goddesses, at once polite and insulting, and in the treatment of genre (this is no grand epic, but truth, *res vera agitur*). The device of invocation, which here so firmly suggests an opening, palpably and cheekily draws attention to the structural audacity, and points the change to a manner displayed both as epic and as non-epic.[60]

---

[59] The emphasis with Creticus is not on philosophy, and he is probably differentiated from its hypocritical devotees: *sed* most naturally marks a distinction, he is contrasted in the openness of his behaviour, and 83 f. (after 79–82) suggest that he is not one of the previous group. 77, then, probably does not make it clear that he is a Stoic; he is connected with the *Stoicidae* through Domitian's revival of the Lex Julia, but is not therefore made one of them.

[60] For such obtrusion note 15. 72, which marks a return after only a sentence of digression; there it is the emphasis itself that is the audacity. The effect here is only heightened by Virg. *Ecl.* 6. 13 *pergite, Pierides*, after a clear introduction. The joke in 35 f. (which I must confess to liking) turns of course on the status of *puellae*, a word not high in register and unsuitable for addressing goddesses, but cheekily presented as praise for

The playful rise bears a strong and important relation to what follows. In the main section of the poem there is a sufficiently obvious disparity between the apparent pretension of manner and the low and banally real subject-matter. Juvenal is also exposing the pretentious and misplaced pomp of Domitian and the unreality and falsity of the environment of flattery that encloses him. So *itur ad Atriden*, 'he proceeds to the son of Atreus' (65), not only plays with epic but also derides the contemptible Domitian, no epic king, yet infinitely vain. And yet Juvenal's own narrative achieves, not exactly elevation, but startling breadth and intensity: it portrays not just a ludicrous incident but a political world, and especially (what mattered most to Roman historiography) the relations of the emperor to the great. Between the two colourful and comic pieces of narration (37–72, 119–49) comes the catalogue of advisers. The catalogue itself mocks grander poetry; but it gives a depiction of this world that is wide in range, piercing, for all the sprightly humour, and more forceful in its political engagement than is usual in this poet.[61] Ideas of war and death run through it, but to display either unheroic and sinister violence or unheroic and untruthful want of courage. The frivolity of the main subject is given a further twist at the close, where Domitian's absurdities are preferred to his terrible slaughter of aristocrats (150–2).

The whole form of narrative, with its grandiose connotations, Juvenal not only contorts again and again on a small scale into the discourse of satire, but also handles on a large scale with a conscious lack of proportion and of effective story-telling. So the long catalogue of Domitian's 'friends' soon issues in their dismissal: the narrative is deliberately lamed, the satire pointed.

The moment of ascent at 28–33 has thus a very rich significance for the poem. For all the strong and obvious connection of the two parts of the poem in their basic theme, we should particularly appreciate the differences. The first part strikes us as essentially limited and self-contained rather than pregnant with political

females who must have aged (cf. Plin. *NH* ii. 17). *induperator* (cf. Skutsch on Enn. *Ann.* 78) is found in Ennius and Lucretius, and at Juv. 10. 138; its application to the post-Republican *princeps* is particularly striking.

[61] There is little humour in 78–93. 98 and 106 advertise the actual genre. As to the particular relation with Statius' lost poem see Tandoi (1985); and, for 'Probus', Billanovich and Monti (1979), 373–95; Reeve (1984); Jones (1986). However, the metrical irregularity in the second quoted line is most disquieting.

suggestion: it is significant that Crispinus appears at 108 f. merely as one not particularly notable figure in the catalogue. The first part has no epic associations; its manner is direct and suggests invective more than it does the relative coolness of voice in the narrative.[62] In retrospect, the picture of Crispinus accommodates itself into the larger portrayal of those wicked times; and the very notion of ascent fits into the large and evident symmetry whereby Crispinus' graver misdeeds are touched on, and quitted, at the start, Domitian's touched on at the very end. The poem actually coheres effectively; but it has also a dynamic structure in which the movement from the part that emerges as a prelude brings out sharply the character of the rest. That structure thrusts genre into the centre of our view; the results are intriguing, discordant, and manifold.

The authors of this period are far from indifferent to structure, to which their culture was highly sensitive; some of them, however, treat structure in a manner self-consciously unstraightforward. We have seen how unsatisfactory it would be either to play down their audacity or to make it prove a work lacking in cohesion. We have seen repeatedly the cohesion of the boldest works, and the complicated relationship in particular passages between cohesion and excursion. We have also observed the importance of overall design, and of decisive movements within a work. Large differences have also appeared, which relate, in part, to genre; the different presuppositions of prose and poetry are particularly striking. Connections too have been seen between genres, even in large design: so in the pattern of rising greatness that we have dwelt on, with its manifold variety of treatment and the very different ways in which greatness is complicated. It has also emerged that structure is an indissoluble element of a work's force and nature, not simply an abstract requirement to be satisfied; nor can we separate radically the many and interwoven scales on which it operates. It is for these reasons that in structure no less than in the detail of passages the essential character of each author appears.

---

[62] Note the metaphor from drama at the start. Even if Courtney were right about 17, the poet would be dissociating himself from epic; but *perhibent* must refer to the proposition, for to use it of a mode of expression (not a name) would so far as I can see be unexampled.

6

THE GODS IN MYTHOLOGICAL
POETRY

WE have considered some important aspects of these writers' art, and of differences and relations between writers and genres. This last section of the book will seek to provide the discussion with more dimension and substance, and to give a solider and richer sense of writers and genres, in regard to the book's primary areas of concern. Our attention will now be concentrated almost entirely on the 'highest' genres in poetry and prose, on epic, tragedy, philosophy, and history; in prose we shall confine ourselves somewhat less rigorously. We shall mostly consider sizeable but delimited episodes or passages, and shall view these authors handling themes of special significance for our inquiry. It must be stressed that for the most part the section is not at all attempting a balanced or synoptic survey of how the writers treat these areas. We shall rather be watching their art at work and seeing some memorable and suggestive instances of what these genres can do on these subjects. Still less is the section attempting to outline the views of the authors on these topics. Although we will often be concerned by the relation of art and thought, our predominant interest here is in art; and the authors' actual opinions will often appear less readily accessible than might be supposed. Finally, although some links, conclusions, and generalizations will be suggested, it is my hope that the reader will principally feel characteristics and differences through immersion in the successive passages and the discussion of these; the preceding chapters will make the more evident the focuses of our interest.

The first pair of chapters will see poetry and prose at their most widely divergent. The gods as treated in mythological poetry furnished the most spectacular ingredient of that unreality which was and was said to be a crucial aspect of high poetry. They mark out more than any other area of content the gap between elevated poetry and prose. They indicate too very strikingly the gap between philosophy, as handled by Seneca, and history, as handled by Tacitus; again approaches to reality and truth are of prime significance. Together with the difference between poetry and prose here in relation to truth go differences in relation to greatness. The gods in serious prose are supremely exalted beings; they are essentially treated as an object, and a source, of grandeur. In tragedy and epic, for all the connections between greatness and unreality, the unreality of their gods is strongly conjoined with a conspicuous element of lightness, of grandeur modified and mingled with detached play. On this element particular emphasis will be laid: such play, and such complexity, are in general especially important and are taken especially far in high poetry, and they form some of its most distinctive features.

The second pair of chapters will see poetry and prose, and philosophy and history, at their closest. The theme of valiant death brings us to the heart of the ideals and the moral world which these genres present to us; and it shows their grandeur and their evocation of greatness in spirit at their strongest and most unqualified. The chapter considering high poetry on death will select much more distortingly than that considering high poetry on the gods, and will single out passages where grandeur and sublimity appear most unmixedly. Even so, the complications so characteristic of poetry will prove by no means absent; this too is revealing.

The whole scheme should thus enable us to gain a feel for genres at their furthest distance and at a point of central and significant convergence. But our interest is by no means confined to the broadest aspects of the genres and of greatness and reality. We are as ever much interested in the individual writers; and the handling of greatness and reality is here to be perceived through the detail of each extract. This detail includes the specific aspects of wit and extravagance, which we can now see in larger contexts of passage and of content, and the aspect of structure and form, which we can now observe more fully on a circumscribed but substantial scale.

We shall pursue a little the matter of unreality in the divine world of these poets. The theological world of high poetry, anthropomorphic and vigorously polytheistic, derives its origin from epics 800 years old. For our purposes, one need not describe the treatment of the gods in the most important models for epic, Homer, Virgil, Ovid; nor need we here attempt to recover the beliefs of educated Romans at this period. The central and simple point, that in these poets' gods there is a large element of palpable untruth, emerges very plainly and fully from the remaining literature as a whole. It is not only that the presentation of the gods by these genres is often treated in prose and low poetry as conspicuously unreal, unreality itself being seen as an important feature of high poetry. From the other writing of this epoch it is also abundantly clear that, whatever allowance one makes for conventions in prose and so forth, there was much in this world of the gods which was remote from anything a well-educated person might think likely. The next chapter will make that sufficiently apparent. If a well-educated person held any firm convictions about the nature of divinities, the non-mythological literature indicates that those convictions would probably be derived from philosophy, or else, though this is more uncertain, from the religion of the state. That literature also indicates that opinions thought possibly true would flow from the same sources. What is very improbable is that there would seem any likelihood in notions of gods with all the less edifying features of men, with amours and quarrels, with spite, jealousy, and cunning, with tears and foibles. And yet such notions are seized on with relish by the poets. Nor would all the physical fantasy linked with these gods seem any more plausible. Morally nobler elements are certainly present in the high poetry too; and the poets sometimes make some use of philosophical language and ideas. But there can be no doubt that on its surface the world of the divine would strike readers as in many ways markedly remote from any possible reality. Beneath that surface there may (conceivably) hide a vision of divinity which the author wishes us to believe true; but the surface is in itself a vital aspect of the poetry which a delving for views must not too quickly discard.[1]

---

[1] One or two obvious passages may be mentioned which bear on the unreal element in the divine world of high poetry: [Long.] 9. 7 f.; Plut. *Aud. Poet.* 16a–17c; Petr. 118. 6; Juv. 1. 7–9; *Aetna* 74–93 (85–92); Plin. *NH* ii. 17. Quintilian and Plin. *Ep.* i–ix are particularly rewarding for the outlook on the divine they unostentatiously imply. Some interesting passages in Quintilian: i. 1. 1, 10. 46, 12. 18; ii. 16. 12; v. 11. 42; vi. *praef.* 4; vii. 3. 4 f.; xii. 2. 2. It is the quietness of Pliny's attitude that is most significant (on i. 5. 5 note Quint. x. 7. 14); but v. 11. 3, vi. 16. 3, etc., show that we have to do with no simple literary or social exclusion of the divine. Cf. Bütler (1970), ch. 1. Even Martial assists (e.g. iv. 21 implies that assertive atheism is uncommon). Also noteworthy is the parody of poetic theology in comic prose. So in the *Apocolocyntosis*, humour is significantly obtained from combining poetic matter and historical manner (5. 1, etc.); significantly too, the association is used to mock the pretensions

Seneca's prose and verse contrast strikingly in this respect. In the prose he condemns poetic theology firmly (it was not a feared rival, but a traditional object of scorn in some lines of philosophical tradition). Sometimes he can suggest an urbane tolerance; but the strong rejection underneath is clear. At *NQ* ii. 44. 1 the idea of Jupiter's different types of thunderbolt, used by Ovid, befits only the freedom conventional for poets, *poeticam istud licentiam decet*; the larger context makes clear his utter contempt for the very conceptions, fundamental to epic, of Jupiter hurling thunderbolts or holding council.[2] At *Vit. Beat.* 26. 6 Jupiter simply tolerates indifferently the absurd tales of him in poets, *ineptias poetarum*; the sentence heaps them up in hectic confusion so as to ridicule and disapprove. Still more hostile is the play at *Brev. Vit.* 16. 5 on *poetarum furor*, the madness of poets (inspired or monstrous). Yet Seneca's own poetry revels in mythological deity; whenever it was that he wrote it, he had been concerned with philosophy all his adult life. It is particularly interesting that, even after an unusual moment in the *Phaedra* when the Nurse authoritatively declares the mythological Venus and Cupid to be a fiction (195–203), the poet in the following chorus charms us by his exquisite handling of that fiction, and runs his fingers delightedly and delightfully through tales of divine infatuation. The metamorphoses of amorous Jupiter deplored at *Vit. Beat.* 26. 6 are exulted in here (299–308). The prose probably distorts Seneca's attitude to poetry, as we should expect (see pp. 15–18): we may assume he was often ready to enjoy the gods that supposedly dismayed him. But the prose also makes it obvious that they were in their immediate appearance far removed from his beliefs; and it makes it seem unlikely that he saw in them a promising disguise for philosophical truth.[3]

of history to truth. The type of unreality that concerns us here can readily be separated from any 'reality', i.e. plausibility within the fictional world, created by physical detail; that notion has in any case relatively little potential importance in the divine world of these epics. On the gods in high poetry of our period generally see Schönberger (1965); Burck (1979), 230–7, 286–93, 334–43; Liebeschuetz (1979), ch. 4; Billerbeck (1986); Colish (1990), 252–89; and now above all the excellent work of Feeney (1991). No bibliography can of course be given for Roman religion in general, but MacMullen (1981) may be found a stimulating point to begin.

[2] The notion of grades of thunderbolts Seneca uses himself in his tragedies (*Thy.* 1082). With his attitude to the Etruscans here, not the poets, compare and contrast Cornut. *Theol.* 35 (p. 76 Lang) on οἱ παλαιοί, 'men of old', including poets.

[3] At *Ben.* iv. 8. 1, a highly abnormal passage, the cosmological allegory of Hercules is ascribed to *nostri*, not embraced as an opinion (West (1983), 193f., connects *SVF* i. 514); it only appears at all through the special needs of the argument. It would in any case offer

The contrast of the ode in the *Phaedra* with the Nurse's declaration is scarcely accidental; it brings out the distance of the imagined world from reality, and so enhances the lightness of the ode. Epics can disclose sudden vistas of a philosophical universe which give a teasing or haunting emphasis within the poem to the fictitious qualities of its normal framework. Such moments draw inspiration from earlier epic (Virg. *Aen.* vi. 742–51, parts of Ov. *Met.* xv. 75–478, and also AR i. 496–502). Statius has a brief one at *Theb.* vi. 360–4, where Apollo sings in heaven on a series of issues in natural philosophy. The poet firmly contrasts with this song Apollo's common songs on the deities of myth (358f.). The present song considers the universe in highly philosophical terms. So Statius begins *tunc aperit quis fulmen agat, quis sidera ducat / spiritus*, 'then he disclosed by what spirit the lightning is impelled, the stars led onward' (360f.). This directing 'spirit' is a Stoic conception, craftily delayed so that one could think at first of mythological deities as subject. In immediate contrast Apollo himself then exhibits the most drastically mythical divinity; he speaks of his enslavement to a mortal and his subjugation to Jupiter and the Fates (375f.), and he weeps for a mortal favourite (384). By the momentary fissure the poet brings out the separate and unreal nature of his divine world.[4]

Weightier is Virtue's speech to Scipio in Silius (xv. 69–120). Man's mind is there presented as divine in origin; to follow Virtue, in accordance with that origin and the gods' intention, brings one to heaven (69–89).[5] The thought is thoroughly philosophical; the

little comfort to Stoic interpretation of the tragedies. On the tone of the chorus cf. Henry and Walker (1966), 232f. Zwierlein on 203 wishes to save Venus from the demythologization, but it seems forced to me not to refer *Veneris numen* to the goddess; *Erycina* in 199 is part of the fable. Lucr. iv. 1058 if anything supports this approach; cf. Brown (1987), 200. In *Vit. Beat.* 26. 6 note the twist *si tales deos credidissent*.

[4] *soles* in 362 are far removed from Apollo; 364 picturesquely suggests Epicurean physics: cf. Lucr. v. 536–8, 552f., and also Epic. 26. 41. 21–44 Arrighetti. For such strings of topics see Shackleton Bailey (1952), 309f.; Statius unkindly deprives us of a special opportunity to learn the answers. Tradition makes us too expect mythological gods to sing on mythological gods, cf. VF v. 692f., Stat. *Silv.* iv. 2. 55f. (with Coleman); more widely, Hes. *Theog.* 36–52. The contrast with myth subsists whether or not we suppose that on this occasion Apollo first sings briefly of the gods (Housman (1972), 1206f.). I agree with Delz (1983) that that idea is unattractive, but cannot follow him in taking *orsa deo* 358 with what precedes: the non-terrestrial element in 360–4 is too conspicuously placed for the sequence of thought to work effectively. One should rather postulate that a verse was lost but of different content: it would indicate in some way the novelty of the present performance.

[5] In 88f. rhetoric and even sense seem to make against Delz's punctuation.

moral has significance for the whole poem, but theologically we feel the appearance of a decidedly different world and idiom. The world of the poem normally upholds the traditional barrier between men and gods, earth and heaven: those who defy or approach it are excitingly audacious. Scipio himself has a quite different claim to kinship with the gods: he was begotten by Jupiter in the form of a snake. This radically mythological notion is recalled directly after this passage (138–48). The foreign aspect to Virtue's speech strengthens its impact. Far from supplying the theological foundation for the treatment of the gods in the poem, the passage stands impressively apart, and acquires its weight by emerging, largely, into a less unreal and imaginary presentation of the divine.[6]

Such passages make it the less likely that the poets are predominantly concerned to show in their gods their understanding of divine reality. One might seek to turn their gods, not just their personifications, into demythologized allegories, as some philosophizing writers did with Homer (above all cosmologically). The details would present many difficulties for any wholesale conversion; but even if we persisted, we should not be able to leave behind the surface of the poetry, on which the authors so richly enjoy the anthropomorphic and mythological elements of their divine world. Nor ought we to say that Statius, for example, is only truly interested in personifications and Jupiter. That view would seem evidently false to Statius' poetry of the divine, and would involve various unsatisfactory assumptions: that serious features are the only ones that matter in Statius, that seriousness of impact must be related to likelihood, that it is the ability of a god to cause events which establishes his importance in the poem.[7] All this does not do justice to Statius' pleasure in his prominent,

[6] See on the episode especially Heck (1970). Note on Scipio Sen. *Ep.* 86. 1; the story of the snake is naturally scorned by the historian, Liv. xxvi. 19. 7. Hercules, Bacchus, and the Dioscuri in 78–83 go a little way towards accommodating the passage into mythological epic, but the examples are common in intellectual prose, e.g. Cic. *ND* ii. 62; Tac. *Ann.* iv. 38. 5 (speech); they appear to somewhat different effect in xvii. 645–53. Similarly, the personifications link up with Fides in ii and xiii, but principally of course with Xen. *Mem.* ii. 1. 21–34 (Prodicus B2 DK). One may note that vii. 748–50 does not really infringe the norms of the poem: cf. Val. Max. viii. 15. 7. In Statius the episode of Menoeceus (below) is much less philosophical in presentation than this passage. Valerius has nothing so striking; but note iii. 377–82.

[7] Cf. esp. Lewis (1936), 49–56; note also Schetter (1960), 26–9. As for allegory, it is obvious enough that it was no uncontroversial approach, cf. e.g. Sen. *Ben.* i. 3–4 (p. 17 f.); Plut. *Aud. Poet.* 19e–f; [Long.] 9. 7.

colourful, and frequently entertaining deities, to the pathos he can arouse with them, or indeed to his fascination with gods that are pleading and impotent.

The poets savour and exploit radical anthropomorphism and polytheistic conflict; but they are also interested in elevated images of Jupiter, in moral personifications, and in imposing suggestions of the order of the world (often inextricable from mythology). One need not deny them some concern to represent in their gods divine or at any rate general truth, particularly with regard to human morality. What one must contend positively is that their art feeds not least on the elements remote from possible truth. Unreality itself apart, there are various reasons for this. They delight in the poetic complexity and vitality which they can draw from the divine sphere, in its elaborate relations to sublimity and play. Man-like godhead, the colour of individual deities, and the intricacies of Olympian society offer rich opportunities for paradox and liveliness. Gods also present the furthest extremes; and the mythological relation of gods and men allows especially bold handling of reality and greatness. This divine world had given much to other poets; it is exciting to see how these poets make from its very much their own kind of poetry.

We shall now watch them doing this, in some particular cases, as we consider some specific episodes. They are not chosen, we may reiterate, so as to give a complete or representative picture of the poets' treatment of the gods. The passages in our first part especially will exhibit some of the lighter aspects of that treatment, which have received less than their due of emphasis and appreciation; but some of them will also show strikingly the forceful and elaborate interaction of these with weightier, or darker, aspects to create a complicated and absorbing impact. We begin with a scene less mixed; it illustrates well the poets' enjoyment of their deities, in their individuality and in the complications, personal and conceptual, of epic polytheism. **Valerius** does not in general greatly indulge his gods with exuberant or airy physical fantasy, as we shall see Silius doing, and as Statius does still more; but through the medium of speech he gives them here and elsewhere a bracing vitality. At the end of Book v, Mars and Minerva dispute before Jupiter on the arrangements which Minerva and Juno have been making so that the Argonauts may win the Golden Fleece (618–91).[8] The scene is modelled on the dispute of Venus and Juno at the start of *Aeneid* x. But it is quite distinct in spirit from that episode, which for all its energy and life retains an imposing gravity. Virgil presents a solemn council of the gods, summoned by Jupiter; in Valerius Mars rushes to Jupiter (*ruit*, 623), and plunges into impetuous complaint. Virgil's Venus begins with elaborate laudation of Jupiter (*Aen.* x. 18 f.), as does Valerius' Sol in a parallel episode (i. 505 f.); their openings combine tact and force. Mars starts abruptly, inserting an honorific but perfunctory *rex magne*, 'great king', and soon proceeds to petulant rudeness: *teque ea cuncta iuvant*, 'and you all this delights' (626). Valerius has in mind here the half-comic Ares of Homer (*Il.* v. 872–87); in the *Aeneid* Mars is rarely glimpsed.[9]

The rhetorical organization of the speeches in the dispute must be followed vigilantly: the arrangement of addressees is particularly important and expressive. Valerius' treatment is very different from Virgil's. In Virgil Venus addresses Jupiter throughout, and refers only once to Juno, about whom she is protesting; Juno replies in detail, but to Venus alone. Jupiter addresses the gods in general, though with Juno and Venus in mind. The form is powerfully simple; it effectively opposes Venus' devious propriety and ostentatious humility to Juno's surface of dismissive and embittered directness, and it displays Jupiter's statesmanlike dignity. The speeches in Valerius are much more mobile. Mars at first addresses Jupiter, insulting Minerva in the third person (626), but he shifts to addressing Minerva; he begins doing so with a vague second person plural, that probably includes the Argonauts (*vestro*, 'your', 633), but proceeds to addressing her directly and challenging her to single combat (635–40). The movement and the challenge have rhetorical force; but they none the less express animosity overtaking an appearance of reason, and brutal crudity and violent threats overtaking

---

[8] For this episode (note too the start of vi) see esp. Lüthje (1971), 232–6; Adamietz (1976), 80–2. On the gods in Valerius more widely see Harmand (1898), ch. 10; Mehmel (1934), 89–98; various important passages are discussed by Eigler (1988). One must observe that Valerius can use physical action by his gods concisely but with subtlety and strength, especially in the powerful scenes with Medea and Juno in vi (477–682), Venus in vii (193–399).

[9] The effect of 624–7 is not lessened by the abrupt opening of Venus at Sil. iii. 559–61, Bacchus' forthright speech at Stat. *Theb.* vii. 155–92, or Juno's *magne ... Iuppiter* at Virg. *Aen.* xii. 808 f.

an air of legality. The robust language and conceptions evoke
Homer's gods at their most vigorous and philosophically unacceptable; Mars' unsophisticated character is allowed to glare
through the elegant verse. So an ingenious parenthesis is surrounded by the rough thuggery of *quin age . . . imus nos, protinus imus*
(636f.), 'come on, let us go, go at once' (to my grove and fight it
out).[10]

The last part of Mars' speech reverts to addressing Jupiter, and
once more defends his rights with injured fairness. Yet the final
lines naïvely affect to cloak a ferocious threat to the goddesses,
who are not addressed, in the form of hypothetical argument to
Jupiter.

> ego cara Mycenes
> culmina, virgineas praeder si Cecropis arces,
> iam coniunx, iam te gemitu lacrimisque tenebit
> nata querens. metuant ergo nec talia possint.   (645–8)

If *I* were to plunder [Juno's] beloved temple in Mycenae, or the virgin
goddess's citadel in Athens, your wife or your daughter will at once be
embracing you with groans and tears of complaint. So let them be
afraid, and not be allowed to do such things.

The threat grows more direct as Mars' first sentence changes
from a notional possibility to a vividly imagined future; the last
sentence incongruously mixes a lapidary warning to the goddesses with a plea to Jupiter. For all its transparency, however,
the form suggests inhibitions in Mars, and the complexities of the
polytheistic situation. Mars is aware that Juno is just as much
responsible as Minerva, but he does not feel he can treat his
mother in the speech with at all the same open fierceness that he
treats his sister. As it is, the virtual equality of his treatment at this
moment is seized on and distorted by Minerva: *quin simili matrem
demens gravitate secutus*, 'indeed you were crazed enough to attack
your mother with like harshness' (656). The three gods Mars deals
with require quite different handling, and the hierarchy of family
increases the complications.

Minerva's speech also changes its addressees, but with none of
the tumult and naïvety of Mars': it is both strong and neat. She

---

[10] *sola* in 638 contrasts Minerva's descent alone to her descent with Mars *(imus)*; Leo's
introduction of Juno does not suit the sequence 635–40 ((1960), 239). For the expressive
effect of the address cf. Thuc. iii. 63–6, where the Thebans' bitterness makes them address
the inner section of their speech not to the Spartans but to the detested Plataeans.

begins addressing her adversary directly, like Virgil's Juno, but whereas Juno's opening is darkened by sombre passion (*Aen.* x. 63f.), hers is brightened by mockery (cf. 650) and ringing self-confidence.

> 'non tibi Aloidae quibus haec fera murmura iactes,
> non Lapithae, sed Pallas', ait. (651 f.)

'You have here', she said, 'to hurl those savage noises at, not the sons of Aloeus, nor the Lapiths, but Pallas.'

She contrasts herself with Mars' most memorable human enemies; the names grow shorter, but the shortest, her own, conveys curtly and with trenchant assurance the extreme of might which it embodies. She also here contrasts her style with his.

Mars had moved to abandoned engagement in the second person; Minerva coolly moves to the third. The movement solidifies as she stresses that she and Juno were right to arrange negotiation, not force, and contrasts their procedures with those of Mars: *sic Thraces agunt, sic turbidus iste / si qua petit,* 'that is how Thracians behave, or this turbulent creature here, if there is something he wants' (664f.). The rhetorical strategy itself illustrates the difference in their approaches. The detail too, both elegant and forthright, sets a scornful distance between Mars and Minerva; the final prosaic clause makes him sound spoilt and undisciplined. Yet for the reader Minerva's presentation brings out her underlying resemblance to Mars, in concerns, not in manner: she had been less unenthusiastic about warfare than she here alleges (666f., cf. 286–9). She finally addresses Jupiter directly, not rudely or ingratiatingly (cf. 644f.), but with an appearance of frank simplicity (666). Minerva's nature too is vigorously and subtly displayed and disclosed in this vivacious and entertaining altercation.

With dramatic vitality, Jupiter is made to interrupt Mars, who has started retorting to Minerva. The texture of his speech is more involved than in Virgil. Jupiter addresses Mars in terms not unlike Minerva's: *quid, vesane, fremis,* 'why this roaring, you madman?' (673); but he also addresses all three gods together in terms that wearily imply their essential kinship in purpose and conduct (675f., 689, cf. 673f.). He addresses the goddesses too with direct and emphatic instruction (677–9). His ethos is coherent but complex; and his aloof perspective offers a new and levelling vista of the dispute. Minerva has dwelt on 'pushing everything forward with thoughtless fighting' as the behaviour of Mars (*caeca sed cuncta impellere pugna*, 663); Jupiter, irritated by the behaviour of them all and indifferent to their quarrels, bids them all 'push these matters forward in any way, with any sort of fighting' (*quolibet ista modo, quacumque impellite pugna*, 675). The speech of Virgil's Jupiter (x. 104–13), though it is actually influenced by the debate, achieves a statuesque monumentality which increases the weight of Jupiter, the council, and the coming battle. Jupiter's speech in Valerius, though itself sufficiently grand, offers a wrily reducing view of the situation, and adds to the life and colour of the scene and of Jupiter himself. Virgil's Jupiter trusts to the Fates (x. 113); Valerius', warmly and incidentally, laments their power (686).

The poet plays forcefully in the speeches with the extremes and the categories of mythological polytheism. Minerva continues from her opening (above) with her own threat to Mars:

> neque ego aegide digna
> nec vocer ulterius proles Iovis, excidat iste
> ni tibi corde tumor. lituos miser armaque faxo
> oderis et †primis† adimam tua nomina bellis.　　(652–5)

May I no longer be called worthy of my aegis, or the child of Jupiter, if that raging arrogance does not disappear from your spirit! I will make you loathe arms and trumpets in your misery, and I will remove your name from war.

In the second sentence, with characteristic strength, Valerius presents starkly the drastic paradox of a Mars who shuns war, and ceases to give his name to it; war had been referred to as *Mars* because his being had been so intimately bound up with it, and now that being will change.[11] *oderis*, 'loathe', is placed effectively, and *miser*, 'in your misery', draws out the conception amusingly; but the first clause leads up to the supreme paradox of the second, and the more specific 'arms and trumpets' at the start are outmatched by the general 'war' at the close. Metonymy and the extremes of divine personality are exploited with gusto and animated wit. On the other side, Minerva sets the dissolution of

[11] *primis* is not defended by Virg. *Aen.* vii. 603, where *prima* suits the context; here the word is pointlessly specific, especially after the first clause, and reduces effective wit to incoherence. Perhaps one might read <*pro*>*priis*. Köstlin's *privis* imports dubious vocabulary, particularly in this sense (Housman's conjecture at Luc. v. 612, which I rather doubt, would be more acceptable); Wagner's *numina* spoils the neatness. I do not know whether *excidet* might be preferable in 653.

what is involved in the name Pallas: if she cannot subdue Mars, she wishes to lose her essential nature and glory (her relationship to her father is fundamental to this deity). The play with gods' being and personality is more radical than it could be with mortals, most obviously in the second sentence; it is also more agreeably unreal, if only because gods do not actually alter.

Valerius relishes in this passage the categories of gender. Neither the hierarchy of sexes nor conceptions of the female need apply in the world of epic gods as they might be expected to in that of humans, and the poet enjoys the interplay of these worlds.[12] Mars protests that Jupiter does not let right prevent these female audacities, *neque femineis ius obicis ausis* (627). He implies that wild and cunning lawlessness is typical of females; he also suggests that they should not be allowed such power (cf. 670). On the other hand, when he describes how they would respond to action by him (647f., above), he contemptuously portrays their womanly weakness and tears. Needless to say, Minerva replies not with tears or terror but with ridicule (650) and impervious courage. It is Mars (she indicates) that knows no restraint. To his implications of sexual hierarchy, she opposes the rights of divine society: her speech closes *mas aliquid nequeat, si femina*, 'let there be something the male, like the female, is not allowed to do' (670). Here she meets his gruff and muddled ending (*metuant ergo nec talia possint*, above) with an appearance of sober rationality and neat reserve.[13] Male preconceptions are frequently reversed in literature, but the divine allows special and amusing possibilities. In the whole scene the possibilities of this fixed world are energetically and intricately explored, with vigorous drama, sharp play, and vivid freshness.

Our next scene, **Statius**, *Thebaid*, iii. 218–323, concerns Mars again, and also his mistress Venus (a much grimmer figure in Valerius than in Statius or Silius).[14] Its shape confronts sheerly

---

[12] For philosophers divine gender was a subject of dispute: see Cic. *ND* i. 95, with Pease.

[13] Whatever the text, there will be some play on gender. However, Madvig's *mas ... si* ((1873), 146) for *fas ... sic* is so fitting and spirited that one should probably accept it; the nominative singular *mas* would be effectively unusual. *femina* will have an air of ironic quotation. Shackleton Bailey's conjecture ((1977), 209f.) seems implausible in Minerva's mouth. We must firmly reject the ascription of the line to Mars, with *fas ... sit* (Leo (1960), 240f., cf. Köstlin (1889), 664): this utterance would not suit *ardens* or *quid, vesane, fremis?*, and appears laboured and clumsy.

[14] On the divine in the *Thebaid*, and this episode, see Legras (1905), 157–205; Lewis (1936), 49–56; Schetter (1960), 5–29; Burck (1961); Erren (1970); Vessey (1973, 1986b); Reitz (1985); Ahl (1986). The *Achilleid* is full of interest in this regard, and not only for Thetis. On Venus

a grandiose and disturbing first part with a second part graceful
and amusing. Even in the first part the dark texture is created
from consciously diverse elements. The frightening depiction of
the divine there springs in part from epic polytheism; it cannot
readily or satisfyingly be detached from its fictional and mythological environment. The play in the second part again exploits
the poetic divine and its extremities. The coloration is both richer
and subtler than in Valerius, and the nature and the relationships
of the deities are displayed visually as well as verbally.

In the first half of the episode Jupiter summons Mars to begin
the terrible war of Argos and Thebes; in the second Venus pleads
with Mars, her lover, to refrain. In the first Mars is made a
magnificent and appalling figure, and Jupiter's use of him both
terrifies and surprises us. The very opening sets Jupiter, gazing
from the heavens, against Mars, turbulently warring on earth
(218–22).[15] Mars continues in spirit and appearance his furious
involvement in human fighting even as he returns to the skies (227
etiamnum, 'still', 229 f.); the alarming combination of earthly and
heavenly is imaginatively developed in the suggestions of the language that describes him (223–6). Light from his weapons is made
to display together martial glory, divine greatness, and the ghastly
distortion of celestial radiance.

> clipeique cruenta
> lux rubet, et solem longe ferit aemulus orbis.   (225 f.)

The bloody light of his shield shone red, as the sun was smitten from afar
by that rival orb.

The explicit contrast in the second clause is prepared in the first,
where language apt to the sun (*lux rubet*, 'the light shone red') is
grimly perverted and appropriated by the shield.

This dreadful vision Jupiter does not deplore but deploys. We
feel strangeness even in the insistent demonstratives and the easy
relationship shown in his opening: *talis mihi, nate, per Argos, / talis
abi, sic ense madens, hac nubilus ira*, 'go like that among the Argives,
my son, I ask you, like that—with your sword wet so, and

in Valerius cf. e.g. vi. 467–74, vii. 216, 251–5, 300–6 (a nice twist at 394); ii. 101–6, 196–215
(Statius' treatment of Venus in the episode is more paradoxical and less terrible, *Theb.* v.
135, 158, 280–3). The precise point of ii. 101–6 is made uncertain by the text at 103, where
even Madvig's *tantum* is perhaps on the wrong lines.

[15] The language presses Mars' participation particularly far: cf. e.g. Sil. xvii. 487–90;
VF iii. 83–5; Hom. *Il.* xiii. 298–303; Virg. *Aen.* xii. 331–6.

clouded with this anger that I see' (229f.). One contrasts the Homeric Zeus' embittered address to his war-loving son (*Il.* v. 889–99); and one contrasts Valerius. The paradox intensifies as Jupiter, remarkably, declares it lawful for Mars to inflame in war the very peace over which he presides in heaven: *tibi fas ipsos incendere bello / caelicolas pacemque meam* (234f.). The arrangement sharply opposes *pacemque meam*, 'my peace', to *bello*, 'war', and especially to *tibi*, 'you'. It would be wrong to think that Mars is only a way of denoting war. The poet enjoys exploiting metonymy, but this does not at all exclude the significance of personality; even *te cupiant*, 'let the Argives desire only you' (232) demands a sense of personality for its paradox. The idea of personal encounter is vital to the imaginative power of this scene.[16]

The second part of Jupiter's speech, addressed to the whole company of gods, is still more terrible. The war is grounded on the most solemn element in epic theology, on Fate.

> manet haec ab origine mundi
> fixa dies bello, populique in proelia nati.   (242f.)

From the beginning of the world this day stands fixed for war; the peoples of these cities were doomed to battle at their birth.

In the first clause language of philosophical resonance leads up to the grim *bello*, 'war'; the second presents the conception yet more bleakly.[17] Even Mars is ultimately superfluous: if the other gods thwart him, Jupiter declares he will destroy Thebes and Argos himself (244–52). That final sentence sweeps through moral pun-

---

[16] With *te cupiant* cf. 424 *implet amore sui* after 420–3, and e.g. vii. 703 after 695–7, Sil. xvii. 479–90; further e.g. Sil. iv. 667–81, xv. 130; Stat. *Silv.* iii. 1. 41. As for the scene as a whole, I would certainly agree that Statius exploits with paradox and play different aspects of deity, including that of metonymy (cf. Feeney (1991), 367–71); but it seems to me that Feeney, like others, exaggerates the prominence and significance in the scene of depersonalized allegory. One should bear in mind, besides Homer's war-mad, and faithless, Ares (cf. Feeney, 367f., and note *Il.* v. 889–91, 829–34, cf. xxi. 413f.), Statius' treatment of characters, and especially gods, as extremes. It then becomes hard to see that personality is threatening (teasingly) to disappear, particularly when the conflicts in Mars are going to be handled in such slyly personal terms, and with so lively and human a sense of character. Cf. above Ch. 5 n. 52. For the combination of Jupiter and Mars note not only the start of vii, but vii. 236 / *Mars: ita dulce Iovi*, where the unusual metre strengthens the grimness. In iii. 234 I should like to read *quae*, as Watt does ((1984), 159); I hesitate only over the likelihood of *quae* being corrupted to *cui*.

[17] The importance of Fate and individual destiny from Homer on makes the departure from the epic world seem relatively slight. Cf. VF i. 531–6. The preceding speech of Aletes increases the pathos and irony: note iii. 205f. and 235f.

ishment, divine majesty, and vast images of destruction; it culminates in a picture startling in its conjoined hugeness and
anthropomorphism, and drastic in the personal fierceness and
aggressive power which it expresses. The husband of Juno says he
would destroy her Argos

> licet ipsa in turbine rerum
> Iuno suos colles templumque amplexa laboret.   (251f.)

though Juno herself amid the mighty tumult should embrace in anguish
her hills and her temple.

Mortal behaviour at the sack of cities is here wildly expanded in
scale; the poetry of epic polytheism achieves weird greatness from
Statius' physical and dramatic imagination. Various strands combine into the aesthetic coherence of this fearful speech. Precisely
because he is not presenting a thesis, the poet can seek complexity
of impact, not intellectual disentanglement and clarity; and he
can give darkness its full and sombre force.

The second part of the scene, where Venus pleads for Mars on
behalf of Thebes, has a quite different flavour. The poet disports
himself with much lighter and slyer drama and paradox. The
adulterous intimacy is intriguingly conveyed: Mars' horses know
Venus well (263–5), and she stresses reproachfully how much
more obliging than Mars is her injured husband (275f.). Her fancy
and the poet's proceed to the agreeable paradox that Vulcan
would delight, at her bidding, to make arms for Mars himself: the
poet is manipulating famous scenes from epic to give uxoriousness
this comic and concrete form. The official marriage of Mars' and
Venus' daughter to the founder of Thebes she sets against their
own adultery (271–4, 269); but her impassioned paradox *criminis
haec merces?*, 'Is this the reward for my misdoing?', only underlines
the unseriousness for the reader of immorality among the gods.[18]
Likewise, the amorousness and (restrained) sensuality of the episode are properly at home in the poem only amid the special
atmosphere of the divine. At the close of Venus' speech the poet
enjoys the divine more whimsically. He uses saga to connect the
divine and the grotesque in a bizarre collocation that undermines
the lofty tone of the affronted utterance. 'Is it a slight indignity I

---

[18] The striking *socer* (269) springs from Ov. *Met.* iii. 132, but is used with very different
effect. At 280 we are perhaps to think that Venus breaks off because she has aroused in
Mars an unhelpful enthusiasm for arms.

have endured that the daughter of the goddess Venus [Harmonia transformed into a snake] should crawl lengthily along and spit forth poison on to the grass of Illyrium?', *divae Veneris quod filia longum / reptat et Illyricas eiectat virus in herbas?* (289f.). The grandiose third person *divae Veneris*, 'the goddess Venus', is placed pointedly and entertainingly first; the enjambment and the rhythm in *longum / reptat* show the poet's imitative relish.[19]

The brief and amusing narrative on Mars' reaction to the speech embodies with marvellous deftness of language and awkwardness of action the conflicting sides to the god of war in love.

> lacrimas non pertulit ultra
> Bellipotens. hastam laeva transumit, et alto,
> haud mora, desiluit curru; clipeoque receptam
> laedit in amplexu, dictisque ita mulcet amicis.　　(291–4)

The god mighty in war could not endure her tears further. He took his spear with his left hand from his right, and immediately leapt down from his high chariot. He took her to him and hurt her with his shield as he embraced her; he sought to soothe her with these affectionate words.

The placing of Mars' resplendent compound title highlights his surprising impotence against female tears. His instant leaping down shows him characteristically impetuous and active even in postponing action; but he has no intention of abandoning it. He does not drop his spear, but shifts it; the unusual *transumit* elegantly lingers on the fussy compromise. The clumsy and uncomfortable embrace has an Ovidian humour and point, but the paradox of *laedit in amplexu*, 'hurt her as he embraced her', is subtler and more suggestive. The phrase contrasts ironically with the soothing he undertakes in words.[20]

Mars' speech to Venus displays in its first part an ardent lyricism which is undercut by the passages of narration. Even through the passionate simplicity of the opening we savour the

---

[19] P's *deiectat* is commonly read. It matters little in Statius that the existence of the word elsewhere is dubious (at the Latin rendering of Theod. Mops. *In Tim.* i. 3. 7 *devitare* is preferable); but it is obviously less suitable to a snake. For the paradox with Harmonia cf. Eur. *Bacch.* 1331–3; the transference to Elysium (1338f.) is naturally omitted in Statius, as at Ov. *Met.* iv. 602f.

[20] One may naturally contrast with this treatment of embrace and arms Virg. *Aen.* xii. 433f., Hom. *Il.* vi. 466–74. The varied images in Roman art of Mars and Venus in physical contact do not show the poet's play or complexity: see *LIMC* ii. 1, 544–9 (ii. 2, 408–15). The use of *Bellipotens* is significant again at its other appearances, viii. 384, ix. 832.

paradox created from divine extremes, the contrast with the intense and voluptuous proem of Lucretius, and our awareness of
Mars' priorities and maladroit action. *o mihi bellorum requies*, he
cries, *et sacra voluptas / unaque pax animo!*, 'O my repose from war,
my sacred pleasure, the only peace my mind can know!' (295 f.;
the exquisite *pax*, 'peace', is saved for the close). The speech grows
more entertaining, as Mars (who had previously shown only exultation in his mission, 260) declares that he has not forgotten his
ties with Venus and Thebes. He exclaims

> prius in patrui deus infera mergar
> stagna et pallentes agar exarmatus ad umbras!   (302 f.)

before I do, may I, a god, be plunged into my uncle's waters in hell and
be driven, unarmed, to the pale shades!

Even in the first line Statius enjoys incidentally setting next to the
grandiose combination *deus infera*, 'god, of hell', *patrui*, 'uncle',
with its play on unobvious ramifications in the divine family tree.
In the second line a recurring theme of the passage reaches its
pleasing climax. The wish of the lover, extreme in itself, becomes
more so in the mouth of the god; but to Mars this extremity is
furthered by the thought of losing his arms. A later passage confirms, and extends into weightier irony, the cheerful humour here
on the god's supreme passion for war. Jupiter's ultimate threat
against Mars is to make him peaceful, a gentle and kindly divinity
(*mite bonumque / numen*, vii. 29 f.): no cruel threat, he cruelly
asserts.[21]

In Mars' speech here the dreadful command we heard from
Jupiter becomes a tool for the handling of a tricky situation; tool
and situation display the intricacies of polytheism. Mars stresses to
Venus, not that Jupiter's orders appeal to him, but that no god
could be bold enough to spurn the injunctions of Fate and the
awesome divinity. His essentially grandiose period does not omit a
crude parenthesis in which he naïvely employs the command to
show his superiority to Venus' husband: Vulcan would not have

---

[21] *mitis* is used of deity in its true and proper nature at Sil. iv. 795, cf. Ov. *Met.* xi. 134. At
Theb. ix. 4–7 and xi. 413 f. Mars' bellicosity is perversely excelled by mortals. For the lover's
utterance cf. e.g. Ov. *Her.* 3. 63–6. The love of Mars and Venus, and this episode, are taken
up with intricate and delightful exploitation of polytheism at ix. 821–40, x. 893 f. The
former passage gestures, decorously, towards the Theomachy itself, so disconcerting a
passage for later critics (Hom. *Il.* xxi. 481 ff.; and with *Theb.* ix. 837 cf. *Il.* xxi. 391–417).

been chosen for such a task (305 f.). Venus has succeeded in arousing his jealousy, or pride.

Mars ends by presenting his solution, to go but help the Theban side; he presents it in judicious and responsible language (316). But he springs into immediate and dreadful action. The poet resumes his earlier grimness with a simile from the lightning of Jupiter himself, which embodies his 'anger', his 'fierce commands', and terror and death (*ira* 318, *saeva dei mandata* 321).[22] This simile opposes one which ended the first part of the episode (255–9). There the awed silence of the gods after Jupiter's warnings had been unexpectedly pictured by the tranquil weather of summer, at sea and on land. That evocation had drawn us into its own stillness, as if in a quiet and lasting close; the joyous activity of Mars had abruptly succeeded. Statius' intent use of form strengthens his vigorous confrontation of different aspects of his divine world. But he does not deal simply in large contrasts; fine detail, astounding description, and potent and intriguing combination and paradox inform his rich and brilliant treatment. The extremes and the multiplicity of poetic godhead draw forth the resources of his endlessly imaginative and inventive writing.

Venus leads us—to **Silius Italicus**. The linked pair of episodes chosen here shows Silius exploiting the opposition between the lightest elements of the divine and the weightiness which stamps the central world of his poem.[23] Both these features derive from epic, but the gravity seems fundamental to the conventional idea of the genre and to Silius' poem, the levity, for Silius' reader, apparently alien and remote. This appearance of remoteness the first episode in the pair reinforces; the second changes and confounds it in arresting complication. The first episode seems at the time very much an excursus; it treats of the Judgement of Paris (vii. 437–73). The substantial digressions in Books vi–viii give that part of the poem a boldly excursive quality; this passage, like the digression on Falernus earlier in the book (162–211), has a lightness of tone which intensifies by contrast the general darkness and

---

[22] Divine anger and divine injustice often appear most impressively in contexts (similes, authoritative speeches, etc.) which both set them apart from the main line of narrative and throw them into relief. Cf. e.g. VF iv. 519–26, vii. 567 f.; Stat. *Theb.* iii. 537 f.; Sil. vi. 84 (note also the summary iii. 1 f., outdoing Virg. *Aen.* iii. 1 f.; cf. Sil. ii. 657).

[23] On the second episode see Burck (1984*a*); on the gods in Silius more widely see von Albrecht (1964); Vessey (1972–3); Kißel (1979), 11–85; Burck (1984*b*), 141–4; Küppers (1986), 164–70; Laudizi (1989), ch. 4.

heaviness of the work. It is formally subordinated by its narrative status and position: Proteus tells this story of the past, by way of background, to sea-nymphs anxious about the future. The picturesque world of bizarre or timorous deities (413–30) already removes us from the main world of the poem; and the tale is teasingly distant from the questions of the nymphs themselves.[24] It occupies almost two-thirds of Proteus' speech (437–93), but with salient and mannerist disproportion; even the importance of the forecast that will follow does not make the earlier part seem central in significance. Yet our reactions to the form are complicated by the inescapable memory of Virgil's overwhelming and enigmatic finale to the *Georgics*.

The account of the Judgement distorts obvious narrative to thrust emphasis on to Venus.[25] Silius wishes to show how easily and obviously Venus must win on the home ground of beauty; he also wishes to evoke her alien world with charm and humour. The imposition on Paris of his momentous task appears in a *cum*-clause; it is subordinated to the preparations of Venus and the Cupids (437–40). In that gracefully fluttering scene (441–7), Silius draws out the flavour of his deities; but the eager activity is also made to suggest a very human agitation under the pressure of time (note 444). In *tempora sollicitus litis servasse Cupido*, 'a Cupid, anxious to keep the time fixed for judging the dispute' (441f.), we see entertainingly prosaic conceptions and language applied to the divine.[26] The account gives prominence to its only speech, one by Venus to her sons. It touches incidentally on the general power of love, but stresses most that this is Venus' sphere.

> de forma atque ore (quid ultra
> iam superest rerum?) certat Venus.   (451 f.)

Venus—what can there be left to outdo this?—Venus must contest about loveliness of body and face.

---

[24] For the attractive and foreign world of aquatic divinity, cf. iii. 406–14, and note the contrasts between the martial *raptat* and *pulvere nigrantes* and the marine *perlabitur, fluit*, and *perspicuo* (410, 412, 413), and note *certamine nandi* (413). (In 413 one should read *convertunt*; for the stroke cf. Housman on Man. v. 423–30.) Statius is more extravagant and elaborate (*Ach.* i. 52–60, etc.).

[25] On other depictions of the event see Stinton (1991); Clairmont (1951). Besides Euripides and Ov. *Her.* 5. 33–6 (16. 53–88 I think spurious) cf. particularly Call. *H.* 5. 18–28; Stat. *Ach.* ii. 50–8.

[26] Cf. Hor. *Sat.* i. 9. 35–7, and note perhaps Cic. *Mil.* 28. Compare with this scene Hom. *H.* 5. 58–67, and *H.* 6.

The poet delights in the grand third-person use of the name to embody an extreme, here an ultimate and divine extreme; he postpones it with an agreeably indignant parenthesis. The form of this speech toys with the gods: at first Venus addressing her sons sounds like a human mother (that this should happen when they were alive and safe!); later she sounds like a mortal praying to a god.[27] Family hierarchy too is turned round by this mock-prayer. So it is further when Jupiter is shown in the prayer as subject to the Cupids' power: he is referred to as their grandfather (455). Silius savours in his verse the surprising and unamorous designation.

The arrival of the other goddesses is set in the imperfect (458–65); the advent of Venus is presented with decisive and emphatic perfects (466–9). These perfects are the more striking when what they describe is so atmospheric: the smile and the all-pervading fragrance of the goddess (469 is raptly spondaic). Paris is overwhelmed, and fears, not to choose, but to seem to have been unsure (471): the epigram gracefully registers an extreme. The description of Minerva (458–64) shows with Ovidian particularity how awkwardly out of place she is, as she sets about learning peace with tranquil gaze (*pacemque serenis / condiscens oculis*). The description of Juno points with mythological ingenuity to her humiliation in this sphere, past, present, and imminent.[28] However, after Venus' triumph we turn abruptly to the destruction in war that her rivals successfully inflict on Paris and his city. As the speech goes on, the sphere of love, and of such mythology, is swiftly left behind for the violence, grandeur, and reality of warfare and history.

In the later passage, xi. 385–426, Silius draws to the centre what had seemed so distant and so marginal. The intervention of the

---

[27] For *salvis* cf. e.g. Ov. *Trist.* ii. 206; Spaltenstein is here mistaken. The *si* in 453 produces a common form of prayer (note the parodies in Luc. vi. 706–11; Stat. *Theb.* i. 60–72); the passage is stranger and more paradoxical than Virg. *Aen.* i. 664–6. One should compare generally the scene at Stat. *Silv.* i. 2. 51–46; it is discussed by Vessey (1972).

[28] To explicate 465f. rebarbatively: *iudicium Phrygis* (contemptible beings, cf. e.g. Cic. *Fam.* iii. 10. 10) *et fastus pastoris*, (low beings: cf. e.g. Sen. *Ag.* 731) *et Iden* (the place too whence Ganymede was snatched, cf. e.g. Hor. *Odes* iii. 21. 15f. and esp. Stat. *Silv.* iii. 4. 12–15) / *post fratris* (probably suggesting Jupiter's want of conjugal interest, cf. Ov. *Met.* iii. 265f.; Sen. *HF* 1f.; VF iii. 514, with Eigler (1988), 41) *latura* (for Juno's resentment of Ganymede cf. e.g. Stat. loc. cit.; Ov. *Fast.* vi. 43, *Met.* x. 161; Antip. Thess. cxi Gow–Page; Virg. *Aen.* i. 28) *toros* (for the sexual union with Ganymede cf. e.g. Eur. *Or.* 1392, *IA* 1050, Cic. *Tusc.* iv. 71, Macrob. *Sat.* v. 16. 11).

goddess marks the turning-point of the poem: she and her Cupids cause the depravity of the winter spent in Capua which destroys the vigour of the successful Carthaginians.[29] The effect is audacious, and complicated. We have in the passage on the one hand a grim moral force, on the other lightness and play. The conflict of virtue and pleasure is not really the central preoccupation of the poem, which rather explores different kinds of *virtus*; but there can be no mistaking the importance of the episode for the themes and the plot, and no mistaking the moral outlook of the poet. Yet our strong involvement with the Roman cause, and the delightfulness of Venus and the Cupids, prevent any simple opposition of chillingly frivolous gods with pitiable humanity (as when Venus and Cupid assail Dido); they prevent too any simple disapproval of these gods as the embodiment of immorality. We have a genuine complexity of tone and treatment. And while the gods here triumph easily over the mortals, in accordance with theological hierarchy, in literary terms an element lower than heroism and manly warfare prevails over grander things—and that in epic. The passage has a strong and pleasing sense of overturning hierarchy as well as enforcing it.

The presentation of the divine is dominated by a speech of Venus' to her sons. This forcefully recalls the earlier passage. Venus is no longer in her own sphere, but she speaks with no less confidence, and displays with assured irony her paradoxical superiority over Juno, the patronness of Carthage.

> eat improba Iuno
> et nos (nec mirum, quid enim sumus?) acta secundis
> despiciat. valet illa manu, valet illa lacertis;
> parvula nos arcu puerili spicula sensim
> fundimus, et nullus nostro de vulnere sanguis.   (390–4).

Let importunate Juno, driven on by good fortune, contemn me (it is no surprise—what power have I?). She is strong in hands and arms; I pour forth little arrows, softly, from boys' bows, and no blood comes from the wounds I give.

[29] Cf. xii. 15–26. The historicity of the dissipation is very doubtful (cf. Polyb. xi. 19. 3; Frederiksen (1984), 257). In Livy, Silius' source, it is crucial to the course of events (xxiii. 18. 13; 45. 4), and still more so, on the human plane, in Silius: he removes the force of Hannibal's supposed error after Cannae, decisive in Livy (xxii. 51. 4; contrast the divine intervention at Sil. x. 330–87). Cf. also on Capua Sen. *Ep.* 51. 5.

The first sentence forcefully conveys both character and polytheistic antagonism: the main structure is harshly scornful and
sarcastic, the parenthesis feline. The second sentence sets strong
brevity and vigorous anaphora in one half against slacker length
in the other, and smiling self-depreciation. The language in this
sentence opposes to the physical power and prowess which
command the poem things that sound inferior to them and are
particularly associated with love-elegy. The poet is recalling the
description of the Cupids in vii; *parvulus*, 'little', used of a quiver
there (443), occurs only in these two places of the poem.[30]

Soon the irony gives place to open inversion of the expected
order of things: love, wine, and sleep must vanquish the army
quam non perfregerit ensis, / non ignes, non immissis Gradivus habenis,
'which could not be broken by the sword, or by fire, or by Mars
driving his horses with unrestrained speed' (398 f.). The poet here
gestures towards the tragic lines in which Aeneas comments on
the fall of Troy to trickery (Virg. *Aen.* ii. 197 f.). In Silius, however,
the paradox is much sharper and more piquant; and he creates
here an arresting counterpoint between the voice of his exultant
speaker and his own, as he uses Venus' words to mark weightily
the decisive change in his story. The figure of Mars brings the
triplet and the inversion to a climax through the extremity and
particularity of the gods.[31]

The inversion is elaborated, often more playfully, through
manifold contamination and exchange of language and conceptions between the two spheres of war and pleasure. So at the close
of her speech Venus says of Hannibal:

> segnisque soporas
> aut nostro vigiles ducat sub numine noctes.   (408 f.)

Let him idly spend nights slumbering, or awake, but under our power.

We have seen Hannibal wakeful at night with martial concerns,
as becomes an epic general; but here he is imagined, with an

---

[30] The occurrence of *parvulus* in the *Aeneid* gives it a somewhat special status among
diminutives (cf. also Lyne on *Ciris* 138); but it is none the less significant that these are, if I
have not missed any, the only two passages in Silius where diminutives appear. (iii. 248
avunculus does not count.)

[31] We look back particularly to Cannae in ix, where Mars' warring against the
Carthaginians had been particularly important (438–555). *virorum* in 397 is probably
pointed: cf. 481 and Strabo v. 4. 13.

elegiac and ingenious twist, as awake, but through love.[32] The links within the poem produce an especial force here; the divinities slide forcefully into the pattern of words and master the clause with elegance. Purposeful as is the lightness of tone, the wit detaches and charms us. Still more pointed, and sometimes still lighter, is the assimilation of the Cupids to an army. This is seen most fully and most winningly at the resumption of the narrative.

> haec postquam Venus, applaudit lascivus et alto
> mittit se caelo niveis exercitus alis.　　　　　　(410f.)

When Venus had ended, the playful army clapped, and launched itself from the lofty heavens on snow-white wings.

The words are marvellously ordered. *applaudit*, 'clapped', almost startles us with the Cupids' childish and frivolous delight; the verb in this sense is unelevated. *lascivus*, 'playful', reinforces it; the word it agrees with, *exercitus*, 'army', is kept almost to the end. *exercitus* itself is set amid the exhilarating fantasy of the descent. Even *alto*, 'high', and *niveis*, 'snow-white', conventional as they may appear, are meticulously placed, and delicately enhance the Boucher-esque flurry of the scene.[33]

The effect of the Cupids' attack is not only momentous but morally terrible. Venus' own language can suggest this. In *combibat illapsos ductor per viscera luxus*, 'let the commander drink up degeneracy; let it steal through his vitals' (400), the expression has a moral impact: *illapsos*, 'steal', evokes insidious perversion, and *combibat*, 'drink up', invites us to contrast our reaction to the simply pitiable Dido, who drinks love (*Aen.* i. 749).[34] Venus' *profliganda*, (the army) 'must be vanquished' (398), secondarily evokes *profligatus*, 'dissipated'. But it is in the grim tones of the narrator that the moral significance emerges openly. Like Venus, he dwells on the surprise of this attack succeeding where other things had failed, and so underlines the turn in the plot; but his emphasis is

---

[32] Cf. esp. x. 330–71, vii. 282–7. The effect on Hannibal himself is naturally temporary.

[33] The situation gives *exercitus* a sharper point than *exercitus* at VF vi. 457 (cf. 475f.) or *agmen* at Stat. *Silv.* i. 2. 54 (cf. 56, 66), though in both there is play. 386f. is another important moment for the interplay of language: *caeco* suggests Venus' domain as well as mortal ignorance (cf. Heinsius on Ov. *Met.* iii. 490), *exitio* is a black surprise (cf. VF ii. 102 in its context), and the final *domandi* now conveys action both alien to Venus and natural to her (cf. Nisbet and Hubbard on Hor. *Odes* i. 27. 14, Bömer on Ov. *Met.* v. 370).

[34] Cf. *illapsa* at xv. 95 (Virtue on Pleasure), and the expressive phrasing at Cic. *Fin.* i. 39, with Madvig.

ethical: *intactumque secundae / fortunae ingenium vitia allicientia quass-ant*, 'Hannibal's mind, untouched by good fortune, began to be shaken by alluring vice' (425f.). Like Venus' speech, Silius' narrative presents the change from warlike actions to actions of pleasure, and so significantly transgresses the normal limits of his poetic world (414–19, cf. 400–9); but he closes the sequence with the resounding phrase *miserisque bonis perit horrida virtus*, 'through accursèd good things perished grim virtue' (419). Livy had written *quos nulla mali vicerat vis perdidere nimia bona ac voluptates immodicae*, 'those whom no amount of bad had conquered were ruined by an excess of good things and by immoderate pleasures' (xxiii. 18. 11); Silius tightens the phrase into paradox, and gives it a philosophical tinge. Virtue (courage) of superficially unattractive appearance has played an important part in the poem; it is here overcome by the more flagrant paradox of 'good' that is evil.[35] The two phrases we have quoted from the narrative end the two sections that describe the gods' assault, first on the Carthaginians, and second on Hannibal in particular (412–19, 420–6). Each section begins on the impact of the gods, but finishes with moral summation.

This episode well illustrates the complication and richness of effect and texture which the poets can obtain from their gods. We particularly see how Silius takes an element from within the epic tradition, and uses it, not only to illuminate by contrast the fierce and confined world and ethos that dominate his poem, but to interact with that world and that ethos in striking and bold combination.

We now come to an area where grandeur and moral power have particular scope: we come to places where poets put to use the hierarchical boundary between gods and men. Yet the poetry is anything but simple or predictable. The discussion must pause to expatiate a little on hierarchy; the topic is of considerable importance for the treatment of greatness. The literature of this period shows with ample clarity how there lay before authors familiar orderings of the world into categories held intrinsically superior and inferior, nobler and less noble: gods and mortals, adults and children, men and women, the free and slaves,

---

[35] The idea of truly good things is implied, cf. e.g. Sen. *Ep.* 32. 5, 45. 6, *Prov.* 4. 10, *Helv.* 9. 2, Juv. 10. 3. *horrida virtus* is used of the Carthaginians' opponent Decius at 205. Livy may be inspired by Cic. *Leg. Agr.* ii. 95.

Romans and barbarians, the Senate and lower orders, spirit and body, sky and earth; not even species of animals escaped. How far Romans in general took acceptance or application of each ranking is of course an elaborate and often an unprofitable question. What concerns us is that many of these authors love to explore and exploit, whether earnestly, grandly, or entertainingly, transcendence or transgression of these common hierarchies, actual or attempted. Much other classical literature does the same; but these interests often take on in our period a very individual character, above all in the writers most concerned with wit, extravagance, and complications of sublimity and greatness. This particular boundary between men and gods has naturally its distinctive features, some peculiar or especially pertinent to mythological poetry. It is marked by the spatial division between earth and heaven; individual mortals can conceivably become gods (women—barring metamorphosis—cannot become men); mortals can think to overcome gods physically, though they can never succeed (barbarians—of course temporarily—can defeat Romans). On such features the poets seize with alacrity.

We shall look first at **Seneca's** *Hercules* and principally at the scene (895–1053) where Hercules is sent mad and slays his wife and children. The scene is extraordinary in its boldness of imagination and its sombre and powerful picture of divinity. That picture adds to the complications of response which the episode evokes, morally and aesthetically. It far exceeds in darkness the depictions of the divine in epic; yet it is intimately involved with the mythological world of the play, and cannot be demythologized into veridical statement without singular violence to the poetic creation. In the scene we have an elaborate interaction between Hercules' dynamism, which urges beyond mortal limits, and Juno's evil will, which distorts and repels that movement. That interaction must be seen in the light of the brilliant prologue, where Juno conceives the terrible event.[36]

The prologue consists of a long speech from Juno. In it Hercules is seen passing limits with glorious ease. Through his

[36] For literature bearing on these scenes of the play, see Anliker (1960); 45–8, Henry and Walker (1965); Friedrich (1972); Heldmann (1974), 1–56; Shelton (1978), 17–25; Zwierlein (1984*b*); Fitch (1987), with more literature; on religion in the tragedies more widely see Rosenmeyer (1989), ch. 3, and cf. above pp. 62f. Important too for the scene of madness is the debate on Hercules', essentially future, deity (422–505). On Hercules cf. Galinsky (1972); in our period Stat. *Silv.* iii. 1 offers a particularly memorable treatment.

successes he has defeated the goddess, and, in capturing
Cerberus, has defeated the underworld and its ruler (116, 58, etc.;
48, 65). His apotheosis seems assured by Jupiter (23, 121f.) and
already assumed by men (39f.). The triumphs of virtue and
prowess are darkened by Juno. Her hatred affects to believe that
Hercules intends and would be able to conquer Jupiter and
heaven (63–75). The poet delights to linger on this false and
exciting notion. He fluently has Juno devise ingenious support
for it in Hercules' past actions and violent nature; he makes it
surpass and sweep on from the section on the conquest of Hell
(46–63). We are made to relish a conception unreal even within
the world of the play; we relish it partly in its very unreality,
partly for its imaginative daring. Hercules will not reach the
stars slowly and gently, like Bacchus: *iter ruina quaeret et vacuo
volet / regnare mundo*, 'he will seek his path by destruction and will
wish to reign in an empty sky' (67f.). The contrast enhances the
vividness and force of the first clause; *vacuo*, 'empty', vigorously
implies.[37]

The goddess means, however, to reverse Hercules' past break-
ings of boundaries, and prevent or at least spoil his future ones.
This is no satisfying reassertion of a moral order. It was Hercules' deification that was morally satisfying; her maddening of
Hercules will befit her own extreme malevolence. In saying it
would be 'worthy of a stepmother', *dignum noverca* (112), she consciously understates. His invasion of the underworld and his
aspiration to escape death will be answered by the monstrous
invasion of infernal powers into Hercules and death into his
family (88–91, 96, 104). Such reversals will not be produced by
the innate superiority of the goddess: no one can conquer Hercules but himself (84f., 116). Juno's perversion and turning round
of the theme of conquest presents in language the furthest glori-
fication of the human hero; it displays the divine in its most
hideous aspect morally—and its most incredible philosophically.

It would be superficial to allege that Seneca wishes us to
attach little importance to the divine because he brings on the
goddess at this point, omitting the premature appearance of gods

[37] Violent language for the passing of bounds is used characteristically of Hercules in
the play: cf. e.g. 47 *effregit ... limen*, 57 *rupto carcere*, 237 *rupto obice*, 279–90, 566 *fatum rumpe
manu*.

from the machine which begins the madness in Euripides' *Hera-cles*.[38] That expressive stroke was highly audacious even for Euripidean drama, where gods normally appear only at start or end; we can scarcely assume that Seneca would naturally have re-peated it, when the gods come as characters nowhere else in his plays. Rather the appearance of Juno here marks the importance of this element; the prominence and weight of later references confirm it. So Hercules ends his first speech boldly calling on Juno to send any further labour: *quid vinci iubes?*, 'what do you order me to conquer?' (615); the prologue tells us the sinister answer.[39] At the very moment when Hercules discovers what he has done, his father tells him that the grief is his, the crime Juno's (*crimen novercae*, 1201). The play does not in my view prompt us at all sufficiently to remove the divine into Hercules' psyche, and if we do so we rob many striking moments of their strength and elegance.

Seneca's treatment of Hercules' madness obviously differs from Euripides' by depicting it as if on-stage. Still more important, however, are Seneca's great expansion of the ceremony of sacrifice before the onset of madness (895–939), and the visions he gives the mad Hercules before he begins the slaying of his family (939–86). The slaughter itself occupies less than half the scene (987–1053). This arrangement intensifies and enlarges the place in the scene of the divine and Hercules' relation to it; on this aspect we shall concentrate.

The litany at the start (900–8) calmly and colourfully evokes the deities of myth; its mood and order contrast simply with what is to come. Yet the traditional catch-all phrase that ends it takes intriguing turns.

> fraterque quisquis incolit caelum meus
> non ex noverca frater. 					(907f.)

[38] To be seen thus rather than as a second prologue: cf. with 815–25 *Ion* 1549–54 and also *El.* 1233–7. The killing of Lycus further suggests the last part of a play: cf. Kambylis on *Antiope* xlviii. 46ff. Kamb. Sen. *Tro.* 683 (cf. Eur. *HF* 495) confirms that Seneca will have used Euripides directly; the use of other models, though possible enough, has not to my mind been shown probable. On the nature of Juno in the play I very much agree with Zwierlein (1984*b*), 12–18.

[39] The point remains, though more weakly, with E's *quae*, accepted by Zwierlein; but A's *quid* seems more fitting to context and close. We are to wonder what if anything Juno can now impose after this extreme achievement, not which miscellaneous items are left on the list. For the direct address to Juno compare Hercules' magnificent cry at Ov. *Met.* ix. 177–9.

... and any brother who inhabits the heavens and is not a brother from my stepmother.

Much is conveyed here: we are reminded of Juno, shown this human's kinship with the heavenly gods he prays to, and shown his zeal for peace (it is Mars that he does not wish to summon). But all this is communicated through the distancing medium of ingenious play on polytheism; both the ingenuity and the play of the first line are surpassed in the second, which is pleasingly conjoined in asyndeton and creates with *frater* a pleasing 'circle'.[40] The first part reaches a climax as Hercules utters prayers *Iove meque dignas*, 'worthy of Jupiter [to whom he is to pray] and of myself' (927). In those prayers he does not, as he has been urged, seek rest for himself (rather the contrary, 937–9): he prays for peace throughout the universe (926–39). The magnificence and moral nobility of his conception are grandly linked, by the phrase quoted, to a sense of his own worth; and the violence of Hercules is seen, as in the preceding chorus, to subserve the cause of harmonious order.[41] The proud combination of his name with Jupiter's is actually paradoxically ironic: Jupiter's universe cannot match the loftiness of this human's imagination. The gap is made the clearer by Hercules' prayer that the lightning sent by angry Jupiter will cease (*nullus irato Iove / exiliat ignis*, 932 f.). Even apart from the divine action about to come, Hercules' prayers to Jupiter are after their opening (927–9 *cursus*) palpably doomed to go unanswered. It is not Hercules' inadequacy that this discloses.

Abruptly Hercules' order is disrupted by the chaos, mental, imagined, physical, that Juno creates. In his visions the poet's fantasy, liberated from reality even within the mythical world, moves with wild freedom; yet he retains with that reality a forceful contact, and so increases the strangeness and power of his conceptions. The language furthers the union of sublimity and complication. At least Hercules' wish that the stars should continue

---

[40] Cf. *soror* at Stat. *Theb.* viii. 502, and the whole passage.

[41] Something must be said of 920–4, the speech which the prayer succeeds. *utinam ... possem* (cf. *Thy.* 893 f.) and *tinxisset* in my view indicate allusively but firmly that Hercules *has* complied with Amphitryon's direction to wash off Lycus' blood: had he not, he would have been pouring libations from it. The language of human sacrifice in 920–4 seemingly carries Hercules' traditional violence to a hideous extreme, but the lines turn to show the shocking wish (cf. Hom. *Il.* xxii. 346 f., etc.) as paradoxically justified. The versification at 924 enhances the strange and daring moral elevation. Otherwise Fitch (1987), 26, and on 918–24.

their movements undisturbed (928f.) had seemed likely enough to be fulfilled; but in his first speech the celestial world itself is violently disturbed. The sun yields to the stars and the constellations of the year are about to be disarrayed (939–52). The unreality of this *falsum ... caelum*, 'untrue sky', is brought out by another speaker (954); but the vision remains a magnificent expression of the disorder Juno brings. Yet the poet makes us dwell with some pleasure on the exciting and multiply fantastic image of the Lion (Leo) leaping across the sky to break the neck of the Bull (*frangetque tauri colla*, 952).[42]

The second vision makes Hercules attempt to assail heaven. In the prologue such an assault had been falsely predicted by Juno; now it appears directly, though without reality, and is willed by Hercules, although Hercules' will has been deranged. Yet, even while Hercules' mind is unconstrained by truth or morality, the attempt still expresses his greatness of spirit. The whole passage offers us physical and mental sublimity, though the sublimity is complicated and distorted by madness and by style. Hercules' father bids him restrain the impulse of a breast insane yet great, *pectoris sani parum / magni tamen* (975); the comment is to reinforce our appreciation both of ethos and of effect.

As in the prologue, Hercules turns to the last unconquered division of the universe: *immune caelum est, dignus Alcide labor*, 'the heavens have been free from me: they are a labour worthy of Hercules'. The third-person name here falls in a superb extreme of grandeur and pride; Hercules considers not his worthiness of heaven, but heaven's of him.[43] We contrast the bearing and formulation of *Iove meque dignas*, 'worthy of Jupiter and of myself' (927, above). At first, Hercules seems to consider not conquest but the ascent in apotheosis which truly awaits him. Even so, he does not need Jupiter's promise: *quid si negaret? non capit terra Herculem / tandemque superis reddit*, 'no matter if he now refused me: the earth

---

[42] It is of course significant that the lion, Hercules' first conquest (964), now resumes its destruction. The poet is not much interested in depicting madness with supposed clinical authenticity: [Hipp.] *Reg.* iv. 89. 7, misunderstood by Joly, has little bearing here. (τὸ ὑπάρχον, if genuine, denotes not τὸ ὑπεναντιούμενον but the heavenly body; for τούς, τὸ should surely be read.)

[43] For *dignus* cf. e.g. *Tro.* 307f.; but more esp. pp. 220f. below. One should compare with 955–7 the superb and preposterous vaunt of the Lesser Ajax at *Ag.* 545f. over the gods and over divisions of the universe; order is grimly reasserted by 556. (The correspondence helps establish that 545f. are genuine, cf. Zwierlein (1977), 174f., against Tarrant; *fulmen* points to Jupiter, its proper user.)

cannot contain Hercules, and yields him, at last, to the gods' (960 f.). The brisk shrug of astounding impiety confronts the easy sublimity of astounding pride; *tandem*, 'at last', even complains of the delay.[44] This is not mere pitiable megalomania; Hercules' words befit, though they pervert, his stature, and we must relish as well as regret their amazing extravagance.

He proceeds to the plan of attacking heaven, because Juno opposes his arrival and Jupiter despite his son's threat does not instantly override her:

> dubitatur etiam? vincla Saturno exuam
> contraque patris impii regnum impotens
> avum resolvam.   (965–7)

Is there hesitation still? I shall free Saturn from his chains: against my wicked father's ferocious rule I shall unloose my grandfather.

Hercules is so remote from fear or respect that a mere moment's pause is offence enough to decide his anger.[45] Seneca is deliberately pushing the hero's audacity so far as to modify our involvement through a sense of the poet's own self-conscious extremity. This is as usual a matter of content and language together. Thus the brevity and the plain vocabulary of the opening question contribute to the modification. Modification springs too from the almost entertaining obviousness of the irony in *impii*, 'wicked': the word implies wrongs against kin or gods, wrongs at least as evident in Hercules' own action as in Jupiter's actions against Hercules and Saturn. And modification comes especially from *avum*, 'grandfather'. The ingenious play with polytheistic kinship deliberately complicates; the word is placed at an emphatic point, and one where we expect something more terrible than a word suggesting an old man.

The hero elaborates his plans to scale heaven. The piling up of mountains with such a purpose was a topic of familiar sublimity; but the strange physical detail complicates again. So the Thessalian mountains aptly 'full of Centaurs' (*plena Centauris iuga*, 969) cannot be taken with straightforward seriousness—though

---

[44] Cf. e.g. Luc. vii. 72–4 (note 240–2).

[45] For different play with unremarkable hesitation cf. *Tro.* 658, *Med.* 988 (I should prefer to punctuate after *potens*), and also [*HO*] 987. The gate of heaven (962–4) is common enough in such contexts (e.g. Cic. *Rep.* libr. inc. fr. 6, cf. Varr. *Men.* 560 Astbury (both Hercules); Enn. *Var.* 24 Vahlen; Sil. xv. 78; for the original conception cf. Worthen (1988)). But Seneca employs this boundary with radical and self-conscious physicality.

the Centaurs lack the amiable and Asterician absurdity of the browsing goats on the rock which the Cyclops hurled (Demetr. *Eloc.* 115). However, even within Hercules' vision the gods reimpose their limits: a Fury assails the Giants that Hercules has released and shuts them back in Hell (982–6).[46] With the closing of a gate Seneca brusquely curtails Hercules' fantasy, and his own: the rule of the gods is wrested but not destroyed by poetry.

The terrible slaughter of Hercules' family actually involves a descent from the splendour of fantasy: this increases its starkness and horror. The divine at first recedes from the surface, though it remains underneath as the cause; it returns at the climactic moment when Hercules slays his wife and the child she is holding. Here Seneca makes Hercules believe that his wife is Juno (1010 f., 1018 f.); at the moment when Hercules thinks he is triumphing over the goddess, the goddess is triumphing over him. At this astonishing twist, we detest the goddess's ingenious malice; but we also delight in the poet's malicious ingenuity. The imagined killing of an immortal wildly violates both hierarchy and mythical reality; but there is not here the grandeur of Hercules' earlier defiance. His conceptions and his violence are inglorious and uncouth: even if Juno hides in Jupiter's lap, he will carry her off (1010 f.).[47] His manner at the moment of supposed victory has nothing magnificent.

> teneo novercam. sequere, da poenas mihi
> iugoque pressum libera turpi Iovem.
> sed ante matrem parvulum hoc monstrum occidat. (1018–20)

I have caught my stepmother! Come into the palace; pay me your penalty, and free Jupiter from the weight of your shameful yoke. But let this small monster perish before its mother.

The second line has Hercules now kindly establishing proper hierarchy in heaven; but Jupiter's marital enslavement, though a striking idea, is scarcely dignified. The last line carries on the

---

[46] The lines must, I think, be understood thus: the pointless inconsequence and weak incoherence of the paragraph, if Hercules were the object of attack, could not be excused by the insanity of the speaker. The driving back of the Giants is omitted with grim force and characteristic obliquity. With Seneca's treatment of the mountains contrast Man. i. 424–8.

[47] For the structure cf. Ov. *Met.* viii. 394 f. Against Hercules' words may be set the magnificent utterance of Achilles at Hom. *Il.* xxii. 20, unspecific, hypothetical, angrily recognizing the limits of mortality.

ingenious distortion with pathetic paradox: *parvulum*, 'little', in sense and colour suits not a monster but his son. The simple first line, devastatingly false to the reality before his eyes, also marks the grammatical inversion with which he conceives himself in relation to Juno. It is his stepmother that is performing the action on him, as his stepmother; it is he that will pay her the penalty. His final speech, with a new demented shift, and a new humiliation, returns to the language of ceremony as he dedicates his sacrifice to Juno. The vow he has accomplished was worthy of her, he says, *te digna* (1038). The irony looks back to the prayers worthy of Jupiter and himself (1038), to the ascent of heaven worthy of Hercules (957), and, above all, to Juno's modest claim to be planning something worthy of a stepmother (112). The uses of the phrasing mark the grim supremacy of hierarchy and of evil.[48]

Two points must be noted from the profound final scene. Firstly, while it stresses the power of Juno over Hercules in the madness, it also presents Hercules' final endurance after it as an achievement of Herculean courage. Immediately after the daring fusion in which Hercules calls his own hands 'stepmotherly' (*o novercales manus*, 1236), he is told that to endure all his woe needs Hercules, needs his extreme of valour (*nunc Hercule opus est*, 1239).[49] In a conception related to philosophy, but sharpened by the mythological theology, the great human retains his greatness in despite of the divine. Secondly, however, Hercules' real apotheosis is affirmed: affirmed decisively for the reader, but in the most delicate and fleeting manner. In the last line of the play we are told that the land where Hercules is invited, for purification, is wont to make gods innocent: *illa te, Alcide, vocat / facere innocentes terra quae superos solet.* We are drawn into the bold paradoxes of heavenly beings not innocent, but made so by an earthly land (*terra ... superos*); it is only the final word *solet*, 'is wont', which allusively implies that Hercules as well as Mars (1342f.) will be a god. So quietly does Seneca bring about that transcendence of

---

[48] The lines might be sarcastic, as Fitch suggests; if so, irony remains. But Amphitryon's speech would follow less effectively, and *te digna* work less well.

[49] The effect of the resounding *novercales* is strengthened by the abnormal metre: see Zwierlein (1984a), 229f. With 1239 compare and contrast Eur. *HF* 1250, 1347–51. For the treatment of the name cf. Sen. *Tro.* 614; the employment of Hercules' name to register an extreme, in speeches by or to him, acquires in this scene particular force and intensity. Among Seneca's plays such employment of names, common in the period, is particularly prominent in this play, the *Troades*, and the *Medea*.

divisions which through the course of the play had been so vehemently challenged and so forcefully perverted.

At the end of *Thebaid* x (827–939) **Statius** shows Capaneus, one of the Argive leaders, scaling the walls of Thebes with a ladder, defying the gods, and being slain by a thunderbolt from Jupiter. The passage, by no means expectedly, explores related areas to Seneca's, but to quite different purpose. Again there is moral complexity, but of a very different kind; there is not here the same appalling rift between hierarchies of morality and of power. Again the poetry is strange and audacious, but the complications of poetic tone are much richer than in Seneca. Statius, being an epic poet, and being Statius, treats the physicality of transcendence far more colourfully and weirdly than Seneca, and the episode stands at a greater distance still from unentangled seriousness of impact.

The episode before has shown the boundaries between man and god being transcended in a fashion harmonious and morally almost straightforward. The youth Menoeceus has slain himself to save Thebes, in accordance with an oracle: virtue with an ease as of nature brings him to deity. The very clause which shows him attaining it slips in with self-conscious smoothness (780–2; cf. 665, 680). As he goes, the crowd already hail him as a god (*deumque*, 684: the shortest predicate in the line is its climax); as he stands on the walls to die he has already a divine appearance (759), and his 'looking down on the warfare of men' has a symbolic force (*despexitque acies hominum*, 760).[50] He is assimilated and passes to the divine through a divine element in himself: this is stressed when Virtue descends from her place in the heavens and leaves in his heart—herself, *seseque in corde reliquit* (672). Stoic conceptions inform the passage deeply; yet that very phrase we have just quoted gains its paradox from the mythological framework, which is vigorously present. Statius plays audaciously with the combination of philosophy, myth, and epic convention in 639–49 when Virtue prepares for her epiphany: he makes the goddess that personifies a virile quality betray her unfeminine deity despite disguise as a woman, like Hercules in female attire

[50] Compare further the notion of the wise man looking down on humanity from above, e.g. Sen. *Ep.* 92. 32; Lucr. ii. 1–16; Stat. *Silv.* ii. 2. 131 f., with van Dam's note and Nisbet (1978), 11 f.; Sil. xv. 106 f. (compare Daniel, *Cumb.* 1–16). On Menoeceus' deification note also xii. 76–9; for the episode cf. Schetter (1960), 12 f., 41 f., Vessey (1971).

(641–9).[51] Yet the episode, though conscious in its daring, possesses a large and noble simplicity and rectitude.

Capaneus' episode is intended to contrast with Menoeceus' strongly. That is made evident enough when Capaneus declares that lofty *virtus* (courage) bids him attack Thebes at the place where Menoeceus died, and explains the 'command' with an impious defiance (845f.). We naturally compare the celestial Virtus; yet this episode neither presents a blunt moral antithesis between Menoeceus and Capaneus, nor limits its concerns to morality.

The physical division between earth and heaven is forcefully exploited, as in the earlier episode, but here in a boldly and giddyingly concrete manner. Capaneus' mounting of a ladder is turned with remarkable extravagance and fancy into a movement from the earthly towards the heavenly realms; Statius does this not merely as a passing conceit, but with sustained particularity. The episode begins:

> hactenus arma, tubae, ferrumque et vulnera; sed nunc
> comminus astrigeros Capaneus tollendus in axes.   (827f.)

Hitherto our matter has been arms and trumpets, swords and wounds: now I must raise Capaneus to the starry heavens to attack them at close quarters.

The work ascends in literal and poetic sublimity, even from the grandiose material of epic; the bunched enumeration of the first line yields to the lofty sweep of the second. Yet there *comminus*, 'at close quarters', suggests a disconcertingly physical combination of the celestial and the military.[52] Capaneus' own initial feelings are not rapt, like Statius', but blasé: *iam sordent terrena viro taedetque profundae / caedis*, 'the man is now wearied of mere earthly things, and tired of slaughter in the depths' (837f.). *terrena*, 'earthly things', and *viro*, 'man', are juxtaposed to show the hierarchical audacity, like the bold perspective of *profundae*, 'in the depths'. The humdrum verbs take daring to an extravagant and almost entertaining point.

---

[51] Compare Williams's note; cf. now Feeney (1991), 383f. In 672f. the sex of Virtus is used to give an intimate warmth and a light sensuality to the contact of man and goddess; note *pectora*, and the more stridently amorous language transformed by Silius for the action of Fides (ii. 517f.).

[52] Cf. *Aetna* 51f. (where the combination is partly polemical), and the whole passage. For the episode see especially Klinnert (1970), 47–59.

The narrative removes Capaneus vertiginously from the earth. In a dithyrambic union of the familiar and the weird, he is said to carry his ladder (grandly described) to be a journey in the air for himself (*aerium sibi portat iter*, 842). The gods see *in media vertigine mundi / stare virum*, 'the man stand in the middle of the whirling sky' (918 f., below); 'stand' and 'man' are both placed so as to strengthen their paradox after the imposing phrase on the heavens. The divine perspective is used still more arrestingly when the gods fall suddenly silent as 'Capaneus was heard in the midst of the stars', *mediis Capaneus auditus in astris* (898).[53] The phrase in its setting suggests the dramatic and startling intrusion of the scornful hero into the region of the gods. The poet uses the physical boundary between the mortal and immortal worlds with unsettling vividness and bewildering unreality.

Capaneus' ascent is made repeatedly to recall the assault of the Giants, and the like; yet it is also differentiated: it produces no real threat to the gods. In practical terms, Capaneus' wish to fight the gods is wild folly; but Statius with subtle poise has him leave Jupiter entirely unperturbed, the other gods, in spite of themselves, not free from anxiety. The hierarchy of gods and men remains firm, but Capaneus' fierce courage can just seem, though in vain, to shake it. Jupiter, who had been fearful of the Aloidae (852), laughs at Capaneus' mad blasphemy (*furentem / risit*, 907 f.), and speaks with relaxed surprise of mortal ambition (909 f., *quaenam spes hominum ... !*). As for the others

> pudet ista timere
> caelicolas; sed cum in media vertigine mundi
> stare virum insanasque vident deposcere pugnas,
> mirantur taciti et dubio pro fulmine pendent.[54]   (917–20)

The heavenly gods were ashamed to fear such things; yet when they saw the man standing in the middle of the whirling sky and demanding mad battle, they felt silent wonder, and suspense for the thunderbolt, of whose success they were unsure.

---

[53] I agree with Williams, against Housman, that *quierunt* should be read in 897; Hill's helpful account yields a somewhat flaccid narrative, and does not explain *ecce*. In 918 Statius is presumably adapting Ov. *Met.* ii. 70; we may also hear the sense 'dizziness' in the background. Williams's 'right at the centre of the universe's revolution' seems philosophically dubious.

[54] P's *pallent* ruins the sentence and leaves *mirantur taciti* very weak. The use of *pro* is the same whether the verb is of fear or of anxiety; it makes little difference to the sense whether we read *dubio* or the conjecture *dubii*, though *dubii* places the emphasis somewhat more

The sentence is exquisitely contrived to evoke, not terror, but the shadow of fear; to portray at the same time as this the hopelessness, and the fearlessness, of the mortal's attempt; and to paint the emotion of the gods as just slightly unbefitting. The polysyllabic *caelicolas*, carefully chosen and placed, catches the gods' sense, as well as the narrator's, of the shame of their being afraid. For the stark notion of fear the last line gently and smilingly substitutes weaker feelings and softer expressions. The start of the next book goes further for Capaneus, after his death: it has the other gods congratulate Jupiter as if he had beaten the Giants (the real difference is still plain); and it has Jupiter himself not deny Capaneus' deeds all praise (*ipsi non inlaudata Tonanti*, 11).[55]

That passage seals the mixture in the action of folly, wickedness, and splendour. The first words densely and paradoxically mingle those ideas in a weighty subordinate clause: *postquam magnanimus furias virtutis iniquae / consumpsit Capaneus*, 'after great-spirited Capaneus had ended the madness of his wrongful courage' (xi. 1f.). Framing the action on the other side of the episode (x. 827–36), Statius uses length rather than brevity, and unresolved alternatives more than combinations; but again he calls forth a complex and ambivalent response towards what might look an impressively simple impiety. He sets out in profusion possible causes of what Capaneus did ('whether it was that ... ', *sive ... seu*, etc.), and hence possible evaluations. We might have to do with the inspiration of hellish evil, or with *virtus*, 'courage, virtue', exceeding limits (a light paradox), or with a more straightforward rash heroism, or with the result of divine supremacy, whether generous to the great or sinister to the wicked (831–6).[56] The author permits these thoughts to resound discordantly together. Their tumult largely enhances the air of furious sublimity he has already created, though not without self-conscious play (at 831f. his madness and the Muses' daring

effectively. *timere* gives a better sequence than P's *timeri* (accidentally omitted by Hill?). It is here used of a possible future, not an actual present, action; for this use of *pudet* cf. e.g. Sen. *Prov.* 3. 3; Luc. ii. 446.

[55] Somewhat differently xi. 123f.; *ausus* conveys Capaneus' courage through paradox and disapproval while showing Jupiter's absolute supremacy, cf. x. 938f.

[56] At 835 *fata* (P and most MSS) seems preferable, in this causative context, to *fama*. The greatness of Capaneus' coming death has won him the favour to achieve what he does. It scarcely fits the text to have the various possibilities depict the judgements of hell, earth, and heaven; no more does it (cf. xi. 11, etc.) to view Capaneus as an embodiment of the demonic (or Pluto as the devil).

incongruously echo the impious mortal's). Yet luxuriant sublimity and mortal magnificence are repressed by the grim and lingering final phrase on human folly and divine control, *blandae superum mortalibus irae*, 'the alluring anger of gods to men'.

We are to react to Capaneus with a paradoxical mixture of moral attitudes; but the complexity and discord extends to the aesthetic impact of the passage. We see this especially in Capaneus' own speeches. Thus there is an obvious interval between the first and the last. In the first, for all the moral complication, his *hac me iubet ardua virtus / ire*, 'this is the way my lofty courage bids me take' (845f.), has a strong and noble grandeur.[57] In the last, where he proposes to use Jupiter's lightning to rekindle the flame of his torch (925f.), the poet's ingenuity and mischief obviously preclude a straightforwardly emotional response. There is a certain appeal in Capaneus' own blending of defiant frivolity and single-minded war-lust, but any admiration or dismay is amused and distant. A richer and more complicated extravagance appears in his speech of challenge to the gods at 899–906. The extremity of his blasphemy and valour flout mortal limits so dizzyingly that one feels mentally too in empty air; yet the wild splendour of the transgression thrills. At the same time, Capaneus' insults display such gusto, and deploy mythology with such denigrating address, that one is diverted and entertained. Not only heroism, folly, impiety but sublimity, lowness, and unreality are headily compounded.

In the speech Capaneus exploits the hierarchy among the gods even as he wildly contemns the hierarchy placing men below gods; his exacting standards cause him to dismiss the idle Bacchus and Hercules and call on Jupiter himself.

> pudet instigare minores:
> tu potius venias; quis enim concurrere nobis
> dignior? en cineres Semeleaque busta tenentur:
> nunc age, nunc totis in me conitere flammis,
> Iuppiter! an pavidas tonitru turbare puellas
> fortior ... ?   (901–6)

It shames me to goad on lesser gods; do you come instead. Who could be worthier to fight with me? Look! Your Semele's ashes and tomb are

---

[57] One should compare Coroebus at i. 644f. *mea me pietas et conscia virtus / has egere vias.* Coroebus, while defying the divine like Capaneus, attains a moral superiority to the god, and even *pietas*; contrast Virg. *Aen.* viii. 131.

captured. Now, now, Jupiter, come strive against me with all your fire! Or are you bolder at alarming timid girls with thunder?

pudet, 'it shames me', delightfully exhibits a weary scorn. At first, Capaneus addresses Jupiter without mentioning even his name (we are to gather it from the context and what follows); here fantastic pride combines with the excitement of direct challenge. *dignior*, 'worthier' (903), locates the standard of greatness not in the gods but in himself: the word begins the line with over-whelming and preposterous audacity. We are raised into still higher and more incredible regions by his superb open gesture when he calls on Jupiter, not in despair but in martial courage, to send his thunderbolt against him (904). The god's name now falls with immense force and daring. The appended provocation draws us into much much less grandiose and more amusing poetry. The taunt has a warrior's crudity; but it also ingeniously combines undignified matter with a cunningly barbed reuse of the myth of Semele.[58] Our reaction is not simply the aghast dismay of the other gods (906).

This episode provokes clamorously contrasting responses, pushes extravagance and unreality to the wildest and strangest point, and yet exhibits sure poise and deft precision. The conflict of man and gods excites Statius' poetry to one of its most astounding flights; but all the time we feel the poet's easy and unshaken mastery over his medium and his universe.

These scenes display vividly the imagination and life with which mythological poetry invests its world of the divine. The complications of effect so important to high poetry have appeared with particular force; the relations between unreality and magnificence, play, and so forth have proved particularly elaborate. And for all the connections between the episodes, we have seen in this vital sphere the exhilarating fertility and diversity of the poets.

---

[58] With his lightning Jupiter had, not intended to frighten her, but been tricked into killing her; his love for her, implied in 903, makes the suggestion the more cruel.

7

THE GODS IN PROSE AND IN LUCAN

IN this chapter we shall concentrate chiefly on **Seneca**, whose works dwell far more on the divine than any other writer's in prose.[1] By considering some particular passages, we shall be able, among other things, to savour the difference of his philosophical writing on the the divine from writing on the divine in poetry. We could have made that difference seem smaller, at least theologically, by concentrating on certain types of passage in poetry, and by taking less interest in play; our purpose, however, is not to arrive at an absolute measurement of the interval but to glimpse characteristic differences between the genres in scope, atmosphere, world, and manner. Many divergences are obvious, but less simple than they appear. From the harmony and theological optimism of Seneca's explicitly Stoic universe poly-theistic discord, and sinister or entertaining anthropomorphism, utterly disappear. The tone is thus simpler and more uniformly serious; but Seneca is often eager to display the paradox and strangeness of conceptions which can so overstep familiar hier-archical limits. We lose too the particularity with which poetry depicts its gods; but Seneca's language and imagination commonly make his gods vividly accessible to the reader. The question of actuality makes a fundamental difference, but is especially complicated.

The gods of poetry are to a large degree felt to be unreal; Seneca in a broad sense believes in the truth of his depictions, and seeks to make the reader embrace that truth, through the sense of reality and persuasiveness which his writing creates. But Seneca is not merely hammering home a tight and lucid dogma: Stoicism did not compel a ferocious delimitation. God was identified, in the foremost line of classic theory, with the mind running through the universe. But there had always been present other conceptions too, and complications: thus Stoicism also had a place for plural

---

[1] On God in Seneca see, among other works, Motto (1955*a*); Richards (1964), esp. ch. 4; Dragona-Monachou (1976), ch. 6; Scarpat (1977), esp. ch. 1; André (1983).

gods.[2] On the precise nature of God or gods, and the degree to which they possessed personality and interacted with men, Stoics of the Imperial epoch especially could show a large fluidity. Stoicism in general favoured multiple levels of interpreting and expressing reality, rather than univocal flatness. Thus we cannot know quite how far Seneca takes belief in the personality with which his language normally invests his deities (cf. pp. 232f.). Besides this, Seneca does not generally offer a full and total portrayal of divinity as he conceives it, but rather selects particular aspects, to suit his argument (as a rule anthropocentric). From these he frequently produces forceful pictures, most commonly fleeting. For all the underlying unity of Seneca's thought, even the more substantial pictures vary strikingly in the dominating impressions of deity which they leave. Their life, colouring, and shape are the creation of Seneca's writing. And in writing so often figurative, imaginative, paradoxical, and extreme we must encounter reality and truth through the literary experience, and not seek too meticulously to disentangle presentation from belief.

Thus, despite the large and real difference between high poetry and philosophy in respect of reality, we see in Seneca's prose no simple specimen of writing that straightforwardly communicates propositional truths; rather we see work in which a complicated relationship exists between reality and art, and where art and imagination have large significance and ample scope. The comparatively extensive passages we discuss will illustrate the range of Seneca's depictions, and the power of his writing to give them substance and force, and through them to win and inspire.

The *De Providentia* explicitly concentrates its attention on one aspect of the long-lived debate about providence: on the question why good men suffer bad fortune.[3] Seneca concentrates his skills

---

[2] Plural gods explicitly worked in, *SVF* ii. 1049, etc.; in Seneca there is most commonly little important difference between *deus* and *dei*. God νοῦν κόσμου πύρινον: *SVF* i. 157 (etc.); later at least, a pervading πνεῦμα νοερόν, Posid. fr. 100 EK (etc.). God might also be identified with the cosmos, and so forth (*SVF* ii. 527, etc.). The variety of Stoic notions, in the same thinkers, was familiar: see the hostile treatment at Cic. *ND* i. 36–41. Note too the presentation as alternatives of the conceptions mentioned at Sen. *Helv.* 8. 3. The best way to begin on the cosmic ideas is perhaps to read Diog. Laert. vii. 136–43, not regarding the doxography too closely (see Kidd (1988), i. 405f.).

[3] Note the placing of this topic in Nemesius' discussion (*Nat.* 366–8). Even in regard to individuals, the ancients were at least equally interested in the unpunished bad (cf. e.g. Plut. *Ser. Num.* (548a–568a)). The treatment of providence most illuminating for Seneca and the tradition is Philo's *De Providentia*, mostly conserved in Armenian (see the edition of

of art and thought on painting the relationship between the good man and God or the gods. He must so draw it that it vividly and acceptably unites divine concern for the good and the divine infliction of misfortune; and he must colour it with an ethos that appeals and excites, and renders complaint ignoble and dull. In relation to this second aim, an inspiring sense of moral greatness is vital to Seneca's persuasion. To pursue this aim further, and at the same time to challenge and unsettle us, Seneca pushes what is conceived as an apparently paradoxical position to extremes of paradox. He would rather be provocative, robust, and arresting, than bland, safe, and anodyne. Human loves, hierarchies, and activities form a prime resource for making the theology tangible and tolerable, but also for making it startling and strange.

At I. 5 Seneca pronounces that 'between good men and the gods there exists friendship', *inter bonos viros ac deos amicitia est*. We are already to be struck by such human language and so close a relationship. The loftiest associations of divinity have been implanted by the preceding paragraph; and Seneca now underlines by his diction the startlingly human sound of 'friendship'. So he adds on to the phrase quoted the discordant combination *conciliante Virtute*, 'they have been made friends [almost, 'introduced'] by Virtue'. But the privilege and the compatibility go further:

amicitiam dico? immo etiam necessitudo et similitudo, quoniam quidem bonus tempore tantum a deo differt, discipulus eius aemulatorque et vera progenies, quam parens ille magnificus, virtutum non lenis exactor, sicut severi patres durius educat.

Do I say 'friendship'? Rather, a close bond, and a likeness: for the good man differs from God only in time [duration]; he is his pupil, his imitator, and his true offspring, whom that great-spirited parent, not mild in his insistence on the virtues, like stern fathers brings up somewhat harshly.

This sentence progresses adroitly, unexpectedly, and expressively. It reaches new extremities of intimacy, and of likeness; but it also presents the imposition of suffering which is to result from so near a relationship, and from the demands of a likeness which has

M. Hadas-Lebel). For Chrysippus' περὶ προνοίας see Gercke (1885), 705–14; *SVF* iii p. 203; Gigante (1979), 315. On Seneca's work see Köstermann (1934), 7–28; Grimal (1950); Abel (1967), 97–123; Motto–Clark (1973); Wright (1974), 48–54.

to be achieved. We discreetly shift from an association of equals to a hierarchical relationship, where severity becomes intelligible. The inviting climaxes come especially from the heavy rhetorical movement at the start and from the still warmer *vera progenies*, 'true offspring', which ends its tricolon. 'True' enhances the glory and the reality (there is a contrast with myth); but it also prepares for the radical consequences of the image, or truth, which are to be drawn in the unlooked-for relative clause that succeeds. In that clause, human conceptions draw us on towards the more formidable doctrine. *exactor*, 'enforcer', and also *magnificus*, 'great-spirited', although transformed by their contexts, are yet words of very human ring; *sicut severi patres*, 'like stern fathers', presses the human analogy explicitly.[4] But after *severi*, 'stern', and the forceful litotes *non lenis*, 'not mild', all issues in the restrained *durius*, 'somewhat harshly'. The new-born paradox is not at first treated too roughly.

Even by the end of the paragraph it has acquired a slightly harder surface. Seneca is still deploying human notions to make the conception more vivid and more acceptable: we are happy for favoured slaves to live loosely (says Seneca), but not our sons. God, he proceeds to say, *bonum virum in deliciis non habet: experitur, indurat, sibi illum parat*: 'the good man is not God's darling; he tries him, hardens him, and prepares him for himself'. Subtly exploiting hierarchy and language, Seneca at first makes as if to deny intimacy and warmth, but only to replace a superficial fondness with a relationship that goes to the depths of each side's nature. The profound *sibi illum parat*, 'prepares him for himself', wonderfully conjoins a stress on true closeness with the implication that that closeness inevitably demands suffering.[5]

Thought and paradox develop further as Seneca uses human hierarchy afresh, this time the hierarchy of sex. He now inventively contrasts fathers with mothers. Mothers are to win our disapproval for the womanish softness with which supposedly they want their sons to be treated; whereas

[4] For *exactor* cf. Quint. i. 7. 34. The device *amicitiam dico?* recurs in Seneca only at *Ep.* 99. 27. Cf. e.g. Plin. *Ep.* vii. 6. 1.

[5] The language lightly suggests the possibility of an afterlife in the heavens, cf. *Ep.* 102. 29. The hierarchical contrast is very differently exploited at John 8: 35, *Gal.* 4: 1–7. For *in deliciis* cf. e.g. *CLE* 403. 3 *deliciumque fuit domini, spes grata parentum*, 1867. 2, Sen. *Ep.* 12. 3.

patrium deus habet adversus bonos viros animum et illos fortiter amat et
'operibus' inquit 'doloribus damnis exagitentur ut verum colligant
robur.'   (2. 6)

It is a father's spirit that God shows towards good men; he loves them
strenuously; 'let them be harassed', he says, 'by labour, sorrow, and loss
so as to gain true firmness.'

Thanks to the context, *patrium*, 'a father's', strongly emphasized
by its separation from *animum*, 'spirit', combines with suggestions
of love emphatic suggestions of severity.[6] Unrelenting *et*s hasten
us on, first to the impacted and discordant combination *fortiter
amat*, 'loves strenuously', and then to the alarming speech of the
loving deity. There what in its main clause sounds like a maledic-
tion flows (as the rhythm suggests) into the stern justification.

Later this image will reach a still more exacting form as Seneca
assimilates the gods' treatment of us to that of Spartan fathers who
have their sons fiercely flogged in public to test their courage (4.
11f.). Seneca is there at once extreme, self-conscious, and insistently and insidiously persuasive. The physical and emotional
horror, and the paradox, are extravagantly and ingeniously
embraced: the Spartan fathers *laceros ac semianimes rogant perseverent
vulnera praebere vulneribus*, 'ask their torn and half-dead sons to
continue giving their wounds to be wounded anew'. But characteristic phrases appeal, though not without flourish, to our belief:
numquid tu ... credis?, 'surely you do not think' that these fathers
hate their sons; *quid mirum si ... ?*, 'what wonder that' the gods test
hardly, *dure* (for no proof of virtue is soft)? In the second instance
Seneca supports his persuasion by dextrously opposing *dure*,
'hardly', and *molle*, 'soft': the latter word suggests feeble
effeminacy, and Seneca cunningly excludes any middle ground.[7]
Words by now familiar, like 'hard' (*dur-*) and 'brave' (*fort-*),
undergo modulations in the passage: some of those modulations
daunt, some conciliate.

Very shortly after the passage on fathers and mothers, Seneca

---

[6] With both 2. 5f. and 1. 5 compare the much kinder picture of God as a father in Philo,
Prov. ii. 15 (though presumably Judaism has some influence here). For the use of military
hierarchy in 4. 8 cf. e.g. Plat. *Ap.* 28d9–e (cf. Epict. i. 9. 24, etc.); Epict. iii. 24. 32; Sen. *Ep.*
120. 12; Rutherford (1989), 240f. The literal statement in Diog. Oen. fr. 103. 4f. Casanova
gives us a revealing contrast with the Epicurean ethos.

[7] Cf. e.g. 3. 5 (with Plut. *Fort. Rom.* 317d). For the Spartan floggings, sometimes fatal, cf.
Tigerstedt (1965–78), ii. 147f., 166; note Holford-Strevens (1988), 6 n. 38. Cf. also Petr. 105. 5.
With *vulnera praebere vulneribus* cf. Sen. Rh. *Contr.* i. 8. 3.

goes on to present the gods, not as fathers, but as spectators of gladiatorial games that enjoy the virtuous suffering of the great (2. 7–12). This potentially appalling image of the God who is 'most loving of the good', *bonorum amantissimus*, Seneca arrives at in full awareness of its extremity and its paradox.[8] It is presented as Seneca's own fancy; he tempts us to think him and his gods alike capricious and heartless. At the start we have *ego non miror si aliquando impetum capiunt ...*, '*I* should not be surprised if the urge does not sometimes seize them ... '; near the close, *inde crediderim ... : non fuit dis immortalibus satis spectare Catonem semel*, 'that, I would think (is why Cato needed two attempts to kill himself): the immortal gods were not content to watch Cato only once.' The latter sentence, indeed, shows such extravagant ingenuity in combining historical fact with Seneca's wild idea as must certainly complicate our response. And yet the language and the assurance of the writer finally succeed in making the whole conception an extreme and potent image of the gods' loving delight in the virtuous and of the splendour of virtue (nothing else truly matters). The love comes in explicitly only at the close, after teasing delay. *quidni libenter spectarent alumnum suum tam claro ac memorabili exitu evadentem ... ?* (2. 12), 'of course they were glad to watch him whom they had nurtured go forth with so glorious and memorable an end ...' The gods of epic, we are to remember, lament to see their progeny die; this sentence presents the contrary. Thanks to *alumnus suus*, 'him whom they had nurtured', the warmth of love now tinges the writing; what appeared stark and searching paradox in the first half of the sentence in the second resolves itself into glory. The paradox and extremity make Seneca's communication arrest and challenge us; simultaneously his self-conscious daring detaches and fascinates one part of our mind. In this passage generally, a noble and inspiring picture of the relation between god, man, and virtue expresses itself through paradox and extravagance, graphically, demandingly, intriguingly; it also triumphs over paradox and extravagance with ostentatious bravado.

The strenuous combinations in the presentation of God appear

---

[8] For the epic origins of the idea see Griffin (1978). Seneca has usually no liking for the arena: cf. *Ep.* 7. 2–5, 95. 33, *al.* With the present passage contrast Cic. *Fam.* vii. 1. 3. For the idea of gladiatorial courage as morally uplifting cf. (e.g.) Plin. *Pan.* 33. 1.

even at the end of the piece. God's speech expresses in its form, and displays by its content, his active love for the virtuous. But it becomes increasingly bracing, and finally stresses how easy it is (physically) for humans to die: the ease of dying manifests God's love. The conception deliberately defies the weak responses of ordinary men.[9]

The first half of *De Beneficiis* iv (1–25) offers a picture of deity very different in its colouring and impact from that of the *De Providentia*. This is not a matter of large inconsistency. Seneca wishes to concentrate on other aspects, presents those aspects with engrossing power, and develops them to imposing and magnificent extremes. The concern of *Ben.* iv is principally with the intrinsic value of conferring benefits; to suit the thought, the gods appear chiefly in their universal and benignant generosity. It is not a question of tight argumentative necessity: Seneca wishes also to explore these sides of divinity in their own right, and to give his outlook a cosmic dimension. The extremity is meant to be felt. Indeed, in the later part of this book itself the presentation of the gods is modified. This happens in the intricacy of argument; yet we are assuredly intended to notice and appreciate this shift for itself. Seneca often likes to limit and qualify after open extravagance of thought; in him sobriety and ardour perpetually modify and support each other.

In the part of the book where the gods appear most, we see them not, as in the *De Providentia*, narrowly, intimately, sternly involved with the virtuous, but broadly, impersonally, munificently outpouring good things to all mankind. The gods are themselves given a much less vigorous air of personality; they act through the universal order, and the abundant particulars, of the world. This world of endless gift is a picture and a system which Seneca opposes pugnaciously to Epicureanism, where the gods do not interact with the rest of the world, a world of undesigned chance. The emphasis on philosophical systems, largely absent from the *De Providentia*, increases the generality and breadth of the depiction. At the same time, Seneca's picture is not to seem, as he

---

[9] Cf. Sil. xi. 187–9; Plin. *NH* ii. 156; contrast Philodem. *De Morte* iv col. 37. 27–38. 3 (Gigante (1983), 181). Seneca intensifies the challenge through graphic physicality in his individual treatment of a common device, that of enumerating means of suicide (cf. Winterbottom on [Quint.] *Decl. Min.* 260. 24).

wishes Epicurus' to seem, bizarre and recherché. It is to be attractively harmonious and grandly evident.[10]

The difference of temper between Seneca's two treatments is
seen strikingly on the theme of luxury (ever opposed to virtue). In
the *De Providentia* we hear God tell the virtuous that he has deceived 'the others' in surrounding them with the false good things
of luxury (6. 3f.). Divine concentration on the good is taken to a
grim and unusual extreme in this language of deception (contrast
Ben. iv. 17. 4). In *Ben.* iv, not luxury directly, but the abundance of
delightful things which makes luxury possible, and the ease, and
every human art, all spring from God, who has not seen only to
our necessities: *usque in delicias amamur*, 'his love for us extends to
the daintiest pleasures' (5. 1).[11] This benevolent indulgence rings
very differently from *bonum virum in deliciis non habet*, 'the good man
is not God's darling' (*Prov.* 1. 6, above). Divine generosity is now
taken to an extreme that is intended, from Seneca, to arrest. Even
the underlying thought of the passages implies a divergent
approach from the *De Providentia* to the material world, and to the
significance of anything besides virtue. But this divergence has
been sharpened and pushed to extremity by the language and
presentation; in consequence the gods are portrayed in dramatically different colours.

The superabundant generosity of the gods is expressed through
the superabundance in Seneca's writing here. Streams of such
words as *tot*, 'so many', and *unde*, 'whence?', pour forth in overflowing rhetoric the bounties of heaven. They express too the
contagious fervour of Seneca. The very size of the longest digression on the gods (4–8) serves the same purposes. Yet Seneca's
persistent liveliness and alertness of thought prevent any lax flac-
cidity; his thought draws out with insistent ingenuity and energy
the multifarious and all-supplying kindnesses of God. The com-
bative zest of the discourse, particularly against Epicureanism,
makes it all the more sharp and forceful.

We shall mention one or two passages, giving particular notice

[10] Note esp. 4. 2; cf. e.g. *SVF* ii. 1115. For the picture in general cf. particularly Cic. *ND* ii.
115–68 (e.g. 133, 140). The Epicurean side is now further and forcefully represented in Diog.
Oen. frr. 18–19 Casanova.

[11] Seneca takes to an extreme a conception unwelcome to Epicureans. Cf. Philodem.
περὶ θεῶν iii col. c, *SVF* ii. 1124; Cic. *ND* i. 121, Plut. *Non Posse Suav.* 1102f–1103a. On the
treatment of luxury note Cic. *ND* ii. 160; contrast in *De Beneficiis* itself above all Demetrius'
speech at vii. 9f. (cf. iv. 6. 2 with vii. 10. 2).

to Seneca's significant handling of length and brevity, of lavishness and control. In 25 the author sets forth the gods as a pattern
for our own disinterested generosity; the conception is made to
manifest a hierarchical and emphatically Stoic universe. A lavish
sentence (2) opens with a commanding *vide*, 'see'. Its parts expand
from *quanta cottidie moliantur, quanta distribuant*, 'how many things
they set in train each day, how many they distribute', to the length
of the final member, with its loving evocation of benevolent action
and concrete result:

quantis imbribus repente deiectis solum molliant venasque fontium
arentis redintegrent et infuso per occulta nutrimento novent.

how many showers they cast suddenly down to soften the earth, and
restore the dried-up waters of springs, renewing them by nourishment
poured in through hidden ways.

The remainder of the sentence, by contrast, is pointedly brief and
plain: 'all this they do with no reward, no gain that comes to
them', *omnia ista sine mercede, sine ullo ad ipsos perveniente commodo
faciunt*. The final sentence of the paragraph is still less fluent and
less elevated: *pudeat ullum venale esse beneficium: gratuitos habemus deos*
(25. 3). 'Let us be ashamed that any benefit of ours should be had
on sale: we've got gods who act for nothing.' The curt, colloquial
ending is very Senecan. Here the effect is to produce in the last
clause a jarring combination of words which defies the hierarchies of language: adjective, and verb, hardly befit the gods.
However, by adopting the low style of a mercenary attitude,
Seneca wryly shames us into rejecting that attitude. The abundance of what precedes shows what overwhelming beneficence is
actually implied; now the brusque, dry expression holds in and
contains, but also validates and gives authority to, the opulence of
the earlier description.

   Chapters 5–6 assail the Epicurean notion that the gods confer
no benefits; they are splendidly organized in the length of their
sentences.[12] 5. 1–6. 4, after the interlocutor's blunt allegation 'God
does not give benefits', *non dat deus beneficia*, presents a continuous
cascade of questions. The sequence starts with pungent brevity

---

[12] The idea that the Epicurean gods give no benefits is naturally more prominent in
their opponents, e.g. Plut. *Non Posse Suav.* 1103d; but cf. esp. P. Oxy. 215 col. ii b. 10 f. *nihil agit*
(4. 1) is used several times in Cicero's attack, *ND* i. 116, 123, ii. 59, taking up the Epicurean's
own phrase, i. 51, cf. Epic. 5. 1 Arrighetti.

and torrential anaphora, and a series of questions in *unde?*, 'whence?'; to brevity, anaphora, and *unde* it at last returns (6. 3), having gradually expanded further and further. The sentence before this return is particularly lengthy. It conveys the glory of the world; it shows how the world excels a magnificent palace, which the interlocutor would certainly think no mean gift. There is nothing flabby about the size of the sentence. The elaboration enhances God's gift; but it also shows Seneca's whimsical ingenuity, and a certain sprightly irony at the outlook of those devoted to luxury. So: 'he has built you a vast dwelling, without any fear of collapse or fire', *ingens tibi domicilium sine ullo incendi aut ruinae metu struxit.* Astounding generosity informs the whole clause; but *sine ... metu*, 'without ... fire', vivaciously intrudes a cunning and unelevated thrust amid the grandiose transfiguration of ordinary reality. 'The roof' of the world (better than golden or coloured roofs in palaces) 'shines in one way at night, in another by day', *tectum vero aliter nocte, aliter interdiu fulgens.* The real splendour of the sky gleams through this deliberately colourless understatement, and its true marvel appears through the wry presentation of it as superior gimmickry.[13] All the long and lively development in the sentence is set sharply against a few plain words, which starkly and neatly recur to the interlocutor's absurd claim: *negas te ullum munus accepisse?*, 'Do you say you have been given no gift?'. The *élan* of the rhetoric, the mobility of the language, and the vivid unfamiliarity with which different spheres are combined, turn well-known lines of argument into a fresh and sparkling depiction of the universe as a present.

We turn to a smaller scale of art. The first sentence of the book in which the gods are presented, short though it is, nobly and vigorously communicates their inconceivable beneficence; it does so in part through its shaping. *di vero tot munera, quae sine intermissione diebus ac noctibus fundunt, non darent* (3. 2), '(if one's own advantage were the only reason for conferring benefits) the gods would not make all those gifts which they pour forth without ceasing, day and night.' In Seneca's order the abundant clause which evokes the gods' actual munificence is set against the short and cold *non darent*, 'would not give'; against the bare *darent*, 'give', is set the rich verb *fundunt*, 'pour forth'. The metaphorical suggestions of that

---

[13] In Shakesp. *Ham.* II. ii. 300–4 Wells–Taylor (1230–4) the imagery has become less pointed and more magnificent. At 6. 1 *deus* must indeed be supplied, but before *metalla.*

word are more fully drawn out a little later, when Seneca bids
one consider the men who complain at their lot:

invenies non ex toto beneficiorum caelestium expertes, neminem esse
ad quem non aliquid ex illo benignissimo fonte manaverit.   (4.3)

You will find them not wholly without share in the benefits of heaven,
no one to whom something has not flowed from that most bountiful
spring.

Here too shaping is important. The first half, elegant but plain,
is in the second restated with warm and compelling language.[14]
In that half itself the words are very simple as far as the pointed
and emphatic *aliquid*, 'something'; then the utterance fills out
amply with the expressive and alluring image. *benignissimo*, 'most
bountiful', unites the image with the moral quality. *manaverit*,
'has flowed', is a richer word than *fluxerit* would have been; it
colourfully and seductively presents the enjoyment of some
benefits by the most unfortunate as an embodiment of the gods'
overbrimming and impartial generosity. The obvious problems
in that thought Seneca will on this occasion shelve, and stress
only the positive aspect; by his language he means to capture our
imagination for his depiction of the gods.

We must add a word on a passage which entangles matters.
Seneca ends the ostensible digression 4–8 by answering an
objection: that all he has described is provided not by God but
by nature. He retorts, in accordance with Stoic doctrine, that
God and nature are one: God has many 'names' (Jupiter, Fate,
etc.), which denote the self-same being (7–8). The passage is
often taken out of context to demonstrate Seneca's impersonal
view of the divine.[15] It may indeed present his ultimate opinion,
and he frequently moves in his work between God or gods and
(a personified) Nature; none the less, the tendency of his language in general is to present the divine as if endowed with some
kind of personality and with quasi-human love. How far this is a
matter of presentation, how far of actual feeling or belief, we
cannot hope to determine with precision; but divine concern for
men is important to Stoicism, and we should not too rigidly
circumscribe the conceptions that readily flow from such a

---

[14] In the preceding sentence *tantam* is a conjecture, and an unsatisfactory one, for the
corrupt *tam* of N¹. There are various possibilities, e.g. *iam* ('already').

[15] Cf. esp. *NQ* ii. 45 (which is also called forth by its context).

view.[16] Of this passage in relation to its context we must note two things. On the one hand, the personality of the gods has in the book so far been felt relatively faintly, their affinity to men has not been very forcefully portrayed; hence the explicit consideration of aspects which might seem to tend away from humanity will not here jar too harshly. On the other hand, it is actually essential to Seneca's case here that God should be sufficiently a person to have a generous will, without which he could not confer 'benefits' in the sense that Seneca means and requires. Seneca discreetly fails to confront this crucial question of personhood directly or clearly; what he does is so to write that 'God' appears the pre-dominant aspect of the divine force, and that his language suggests in 'God' a sort of person acting with will (note *beneficio eius*, 'by his gracious act', at 7. 1). The plenitude of 'names' is made tacitly to reflect God's manifold, all-pervading, and abundantly generous activity: he and his gracious action have made and fill this universe of benefit, and 'he can be styled by as many titles as he has bestowed gifts', *tot appellationes eius possunt esse quot munera* (7. 2). The passage does not actually detract from Seneca's picture of the universe and of divine bounty. It increases its solidity and depth, and broadens its range.

After 25, however, which ends the first half of the book, Seneca does deliberately modify the impressions he has given of the gods (cf. p. 228). They now appear more discriminating. It is good men they are concerned with; although they have conferred some benefits on all mankind, good and bad alike, this is only because it was not possible in these cases to confine them to the good (28). The shift in emphasis, and the actual change in depiction, are meant to be seen. 26. 1 strongly indicates a turn in direction, and the movement is marked by recalling and recolouring matter from previous passages, including very recent ones.[17] The style is now stamped by subtlety and the drawing of distinctions: so *mul-tum enim refert utrum aliquem non excludas an eligas*, 'it makes a great difference whether you do not exclude someone or you choose him' (28. 5). Seneca now makes manifest the selectivity and the lavishness of his earlier depiction; but it must not simply be forgot-

---

[16] Cf. e.g. *SVF* ii. 1192, 1118 (more warmly developed e.g. Marc. Aur. ix. 27); Cic. *ND*. ii. 164–7 (more warmly e.g. Marc. Aur. ix. 11); *SVF* iii. 584 (more strongly Epict. ii. 17. 29). Epictetus is particularly notable in this regard.

[17] So with 28. 1–3 cf. 3. 2 (kings), 4. 3, 5. 3 (*commercium*), 23. 1, 25. 2.

ten for this rectified version. Both together contribute to the complex picture we are to receive from the whole book of divine action and of Seneca's thought.

The prologue to Book i of the *Naturales Quaestiones* offers us deity in a different light again. We find too a treatment of the boundary between man and God which it is striking to set against the treatments of that boundary which we considered in mythological poetry. We shall deal with this second aspect first. Through his language Seneca here exploits audaciously the physical and the hierarchical structure of the universe.[18] Man is boldly and disconcertingly made to exceed the expected limits of that structure, yet without any violation of the natural order and even without any sense of heroism. This is part of the wonder. We have to do here both with characteristic features of Seneca's philosophy and with lavish developments in this particular passage.

In this book (certainly not the first in Seneca's own ordering) Seneca considers phenomena of the skies; the prologue portrays the study of God and the heavens as raising us to the divine.[19] Man's likeness to God now admits him to God's world, in this life; what lifts him thither is not virtue even in part, as we would expect, but knowledge and the intellect. The context, as so often, gives the impulse, but Seneca's writing develops the basic conception with startling extremity and vividness. Physical transcendence and philosophical knowledge coalesce in Seneca's impassioned contemplation of tranquillity. We are not shown the struggle of the upward journey, or God's active love for the wise man, only the calm of the spirit viewing the heavens and knowing the supreme objects of knowledge.

Seneca often uses the image of the philosopher or his mind ascending to what he contemplates. Here the immersion of the living man is so full and physical, the abandonment of the world so nearly complete, that it is as if a celestial existence after death were in question. Thus, in a picture usually associated with the

[18] [Aristot.] *Mund.* 400ᵃ3–34 presents with particular force this common philosophical structure, where earth and heaven are contrasted and God is located in or linked with heaven.

[19] The book actually concerns phenomena that Seneca locates in the air, not the heavens; I suspect that, despite *praef.* 14 and the division in ii. 1, Seneca is permitting himself to connect the two, and so aggrandize his subject. One may add that theology itself is quickly and explicitly abandoned at 1. 4. If the prologue was written for a different context, as is contended by Gross and others (Gross (1989), 12–15, 318 f.), that context will clearly in turn have directed Seneca's presentation.

blessed dead, the mind looks down on the tiny earth from above, and marvels at mortal ambition (8–10). There is no magnificent usurpation of a higher realm, as in the passages on Capaneus and, more paradoxically, on Hercules. The mind belongs here, is established and at ease.[20] *nec ut alienis sed ut suis interest: secure spectat occasus siderum atque ortus* ... (12), 'it acts as if amongst things that are its own, not another's: untroubled it watches the rising and setting of stars ... '. The first clause uses basic vocabulary with bold surprise but also with strong simplicity. *suis*, 'its own', to which the clause builds up, makes the mind appear related to, and even in unruffled ownership of, the heavens. The word takes up the forceful phrasing of 11: *sursum ingentia spatia sunt, in quorum possessionem animus admittitur*, 'above there are vast spaces, which the mind is allowed into possession of'. The author is making a pointed contrast with the little empires of man below; but the language still vigorously creates a sense of having, and of having lawfully. *secure*, 'untroubled', would not in itself seem a strange state of mind for the astronomer, but the context transforms it into a remarkable and intimate unconcern. Even earlier, in *inter ipsa sidera vagantem*, '(the mind) wandering among the very stars' (7), the verb, which on the most literal level suggests the star-gazer's vision, in its context evokes unconstrained liberty and almost a relaxed stroll.

The mind, or spirit, is only following its true nature; but as it does so, man leaves his human status. We are to feel both how easy and natural is this ascent to heaven and how excitingly and strangely it bursts the hierarchical structure. At the climax of the prologue, after dwelling on questions about God which the mind will become able to answer, Seneca demands

haec inspicere, haec discere, his incubare nonne transilire est mortalitatem suam, et in meliorem transcribi sortem? (17)

To examine, learn, and devote oneself to such things: is that not to leap over one's mortality and to be transferred to a better rank?

The image of ascent and of dwelling in the heavens is here at first suspended for the more ordinary denotation of inquiry; but that makes Seneca's claim the more startling and the less smooth.

---

[20] Seneca takes his starting point from the idea that the soul derives from God (the cosmic πνεῦμα) and so is divine, and at home in the heavens: cf. e.g. *Helv.* 6. 7f., *Ep.* 120. 14 (cf. Posid. fr. 99a EK; Marc. Aur. xii. 26); 79. 12, 92. 30–3. Axelson rightly denies that death

transilire, 'leap over', is a dramatic verb; but still more arresting is the *trans-* verb in the next clause, and the prosaic language used there, which turns this figurative apotheosis into a definite and as it were official alteration of status.

A much earlier sentence challenges us by presenting contemplation of the heavens both as the transcendence of mortal limits and as the only way for man not to be contemptible. *o quam contempta res est homo nisi supra humana surrexerit!* (5). 'Ah, how despicable a thing is man, unless he rises above what is human!' The form unites emotion and conscious paradox to resonant effect.[21] The context enlarges the paradox. It reveals that *humana*, 'what is human', which man must transcend, includes not only the life of the body (what precedes) but, more startlingly, the soul's conquest of vice (what follows): and yet it shows contemplation of the heavens as itself the true goal of being human, the full and perfect good that belongs to humanity, *consummatum ... plenumque bonum sortis humanae* (7). On the one hand, the prologue is rarefied and extreme in thought and conception, for all the importance in Seneca elsewhere of contemplating the skies, and for all the significance to him of knowledge and reason. On the other, the ascent —however far a creation of Seneca's language—is within our reach, and near at hand. We see Seneca himself (3) engaged in the very contemplation and inquiry which are given such transcendent power. We stand far from the strenuous and heroic world of the *De Providentia*, let alone from the assault of Capaneus.[22]

How is God presented in this prologue? He is shown to us above all as the object of philosophical knowledge; the presentation is intellectual, aloof, and overwhelming. We see the supreme greatness of God's place in the vast and glorious structure of the

is in question here ((1933), 21 n. 9); *domicilii prioris* in 13 if sound would be an extreme instance of Seneca's appropriating the language of death, though *Ep.* 65. 16f., 21, Cic. *Tusc.* i. 51 might tempt one to suppose corruption in *prioris* (e.g. from *praesentis*, cf. *Vit. Beat.* 6. 1, etc.).

[21] Cf. esp. *Const. Sap.* 6. 3. Seneca is connecting *homo* with *humanus* etymologically, and probably connecting both with *humus*, rightly (cf. Maltby (1991), 281, 284). It is rewarding to consider both Montaigne's comments (pp. 588f., éd. Pléiade), and Molière's ironic use of such notions in *Les Femmes savantes* (i. 1. 44f., etc.). Compare Aristotle's rebuttal of traditional wisdom at *Nic. Eth.* x. 1177[b]31–4.

[22] Above, pp. 216ff. One may note the use at *Prov.* 5. 10f., in a somewhat different context, of the myth of Phaethon. There what poetry had made a rash violation of mortal limits becomes in philosophy an admirable deed of intrepid virtue: *est tanti per ista ire casuro*. (In Ovid Phaethon displays an incipient but misguided heroism; it will evaporate abruptly.) For contemplation of the heavens, and the divine, cf. esp. *Helv.* 8. 4–9. 2, *Ben.* vi. 23. 6, *Ep.* 110. 9f., *Brev.* 19. 1f., *Ep.* 95. 10–12.

universe which philosophy perceives and which Seneca powerfully depicts; we see too the large general questions about his
interaction with the world which have occasioned such endless
debate and dispute; and yet the mind can rise to true knowledge of
something so great and so obscure. This knowledge Seneca tinges
with the suggestion of personal relationship, but in such a way as to
imply extraordinary privilege rather than glowing warmth, and to
throw the accent onto intellectual understanding. So

(virtus) animum laxat et praeparat ad cognitionem caelestium, dignum-
que efficit qui in consortium <cum> deo veniat.   (6)

virtue frees the mind and makes it ready for obtaining knowledge of
heavenly things, and worthy to enter into the society of God.

'Entering the society of God' essentially denotes the same activity
as 'obtaining knowledge of heavenly things'. *consortium*, 'society',
ordinary and uncolourful, produces a startling combination with
deo, 'God', and thus conveys the amazing fortune of the mind, in its
easy commerce with the divine. Seneca stands back from the
language of love.

   Notable too in that sentence is the suggestion of process, initi-
ation, and final attainment. The same notions inform the great
moment at 13. It is the sense of intellectual and literary climax that
gives the mind's arrival at knowledge there its momentous power.
Seneca has earlier described how he himself in studying the universe and the divine learns *quid sit deus*, 'what God is' (3). A long
passage has told of the mind's understanding and contemplation
in the heavens, when it has risen there (7–13). At the culmination of
this passage, God himself returns.

illic demum discit quod diu quaesit, illic incipit deum nosse. quid est deus?
mens universi. quid est deus? quod vides totum et quod non vides totum.

There at last [in the heavens] the spirit learns what it has long sought to
discover: there it begins to know God. What is God? The mind of the
universe. What is God? The whole that you see, and the whole that you
do not see.

   The first sentence not only describes and constitutes a climax to
quest and passage, but itself builds up, with potent anaphora, and
with plain but subterraneously emotive language, to two words
which now carry immense weight, *deum nosse*, 'know God'. The
combination in its context is to seem astonishing: God can actually

be known. *nosse* contains the suggestion of personal acquaintance; but its primary force is intellectual.[23] Having now reached this great point, Seneca does not, as we might expect from the start of 12, dilate with Platonic intensity on the spirit's rapturous experience; he promptly transforms his discourse, with thrilling suddenness. We are now directly confronted with the supreme question 'what is God?', which has been invested with such grandeur and mystery; we are no less directly confronted with the answers. Seneca is here in part delivering on the most elemental level some of the knowledge that the mind will attain (so the connection of the sentences must imply, cf. 16): he himself, immersed in celestial study, speaks with oracular and exciting authority. The passage will develop into more argumentative exposition, but that in turn will lead us back into the glory of knowing such truths (as Seneca himself in some sense seems to) and of exploring God's relation to the world (as Seneca actually does). The words quoted are also meant to suggest the relationship between mind, God, and cosmos which underlies the process of knowledge through philosophy and contemplation of the heavens, and which makes that process astounding. Seneca's answers may appear simply to present standard Stoic doctrine; yet they are dense and pointed, as the context makes apparent. God is himself mind, and thus accessible to us; but he is the mind of the universe, and even the universe itself, which we contemplate. Hence he is both akin to us and incomparably greater. The passage, in its setting, is sublime; yet there is a self-conscious theatricality in Seneca's abruptness and assurance, and an ingenious elegance in his form, which lightly complicate that sublimity.

More obtrusively, the actual close of the prologue deliberately brings this intellectual presentation of God to an appearance of incongruity. Seneca turns from the language of deification to answer drab objections about the utility of such pursuits; through these pursuits, he says, he will at least know that everything (else) is small, once he has measured God, *sciam omnia angusta esse mensus deum* (17). The words are full of significance and irony: God, not man, is made 'the measure of all things', and the world of utility

---

[23] *Cf. Ep.* 90. 34; compare and contrast 31. 10. Note the choice of the more markedly intellectual *mens universi*; contrast *animum ac spiritum mundi* at *NQ* ii. 45. 1 (the whole passage is relevant).

becomes too petty to trouble about.[24] None the less, the combination *mensus deum*, 'having measured God', pushes intellectual and definite knowledge of the deity to a bizarre extreme; at the same time, the sentence holds in and partly reduces the grandeur which Seneca has amassed in this austere but enthralling proem.

We have seen something of Seneca's power, splendour, and diversity in handling the gods, and given body to our initial remarks. We may draw out here one or two further thoughts. Firstly, the general greatness and sublimity of Seneca's conceptions and treatment have been obvious; we have seen the connection of these with moral grandeur in the *De Providentia*, and in the prologue to *NQ* i with transcendence of hierarchy. The elevation, however, is no bland dignity: lavish extremes transport and sometimes disconcert, dashes of unelevated vivacity produce spice and freshness, paradox arrests and gives us pause. This brings us to a second point, on the relation between manner and truth. It will have been apparent how features of manner like paradox and extravagance that are shared with mythological poetry serve the imaginative development of each passage; it will also have been apparent how in Seneca's philosophical writing these elements become more vigorously purposeful, and sometimes more forcefully challenging and unsettling, than in the more unreal world of mythological poetry. The relation of artistry and truth in Seneca here is in some respects complex and elusive; but the importance of truth also makes us feel the artistry as particularly dynamic, bold, and exciting.

From the rich presentation of divinity in Seneca we turn to the utterly different treatment in **Tacitus**.[25] His handling of the divine in his historical works illustrates rewardingly the elaborate relationship there between intellectual and emotional elements, and between truth and greatness. The most fundamental aspect, however, is simple and negative: the divine, which so fills and irradiates the philosopher's writing, has by comparison a faint and shadowy presence in the historian's. The contrast is in part a token of the difference between the genres, as treated by the two authors. That difference will itself be connected with differences

---

[24] Man as measure: Protag. B1 DK; cf. Sen. *Ep.* 71. 6. On the thought note also *NQ* vii. 30. 3 *maior pars sui operis ac melior*.

[25] See particularly Kroymann (1969); Burck (1961); Syme (1958), ii. 521–7; Häußler (1965), 377–89; Scott (1968); Riposati (1983); Colish (1990), 304–9.

in the authors' own beliefs and intellectual temperaments, though the relation between Tacitus' beliefs and his work can hardly be determined with precision. Tacitus adopts a genre which narrates human events from a critical stance: it is wary over supernatural intervention and metaphysical commitments. Even Livy is no exception to this tradition; and Tacitus gives in general a particular importance to the presentation of the writer's critical mind.[26] Some light is thrown on the intellectual contrast with philosophy, and on the distinctive character of history, by two authors of our period who write in other kinds.

The **Elder Pliny** writes within the domains of natural philosophy, but without allegiance to a philosophical school. Near the start of his work proper, he enhances the greatness of nature, cosmos, and sun by deploying philosophical, especially Stoic, notions of their divinity (ii. 1f., 12f., 27). But it is that greatness itself, and physical reality, that matter to him, and the theological belief is handled gingerly.[27] In his general treatment of religion here, he displays metaphysical confidence only negatively, by colourfully assailing unenlightened conceptions, practices, and attitudes. On the truth of the notion he chiefly discusses, that the gods are concerned with men, he conspicuously declines to adopt an opinion. The avoidance is not to seem feeble. Such shrewd caution suits Pliny's whole scholarly manner and position; we are meant to think well of its judicious restraint, and to contrast the enlightened reserve of Pliny with the gloomy and chaotic credulity of mankind. The stance, in a work on nature, very strikingly exemplifies an intellectual tradition on the divine for non-philosophers; the still greater reserve of history has a broad intellectual background.

The **Younger Pliny's** *Panegyricus* freely uses a benevolent and

---

[26] Livy makes plain his reserve and rationality, though he urbanely affects to adopt, as a patriot and antiquarian, what he is very far from committed to intellectually. Thus his elegant remarks at *Praef.* 6f. (cf. v. 21. 8f.), and xliii. 13. 1f., are meant to display his critical consciousness; i. 4. 2 presents a pleasing example of aloofness to begin Roman history. (*seu ita rata* is exquisitely sceptical; compare the material and treatment of Dion. Hal. *Ant.* i. 77. 1–3.) See esp. Kajanto (1957). The choice of genre may commonly be linked with other choices, and, more obviously in the case of prose, with beliefs; we glimpse some of the intricacies, however, in Posidonius', very moralizing, history (cf. frr. 58–60 EK, 67, 266, etc., T 80; Kidd (1989)), and in Livy's overtly philosophical works (not merely dialogues), and even Pollio's (Sen. *Ep.* 100. 9).

[27] One should also compare with 12 f. (cf. *SVF* i. 499) the more openly figurative passage on the earth at 154–9.

moral picture of the gods to add magnificence to political events and to the figure of Trajan. The genre of oratory permits, and Pliny's purpose encourages, a firm assurance in the presentation of the gods as active in human affairs. His treatment forms part of a ceremonious language of praise; it is significant that at one point he can momentarily adopt a position of agnosticism on the gods' involvement with men (80. 4). The contrast with history is obvious: the flow and ease of the speech's metaphysical assumptions and laudatory manner would be alien to history and its sober and exacting scrutiny.[28] Yet Tacitus too, in very different ways, can use the language of divinity to lend grandeur to history, and can even suggest, very discreetly, the possible or probable will of heaven through seemingly supernatural events.

However, Tacitus' treatment of the divine is stamped above all by his historian's wish to display his critical caution and subtlety, and, not least, his aversion to facile acquiescence in the miraculous. At *Hist.* iii. 33. 2, for example, we see Tacitus showing at least reserve over an instance of supernatural intervention. He ends his shocking account of the sack of Cremona with a remarkable detail:

cum omnia sacra profanaque in ignem considerent, solum Mefitis templum stetit ante moenia, loco seu numine defensum.

While everything, sacred and otherwise, was collapsing into the flames, there remained standing, alone, the temple of Mefitis in front of the city walls, protected by its position or by divine power.

Like alternatives on motivation, the alternatives here parade both acuity and restraint. *loco*, 'by its position', which neatly gives point to *ante moenia*, 'in front of the city walls', shows Tacitus' shrewd and dry practicality. The first clause of the sentence, taking up references to temples earlier in the account, suggests the difficulties Tacitus notices in the supernatural explanation. None the less, the order of the alternatives prevents too pat a cynicism, and the mind is momentarily intrigued by the notion of divine intervention so curiously and disconcertingly limited. In their effect,

---

[28] Some passages noteworthy in regard to divine action: i. 3–6, 8. 2, 10. 4, 67. 5–68. 1, 72. 3f., 74. 4f., 94. Pliny's references often spring from given particulars in events and the like. The references to the gods in Dio's orations on kingship are naturally less specific, and are more expansive and wide-ranging. Note esp. i. 37–47, 67, iii. 50ff. On these orations generally see Moles (1990).

the evasiveness and the critical manner contain and throw into relief the lavish emotion of the whole passage.[29]

A more complicated example appears at *Hist.* iv. 81. Tacitus exhibits his intellectual restraint; but the divine is also given, and confers, imposing potency and elevation. He is recounting what seem like miraculous events in Egypt which were held to show the gods' favour for Vespasian. Even here, where he accepts the events themselves, he contrives to maintain an air of critical detachment and intelligence. In the case of Vespasian's healings of two men (81), he makes clear his supposedly exacting and penetrating approach to evidence (there are eye-witnesses, with no personal motives left for deception (3)). He indicates, through the mouths of doctors, that medically the healings need involve no miraculous element, so that the gods might have operated (if at all) through ordinary nature (2). He characteristically shows himself more wary over the divine significance than over the occurrence itself, and presents the divine interpretation as the opinion of others (1); and he distances himself from the superstitious Egyptians (1).[30] Yet Tacitus' very caution gives solidity to the event; his very openness in interpretation, while making the thought of divine favour less evident, makes it also excitingly mysterious and suggestive. After all Vespasian's dubiety and the doctors' expatiation, and after the build-up of cola to the plain action *iussa exsequitur*, 'he did as he was bidden', the result follows with dramatic and challenging power. *statim conversa ad usum manus, ac caeco reluxit dies* (81. 3). 'At once, the injured hand was restored to use, and for the blind man the light shone.' The sentence wonderfully and significantly conjoins in its rhythmically twinned clauses the prosaic and the exalted; but the crucial word is the opening *statim*, 'at once'.[31] The numinous force of the moment is strengthened by

---

[29] Since Tacitus places the sentence after the close of the main account, as something noteworthy, he must intend *numine* to refer to supernatural power, not merely fear of that power (cf. Wellesley ad loc.). The impersonal *considerent* suggests the same. (For 35. 1 cf. ii. 70. 1.) A few inscriptions survive to this interesting goddess, but one should not exaggerate the prominence of her cult; for Tacitus she is evidently a deity far from the first rank of fame and splendour, and this makes the event the more striking.

[30] The doctors' pragmatic ending is nicely cynical; but the language would not support the notion that Tacitus is mocking their pomposity (as is perhaps suggested by Syme (1958), i. 206). On the events cf. Henrichs (1968).

[31] Set against this sentence Suetonius' quiet *nec eventus defuit* (*Vesp.* 7. 3; ὑγιεῖς ἀπέφηνε, Dio (Xiph.) lxvi. 8. 1). Suetonius does not show the same critical concern as Tacitus, either; with Tacitus' reported clause in 81. 1 cf. in the Dio the direct τὸ μὲν θεῖον τούτοις αὐτὸν

the episode that follows: there Tacitus again shows caution and care, and again in doing so he forcefully presents the operation of the divine, this time with less real possibility of doubt.

These chapters carry through and advance the treatment earlier of divine indications that Vespasian would become emperor (ii. 1. 2, 78). Tacitus had there combined suggested or actual acceptance with mockery for easy and adaptable credulity. At the opening of the work he had accented still further his critical canniness.

occulta fati et ostentis ac responsis destinatum Vespasiano liberisque eius imperium post fortunam credidimus.   (i. 10. 3)

What fate kept secret, and that Vespasian and his sons had been shown to be ordained for empire by portents and oracles: that we believed [only] after their triumph.

The sentence is maliciously constructed: the bulky and grandiose clause *et ... imperium*, 'and ... oracles', follows a brief colon that contradicts it, and is followed by a brief clause that shrewdly deflates it.[32] The first person plural actually increases the historian's wry and ironic detachment. In all this Tacitus aims, not to be rigorously consistent, but to show his critical stringency, and yet to give a mounting impression of divine purpose behind Vespasian's emergence from the tumult after Nero. We begin to see the artistic and intellectual complexities in Tacitus' handling of the divine.

We must stress once more, however, the great importance to Tacitus of exhibiting caution, sobriety, and intelligence. He reinforces this appearance, like the Elder Pliny, by cool or pungent disdain for the ready belief of the unenlightened. So at *Ann.* i. 28. 1–3, when ignorant soldiers see divine significance in an eclipse, Tacitus presents their theology and behaviour as grotesque and almost exotic; this also fits his whole depiction of the mutinous soldiers, which is marked both by perception and by hauteur. The 'ignorant' and their beliefs in portents are loftily contemned (*imperiti*, *Hist.* iv. 26. 2; cf. *Ann.* xiv. 22. 1f.). A Gaul who leads a

ἐσέμνυνεν (the language is like Dio's own). Tacitus' following digression on Serapis (38f.) adds an air of scholarly detachment, while deliberately interrupting our involvement in the narrative.

[32] Commentators take *occulta* as part of the belief, which seems less coherent. Contrast *Agr.* 13. 3 *monstratus fatis* (assuredly 'marked out by fate', not 'shown to the fates').

revolt and lays claim to deity Tacitus regards with unbounded
scorn (*Hist.* ii. 61): this is a disgusting interruption (*pudendum dictu*,
'shameful to say') to grand events and by implication to his history. It is not the impiety but the absurdity which he deplores. He
narrates with cruel impassivity and superior wit how the 'stupid
crowd', *stolidum volgus*, think their compatriot invulnerable when
the beasts do not tear him in the arena—until he is slain there. He
thus manifests with force his own intellectual loftiness: he wishes
to appear as an aristocrat of the mind.[33]

Yet, despite Tacitus' normal reserve over asserting the action
of the divine, there are occasions when he seems to assert it
unreservedly. The rupture is real and intentional: from so aloof
an author such moments arrest and impress. Most of the passages
where these moments occur are in themselves unusual, and stand
outside the sequence of annalistic narrative. In them we see
Tacitus both stepping back to obscurer levels of causation, and
allowing a freer rein to his (calculated) emotion. The character of
the passages gives them particular impact, but they often have a
rhetorical liberty which sets them apart from the meticulous
exposition of events. This invites us to see in the statements on the
gods bold gestures which express the narrator's feeling and colour
the reader's response, but are as statements incalculable. All such
statements in these unusual passages we are meant to regard as
belonging to a somewhat looser and less literal mode of discourse
than the central narrative, which remains distinct. How far the
language they use may be taken as itself figurative and unmeta-
physical, varies from passage to passage; however, the expression
often forcefully conveys or effectively suggests an appearance of
assertion more impressive and exciting than mere cliché or decor-
ation. This view is supported by Tacitus' great care over the
placing of such moments, by his restricting them generally to the
unusual passages in question. But this restriction helps to demonstrate too that the purpose of these moments is essentially artistic,
and that greatness and emotional force are now paramount. This
will become evident enough from the moments themselves; and
will be further confirmed when we consider the 'assertions' that
do appear within the main narrative. The general distribution of
these moments shows further Tacitus' finesse in handling the
antagonistic claims of the grand and the critical, which are both

[33] On Mariccus cf. Graßl (1973), 93 f., 180 f.

so important to him. In his treatment of the gods as a whole he wishes the display of intellectual rigour to set off by contrast the freer heightening in some passages of emotion and greatness; but he does not wish the rigour to be seriously compromised. The two crucial elements may interact with each other, but not interfere.

Hist. i. 3. 2 and *Ann.* iv. 1. 2 retain the form of intellectual argument. Even here the reader should feel that the form, while affecting our impression of Tacitus, serves chiefly to sharpen the audacious stroke, and not at all to persuade. It also gives the talk of gods more impact than a mere figure of speech; that impact is especially evident in the passage from the *Histories*. At *Hist.* i. 3. 2 Tacitus ends the second half of his prologue, where most uncharacteristically emotion and style have poured in flood (p. 56).

nec enim umquam atrocioribus populi Romani cladibus magisve †tustis† indiciis adprobatum est non esse curae deis securitatem nostram, esse ultionem.

Never has it been demonstrated by more terrible disasters for the Roman people or by clearer signs [here portents, etc., are in question] that the gods are not concerned to keep us safe, but that to punish us, they are.

The first half *nec ... est*, 'never ... indications', forcefully combines language of lavish emotion and of proof; the final statement, with its trenchant asyndeton, its theatrical generality, and its sombre yet moral vision, excites us as a boldly expressed response and inspires our feeling towards the grand and terrible events. What matters is not (it need hardly be said) our ratiocinative conviction of its truth.[34]

Ann. iv. 1 marks what Tacitus thinks the decisive turn in Tiberius' reign by expatiating on Sejanus. He gained his power over Tiberius

non tam sollertia (quippe isdem artibus victus est) quam deum ira in rem Romanam, cuius pari exitio viguit ceciditque.

not so much through his cunning (for he was later defeated by the same skill) as through the anger of the gods against Rome; for her his flourishing and his fall were equally disastrous.

[34] Luc. iv. 807–9, the probable source, does not use the language of proof and inference, and is characteristically bitterer. It is hard to find a satisfying parallel for *iustis* (Rhenanus), which did not content Heinsius and others. Meister's *iustis vindictis* does not suit the train of thought (and see Heraeus). Something like *claris* might be worth considering. One should

The parenthesis, rough in form and oblique in thought, renders all the more startling the sudden appearance of heavenly wrath. The show of argument counts for something (though the proof of divine action could not be slighter); but again what matters is palpably not the theology but the colouring of the events and the momentousness of the passage.[35] The relative clause at the end partly reinforces the argument (the divine explanation offers coherence); but chiefly it throws emphasis on to Rome.

Such language appears naked and unsupported at *Ann.* xvi. 16. 2, where Tacitus, dwelling powerfully on the deaths under Nero, declares that a single collective treatment would not suffice for such anger of the gods against Rome: *ira illa numinum in res Romanas fuit* ... The role of the gods is again to confer greatness and emotional power on the events: the gods are not here themselves the main focus of the thought. These concerns are still more obvious in the climax of the excursus at *Hist.* ii. 38 (p. 52). Tacitus is arguing that the armies of Otho and Vitellius were not likely to behave differently from those in earlier civil wars: *eadem illos deum ira, eadem hominum rabies, eaedem scelerum causae in discordiam egere* (ii. 38. 2). 'The same divine anger, the same human fury, the same motives for evil deeds drove them too to civil conflict.' The rhetoric, extravagant for Tacitus, does not merely press a case: it emotively presents a vast and impassioned historical vision. It is this, not the argument, that is subserved by the anger of the gods, itself unargued. The opposition of gods and men makes the gods seem more than a mere periphrasis for misfortune. The shrewder *scelerum causae*, 'motives for evil deeds', at the close, is meant to show Tacitus retaining even here his firm contact with human realities.

For all the intricacies, we have so far seen an essentially sharp division; the passages which assert the gods' impact vigorously have a special character which illuminates both the passages themselves and Tacitus' careful manner within his main narrative.[36] In the *Histories*, and in the *Annals* before Nero, the main narrative very rarely allows such direct assertion of the gods'

read Lipsius' animated and characteristic note on the thought; in general 'he remarks of 16th–18th-cent. commentators on passages concerning the divine are full of interest for the perspectives and contrasts they suggest.

[35] For the form cf. *Ann.* v. 4. 1.

[36] Less vigorous is *Hist.* iii. 72. 1 *propitiis, si per mores nostros liceret, deis*; the unusual nature of the passage, and its emotional force, are plain.

agency. At *Ann.* iv. 27. 1 ships arrive opportunely *velut munere deum*, 'as if by the gods' gift'; but the evasive *velut*, 'as if', is vital. The only passage that will really answer (if I have missed none) is *Hist.* iv. 78. 2: here the barbarians' sudden loss of courage occurs 'not without divine aid, too', *nec sine ope divina*. Even here the negative expression (which echoes Sallust) may be contrasted with the resounding directness in the passages above. Tacitus is notably freer in employing a personified Fortune: such language carries less intrinsic suggestion of belief either in personality or in causative power.[37]

The Neronian books show a somewhat less restricted use of the gods within the narrative. It seems hard not to connect this with other features which suggest that these books formed the climax of the *Annals*. It appears probable in any case that the increase is linked with the desire to make the narrative greater and more intense. However, even this fairly slender relaxation is not straightforward. In the 'unusual' passages the gods had always been presented in anger. Such grim but vestigially moral grandeur appears here too; it is counterbalanced, however, by the still bleaker grandeur of assertions that the gods showed themselves indifferent to virtue and vice. These opposed aspects, which conspire in creating darkness of atmosphere, also keep the reader's impression of Tacitus complex. The narrative cannot seem to have become credulous or facile in its handling of the divine.

Tacitus describes with a memorable sentence the night on which Nero has his mother murdered: *noctem sideribus inlustrem et placido mari quietam quasi convincendum ad scelus dii praebuere* (xiv. 5. 1). 'A night radiant with stars and still with an untroubled sea was provided by the gods so as to [*or*: as if to] prove the crime manifestly.' We move grimly from the tranquillity of nature to crime to the gods; the gods contribute both to the poetic elevation of description and to the moral greatness of sin. We are uncertain

---

[37] Cf. esp. *Hist.* ii. 1. 1, 12. 1, iv. 47 (almost poetic, cf. Sen. *Tro.* 4–7, Hor. *Odes* i. 34. 12–16), *Ann.* iii. 18. 4, iv. 1; unpersonified, but with more sense of real causation, *Hist.* iii. 46. 3. For extremes of personification see Plutarch's pieces, *Fort. Rom.* and *Fort. Alex.* (316b–326b, 326d–333b, 333d–345b); these offer a striking contrast in what genres of prose can allow themselves. The whole subject of Fortune in the literature of this period is one I omit with regret. *Hist.* iv. 78. 2: commentators cite Sall. *Hist.* iv. 60 Maur. *non sine deo. Hist.* i. 29. 1 obviously does not belong here. For *velut* in *Ann.* iv. 27. 1 cf. Polybius' use of ὥσπερ and the like, Ziegler (1952), 1538f.; one should contrast the plain *Fors* (*fors*) *oppressit* at the start.

how far their status is figurative or actual, and the ambiguous *quasi*, 'as if to, so as to', increases the uncertainty.[38] But in this author their appearance as subjects is surprising and extremely powerful. This sentence introduces the protracted execution of the deed; but near the close of his account of its aftermath, Tacitus enumerates the many astounding prodigies that ensued, and confirms that they were meaningless (*inrita*):

quae adeo sine cura deum eveniebant ut multos post annos Nero imperium et scelera continuaverit. (12. 2)

These were all occurring without any involvement from the gods, so much so that Nero prolonged for many years thereafter his reign and his crimes.

The author drily shows, with argument, that there is no divine significance in the prodigies (the factual truth of which he has chosen not to question). The intellectual manner and tone also set off the latent emotion and grandeur. The sentence implies not merely the pointlessness of the prodigies but the gods' indifference to punishing Nero. This potent thought is intensified by the force of language in the second clause. 'Eight' would have sounded rather different from 'many'.

Still more impressive is xvi. 33. 1, where a loyal friend of Barea Soranus is stripped of his wealth and sent into exile. The sentence begins with the 'example of fine action' he offers (*honestum exemplum*), and ends with 'the gods' impartiality towards good examples and bad', *aequitate deum erga bona malaque documenta*. The outspoken utterance carries immense force. Yet it is grounded on facts, which are grimly faced; *aequitate*, 'impartiality', enhances the impact by its bitter restraint. Tacitus does not mention here that the man was recalled two or three years later.[39] The passage is separated by no long interval from the appearance of the gods' wrath in the excursive xvi. 16 (above), or from the climactic sentence within the narrative at xvi. 13. 1. Tacitus there begins to close his account of the terrible year in which Piso led his conspiracy against Nero. *tot facinoribus foedum annum etiam dii tempestatibus et morbis insignivere*. 'The year defiled with so many crimes the gods

---

[38] On Tacitus' use of *quasi*, etc., see Wölfflin (1867), esp. 120.
[39] Dio lxii. 26. 2 (Xiph.). Tacitus' phrase has probably suffered some corruption, but it does not affect the basic sense.

themselves marked out with fearful weather and disease.' The year is summed up with grim alliteration, and then rises to a new pitch with the surprising introduction of the gods. As with Agrippina's murder, their status is indefinite (again they are linked with the weather); the dark possibility of divine retribution lurks in the expression. The emphasis falls on the history and the dramatic gesture, not on theology or belief; the literary force of the moment is great, such is its placing, and so lavish is the description that follows.[40]

All this shows how Tacitus' handling of the divine revolves around the concerns which are so vital to the genre as he treats it: to display the historian's critical mind and to render the work great and affecting. We have seen not only how anxiously and skilfully these concerns are reconciled and how subtly they can interact, but how Tacitus' treatment fits in with the particular quality of his work. We have also incidentally implied, and supported, a sceptical position on the author's belief in his more definite utterances, on the extent to which one should suppose he was expressing his convictions and the extent to which it is important for the reader to think that he is doing so. Our position will seem self-evident to some, paradoxical to others. In connection with this secondary matter, let us add a word on *Ann.* vi. 22.

In this passage, most exceptionally, the author affects to show us himself reflecting on superhuman causation in general. We should note, firstly, how he parades his brooding uncertainty: *sed mihi haec ac talia audienti in incerto iudicium est*, 'as for me, when I hear such things, my verdict is uncertain' (as to whether mortal affairs are directed by fate or chance). He then expounds three differing sets of opinions, eloquently and thoughtfully, but without any commitment. This accords with his wider intellectual stance. Secondly, the options he thinks worth considering stand remote from the conception of divine anger which predominates in his dramatic language. He presents two philosophical systems and, with less respect, astrology; the philosophies are Epicureanism and, essentially, Stoicism, modified by a seemingly Platonizing

---

[40] One might also mention xiv. 22. 4, Nero's illness *iram deum adfirmavit*; however, Tacitus might be simply reporting, not adopting, the interpretation. At all events, tone and placing would scarcely suit the supposition that Tacitus has there on the impulse of the moment revealed his real beliefs (cf. Koestermann ad loc.).

element.[41] Angry gods do not belong in either Stoicism or Epicureanism, and here gods enter at all only in the Epicurean denial of their concern with men. We could not make the passage appear unimportant merely by pointing to less respectful remarks on philosophy in Tacitus. It is above all to philosophy that one would expect intellectuals of this period to turn for possibly valid opinions on the divine, and there might well be an element of selection and even artifice in Tacitus' usual pose (in this very passage he takes pains to avoid naming schools). However, this passage itself is no uncontrolled outpouring: it has its own historiographical tradition, and need not offer us a simple photograph of Tacitus' unchanging theological position.[42] But the passage is at all events present in the text, it makes an impact (not an unweighty impact) on the reader, and it is intended to sound like personal thought, much more so than the moments of assertion. Given this, both the reserve which the passage displays and the theological world which it moves in discourage us from imagining that Tacitus intends his reader to construct any definite system from his other utterances, or to take those utterances as a revelation of decided belief.

The contrasting viewpoints used in the Neronian books form a further obstacle to such a notion. Not that they would lend it any positive support if they could be reconciled with each other and with earlier pronouncements: uniformity here would hardly prove belief. And it is assuredly unlikely that Tacitus supposed readers of history to seek the tight cohesion and consistency of theology which they might (perhaps) have looked to find in philosophy. He certainly evinces no anxiety to show himself consistent. To him local effect, accumulated atmosphere, and the whole intellectual feel of the work are very much more important.

We close this pair of chapters with a word on **Lucan**, whose treatment of the divine can only be properly appreciated after considering epic, history, and philosophy.[43] He daringly ignores

---

[41] On the doxography cf. Theiler (1966); Dillon (1977), 294–8, 320–6; Sharples (1983), 13f. On astrology, Tacitus wishes to distance himself from the ready and thoughtless acceptance we might have inferred from 20f.; his tone on this subject naturally varies, and he evades commitment as to truth (cf. *Hist.* i. 22, ii. 78. 1 (*superstitione*), *Ann.* iv. 20. 3).

[42] Note esp. Polyb. xxxvi. 17.

[43] On Lucan and the divine see Friedrich (1938, 1954); Jal (1962); Piacentini (1963), 12–18; Dick (1967); Le Bonniec (1968); Ahl (1976), ch. 8; Narducci (1979), esp. 39–79; Lausberg (1985) 1605–11; Johnson (1987), ch. 1; Veyne (1990).

one of the principal features differentiating epic from history, and shows us no scenes on Olympus, and almost no mythological deities. He is not just aiming at truthful realism, or at the manner of history: his emotional involvement with the gods is as far removed from the historians' reserve as possible, and we have already seen that his handling of the divine shows no simple insistence on credibility.[44] The very defiance of genre, and the aesthetic bleakness, form part of his object; and he is theologically defiant too. In contrast with all standard views the divine in the poem is normally both malevolent and immoral; the gods normally further Caesar's shocking cause. We are far from the satisfying universe of Seneca's prose. In Seneca Fortune is usually seen as fighting, the gods as aiding, the good; in Lucan gods, Fortune, and fate are generally united in evil. This pointed union does not make the gods a synonym for impersonal destiny: the gods' malicious will is crucial to the poetry, and in this work we cannot meaningfully go behind the poetry in dividing the figurative from the actual. It is far from clear that we are to think the conception of deity true outside the world of the poem. Indeed, a singularly noble and impressive speech by Cato (ix. 566–87) offers us a morally satisfactory picture of God, quite different in approach to that of the poem, and straightforwardly Stoic. One might incline to see here the equivalent of those moments in mythological epic where the divine fiction parts, and a less unreal world is glimpsed (pp. 188f.).

The conception of the divine in the poem makes its impact partly through the intrinsic force of its pessimism, and partly through Lucan's writing, in particular through his use of his own voice. In form and feeling the narrator's handling of the gods stands close to his characters', far more so than in ordinary epic. There is no 'objective' description to make the gods vivid. The poet like the characters prays, protests, and condemns, and the divine gains its lively presence above all from commentary, sombre with passion or sparkling with wit. Abuse of the gods can spring from distress, in Lucan's own narrative and elsewhere: the poet's usual outlook, while true within the world of the poem, also expresses his emotional response to the events. Subjectivity and objectivity cannot readily be sundered.

Two passages will illustrate the vitality of Lucan's treatment. In

[44] pp. 66f.; and note above all vi. 464f. and the whole passage.

the first the divine world of the poem is powerfully displayed
through contrast between the utterance of passionate engagement and that of narrative; both are delivered by the poet. At iv.
110–21 Lucan prays to Jupiter and Neptune to make last for ever
the storm and the flood which have held Caesar's army trapped.[45]
He removes the prayer yet further from the reality of the poem by
departing from its conventions and addressing the prayer to distinct and decidedly mythological deities. Neptune is *sorte secunda /
aequorei rector ... tridentis*, 'you who were allotted second place to
rule the trident that commands the sea' (110 f.). Lucan makes a
whole series of requests, in particular for diverting the inland
waters of the earth to inundate the region. This transposes into
an unattainable wish Ovid's mythical picture of the gods causing
the Flood (*Met.* i. 260–85); the use of geographical realities here
only exacerbates the air of fantasy.[46] In the prayer, then, the poet
presents colourfully and incredibly the idea of deities who inter-
vene for good. His own emotional manner recalls the impassioned
outcries of characters in Seneca's tragedies who are overwhelmed
by events; he offers us too the deeper pathos of his seeking to avert
the civil war. He also enjoys the paradox of desiring what sounds
like disaster for the earth in order to benefit it.

The hopeful conception of the gods, and the ardent prayer, are
demolished when Lucan drily resumes his narrative voice, and
shows us the drab and terrible tenacity of the divine in evil. The
transition runs thus:

> huc stagna lacusque
> et pigras ubicumque iacent effunde paludes,
> et miseras bellis civilibus eripe terras.
>   sed parvo Fortuna viri contenta pavore
> plena redit, solitoque magis favere secundi
> et veniam meruere dei.   (118–22)

Pour out here, Neptune, pools, lakes, and sluggish marshes, wherever
they lie; and so snatch the wretched earth from civil war.

But Fortune was satisfied with the slight fear Caesar had suffered, and

---

[45] On the events cf. Caes. *BC* i. 48–55; App. *BC* ii. 167–9. See also Metger (1957), 93–108;
Morford (1967a), 44–6.

[46] The impersonal form of 114–17 is striking, but not actually discordant with the prayer;
cf. e.g. Sen. *Phaedr.* 674–7. None the less, the gods acquire from those lines a further
unreality within the unreality of the prayer. However, *concussa* in the context intriguingly
suggests, but does not demand, the action of the trident. Cf. Ov. *Met.* i. 283, etc., and
conversely Sen. *NQ* iii. 29. 1; note Hdt. vii. 129. 4. For the phrasing in 110 f. cf. VF i. 615–17.

returned in full; the gods, favouring him, supported him still more than their wont and so won pardon.

We see here how at the climax of the passage the wildly copious rhetoric of the prayer yields to a single line, simple, intense, and magnificent. But all is in vain, as we always knew; the gods of Lucan's world belong with Fortune, and will not seriously abandon evil. The language of the last three lines, though unexcited in appearance, is pervaded by irony and bitterness. The final phrase, marked out by the verse, is particularly mordant. The gods are no expected object for forgiveness (the placing of words heightens the paradox); in this poem the idea deviously implies that a mortal has been angry with them (ii. 93, ix. 1103). Here they 'win' pardon by their action from wicked and much-favoured Caesar; they do nothing to win it from the human race, whose hopes they hereby crush. 'Fortune' could not be substituted for 'the gods' without losing all the cool sarcasm. In these three lines the strength of the contrast with what precedes, the elegance of the casual resumption, and the sharpness and ill-will of the phrasing give the picture of grim and deplorable uniformity a compelling vivacity and animation.

The poet's discourse stands still further to the fore at vii. 445–59. Lucan here reaches the climax of the emotional and mannerist expatiation with which he has deferred for 73 lines his incipient account of Pharsalia. With a sudden impetus he declares:

> sunt nobis nulla profecto
> numina; cum caeco rapiantur saecula casu,
> mentimur regnare Iovem.　　　　　　　　(445–7)

We have indeed no gods; since the ages are snatched along by unseeing chance, we lie when we say that Jupiter reigns.

The audacious and surprising declaration carries great force. The first clause is bleak and imposingly simple; the last communicates a more biting and personal blasphemy. *numina*, 'gods', and *casu*, 'chance', fall resoundingly and grandly, helped by their place in the line and the alliteration; the name of Jupiter enters rather with curt, harsh irony. The strident Epicureanism is pressed home by a series of forceful questions: how can Jupiter, if he is involved with human affairs, fail to respond to this supreme

wickedness?[47] The stance shocks and excites. We should not
make this passage the key to the theology of the poem: it is palpably at odds with the poem's world. The line of argument looks
strange and futile when the gods have positively and persistently
promoted the cause of wrong. Rather, we are to see the lines as an
outburst, and to be struck by the emotion which drives the poet in
his supreme distress to abandon the universe of his poem. The
cleverness of his argumentation adds a touch of incongruity, but
that is wholly like him.

The conception and the feeling are abruptly and arrestingly
altered when at the end of the section the poet's ingenuity secures
revenge:

> cladis tamen huius habemus
> vindictam, quantam terris dare numina fas est:
> bella pares superis facient civilia divos. (455–7)

Yet we have got our vengeance for this slaughter, in so far as it is lawful
for gods to be punished by men: the civil wars will produce gods equal to
those on high. [The Caesars will be deified.]

Neither the means of revenge nor even the offence fit intellectually the earlier notion of divine indifference; emotionally
directness, power, and abundance are rudely cut short. But this is
all what Lucan intends. The sudden shift of thought and manner;
the bizarre satisfaction (*habemus*, 'we have got', is full of ethos); the
ironic piety of the appended qualification; the brilliant and unexpected idea; the adroit and intrepid expansion of the target to
include the emperors: all this keeps us from any simple participation in Lucan's grief, and even delights us. We enjoy the resource,
energy, and heroic impudence with which the poet entangles and
worsts his superiors in the cosmic and the political hierarchies.[48]
In this whole passage it is not Jupiter and his thunderbolt that
capture our imagination, but the poet's lively and rebellious
engagement with the divine.

We have now tasted the different universes displayed by this

[47] One must remember that Cassius (451) was an Epicurean: this nicely and polemically
sharpens in 449–51 the absurdity that anti-Epicurean opinions would entail. *nobis* in 445
are of course mortals, as the following words and 454 make apparent. With the placing of
regnare Iovem contrast both Hor. *Odes* iii. 5. 1f. and Ov. *Met.* xiii. 842–4.

[48] With 459 cf. esp. vi. 809. It is interesting to compare with Lucan's treatment of the
imperial cult here the simpler and less imaginative contempt of Pausanias' forceful aside
(viii. 2. 5).

literature; and various generalizations and comparisons have been made in passing. We need only revert briefly to our major themes in regard to this chapter. In mythological poetry, on this area, we had witnessed manifold complications of tone, and highly involved relations between greatness and unreality. The prose has been tonally simpler, but has offered no single and simple reality to set against the unrealities of poetry. Prose has presented large divergences of tradition and treatment, and individual authors' approach to truth has been far from straightforward. The immense distance between Seneca and Tacitus in this region of subject-matter is both evident and important. Tacitus displays for the most part his intellectual reserve. He will sometimes relax in his language the astringency of his attitude towards truth, in the pursuit of magnificence: the two motives have here a tendency, which he controls and exploits, to pull in opposite directions. Seneca presents with assurance of tone what is broadly to seem both grand and real. In some ways the universe of his philosophical truth surpasses in lavishness the universe of poetic fiction: there the hierarchical boundaries are more tightly guarded, the divinities less loving. However, the solidity and the shaping of Seneca's reality owe not a little to his own language and imagination, which mould and animate it. Finally, in epic Lucan strips away poetic fiction, but to produce a universe which is strange as well as austere, and which is strongly conjoined with the subjectivity of the author's voice. The complexity of effect is very considerable. The passage we have just considered, in its subjectivity and its seeming immediacy, in its despair and its wit, confronts us with complication quite differently from the fiction and relative detachment of mythical narrative; but it does so with no less vigour. To contemplate the higher genres from the viewpoint afforded by this subject is to see the remarkable breadth and intricacy that this literary landscape can assume.

8

DEATH IN PROSE

THE subject of death brings the non-comic genres to their nearest contact. As we have seen elsewhere, significant death serves more than anything to mark out high literature, and it offers it supreme opportunities for sublimity. Furthermore, the literature of this period is especially pervaded and perfused by shared conceptions of noble death: conceptions not of the relation of death to an afterlife, a subject on which even the philosopher offers no fixed doctrine, but of violent death, resolutely faced, as an achievement and a victory over fortune, slavery, physical power. The origins of these conceptions are manifold; the reasons for their importance in this literature are also manifold, and the relative weight and the connections of those reasons can hardly be determined at all closely. Our object here will be to consider some individual treatments of death.[1]

In order to concentrate our attention on the most comparable aspects, we shall look mostly at death in regard to the person that undergoes it, not to the bereaved, and at death valorously endured, especially death deliberately inflicted by others or the self; and we shall look principally at accounts of particular deaths, rather than at reflections on death in general. We shall be concerned to see in prose not only the primacy of moral greatness but how the authors convey and handle that greatness; we shall be interested too in the varying relations of their accounts to reality: physical reality, historical reality, the reality of recent experience, and the reality of the present and of philosophical truth. We shall be interested at the same time in the role and use of the author. All

---

[1] It is evident that we could not advance an explanation purely in terms of what the upper classes suffered and feared during this particular period. In the material of the Elder Seneca we see the characteristic stances and tones of our period on this subject already established and popular; and in the case, say, of Statius, directly political influence seems highly improbable. For historical and other aspects of heroic death cf. Hirzel (1908), esp. 433–68; Grisé (1982); Griffin (1986). It is noteworthy for genre and the period that even Martial can celebrate valiant deaths, e.g. i. 42; note also v. 69 (cf. Sen. Rh. *Suas.* 6). Many passages relevant to death have inevitably been mentioned in earlier chapters; a broader consideration would certainly embrace Petronius.

this will throw light on the character of the particular genres and writers: we shall see the specific consequences of generic features, and significant aspects of the authors' individuality, in the differing and related treatments of what is perhaps the most important theme in the literature of this period, and the one by which it most deeply affected its European successors.

We begin with **Tacitus**. One may start by stressing that truth is vital to the impact of the deaths that he narrates. Their literary force rests above all on moral response, and the moral response is to be affected by our knowledge that these events are historically true and truly told, and by the discrimination and justice of the assessing narrator. Tacitus' treatment is intensely concerned with evaluation, and his language characteristically emphasizes the severity, the vehemence, and the nuanced finesse of his judgements. He presents death and behaviour in regard to death as contributing to the achievement of good or evil fame; this fame has a special character and reality when the deeds are unquestionably actual. It will also inspire or deter men to come; but that aspect is perhaps foremost a way of expressing the fame itself. And in the realization of this fame both the author and his readers are not without a part to play.[2]

We look now at some particular narrations of death. In *Hist.* ii. 46–50 Tacitus describes the suicide of the emperor Otho; in the tradition followed by Tacitus, Otho slew himself after a defeat by no means fatal in order to prevent further civil war.[3] First a word on Tacitus' account in relation to others. It is clear from other

---

[2] Some characteristic expression with regard to evaluation: *Hist.* i. 72. 3 infamem *vitam* foedavit *etiam exitu sero et inhonesto*; iv. 60. 1 *donec egregiam* laudem *fine turpi* macularent . . . *vitam orantes*; *Ann.* i. 53. 5 *constantia mortis haud indignus Sempronio nomine; vita degeneraverat*; ii. 63. 3 *multum* imminuta claritate *ob nimiam vivendi cupidinem*; xvi. 11 *ne vitam proxime libertatem actam novissimo servitio* foedaret. On the relation of literary appeal, morality, and fame, compare *Ann.* iv. 33. 3 not only with *Hist.* i. 3. 1 but with *Ann.* iv. 35. 3. It is not our purpose to ascertain Tacitus' exact and real opinions about death; but it would in my view be hazardous simply to assume that *Agr.* 42. 4 proves in Tacitus even at that time a fixed disapprobation of 'useless' deaths. One cannot so lightly disregard the pressure of the context. As to historical truth, it is fascinating to see the emphasis placed by a modern *poet*, Geoffrey Hill, on bearing witness to historical events, not least appalling death (see esp. *Collected Poems* (1985), 199–201).

[3] Cf. Mart. vi. 32; so the source which lies behind the accounts of Tacitus and Plutarch (*Oth.* 15–18), and also behind most of Suetonius' (*Oth.* 9–12) and Dio's (lxiv. 11–15). For the possibility of controversy cf. Suet. 9. 3. On the historical situation see particularly Wellesley (1971). For Tacitus' scene see Voss (80f.); Heubner (1963–82), ii. 181–90, and the works he refers to; more widely, see Marx (1937–8); Schunck (1964). Sen. Rh. *Suas.* 6. 16–27 is of course an important passage for the treatment of death in this genre.

accounts, particularly Plutarch's, that Tacitus' narrative owes a great deal to his lost main source. But since the other authors are no mere transcribers either, we should not attempt to fix Tacitus' own contribution with undue confidence; nor should we exaggerate the differences between the accounts in order to show Tacitus' superiority and originality. We should rather note principally the effect and the particularities of Tacitus' account as such. Even the smallest detail is of consequence in so charged and momentous a narrative. Thus Tacitus writes

vesperescante die sitim haustu gelidae aquae sedavit. tum adlatis pugionibus duobus, cum utramque pertemptasset, alterum capiti subdidit. (49. 2)

Evening was coming; he quenched his thirst with a drink of cold water. He had two daggers brought to him, tested them both thoroughly, and put one under his pillow.

Plutarch and Suetonius say almost precisely the same (Plut. *Oth.* 17. 1, Suet. *Oth.* 11. 2), but join the two actions into a single syntactical structure. Tacitus' style allows the first austere and practical action to drop into our minds with that deliberate and poignant significance which small and simple events can acquire in a narrative progressing to expected death.

In presenting the death itself Tacitus aims for grandeur and authenticity. Plutarch, with a light dramatization, shows us Otho 'planting the sword straight with both hands' (17. 5); Suetonius offers us animated detail: 'he transfixed himself with a single blow, underneath the left nipple' (11. 2). Tacitus tells us simply that *in ferrum pectore incubuit*, 'he fell onto the sword with his chest', and that those who then came in *unum vulnus invenere*, 'found a single wound' (49. 2 f.). The first phrase is nobly restrained; there is only *pectore*, 'with his chest', to make the physicality felt. The second phrase concentrates on the channel of historical evidence, not on reconstructed drama; yet in its stern allusiveness it starkly implies the decisiveness of Otho's deed. It is also important to the spirit of Tacitus' account that this should be not a witnessed suicide but a deed performed in isolation. Public in purpose and significance, the act is in performance quiet and intensely private.

It is evident how, as in so many accounts of valorous death, the calm of the protagonist is set against the emotion of other people. In this episode, however, we see a remarkable interaction

between life and death, between the individual and others. Both
the altruistic aspect of Otho's deed and the aspect focused on
himself contribute to the nobility and strangeness of the episode.
On the one hand, Otho is performing his deed for the good of
others, and acts not simply in large and general patriotism but
with close and practical concern for individuals. When his decision is made and announced, he does not act at once. Calmly
and elaborately, he works at securing the safety of those who
might be in danger, arranging transport and destroying letters,
quelling disorder. In talking to individuals he dexterously and
courteously handles the nuances of age and rank (48. 1). He
behaves as if he were immersed in the intricacies of life, which he
has renounced; even money he gives away 'sparingly, not like a
man about to die', *parce nec ut periturus* (contrast Plut. 17. 2): the
explicit phrase is both shrewd and resonant. He can do all this, we
are made to infer, precisely because he has truly relinquished the
ignoble desire to live (cf. 47. 3, with which *placidus ... coercens* 48. 1
is linked). In the speech he makes to his soldiers, his emphasis is
not so much on the Roman state as on the men he is addressing
(one may contrast Plutarch and Dio). Not that Tacitus doubts
Otho's wider purpose; but his warmth to his men shows his
engagement in the demands of the moment, and his concern for
the body with which he had been most closely bound (33. 3).[4]
Even towards his enemy Vitellius he is magnanimous (47. 2, 48. 2).
That magnanimity and freedom from bitterness is made possible
once more by his embrace of death: he needs no consolation for
death (47. 2); to indict gods or men would evince a wish to live (47.
3; cf. ii. 53. 2).

All this moving and concrete altruism coexists with a no less
admirable absorption in himself and the glory of his deed. His
own contemplation of this glory is presented with stylized grandeur: Otho speaks with uninhibited and magnificent assurance of
his own act and fame. His speeches (47, 48. 2) splendidly interweave these elements, not to undermine the altruism, but to
display the manifold nobility of Otho's deed. So his first sentence

---

[4] On Otho and the army, cf. Campbell (1984), 365–70. Otho will doubtless have wished
his act to be seen as large in purpose too; it is not quite uninteresting to note the *Pax Orbis
Terrarum* of his earlier propaganda (*RIC* I^2 258–61). For the emphasis on taking action for
the safety of others cf. Plut. *Princ. Inerud.* 781d, Sen. *Prov.* 2. 11 on Cato.

ends *nimis grande vitae meae pretium puto*, (to expose you to further danger) 'I think too great a price for my life'. This altruism and apparent modesty are followed by the more self-contemplating *quanto plus spei ostenditis, si vivere placeret, tanto pulchrior mors erit* (47. 1), 'The more hope you display—were it my intention to live—the more splendid will be my death.' The thought is now less simple in presentation. *mors*, 'death', without *mea*, 'my', answers *vitae meae*, 'my life'; *pulchrior*, 'more splendid', shows the act morally, but for itself, as a specimen of courage almost aesthetically attractive. In 47. 2 we see a converse movement. Otho at first declares, 'let others hold the imperial rule for longer; let no one leave it with such fortitude', *alii diutius imperium tenuerint; nemo tam fortiter reliquerit*. The form of the wish turns a kind of epitaph into an indirect, but magnificently chiselled, declaration of achievement. The self-regard is evident; earlier too the brevity of Otho's reign (three months) had been deflected from a ground for scorn into a device for praise (47. 1). But he then asks with ardent emotion, 'shall I let the state be robbed of so many Roman soldiers?', *an ego . . . patiar?* (47. 2). Even in declaring that he will end the civil war he dwells on his reputation: *hinc Othonem posteritas aestimet*, 'let it be from this deed that posterity judges Otho' (47. 2). The use of the name in the third person has a superb detachment and pride. Otho is aware of his less admirable deeds, but they do not disturb the statuesque ease of this heroic confidence.[5]

Tacitus offers us this supreme nobility; but intellectually his judgement is to be seen as detached. Otho's wish about posterity, *hinc Othonem posteritas aestimet*, Tacitus accedes to only in half; he answers it with the balanced verdict:

duobus facinoribus, altero flagitiosissimo altero egregio, tantundem apud posteros meruit bonae famae quantum malae.   (50. 1)

By two deeds, one wicked in the extreme [the killing of Galba], one splendid, he won with posterity exactly as much good repute as bad.

---

[5] For the use of the name compare especially Germanicus at *Ann.* ii. 71. 3. In 48. 2, where Otho consoles his anxious nephew (*PIR*[1] S 110, Syme (1980), 99 n. 15), he shifts strikingly from allaying the nephew's own fears to dwelling with pride on his own achievements; contrast Plut. *Oth.* 16. 2. The speech in 47, probably answering to a speech in the main source, was no doubt composed freely; but note Suet. 10. 1 for Tacitus' content as regards the men. As to the general grandeur of Tacitus' account, note how he avoids the earlier suicide of the messenger (Suetonius, Dio; contrast iii. 54. 3); and how he avoids suggesting Otho's snores (ii. 49. 2; contrast Plut. 17. 3).

The balance comes from Tacitus' source.[6] The verdict is intended to seem final, just, and not stridently individual: as commonly, Tacitus draws no sharp distinction between his view, that of the time, and that of posterity. Certainly he does not dissent from a low estimate of Otho's life in general, as in the versions of Plutarch and Dio; but his less obvious choice of the murder and his more allusive expression give an air of penetration. Indeed, it is precisely because he has generally portrayed Otho in so sordid a light that the laudatory effect of the present narration becomes critically acceptable. Tacitus suggests in his account of the death many pointed contrasts with Otho's past conduct, and he forcefully reminds us of what people supposedly thought about Otho before his great deed (ii. 31. 1). Tacitus often likes to display his sense of the mystery and moral complexity of human behaviour, especially as shown by death; but he has also subtly suggested throughout that Otho is a man to surprise expectation. In his evil deed and in his good, and more widely too, Otho passes beyond the limits of the facile voluptuary. Not only in judgement but in the depiction of men Tacitus exhibits the depth and the organizing breadth of his mind and art.[7]

We turn in a moment to the death of Seneca; but we shall first consider an unexalted death, which illuminates by contrast the treatment of Seneca and Otho. This is the death of Messalina, the wife of Claudius, killed after her 'marriage' to C. Silius.[8] Tacitus' narration enters the physical happenings with dramatic intensity; but every physical moment has moral force, and the account is

[6] Plut. 18. 3, Dio lxiv. 15; there is a split between the various derivatives of Dio. *meruit* implies that the reputation is achieved, not merely deserved: cf. 31. 1, where the contrast of time shows this clearly; the phrasing in that passage is very plainly echoed here (there *quo egregiam Otho famam, Vitellius flagitiossimam meruere*). This is indeed the commonest use of the expression: note Quint. x. 1. 116!

[7] i. 22. 1 *non . . . mollis et corpori similis animus*; ii. 11. 3 *famae dissimilis*; i. 71. 1 *contra spem omnium. falsae virtutes* there in part suggests the thought of the time, and, though the phrase is for Tacitus just, it also contains an irony. Contrasts between Otho's death and the past: cf. e.g. i. 21. 2 *apud posteros*; *acrioris viri esse merito perire*. With this perverted desire for fame we ironically contrast his actual death; ii. 50. 1 heightens the opposition. Also contrast i. 44 with his outlook here (in turn cf. Vitellius at ii. 70. 4). One must contrast too his conduct here with that over the praetorian riot, and particularly his speech (i. 81–4); cf. Keitzel (1987). On Tacitus' depiction of Otho cf. Shochat (1981); one must at the least say, however, that Tacitus does not intend his favourable remarks to seem like self-exposure, but rather like deliberate justice.

[8] On Tacitus' account cf. Seif (1973), 135 f. The events are discussed by Meise (1969), ch. 6; Levick (1990), 64–8. There is no detailed narrative of the killing save Tacitus'; but note esp. [Sen.] *Oct.* 951 *cecidit diri militis ense*.

vigorously evaluative. The death is marked by perversion and
degradation at every turn; but the values of the author, stern,
grand, and strong, make the total impact of the passage (*Ann.* xi.
37–38. 1) impressive and exciting, not merely squalid and repulsive.

Tacitus' narrative of the death, though only a few sentences in
length, avoids a straightforward progression; the structure is
expressive. Tacitus focuses his account on the moment when those
who are to kill Messalina arrive. He begins with Messalina being
found by her killers (37. 3); he then proceeds backwards to tell how
Messalina's mother had been urging her to slay herself at once; he
returns to the moment of arrival, and in three lines describes the
killing. The arrival is the moment of recognition for Messalina,
when her vain hopes, her rage, her laments, and all her long folly
yield to stark reality: *tunc primum fortunam suam introspexit*, 'then for
the first time she realized her lot'. The sentence goes on promis-
ingly *ferrumque accepit*, 'and she took the sword'; but with typical
Tacitean distortion it runs on sadly *quod frustra iugulo aut pectori per
trepidationem admovens ictu tribuni transigitur*, 'her efforts to apply it to
throat or breast were rendered vain by her terror; a stroke from
the tribune pierced her through.' The last three decisive words
bring out the fumbling attempts of the participial clause. We are
intended to despise this weakness: Tacitus shows no indulgence to
her supposedly feebler sex.[9]

Before the arrival too we see her moral failure. The astounding
pride, *superbia*, she had been showing (37. 1), might have made us
expect a spirited end; but the exhortations of her mother—a
woman, too—serve only to bring out her ingloriousness:

sed animo per libidines corrupto nihil honestum inerat; lacrimaeque et
questus inriti ducebantur, cum impetu venientium pulsae fores, adstitit-
que tribunus per silentium ...   (37. 4)

There was no nobility in her mind, ruined by all her lust. She was
continuing her futile tears and laments when the doors were struck as the
men thrust in; the tribune stood there in silence ...

The thrilling force and sharpness of the moment, aurally and
visually, condemn and end her ignoble inertia. We are naturally to
contrast her with her lover, who simply begs for his death to be

---

[9] For the standard presumptions about women and courage cf. e.g. Plin. *Ep.* vii. 19. 7;
Quint. v. 11. 10; Sen. *Marc.* 16. 2; Tac. *Ann.* xiv. 35. 2 (in each case we have the categories
transcended; cf. further e.g. *Ann.* xvi. 10. 4; Sil. iii. 112f.). For *introspexit* cf. *Ann.* i. 10. 7; *inspicio*
more commonly has such a sense.

hastened (35. 2). He shows the crucial quality of courageous firmness, *constantia*.

Ignobility is not limited to Messalina. The whole event manifests not only evil, but the wild perversions of hierarchy in Claudius' world. Most notably, against the stern and dreadful figure of the tribune is set the freedman Euodus, who is in charge of the operation; we are shown him *increpans multis et servilibus probris*, 'abusing her with many insults of a slave's sort' (37. 4). The ugly and tangible breach of rank in this behaviour suggests and expresses a larger inversion: freedmen are really still slaves, and yet it is freedmen who dominate the emperor, and a freedman Narcissus, not Claudius, who has ordered the killing. The bizarre Claudius, in contrast to the whole emotional episode, evinces no reactions to the death whatever (38. 2 f.).[10]

Tacitus treats at particular length the death of Seneca, whom Nero made to kill himself after the conspiracy of Piso (*Ann.* xv. 60. 2–65). One aspect of the passage that will particularly interest us is the significance of genre, as the historian writes on the philosopher. It is evident that Seneca himself, as Tacitus makes apparent (64. 3), had in mind the death of Socrates, as recounted in the *Phaedo*; but Tacitus' narrative differs deeply from Plato's. Plato, using a speaker who was present at Socrates' death, offers the account of an eye-witness and disciple. Indeed, the present events were narrated by the historian Fabius Rusticus, who was a friend of Seneca's, and stood far closer to them than Tacitus; his account, one might plausibly surmise, evinced his feeling for the philosopher.[11] Tacitus, though his narrative arouses our admiration for Seneca, writes from a position of distance. The death took place over fifty years before, Tacitus has no personal connection with Seneca, and he does not espouse his, or any, philosophy.

---

[10] For the perversions in regard to freedmen cf. e.g. xi. 35. 1; xiii. 2. 1 *neque Neroni infra servos* (i.e. freedmen, cf. Plin. *Ep.* viii. 6. 10) *ingenium*, 6. 3; *Hist.* v. 9. 3 (Antonius Felix) *ius regium* (in Judaea) *servili ingenio exercuit* (cf. Suet. *Claud.* 28. 1). See further for the outlook on freedmen *Ann.* ii. 12. 3, xv. 54. 4; conversely note ii. 39. 1, a slave acting *non servili animo* (cf. Sen. *Ben.* iii. 23. 3). Cf. also Weaver (1972), 10 f. Note esp. the perversions in [Sen.] *Oct.* 947–51, Messalina *famulo subiecta suo*.

[11] Cf. *Ann.* xiii. 20. 2 *sane Fabius inclinat ad laudes Senecae, cuius amicitia floruit*; these events: *Ann.* xv. 61. 3 (fr. 3 Peter). Other accounts were assuredly known to Tacitus, in particular the hostile account which probably lies behind Dio's (lxii. 25. 1 f.). On Tacitus' treatment (and on his attitude to Seneca) see Dürr (1940); Alexander (1952), esp. 342–50; Dyson (1970); Treves (1970); Griffin (1976), 367–83, 427–44; Fabbri (1978/9); Döring (1979), ch. 2, esp. 37–41; Maurach (1991), 43–7.

The historian's testimony is to be the more moving precisely because he writes without partiality or ideological predisposition in favour of the philosopher. He respects Seneca for realizing his own ideals (cf. 63. 3 (45. 3), 64. 4); but it is more that on the common ground of courage in death the values of historian and philosopher come nearest to converging.

The separation of historian and philosopher is to be felt even in details. When Tacitus refers to the hemlock that Seneca had long planned to take, he calls it 'that poison with which those condemned in the Athenian public court were destroyed', *quo damnati publico Atheniensium iudicio extinguerentur* (64. 3). To write 'that poison with which Socrates was killed', though this is what Tacitus means, would be alien to his ethos.[12] Two linked moments are of more particular significance here; one comes after Seneca's death. Tacitus says that he has quoted verbatim the uninhibited words of Subrius Flavus to Nero,

quia non, ut Senecae, vulgata erant, nec minus nosci decebat militaris viri sensus incomptos et validos.   (67. 3)

since they have not, like Seneca's, been published, and it is no less fitting that people should learn of the unpolished and forceful sentences of the soldier.

Tacitus gives the philosopher no advantage over the blunt military man in valour or significance, only in literary style (this intensely artistic culture looked for verbal elegance at such moments).[12] His approach to courage of different kinds is open, rather than hostile to Seneca. He has earlier described how Seneca dictated eloquent utterances to scribes even as he was dying, *quae in vulgus edita eius verbis invertere supersedeo* (63. 3): 'As they have been published in his own words, I refrain from paraphrasing them.' This clause makes still more unlikely any intention to mock; but we are to be struck by this unemotional close to the first part of Tacitus' account, with its careful and prosaic justification of the historian's procedure.[14] The writer, and the

---

[12] The subjunctive must essentially be attracted, *pace* Fabbri (1978/9), 424: the phrase does not suit Seneca's mouth.

[13] For the limitations of the military with words cf. *Ann.* xv. 26. 3, *Agr.* 9. 2. Note that Subrius' utterance lay in some form before Dio (lxii. 24. 2).

[14] *invertere*, a highly uncommon expression, draws attention to historians' regular avoidance of verbatim report. Hartman's *meis* is not unattractive.

very particularities of his technique, obtrude themselves, precisely with a view to conserving Tacitus' distance: no one would have been likely to wonder at the omission. There is also a touching suggestion, just beneath the surface, of the respect of Tacitus the writer for Seneca the writer at the time of death. The later passage confirms this. Earlier Tacitus had treated with lofty indulgence Seneca's *ingenium amoenum et temporis eius auribus accommodatum*, his 'pleasant talent, suited to the ears of the time' (xiii. 3. 1).

Subrius' ethos is far from undermining Seneca's. Indeed, between the two passages Tacitus mentions a rumour that Subrius planned, with Seneca's knowledge, to have the virtuous Seneca made emperor, after killing not only Nero but Piso; in this regard Tacitus quotes a pithy and contemptuous remark ascribed to Subrius on Nero the lyre-player and Piso the performer of tragedy (xv. 65). The rumour is seen as quite uncertain; but the passage none the less evokes Subrius' manner and suggests the moral kinship between his world and Seneca's. The effect of the passage is more complex, however. It is placed immediately after the account of Seneca's death, which has closed nobly and almost warmly. The dubieties of history, the laudatory but incriminating rumour, the unelevated and satirical wit of Subrius' remark, remove our emotions from involvement in the narrative and show us Tacitus standing back.

Tacitus' organization of his material conveys the movingly involved relations of philosophical beliefs with other things, physical actualities and human emotions. What comes immediately before the actions of suicide Tacitus divides firmly into two parts (62, 63. 1–2). In the first Seneca appears as the heroic philosopher. Unmoved by fear, he exhorts his weeping friends to philosophical restraint; he proudly arraigns Nero and dwells on his own glory (both with some rhetorical purpose). He bequeaths his friends the memory of his life, depicted in their minds, *imaginem vitae suae*; this is now his only possession, but his most splendid, *pulcherrimum*. If his manner includes more pride and more strenuous harshness than that of Plato's Socrates, so irresistibly light and at ease, that is part of the whole character of the age, as well as of Plato's Socrates. In the second part, Seneca's stance is slightly but beautifully complicated by love for his wife. His attitude grows a little weaker and softer, *paululum ... mollitus*, as he begs her not to carry her grief to extremes.[15] He assumes that she will live on, and imagines her too dwelling on his life of virtue; but she resolves to die herself, and without compulsion. Seneca sweetly and graciously permits her to upstage him. His elegant words to her mingle self-conscious heroism with the courtesy of the loving husband: ... *sit huius tam fortis exitus constantia penes utrosque par, claritudinis plus in tuo fine* (63. 2), '... let us have the courage of so brave an end in equal share, but let you have the greater glory in your death'.[16]

In describing Seneca's motivation here Tacitus implies both his generosity and his love. In the values of this period the love of a wife can lead men to ignobility; but Tacitus' phrasing portrays Seneca's tenderness warmly. We none the less see the appearance of a different and less sublime sphere of feeling. Seneca accepted her decision *gloriae eius non adversus, simul amore, ne sibi unice dilectam ad iniurias relinqueret* (63. 2): 'He was not hostile to her winning glory, and at the same time acted from love: he did not wish to leave his singularly beloved wife to be ill-treated.' In *sibi unice dilectam*, 'singularly beloved', Tacitus uses a turn common in more exuberant genres; here it possesses both intimacy and memorable weight.[17]

In the irony of the uncomplying event, neither the glory nor the ill-treatment is realized. Paulina's magnificent suicide is untidily cut short by Nero, anxious for once about his reputation. Tacitus purposely interrupts the flow of narrative to consider the allegation that she deliberately evaded death; in this context he also describes pointedly the nature of her remaining life.[18] The manner of intel-

---

[15] The phrase *paululum adversus praesentem fortitudinem mollitus* is likely to be corrupt; *praesentem* is still more difficult than *adversus*. *mollitus* is probably sound; the conjecture *molitus* would not suit Tacitus' usage. The exact force of *mollitus* cannot in the circumstances be known.

[16] On *exemplo* just before see Ch. 2 n. 43. In 64. 2 it is wrong to see *famam ... petivisse* as part of the slander.

[17] It is especially common in letters (e.g. Cic. *Att.* i. 17. 4, *Fam.* v. 8. 4; Plin. *Ep.* iii. 3. 1, vi. 29. 1). For the effects of a husband's love contrast esp. *Ann.* xv. 59. 5 (Piso), cf. xiv. 59. 1, and note the attitude of Germanicus, i. 42. 1. More amorous and less admirable than Seneca, but closely related, is Radamistus at xii. 51. 2. On generosity with praise note Liv. ii. 40. 11. It is notable that Seneca at one point feels his resolution of spirit to be threatened, not by his own sufferings but by those of his wife; the relation of love, philosophy, and our sympathies is again complex (compare Mart. i. 13). The role of Xanthippe, and Socrates' attitude, are entirely different: Plat. *Phaed.* 60a, 116b (cf. 116a: the disciples are his truest children), 117d.

[18] The life exhibited few *blandimenta*; she had plainly been very close to death; she showed exemplary fidelity to her husband's memory (cf. e.g. *Ann.* xiii. 32. 3). All this is relevant to the allegation, though it does not settle the matter. Tacitus could obviously have placed the section about Paulina at the end, had he wished; it is interesting that Montaigne does this in his adapted translation of the episode (ii. 35).

lectual history again complicates the impact; but here the historian's voice enhances the nobility of presentation. Tacitus puts on a moral superiority to the crowd; he censures them loftily as swift to believe (and do) the worse, *vulgus ad deteriora promptum* (64. 2). By this superiority he, Paulina, and the narrative are raised.

Paulina's aim for glory is frustrated; Seneca indeed dies nobly but against the excruciating resistance of physical reality. Socrates' death is presented by Plato, perhaps unhistorically, as exceedingly smooth and straightforward. Tacitus retails and accentuates the agonizing protraction and ugly untidiness of Seneca's decease. Tacitus does not commonly offer much physical detail on death, except with some special purpose; the extended account here is quite exceptional.[19]

By a sad irony, the philosophical simplicity of Seneca's diet helps to make his suicide difficult: his blood will not flow away swiftly (63. 3). He severs more veins; no speedy death results. Seneca is exhausted by *saevis cruciatibus*, 'savage agonies'; the language is strong, and no less strong the *tormenta*, 'tortures', used of Paulina's sufferings. The death is made to seem the more extended by the interposition of the passage on Paulina's survival; hence that passage not only complicates, but also increases, the force of the narrative on Seneca (such double effects are characteristic of Tacitus). The very avoidance of swift and flowing narration means that Seneca's death appears the longer drawn out when we return to it; we do so with *Seneca interim, durante tractu et lentitudine mortis*, literally 'meanwhile Seneca, the protraction and slowness of his death lasting on ...' (64. 3). The use of two nouns, not one or one and an adjective, adds to the feeling of prolongation; *durante*, 'lasting on', is expressively applied to the death, not the life or the person.[20] Seneca arranges to take

---

[19] For detail cf. *Ann.* iv. 45. 2, vi. 14. 1, xv. 52. 1 (unexpected means of suicide); vi. 50, xii. 66. 2–67. 2 (deaths of emperors). In Livy cf. e.g. xxxv. 35. 18f., xl. 24. 5–7. None of those passages really resembles this; xiv. 64. 2 (Octavia) gives us a shorter sequence much more briefly, cf. xv. 69. 2. Note the theme of slowness in this part: xiv. 64. 2, xvi. 14. 3, 35. 2, cf. xv. 70. 1; the deaths in this part are especially impressive. This will be partly a question of what came to Tacitus in his sources; but Tacitus will still have exercised the choice to include, most assuredly in this passage, and the effect in any case remains.

[20] Cf. e.g. *Ann.* vi. 50. 3, [Quint.] *Decl. Mai.* 12. 27, Plin. *NH* xi. 283. *tormenta* of physical pain other than literal torture comes only here in Tacitus; Pliny is naturally freer, *Ep.* i. 12. 5 (see p. 269 below) *incredibiles cruciatus et indignissima tormenta*. At *Ann.* vi. 6. 2 (of the mind) the image of torture is felt. *saev-* is used of pain elsewhere only at *Ann.* ii. 69. 3 (with point); cf. xvi. 35. 2 *graves cruciatus*. The point on diet at xv. 63. 3 makes against a negative interpreta-

hemlock, like Socrates; this is couched in a half-sentence syntactically elaborate and involved (for Tacitus). The resonant and premeditated plan is rudely thwarted in three words, forcefully arranged: *adlatumque hausit frustra*, 'it was brought, and he drank it —in vain'. The physical reality of his body blocks the philosopher's intention. The death itself occurs in a participial clause, and is not allowed even the stateliness of closing its own sentence. *exim balneo inlatus et vapore eius exanimatus sine ullo funeris sollemni crematur* (64. 4). 'When he had been carried to a bath and killed by its steam, he was cremated with no rites of funeral.'

And yet, through all the hideous and messy indignity of circumstance, the dignity of the philosopher is conserved, strenuously and the more movingly. Mentally he imposes his will in defiance of events. Just before the very end water is used to warm Seneca's blood, and he grandly converts this physical reality into a libation to Jupiter the Liberator (64. 4). The burial without honour, which we imagine to spring from Nero's hatred, in fact realizes the philosopher's austere and noble plan: Seneca had considered his end even when he stood at the height of his worldly glory, *praedives et praepotens*, 'excelling in riches, excelling in power' (64. 4). Here the philosopher's and the historian's sense of time richly blend. The whole passage presents a narrative on a physical level searchingly unglamorous, and on a spiritual profoundly heroic.

The deaths treated by **Pliny** in his letters are often such as would be treated by history: this area can bring the two genres particularly close in matter. Pliny's manner here too is sometimes nearer to history than we might expect; but the stance of the author, and his style, usually produce a quite different effect from Tacitus. To read Pliny makes us feel the austerity and distance of Tacitus' art, in his fully historical writing: in the *Agricola* Tacitus treats in a very different fashion the death of his own father-in-law (43–6). Pliny's letter on his uncle's death in the eruption of Vesuvius (vi. 16) is designed to form the basis for a (shorter) account in Tacitus' *Histories*. For all Pliny's concern with truth, his personal relation to the subject inevitably gives his warmth a quite different quality, for the reader, from that of the judging historian. This

tion of that moment (cf. Dyson (1970), 78); *Ann.* xv. 69. 2 and xiv. 64. 2 do the same for xv. 64. 4. One cannot separate the words from the evident current of pathos. None the less, I agree with Dyson that the account has a deliberate strangeness.

aspect blends with style and ethos. Tacitus avoided the snores of Otho; Pliny dwells on the snores of his uncle (which he evidently knew well). He does so in order to emphasize his uncle's tranquillity. He takes up tranquillity and sleep very differently at the end: *habitus corporis quiescenti quam defuncto similior*, 'in the position of his body he looked more asleep than dead' (20). The purpose is praise, the tone is quiet; but the tenderness and physical closeness cannot be imagined in Tacitus.[21]

No less alien to Tacitus is the oratorical richness and lavishness with which Pliny elaborates on the physical action of a condemned Vestal Virgin in avoiding the executioner's hand (iv. 11. 9). She was condemned by Domitian, whom Pliny vigorously assails.[22] More usually Pliny writes from a stance of avowed personal engagement; his accounts are infused with the emotion of a friend, and his own responses are one of the prime focuses of our attention. In i. 12 Pliny describes the death of Corellius Rufus, his great supporter and guide in youth, to whom he felt profoundly indebted and attached. Corellius had killed himself at 67, because of a painful illness. In a manner that would be artificial in an ordinary letter, Pliny develops a vigorous account of Corellius' illness over the years. It mingles elevated evocation of Corellius' noble spirit amid his physical afflictions with dramatic and personal recollection. The reader is made to share in the sense of secrecy as Pliny tells what Corellius said about Domitian, who was then alive, to Pliny his special friend. Corellius' slaves and his very wife were absent; even so he looked round anxiously, *circumtulit oculos* (8). Why did Pliny think, says Corellius, he had endured such great pain for so long? 'To outlive that brigand just for one day', *ut scilicet isti latroni vel uno die supersim*. The high political motive is spiced by the racy expression and the personal hatred.[23]

---

[21] The phrase undoes the standard assimilation of sleep and death (Nisbet and Hubbard on Hor. *Odes* i. 24. 5); Stat. *Silv.* v. 3. 260f. is quite different. On the snoring cf. Görler (1979). For Pliny's handling of death see Traub (1955); Bütler (1979), ch. 6; Gnilka (1973).

[22] The line of Euripides quoted in Greek introduces into the account a slight touch of urbane distance; quotations in Greek are of course a device quite foreign to higher genres. It is a familiar citation, like that in 12 (for which cf. Quint. x. 1. 49; Sch. Hom. *Il.* xviii. 20f. (bT)).

[23] Compare conversely for motivation to suicide connected with the political situation Tac. *Ann.* vi. 26. 1 (contrast Dio lviii. 21. 4f.), 48. 1–3 (cf. Dio lviii. 27. 4). On suicide from illness cf. Sherwin-White on 3 here, Trisoglio (1973) on 9. We note that Pliny is concerned to dignify Corellius' gout; for its ingloriousness see above all Lucian's *Podagra*. As to Corellius and Pliny see *Ep.* iii. 3. 1, iv. 17, vii. 11. 3, ix. 13. 6; Syme (1979), 714, (1988*b*), 462, 465f.

By contrast, Pliny's broader narrative describes grandly Corellius' decision to die, once Domitian had expired: *ut iam securus liberque moriturus multa illa vitae sed minora retinacula abrupit* (8). 'Since he could now die in liberty and free from care, he broke off all the many but lesser ties that bound him to life.' The political concern (cf. 12) now takes on the resounding language of liberty so often associated with heroic death. The language shows with firm ease the subordination to these high matters of his love for his family (one of the 'lesser ties', 3); his decision to leave them is turned into a strong and momentary action.

The narrative soon changes to a brisk simplicity and an elemental tension: *iam dies alter, tertius, quartus; abstinebat cibo*, 'two, three, four days passed; he would take no food' (9). Pliny's own experience re-enters: he is sent for as the only person who can persuade Corellius to eat. He lets us feel his importance here, but also his affection: a single active word shows his response—*cucurri*, 'I ran'. Then with expressive drama Pliny arrests this excitement and renders it sadly purposeless in the face of Corellius' obdurate magnificence. A messenger tells Pliny his attempts would be useless. When offered food, Corellius had said simply, κέκρικα, 'My decision is made.' The utterance contrasts with his first: stately and philosophical Greek for pungent and political Latin, a lapidary word for a colourful pair of sentences, death for life.[24]

With Corellius' declaration Pliny leaves the narrative. We linger on the decision, captured in his fine pronouncement, not on the physical moment of death. We see the decision both through the experience of Pliny at the time and through Pliny's continuing emotion, to which he now glides on.

quae vox quantum admirationis in animo meo tantum desiderii reliquit: cogito quo amico, quo viro caream. (10)

The utterance has left in my spirit feelings of loss as much as of veneration: I reflect on what a friend and what a man I am now without.

The two parts of the sentence are linked: he longs for the friend and venerates the man. Pliny holds grandeur and pathos in elegant balance; he is here the channel through which we feel

---

[24] The use of Greek at significant moments, though always stylish, carries varying nuances: for examples cf. Townend (1960). Conceivably Pliny thought Corellius' utterance more original than it was (Cic. *Att.* xiii. 31. 3, Epict. ii. 15. 6, both cited by commentators); Pliny's acceptance certainly makes a striking contrast with the enterprise of Epictetus, ii. 15. 4–13.

both. For the rest of the letter he dwells on his own grief.[25] The various modes of the letter communicate the greatness and sadness of the event, in many ways: through Pliny in the past and in the present, through narrative and reflection, through engaged and enriching eloquence and direct and lucid report. This multiplicity of impact is made possible by the form and range of the genre, as Pliny treats it. It is above all a question of Pliny's open involvement, as a person and as a writer; but the effect could only be realized by an intensely and obtrusively self-conscious writer and man.

Pathos becomes much freer, more direct, and more central when it reaches us through the voice of a grieving friend, not of a narrating historian. Supremely pathetic is **Quintilian's** treatment of his son's death in the proem to Book vi, one of the most moving and distressing passages in Latin literature. And yet it is striking how important even here is greatness of spirit. The passage is illuminated by Plin. *Ep.* v. 16, where the death of a 12-year-old girl evinces 'an endurance, even a courage' (*qua patientia, qua etiam constantia*) which surpasses the hierarchy of age. Her spiritual strength amid physical collapse is grandly depicted; it renders her, almost, worthy of immortality (4, 1).[26]

Quintilian's proem deploys a kind of narrative form, in that he presents chronologically and climactically the sequence of his losses, of his wife and his two sons; but within even the section on his elder son (9–13) he does not narrate so much as expatiate. The emphasis falls at first on the 9- or 10-year-old boy's attainments, which were beyond his age. The child's fatal illness makes its entrance, not to produce a narrative contrast, but to exemplify the summit of those attainments, which was his courage, already fully achieved.

nam quo ille animo, qua medicorum admiratione mensum octo valetudinem tulit! ut me in supremis consolatus est!   (11)

---

[25] To my mind the expression of Pliny's own, properly unconsoled, sorrow is not meant to make the reader think he does not in truth fully accept the rightness and greatness of Corellius' death. I would thus differ a little in emphasis from Bütler (1970), 77f.

[26] The girl's age is given by the MSS *nondum annos xiiii impleverat* (2), against *ILS* 1030: Dressel conjectures *xiii*. It is more cautious to suppose a scribe in error over a fourth *i* than Pliny in error, in his published work, over the age of his friend's daughter at death. Pliny characteristically savours the paradox of her possessing also a girlish charm. On the age of Quintilian's elder son and related matters see Adamietz (1986*a*), 2248. Himerius 8 is worth comparing with the Quintilian for the very different union there of emotion and artistry.

With what spirit did he endure an illness of eight months! How the doctors were amazed! How he comforted me at the last!

The doctors bring in, with no touch of artifice, both drama and corroboration: this is not merely the father's aggrandizement of his son.[27] Pliny also mentions the child consoling the father (v. 16. 4); but here the confounding of roles, marked out by the position of *me*, has a more piercing point.

For Quintilian sets against the heroism of his son his own weakness in not killing himself for grief. His lavish self-reproach assuredly suggests not only the depth of his sorrow but the nobility of his mind (like the self-reproach of Sir Gawain). None the less, there is a significant contrast between the precocious perfection of the courageous boy and the bitterly felt imperfection of the father, who is the true centre of the passage as a whole. He proclaims with grim and authoritative epigram, *nemo nisi sua culpa diu dolet*, 'no one mourns for long save by his own fault' (there is always suicide); yet he continues, with sad resignation, *sed vivimus*, 'but I am alive' (13).[28]

The tragic physicalities of death appear, not as formally the prime concern of the writing, but again as the instrument of the moral argument.

tuum corpus frigidum exsangue complexus animam recipere, auramque haurire communem amplius potui, dignus his cruciatibus quos fero, dignus his cogitationibus? (12)

Could I embrace your cold and bloodless body, receive your dying breath, and then continue to breathe the air that all living men breathe? I deserve these torments that I endure; I deserve these thoughts.

In the first clause we appear in direct contact with Quintilian's terrible experience at the death; but the sentence as it develops is not a simple description of past anguish. The last clause, with its vehement anaphora, forms the true climax. The richest morality

[27] Cf. 10, Himer. 8. 6. On the importance given to the child's promise in oratory note Petr. 117. 6.

[28] Note in relation to *sua culpa* Quintilian's handling of necessity (cf. Hdt. i. 11. 3 f.) at iii. 8. 22 f.; on *cupido lucis*, iii. 8. 46 f. Cf. further for the elevated attitudes he adopts ix. 2. 85 f.; xii. 2. 30; and xi. 1. 9–11. Sen. Rh. *Contr.* v. 1 shows an interesting kinship of material at a far greater remove from reality; note also e.g. Petr. 111. 3. In vi. *praef.* 13 here *et si . . . aetate* is commonly misunderstood: as is shown by the particles and the whole train of thought, Quintilian is saying extravagantly, 'may my, not desire for life so much as willingness to suffer it, avenge you in what remains of my lifetime for my staying alive!'.

and the deepest pathos belong in the passage to Quintilian's present state of mind. And a very immediate present: *cruciatibus*, 'torments', sounds worse than *cogitationibus*, 'thoughts', but it is the very thoughts he is now uttering that furnish his cruellest pain. The sentence turns in on itself in agonized self-reflection. The primary object of the whole passage is to arouse pathos; but the pathos of this climactic section would be both more facile and less intense without the moral elevation and complexity which govern and shape the discourse.

Seneca treats death with an especially evident general, and specific, purpose, to affect our responses to the thought of our own demise. In considering one or two passages from him, we are not aiming to establish his views on death or to discuss their relation to Stoic doctrine. The Stoics had a special reputation for encouraging a courageous attitude to suicide and other violent death; but these topics are more prominent in Seneca than in other Stoic writers. Stoics had always emphasized that death was no evil, and that suicide could be a rational act; what marks out Seneca's writing is not so much his doctrine as the range of his tone and manner. Seneca can write powerfully on death with grandiose or demeaning or quiet or strange and subtle language; he often moves ostentatiously between these registers, and often mingles them in arresting and unlooked-for combinations. There is much behind this variety. Seneca wishes to inspire both enthusiastic heroism and cool disdain (which can be related); his writing and his thought delight to range between sublimity and lowness, between extravagance and sobriety, and to qualify and complicate. The concerns of this pair of chapters give us a special interest in elements of narrative. But we could not give much sense to these without looking a little at other elements too; we shall gain some glimpse of Seneca's richness here in thought and artistry.[29]

We may consider first *Ep.* 24, and especially its handling of Cato's suicide. Lucilius is supposedly threatened with a trial (never referred to again): this furnishes a concrete situation for admonition on pain and death. Seneca partly relishes the element

---

[29] On Seneca and death, and Stoicism, see n. 1 above and Benz (1929); Regenbogen (1961), 451–62; Motto (1955*b*); Tadic-Gilloteaux (1963); Rist (1966), ch. 13; Leeman (1971); Griffin (1976), ch. 11. For the Stoics' reputation on attitudes to death note e.g. Mart. xi. 56. Among the many doctrinal matters I am not concerned to discuss is Seneca's opinion about an afterlife; the least precarious inference from the texts would be that he held no real opinion, but even that would be precipitate.

of personal drama which his genre makes possible. But he is also
pleased to treat the genre audaciously, and to decline openly the
obvious course of encouraging Lucilius to hope; instead he
confronts him with death and pain unsparingly.

Cato's suicide appears frequently in Seneca, and receives
several substantial treatments (*Prov.* 2. 9–12, *Ep.* 24. 6–8, 71. 8–16):
Seneca is not giving a single decisive account like a historian, but
returns to vary, lovingly and ingeniously, an event that is primarily significant for the attitudes it will excite in the present.
Historians talk, at any rate, of noble deeds as being examples, and
the events in themselves certainly matter to Seneca; but the
implications for the reader stand much further to the fore in
Seneca than in history, and the thought and fancy of the writer
exercise a much more conspicuous dominion.[30] Here Seneca uses
spirited play to advertise directly the moral power of the
exemplum and of his treatment, and to advertise obliquely his
inventive art. Before Seneca has mentioned Cato, Lucilius is
made to decry his hackneyed examples and predict that Seneca
will now 'narrate Cato' (*Catonem narrabis*), as he puts it with
sarcastic compression. Seneca meets this forbidding challenge to
his originality and eloquence, and plunges in with a robust 'of
course I will narrate him, and how on that last night ... ', *quidni
ego narrem ultima illa nocte ... ?* (6). He ends declaring, after a
brilliant, and forceful, epigram, *non in hoc exempla nunc congero ut
ingenium exerceam* (9), 'It is not to practise my talent that I am now
amassing these examples.' The hardened lover of Seneca will
recognize that one of the purposes of this statement is, alas,
precisely to draw attention to the talent he has shown—but only
one: he is stressing too his protreptic urgency.

The speeches which are assigned to Cato in Seneca's major
treatments are plainly not to be read, as in history, as if they were
speeches Cato might have uttered; they are to be read rather as
more or less overtly the author's meditation on the event, grandly
delivered by the agent. The start of the speech here strikes
characteristically Senecan notes in defying Fortune with scornful
informality: *nihil egisti, Fortuna*, 'Fortune, you have wasted your

---

[30] For historical accounts of Cato's death see Plut. *Cat. Min.* 63. 70; App. *BC* ii. 406–12;
Dio xliii. 10 f.; Liv. *Epit.* 114, cf. fr. 55 Jal; on the tradition cf. Geiger (1979), 63–7. See also
Tandoi (1965–6). On this letter generally see Maurach (1970), 96–100.

time'.[31] As it proceeds, we see that the frustration of all Cato's efforts for the liberty of others has not affected his own liberty or himself; the theme suits both Cato and the letter. The close of the speech magnificently combines grandeur and repose. *nunc, quoniam deploratae sunt res generis humanae, Cato deducatur in tutum* (7). 'Now, since the state of the human race is [with Caesar's triumph] irremediable, let Cato be led to safety.' Despite the vast catastrophe against which Cato has so laboured, he remains composed; we might ordinarily have expected such an opening clause to be followed by words of despair, but Cato's utterance manifests resigned assurance. The final language is paradoxical but quiet. The name expresses the grandeur of a person who is not trivial in importance when set against the human race; and it expresses too his wholeness: the actual person is untouched by circumstance.[32]

The transmitted facts of Cato's actions become the basis, in Seneca somewhat as in Lucan, for ingenious and morally purposeful commentary. Particularly notable is the handling of the datum that Cato, having failed to kill himself with the sword and been bound up by the doctors, completed the task with his own hands. Appian gives a hideous account of the physical details (*BC* ii. 412); Seneca returns incessantly to the motif with a more elaborate fascination, drawing forth many aspects. He relishes the union of the nasty, and the bizarre, with this extreme of heroism, and he relishes the combination of Cato's violence and his sanctity. Seneca again stands closer to the poets.[33]

The version in *Ep.* 24, like that in *Prov.* 2 (p. 227), suits its setting.

iam non tantum Caesari sed sibi iratus, nudas in vulnus manus egit et generosum illum contemptoremque omnis potentiae spiritum non emisit sed eiecit.   (8)

---

[31] For Cato and Fortune cf. esp. *Ep.* 104. 29 f.; in general see Busch (1961). The standing of the speeches is particularly obvious in the case of that at *Ep.* 71. 15, which has a somewhat different status; there Cato dwells purely on the mutability of all things. For the speech here, note the same opening (*nihil egisti, Fortuna*) to a speech which is explicitly Seneca's interpretation, *Ben.* i. 9. 1. Whatever the text at Pers. 3. 45 f., there cannot be one fixed speech known as Cato's: it would be the boy's own speech, as *non ... laudanda* shows (I incline to favour *morituro ... Catoni / dicere*, like Barr). The speeches in Plutarch (cf. App. 409, and also Dio 10. 5) should be contrasted with ours.

[32] The 'third-person' use of the name is one naturally invited by the extreme figure of Cato. Cf. not only *Prov.* 2. 10 etc., but e.g. Plut. *Cat. Min.* 30. 5, 69. 2, and, even in his lifetime, Cic. *Fam.* xv. 4. 16 (cf. xv. 6. 1; Plut. 15. 6). For *generis humani* cf. *Pol.* 13. 1.

[33] Add to *Prov.* 2. 11 f. *Ep.* 67. 7, 13, 70. 19, 95. 72; cf. also Sen. Rh. *Suas.* 6. 2. On the sanctity of Cato cf. Fugier (1963), 259–70.

Angry now not just with Caesar but with himself, he thrust his bare hands
into the wound, and that noble spirit, which scorned all rulers' power, he
did not let forth but hurled forth.

Cato's vehement determination to die is pushed to the point of
anger with himself for his earlier failure to do so: both the determination and the anger are expressed by the violence of the physical
language. Seneca partly relishes for themselves the physical ferocity and the paradox of the self-violence; the paradox is especially
extreme with a man who so little merits such violence and anger.
To heighten the paradox, the *spiritus*, 'spirit', that Cato treats so
fiercely is also made itself the embodiment of his nobility. Still more
Seneca delights in the language itself, violent but self-consciously
clever; most of all he delights in the toying with verbs that concludes
the sentence and follows the resounding nominal phrase (*generosum
... spiritum*, 'that ... power').[34] But all this is also full of moral
purpose; and that purpose is itself audacious. Seneca here presents
a striking change after the tranquillity of the speech. Cato's anger
with Caesar, and with himself, creates a very different mood from
what we might expect in Stoicism. Seneca is deliberately pressing
the resolution of Cato to a lavish and fiery extreme; he brings to a
climax the animated, eager, and extravagant heroism which has
already roused us in the preceding example (Mucius Scaevola).[35] It
fits both his theme and the large design of the letter.

Seneca's strategy to make Lucilius despise pain and death shifts
openly after this climax; and elevation is gradually but visibly abandoned. Now Seneca starts to emphasize, not that it is heroic to
despise death, but that the unheroic have despised it. Not only must
it be possible for us to despise it, but, as the examples sink lower, we
see that death must be despicable indeed if it can be despised by
those far beneath us in the human hierarchy.[36]

[34] *Ep.* 70. 19 is related but less pithy and, as it were, self-applauding. For the expression of
contemptorem ... spiritum cf. Virg. *Aen.* ix. 205; for heroic contempt of power, which here
answers to the scorn of physical death and physical fortune, cf. *Ben.* v. 6. 6 (Socrates).

[35] Note Marc. Aur. x. 8. 5: one should commit suicide μὴ ὀργιζόμενος ἀλλὰ ἁπλῶς
καὶ ἐλευθερίως καὶ αἰδημόνως. Cato's anger here has different causes, but remains a
striking attribute for Stoic hero in Stoic author. Scaevola's anger with himself (5) has again
a different cause; but his temper and Cato's clearly belong together in this part of the
passage. Marc. Aur. ix. 3. 3 also offers a notable contrast of ethos with the present place.

[36] For the strategy cf. Quint. v. 11. 10; Marc. Aur. xii. 34. 'Contempt' of death is of course
standard language: cf. e.g. Cic. *Div.* ii. 2 (Cicero states the subject of *Tusc.* i); Marc. Aur. ix.
3. 1 gives it a twist (contrast iv. 50. 1, *al.*); Diog. Oen. fr. 75. 1–3 Casanova strengthens it to
καταγελᾶν.

tolle istam pompam sub qua lates et stultos territas: mors es, quam nuper
servus meus, quam ancilla contempsit. (14)

Remove all that grand show you use to hide under and frighten fools:
you are Death, whom [*and*: death, which] my slave, and my slave-girl,
have lately scorned.

meus, 'my', together with *nuper*, 'lately', gives a drastic immediacy
to the hierarchical point. *ancilla*, 'slave-girl', reaches a yet lower
point than *servus*, 'slave'; but the word is followed by *contempsit*,
'has scorned'. The revelation of death does not cause but
abolishes terror, and the grim brevity of the address *mors es*, 'you
are Death', is pronounced not with awe but with dismissal. There
is something grandiose in the defiance of the address; but the
process is now principally one of puncturing grandeur and
exposing truth. Death's real nature is to be shown beneath its
empty claims to a magnificent terror. Other Stoic writers seek to
make death seem trivial; but Seneca's procedure is rendered
particularly arresting by the overt movement of level, and by the
boldness of language and drama.[37]

Before the final section of the letter death is handled in various
different ways again. Particularly notable for us is 19–21; here
Seneca reminds Lucilius how he himself has in a poem treated the
standard theme (*locus*) of death as not a single moment but a
life-long process. Seneca is courteous to Lucilius here, and remarks how Lucilius' treatment shows his habitual grandeur as
well as a particular force and sharpness; he makes no obstreper-
ous remarks on hackneyed material as Lucilius himself had been
feigned to. Seneca's own rendering of the theme aims not so much
for the poet's grandeur as for an elegant and eloquent wit which
makes the idea look both a strange and a persuasive contraven-
tion of the familiar. The moment of death is deprived of its decisive significance. So *cotidie morimur*, 'we die [are dying] every day'
(20): the bold collocation erases division between life and death
and between the humdrum and the momentous.[38] At the same

---

[37] Death made to appear trivial: e.g. Epict. iii. 10. 14–17. For the masks of 13 cf. Epict. ii. 1.
15. The image of *turbam carnificum circa te frementem* (14) probably suggests the triumph-like
advent of a deity.

[38] It does not matter that the phrase occurs also in *Ep.* 1. 2: in both places the setting
makes clear that it is meant to startle. The handling of the water-clock in 20 only confirms
the stylistic level of the passage as not particularly lofty. Donne's felicitous adaptation of
part of the passage raises it somewhat in language; he then trumps it sublimely (*Sermons* ii. 9
p. 202 Potter–Simpson).

time, the context impels us to give particular attention to the
expression of the thought in prose; Seneca's own densely ingenious phrasing does everything possible to encourage this. Not only
when he rephrases Lucilius' own quoted line (21), but in phrases
like *tunc ad illam pervenimus, sed diu venimus*, 'at our last hour we
arrive at death, but we are long in coming', we see an exquisite
neatness and symmetry unattainable in verse. Genre, personality,
expression complicate Seneca's impact: the sombre thought is
variegated by subdued but glancing and many-coloured light.

The last section (22–6), still more emphatically and directly
than 9–14, withdraws from the grandeur of the passage on Cato's
suicide. It does not undermine it, but offers balance, restraint,
caution, which complement and qualify the earlier heroism; the
different aspects together create a rich and subtle picture. Seneca
presents with approval various quotations from Epicurus on
foolish suicide, and judiciously warns against either loving or
hating life excessively.[39] He extends his concerns from Epicurus'
to consider even rational suicide and the suicide of noble men.
The language pointedly recalls the first half of the letter (1–14): a
thoughtless urge to death 'often seizes noble men of the most
spirited and vigorous character (*generosos atque acerrimae indolis
viros*), often the low and sluggish (*ignavos iacentesque*); the former
despise life (*contemnunt*), the latter find it irksome' (25). To make
Lucilius despise death had earlier been Seneca's dominating concern, and *contemnere*, 'despise', and its cognates, had run through
the first part; despising life differs only by a subtle shade from
despising death, but it now forms part of an attitude that Seneca
abjures. *generosus*, 'noble', and *acer*, 'vigorous, eager', have been
used in relation to Cato (8) and Scaevola (5), *ignavus*, 'low', to the
lesser scorners of death (9).[40] The two classes are now conjoined,
not to encourage bravery, but to exemplify irrationality. Even
when reason bids one kill oneself, one should not do so in a
precipitate onrush (*non temere nec cum procursu*, 24): *vir fortis ac sapiens*

---

[39] Note that the remarks of Epicurus may have received from Seneca a more sharply
pointed form. This has happened e.g. at *Ep.* 17. 11, 29. 10, where the Greek survives; and
such is Seneca's standard practice (cf. e.g. *NQ* i. 3. 7 f. with Aristot. *Meteor.* iii. 373ᵃ35–ᵇ10).

[40] For P. Scipio there (Q. Metellus) cf. Liv. *Epit.* 114; Sen. Rh. 6. 2, 7. 8; Val. Max. iii. 2. 13,
etc.; Syme (1939), 40. On the especially paradoxical death through fear of death cf.
Winterbottom on [Quint.] *Decl. Min.* 276. 10; but *est enim*, etc., in 25 shows that the whole
conception of desire for death is intended to seem strange.

non fugere debet e vita sed exire (25). 'The wise and courageous man should not flee out of life, but depart.' The thought does not contradict the *non emisit sed eiecit*, 'he did not let forth but hurled forth', used of Cato; yet in mood the passages contrast strikingly. There the rhetorical device had been used to reject the more familiar term in favour of one that showed a more violent courage; now much the same device is used to return to the more familiar term and invest it with quiet depth.

The whole letter closes evoking the unexalted weariness of life that can assail one. The speech of malaise explicitly includes, with a characteristic twist, a distorted philosophical element. But its issue is not grand: the last two sentences of the letter end with *nausia*, 'disgust', and with *supervacuum*: life is thought 'superfluous'.

This letter, then, affords a striking example of manifest and purposeful shifts in the treatment of death, especially with regard to grandeur. We may continue this line of thought as we consider *Ep.* 77, which presents both forceful contrasts in level and manner between different narratives, and a remarkable and peculiar combination within its principal narrative. The letter includes a sizable account of how Marcellinus, a good friend of Lucilius', has killed himself young, not from an overwhelming cause but because of a wearisome illness (5–9). The first half of the letter (1–9) is fascinatingly perverse. Seneca begins it with a vigorous, and technical, evocation of the external and immediate world (the arrival of ships from Alexandria); but this distant approach to more ordinary epistolography appears only in order to make possible a contrast. The point is that Seneca felt pleasure at his lack of interest in the arrival of these ships, and in news of his Egyptian estates. The structure is devious, and expressive; more insidiously attractive is the sensation of pleasurable detachment from life. With still more remarkable deviousness, the narrative of the friend's death, which Lucilius had not heard of, is not presented as a principal item of news. Rather, it is presented chiefly as a tale into which Seneca has digressed, for illustration, from his exposition proper (*in fabellam excessi*, 10).[41] It will indeed be not unwelcome to Lucilius, Seneca avers, to learn of that most gentle decease (the assumption itself contradicts expectation); but Seneca wilfully, and pointedly, gives his primary emphasis to the moral value of the story.

[41] Cf. for *fabella (fabula) NQ* i. 16. 1, v. 15. 1, *Ben.* vii. 21. 1.

The detailed narrative of a recent death reminds us of the letter of Pliny. However, whereas Pliny wishes his feelings to strike us as subtle, but natural and exactly proper, Seneca aims to run counter to our instinctive feelings.[42] His account mingles, disconcertingly and absorbingly, the heroic, the tranquil, the ordinary, and the weird. It has three main parts: a Stoic friend's speech of advice to Marcellinus, a passage of narrative on Marcellinus and his slaves, and the description of the death itself. The speech of the Stoic recommending suicide is contrasted with the more obvious advice of other friends. Seneca thoroughly endorses the speech, and it provides direct doctrine in an oblique form. Yet the setting and the language make it also compelling drama. Short as the speech is, it changes key headily. It begins:

noli, mi Marcelline, torqueri tamquam de re magna deliberes. non est res magna vivere: omnes servi tui vivunt, omnia animalia; magnum est honeste mori, prudenter, fortiter. (6)

Don't torment yourself, Marcellinus, my friend, as if this were a great matter you were considering. There is nothing great to being alive: all your slaves do it, all animals do it. The great deed is to die laudably, prudently, bravely.

Even this part modulates. The opening is devastatingly relaxed and casual; with easy friendliness and an unexpected cool, it pushes the Stoic notion of life as something 'indifferent' to a stunning and unsettling extreme. The tone alters in the course of the next sentence to become more strenuous and noble. *magnus*, 'great', shifts from its first connotation 'important' to its final connotation 'heroic'. The hierarchical argument has a magnificent scorn; it will be made the more striking when the Stoic later bids Marcellinus show gratitude to those very slaves (8).

After this opening the speech shifts its manner; it shows the triviality of life by depicting it as base and repetitive. It closes: *mori velle non tantum prudens aut fortis aut miser, etiam fastidiosus potest.* 'It is not just the wise, brave, or unhappy that can wish to die, but even

[42] Note Plin. *Ep.* i. 22. 8–11 in comparison with Sen. *Ep.* 77. 5f. Seneca's explicit and emphatic *et non insanabili* (5) is intended to make him sound extreme here even in Stoic terms: contrast *SVF* iii. 757 νόσοις ἀνιάτοις, Sen. *Ep.* 58. 36; the mention of the ψυχή makes *SVF* iii. 768 sound less drastic. Marcellinus is not, I think, made to sound hopelessly lazy: the description of Lucilius' friend in 5 must be read as a compliment, as it would naturally be in any case; *Ep.* 24. 26 confirms the generality of 6, which the argument requires.

the bored.' The adjectives echo and then go beyond the adverbs of the passage above; the weary attitude marked off with disapproval in *Ep.* 24 is now incorporated into the argument for death. It is not so much the argument itself that disquiets as its appearance here: it closes on an almost whimsical note a speech bidding a man to kill himself now. The effect drives home Seneca's extreme and provoking thought with an extremer strangeness.

The narrative on the slaves combines concrete reality with suggestion of the noble suicide. The slaves fear to assist because of the legal consequences, and must be reasoned with (7): these are the complications of the familiar world. Marcellinus himself consoles them as they weep (8): this is the standard conduct of courageous death. The distribution of (small) sums to the slaves mixes the concrete and the benign: we may compare the grander practicality of Otho.[43]

After this harmonious narrative, the death itself shows a more exotic tonality. All the violence of heroic suicide is absent: *non fuit illi opus ferro, non sanguine*, 'he needed no sword, and no shedding of blood' (9). In its place we have this (after three days without food):

solium deinde illatum est, in quo diu iacuit, et, calda subinde suffusa, paulatim defecit, ut aiebat, non sine quadam voluptate, quam afferre solet lenis dissolutio, non inexperta nobis, quos aliquando liquit animus.   (9)

Then a bath was brought in; he lay in it a long while. Hot water was poured in, and he gradually passed away, not without a certain pleasure, he said—the pleasure that is commonly produced by a gentle loss of life. Of such loss I am not without experience myself, since [in illness] consciousness has sometimes left me.

The slow ease of this death is already conveyed in the factual narrative which ends with the langorous double spondee *-im defecit* ('gradually passed away'). The addition of physical pleasure brings a weird and almost decadent element remarkable in this virile writer. The restrained language, the scientific air, the importation of personal experience: all this only heightens the

---

[43] In 7 the absence of a subject for *detraxit* after the preceding sentence is scarcely to be tolerated, the less so with *ipsum Marcellinum* in 8. Perhaps we should read *illo*, with *suasore* and *adiutore* as predicative; it would have been altered by someone who did not recognize the construction, for which cf. Liv. xxxv. 42. 13 (related things e.g. Sen. *NQ* iii. *praef.* 18). What follows shows that this gives a better sense to *adiutore*: the help is needed to deal with the slaves, not to replace them.

piquancy and reality of this soft and perversely agreeable decease.[44]

The letter soon changes its tone. Seneca majestically presents the universal law to which all must conform (12); the individual's objections look foolish and futile. He then rises higher again, with the story of a heroic Spartan boy (14 f.). The force of the examples is increased because boys stand lower hierarchically than men. At first, however, Seneca complicates his effect by introducing that point and the story with robustly entertaining play. *exempla nunc magnorum virorum me tibi iudicas relaturum? puerorum referam.* 'Do you think I am now going to recount to you examples set by great men? I shall recount ones set by boys.' Seneca pretends that his procedure is drearily predictable; he fulfils the expectation (of valiant examples), but unpredictably surpasses it. The brevity of the second sentence gives elegance to the wit and punch to the idea.[45]

The account contrasts radically with the earlier narration; we are to see them as parallel *exempla* (10, 14).

... captus clamabat 'non serviam' sua illa Dorica lingua, et verbis fidem imposuit; ut primum iussus est fungi servili et contumelioso ministerio (afferre enim vas obscenum iubebatur), illisum parieti caput rupit. (14)

When captured he kept calling out, 'I will not be a slave', in that Doric dialect of his. He confirmed the truth of his words; as soon as he was ordered to perform a humiliating task belonging to a slave (the order was to bring a chamber-pot), he dashed his head against a wall and broke it.

The anecdote moves with frightening briskness. The action is grimly prepared at the end of the first half of the sentence; the slight slackening of tone and syntax in the parenthesis only gives the action itself a more savage force. Comparison with other versions shows that Seneca tells the story, and chooses or devises variants, in such a way as to shorten the narrative, to make the violence more shocking and abrupt, to render the defiance

[44] The possibility of pleasure at death was evidently of philosophical interest: cf. Philodem. *De Morte* iv col. 4, col. 8. 30–7 (Gigante (1983), 118 f., 123 f.); those mentioned need not be opponents of Philodemus. *ut aiebat* must go with what follows it; possibly the text needs some adjustment: *Ben.* iv. 14. 1, *Tranq.* 2. 14 are somewhat different.

[45] It is worth comparing Lessing's more complex treatment of the theme in *Philotas*; the soliloquy of Scene 4, however we evaluate it, is full of Senecan spirit. One is interested to note how Fontane uses the common theme of death and law in Dubslav's short monologue, *Stech.* ch. 24; the poignant addition at the end brings out Seneca's exclusiveness.

brusquer, and to limit the element of speech to two crucial words.[46] There could hardly be a starker antithesis to the account of Marcellinus, with its leisured and elaborate social drama, its dramatized philosophical reflection, its meticulous description and exploratory psychology. Here all is brutally heroic. We are remote from the sweetness and pathos with which the children transcend their status in the passages of Quintilian and Pliny. The milieu is as alien as that of Marcellinus is familiar (hence the emphasis on Doric). Slavery becomes, not an ordinary part of the upper-class world, or even an instrument of argument, but the object of blunt and extreme resolve. The noble association of death and liberty that is highly prominent in grandiose treatments of death here receives a singularly curt and concrete form.

After the narration Seneca takes up the boy's words; through metaphor he applies them precisely to the present world. The addressee (not very specifically Lucilius) is harangued for his spiritual enslavement, above all to life and its luxury. Without the ability to die, life becomes debased and monotonous slavery (15), and even, by a final trenchant paradox, a kind of death (18).[47] The converse of the lofty association between death and freedom, that between servitude and life, is here presented by Seneca with the most vigorous lowness and contempt. *saccus es*, 'you are a straining-bag', he says to the man through whose bladder pass so many jarfuls of wine (16). Marcellinus' friend had presented in unheated tones the weary, unelevated sameness of life; Seneca now drives home the tedium and baseness of upper-class existence with colourful satire and unsparing vehemence. We do not here have lowness alone: the very scorn and energy with which Seneca assails his addressee and unmasks his pretensions to noble feeling bear in them a kind of spirit not wholly remote from grandeur. The letter eventually takes up earlier themes and moves to a quieter close.

The two narratives complement one another. Both aim to reconcile us to the approach of natural death, by showing us people who actually choose to die, and before old age. The easy detachment and tranquil end of the one, the hard determination and violent death of the other, are taken to divergent extremes;

---

[46] Plut. *Ap. Lac.* 234b–c gives the closest version.

[47] For this thought cf. Heinze on Lucr. iii. 1045; the placing here gives it special pungency.

but the attitudes they convey to life and death, one coolly dismissive, one fierily heroic, provide diverse but supporting inspiration.
The artist relishes the breadth he displays on a single theme; the
philosopher hems us in from opposing sides.

We end by glancing at a passage with no narration, which still
further illustrates the richness of the relations in Seneca between
grandeur and death. The end of *Naturales Quaestiones* vi (on earthquakes) deals with death from earthquake. The end of the later
Book ii will correspondingly deal with death from lightning; but
the end of vi gains a special urgency from the earthquake that has
just befallen Campania.[48] This earthquake and the fears it might
arouse for ourselves occupy the start and the close of the book.
Seneca is concerned with a cause of death grand, vast, and
terrible: the fear of it he confronts with different tactics, and
variously links it with the general fear of death.

At 32. 3 the argument takes a turn to show that grandiose causes
of death are no different in their result from everyday ones.
Seneca is also using humble causes of death to make us feel the
triviality of life (the ability to live), which can be destroyed by
things themselves so trivial; he means to arouse our scorn and
indifference towards it. It does not matter

quantum ... sit quod (Mors) in nos trahat; quod a nobis petit minimum
est. hoc senectus a nobis ablatura est, hoc auriculae dolor, hoc umoris in
nobis corrupti abundantia, hoc cibus parum obsequens stomacho, hoc
pes leviter offensus. pusilla res est hominis anima, sed ingens res con-
temptus animae.

how large a thing Death brings against us; what it seeks to take from us is
as small as possible. *That*, old age will take from us, or earache, or an
excess of infected liquid in us, or food that fails to comply with the
stomach, or lightly hitting a foot. Human life is a slight and tiny thing;
the contempt of life is a mighty one.

The first sentence neatly and inventively deploys the idea of
greatness to the detriment of life; the chiastic design strengthens
the emphasis on *minimum*, 'as small as possible'. Seneca then
makes human life sound the more contemptible by leaving it as an
unspecified *hoc*, 'that', and repeating it with fresh disdain as he sets
it against a new and inglorious source of destruction. He moves
downwards from old age to the slighter earache, and then from

---

[48] On the date (62) see Hine (1984).

undignified disease to digestion, and down to an absurdly little cause and the unsplendid foot.[49] Direct statement comes in the last sentence, which moves on to a fresh contrast of size and to a heroic ethos. Both words of size, *pusilla*, 'tiny', and *ingens*, 'mighty', have strong overtones, of paltriness or glory; the statement is far more vehement and incisive, in both directions, than the quieter statement of the same antithesis by Marcellinus' friend.

Seneca now moves to inspiring and exciting us by showing us the man who despises death indifferent in the face of nature's vastest terrors. We are to be impressed both by the grandeur of the phenomena themselves, and by the grandeur of the courage which is unmoved by them. An exalted series of anaphora sets the short phrase *securus videbit* or *securus aspiciet*, 'untroubled he will see', against the most lavish depictions of sea, sky, and earth successively in their extremity of destruction. Here apocalyptic imagination rises far above a specific and limited narrative; yet the pictures convey to us the heroic individual in memorable but generalized images of solitary valour. The final part takes a different turn; it deals with earth, which particularly concerns the argument.

securus aspiciet ruptis compagibus dehiscens solum, illa licet inferorum regna retegantur; stabit super illam voraginem intrepidus, et fortasse quo debebit cadere desiliet.

(32. 4)

Untroubled he will look upon the earth as its bonds are ruptured and it gapes open, even if the famed realms of the dead are laid bare. He will stand above that chasm unafraid; perhaps, since he will have to fall into it, he will leap.

The description of the natural phenomenon is briefer here, though superbly extravagant; the description of the man becomes more sharply graphic and localized, and ends with him vigorously turning doom into action. Seneca probably has in mind Livy's account of Curtius, who threw himself on horseback into an abyss, to ensure the eternity of Rome (vii. 6); his own figure acts not out of public spirit but in finely useless self-assertion.[50] In a sense, this deed forms the climax of the passage; but *fortasse*, 'per-

---

[49] Seneca deploys the standard term for earache, used medically (Cels. ii. 1. 7).

[50] *patentes ... ad deos manes* (Liv. vii. 6. 4) will give birth to Seneca's *inferorum regna retegantur*; the phrasing is influenced, as commentators note, by Virg. *Aen.* viii. 243–6 (cf. Sen. *Oed.* 582–5). Castiglioni's *ipsa* for *illa* certainly deserves mention.

haps', withdraws from narrative and throws emphasis on to the ingenuity of the idea. After the expansive magnificence of all that precedes, the last colon is made to fall somewhat drily and curtly; the action is morally extravagant, but in aesthetic impact not straightforwardly sublime. (Curtius' horse makes a difference, too.) At the moment of death itself, Seneca contains the lavish splendour of his description.

The treatment of death, and of grandeur in relation to death, undergoes many modulations in the course of this glorious passage. In its last part, however (32. 9–12), Seneca deliberately and characteristically causes the exalted eloquence to recede. Instead, he develops subtle lines of thought about the general fear of death, which make life and time look arrestingly unfamiliar.[51] The manner and thought are no longer either grandiose or pointedly low, although the purpose of the passage is to counter a fear that makes us low and abject, *humiles*, and magnifies, *dilatat*, what we fear (9). The close is slightly more complicated. It takes up the moment we have just quoted, but in intimate counsel rather than spectacular fantasy. Lucilius is urged:

effice illam tibi cogitatione multa familiarem, ut si ita tulerit possis illi et obviam exire.

Make yourself acquainted with death through much thought, in order that, if so things fall out, you can even go forth to meet it.

The magnificent setting for suicide has gone. The act is described in ordinary and unresounding language, with a suggestion of ingenious and unelevating metaphor: one can go forth from one's home to meet death before it arrives, as a token of friendship and goodwill.[52] Essentially we stand at a 'lower' level of style; yet the

---

[51] The basic thought of 9–11, that our past is past and not ours, comes often in Seneca's writing on death; cf. p. 277 and e.g. Cic. *Cato* 69. But Seneca's expression gives it constant and startling newness: so in 10 *in puncto fugientis temporis pendeo*. As to the part before this, note that in the depiction of the next world (7), where the emphasis is on paradoxical safety, there is a hint of grandeur in the negation of grand causes for death; the language suggests the negative descriptions of heaven that descend from Hom. *Od.* vi. 42–6 (cf. also [Aristot.] *Mund.* 400ᵃ11–14; Sen. *Ira* iii. 6. 1). *locus melior* must suggest a heaven (for men); as to *rerum natura*, cf. *Ep.* 79. 12.

[52] Such action has many gradations in Roman life: hurrying to meet loved ones as they enter, coming out of the house to meet them, coming forth from house or city in more public gestures of affection and respect (these last would not be in place with *familiarem*). Cf., with various intermixtures, Stat. *Silv.* ii. 1. 65f., Tib. i. 3. 92; Ov. *Her.* 8. 97, 6. 143; e.g. Liv. xxiv. 16. 16, xli. 25. 4 (and note Cic. *Fam.* iii. 7. 4). *familiaris* and the like, and *obviam*, are

ease of the language, and the suppression of the valorous action, lightly hint a kind of shadowed nobility. In its plainness and quietness of tone this moment stands remote from the earlier one; yet that moment itself is, like this one, ingenious, complex, and compressed. In Seneca's writing we see both large movements of tone and endless subtleties and complications of nuance.

Not the least result of our discussion has been to confront once more the two supreme writers of prose. Thus Seneca presents his particular deaths with a freer engagement of manner than Tacitus; but the complexities of Seneca's wider approach to death confront us more vividly and directly. The physicality of death and the practicalities surrounding it Tacitus can invest with the most searching and pressing significance: a dramatically potent narrative line is laden and charged with moral weight. We have seen Seneca treating physicality with a wider range, sometimes incorporating it into the discourse of fancy and metaphor, sometimes pursuing it into regions strangely subtle or bizarrely extravagant, which somewhat complicate our response. The limits of space and concern have not permitted us to see the full range of Seneca on death—or indeed of Tacitus; yet in this region too we have glimpsed the vital antithesis between the powerful confinement and self-limitation of the one and the powerful richness and expansion of the other. Their basic approach to death is strongly related; their treatments of it are utterly different, yet alike impress their approach on the mind with unforgettable strength.

in themselves natural for such contexts: cf. e.g. *Ira* ii. 12. 3; Cic. *Tusc.* v. 56 (with a sense of metaphor). On Seneca's use of *exitus*, etc., in relation to death see Armisen-Marchetti (1989), 162 f.

9

DEATH IN HIGH POETRY

Death, so important to high poetry, has appeared many times in the book already. The purpose here is not to offer a representative picture of the treatment of death in these poets; rather the contrary. One fundamental aspect in particular will now pass under-represented. It will already have been seen how high poetry, boldly exploiting this sublimest of subjects, likes to create from it strange and disconcerting mixtures, in which bizarreness and incongruous ingenuity are freely cultivated. The epic tradition of describing wounds precisely, and of varying its deaths within strong conventions, is converted into a source of (among other things) black grotesquerie and macabre elegance. This audacity with genre and with instinctive reactions, though its origins lie in Ovid and even Virgil, is eminently characteristic of the period.[1] We shall see something of the element even here; but we set our faces in a contrary direction. For here we shall consider accounts of particularly noble deaths, accounts where the grandeur and seriousness of each writer is at its highest. We shall thus be enabled to savour the likeness and difference of prose and poetry where they are particularly akin. We shall see too some of the means by which poetry achieves a sense of imposing greatness—a side of the poetry that we must not underplay. And yet even here we shall also see tonal complication at work, in very different degrees; and in this regard the passages are arranged roughly in a rising order of complexity. This will bring out things about the different poets, and especially about those who will abandon nowhere the conspicuous complication of straight

[1] It is instructive to compare the treatment of wounding and death at Juv. 15. 51–92 (a poem highly involved in its handling of greatness, reality, and genre) both because its low deflations of grandeur bring out the distinctiveness of epic modification, and because the interval from Silver epic is often less extreme than Juvenal's schematized parody of epic would lead us to suppose. In general on the handling of death in Latin epic, especially in battle, see Blümner (1919); Fuhrmann (1968); Raabe (1976). AR ii. 100–6 should not perhaps be forgotten. On death, in this book, cf. esp. pp. 72, 74, 90–3, 118 f., 121, 123 f., 168 f., 175 f., 179, 214 f., 216–21.

forward greatness. We will also be concerned by many other aspects of poetry which interweave with these; in particular by reality and unreality, and the handling of form and narrative. Part of the intention is to show the reader the great variety and distinctiveness displayed by these poets even in a type of scene where one might have expected a monotonous uniformity.

We begin with the most straightforward of our passages, one from **Silius**. Silius, as has already been glimpsed, is rich in the grotesque and ingenious treatment of death; sometimes the debt to Lucan is transparent. Our concern here, however, is with the particularly noble episode at x. 215–308, where L. Aemilius Paullus meets his death at the battle of Cannae; that battle his fellow-consul Varro had brought about and he (supposedly) had resisted.[2] Silius here allows the death to become strikingly prolonged: it is not the single moment that we expected. The expectation is created partly by the epic tradition which these poets inherited. It is an obvious and important feature of that tradition that in presenting death it habitually prefers (if one may use an analogy from Greek or Russian grammar) the perfective to the imperfective: death and the act that causes it characteristically form a brief and decisive moment. Occasionally in Homer and Virgil speech from or dialogue with the victim separates the fatal wound and the death; but that does not greatly alter the general sense that death is curtly accomplished, firmly and masterfully concentrated by the poet into one short and final point of time.[3] The preference of the tradition is here eschewed by Silius, not in the direction of realism, but of unreal and magnificent extremes.

Silius gives Paullus a glorious career in the battle from the start of the book (where his eyes are fixed on death, 6–10); at last a huge rock smites him in the face (235–7). Livy has him wounded, by a sling, as the battle begins (xxii. 49. 1); he still participates in it actively and dies near its end. Silius, who postpones the wound, leads us to think when it comes that it will promptly be followed by

[2] On the episode cf. von Albrecht (1964), 121–5; Niemann (1975), 237–45; Ahl–Davis–Pomeroy (1986), 2535f.; on the history Lazenby (1978), 74–56, etc. For grotesqueness and ingenuity see e.g. ix. 321f. (cf. Luc. ii. 203f.), iv. 554–69 (cf. Luc. iii. 583–91); Silius is here characteristically neater and more conceptual, less dense and physical than Lucan. See further e.g. vii. 621–33 (note the mingling of pathetic form and savoured ingenuity in 628–30, *heu sortem necis!*, etc., and the stronger pathos of the close).

[3] In Virgil see notably *Aen.* x. 739–46, xi. 816–31, still decidedly 'perfective' in overall impact; the death of Dido is exceptional.

his death. Just before the wound Paullus has performed a passionate act of vengeance, and the poet intervenes: *hic fuit extremus caedum labor; addere bello / haud ultra licuit dextram*, 'that was the final achievement of his slaughter. It was not permitted that he should lend his hand any further to the war ...' (231f.). The ominous and momentous language suggests that the end will follow at once.[4] The wound itself is so described that it will obviously be fatal. In the simile that succeeds, he is compared to a lion that has beaten off the lighter spears but has at last had the sword go into its chest, *accepit ... tandem per pectora ferrum* (242). Again the fatality seems evident; but Silius here powerfully and significantly presents the imperfective aspect, Paullus and the lion in the process of enduring an uncompleted death.

In the sentence that leads into the simile, two lines describe Paullus wretchedly seating his failing body on a rock; the next line begins *sedit terribilis*, 'he sat there, a terrifying figure' (240). The adjective brings a sudden change of perspective and ethos: the prolongation expresses magnificence too (cf. 263). The lion

> stat teli patiens media tremebundus harena
> ac, manante iubis rictuque et naribus unda
> sanguinis, interdum languentia murmura torquens,
> effundit patulo spumantem ex ore cruorem. (243–6)

stands firm, enduring the stroke, trembling in the middle of the arena. A wave of blood flows from its mane, mouth, and nostrils; and as from time to time it casts forth enfeebled roars, it pours out foaming gore from its gaping mouth.

Here the first main verb, the simple monosyllable *stat*, 'stands', reinforced by *teli patiens*, 'enduring the stroke', keeps a note of heroic spirit running through what follows: the lion's trembling (from the wound, not from fear), its sad and graphic but noble isolation, and the unceasing flow of blood. And yet the last three lines slightly modulate this note through the pitiable and heroic futility of its defeated will to roar, and through the syntactical subordination of that effort to the tide of physical destruction.[5]

After the simile Silius expressively abandons this thread of

---

[4] Note too the prophecy at viii. 666f. *ictu / procumbit saxi*.

[5] On *tremebundus* see Spaltenstein; Heinsius' *fremebundus* (with *impatiens*) sorts ill with 245. *ore cruorem* takes up *ore cruento* 240, which forms the sharpest point of comparison. One may contrast the tonality of Virg. *Aen.* xii. 4–8, which Silius probably has in mind, and also of Luc. vi. 220–3.

narrative; he resumes the death of Paullus only after shifting to a brief scene elsewhere (247–59). The interposition increases the semblance of interval before Paullus' death. It is significant for that death that in this intervening scene an Italian commander fights although prostrate and mortally wounded; he causes Hannibal to ask, with potent and extreme suggestion, if the Italians fight even in death. It is significant too that he receives his death from Hannibal, a wish that Paullus is denied.[6]

We then come back to Paullus; but his death does not come yet. A scene of 33 lines ensues (260–92), to which we will return, before Paullus actually comes to meet his death. When we reach the final scene of his last fighting (292–308), a second simile appears. This transposes the futility in the simile of the lion into something more extravagant, undignified, and detaching. A tigress fatally wounded

> languentem pandit hiatum
> in vanos morsus, nec sufficientibus irae
> rictibus extrema lambit venabula lingua. (295–7)

spreads open its weakening jaws to bite in vain. Its gaping mouth cannot satisfy its rage; it can only lick the huntsmen's spears with its dying tongue.

The bizarre and vivid close takes us beyond unmixed pathos to an almost entertaining degradation.[7] The simile complicates the passage. Partly it absorbs us into itself; partly it diverges purposefully from the main narrative. Paullus, for all the extremity and duration of his state, achieves an extraordinary extreme of martial will. Unlike the tigress, he 'does not allow what remains of his life to pass without vengeance', *nec Paullus inultum / quod superest de luce sinit* (292f., introducing the simile): he rises and slays yet another of the enemy.

And that occurs only in the pluperfect (300): his real ambition is to die at the hand of Hannibal, the glorious encounter he has sought since the start of the book (68–71, 42–4, 51–4). But imperfect circumstance swiftly defeats his imposing yet hopeless aspiration:

---

[6] Since *collapso* 253 refers to Hannibal, as Spaltenstein says, *cum (inversum)* might seem preferable to *cui* in 254 (for the omission of the verb cf. e.g. 277).

[7] 297 may help with the interpretation of Stat. *Theb.* ii. 681; that whole simile may rewardingly be compared with this.

> sed vicere virum coeuntibus undique telis
> et Nomas et Garamas et Celta et Maurus et Astur.

But the man was overcome by the weapons that came on him from every side, from Numidian, Garamantian, Gaul, Moor, and Spaniard.

The verse with grim and neat profusion displays the remoteness of his wish from the actuality. And yet, by a further irony, the death Paullus has had will be desired, and desired in vain, by Hannibal himself (522f.). The poet now matches his earlier pronouncement *hic fuit extremus caedum labor*, 'that was the final achievement of his slaughter' (232), with the stark and decisive *hic finis Paullo*, 'that was Paullus' end' (305). A short obituary follows (305–8). The space between the two pronouncements shows not simply miserable prolongation but extreme and heroic greatness in the midst of a decease long extended. That greatness overcomes death even physically, until the limits of reality assert themselves. It is generally rewarding to compare Tacitus' handling of prolongation on the death of Seneca (pp. 267f.). Again we see both heroism and frustration; but Silius does not show at all that intense and significant treatment of unglamorous and awkward reality which we find in the narrative of the historian.

Before this last passage (292–308) has come one that greatly intensifies its significance. The scene is taken from Livy (xxii. 49. 6–12). Lentulus comes on Paullus dying, and urges him to take his horse and leave the field; Paullus refuses (260–92). For Paullus this is no choice between death and certain life: blood pours from his mouth as he speaks (276f.), and he views his life as ended (283, cf. 295f., 288). None the less, we here see powerfully dramatized the resolve to embrace a noble death; the pathos is only increased by Paullus' state and his resignation.

The speech of Lentulus, though it closes in tenderness, is primarily, and sincerely (262–7), a vigorous appeal to Paullus' sense of duty. Against death are set not the attractions of life but the obligations of patriotism. Juno, in disguise urging Paullus to shun Hannibal, had deployed the same consideration (48–51), and had been angrily refused, and cursed with life (61–5). Lentulus, however, is courteously received: he not only risks his own life in offering his horse, but expresses his appeal with forthright and honest vigour. If Paullus 'deserts the ship' and dies, he says,

> invitus plus, Paulle—dolor verba aspera dictat—
> plus Varrone noces. (272f.)

Unwillingly, Paullus, you will do us—my distress inspires such harsh language—you will do us worse injury than Varro.

The anxious preparation of the first line only strengthens the impacted extravagance of the last words: Varro's name has been made to embody an extreme of damage to one's own country. The contrasting resonance of Paullus' name is to be felt in the sentence too. Yet Paullus, because he is Paullus, resists.[8]

Paullus' speech of reply it is interesting to compare with the speech of Tacitus' Otho (p. 259f.). Both finely unite the public and the personal; but Otho treats his own greatness with a more open splendour of manner than the arch-Roman Paullus. Paullus' speech at first concerns itself not with his own fate but principally with the city's, and at the end he breaks off from himself so as not to delay Lentulus' message to Rome.[9] But when he speaks of his own course of action, we see along with elements of patriotism a proud awareness of his own dignity.

> nec talia Paullo
> pectora, nec manes tam parva intramus imago. (287f.)

It is not such a spirit [as to leave the field] that Paullus possesses; it is not as so lowly a ghost that I shall enter the world of the dead.

The pride here appears in restrained and negative form, and through altitudinous contempt for what would be a most understandable weakness. But the name and *tam parva*, 'so lowly', suggest his own moral, and social, status as almost self-evident.[10]

The name has come only a few lines previously:

> amplius acta
> quid superest vita nisi caecae ostendere plebi
> Paullum scire mori? (283–5)

---

[8] With 273 compare the brilliant point at ix. 637–9 (for the expression cf. Liv. fr. 20 Jal, where *Mario* must be right). The weighting of proper names is important in the whole passage, e.g. 224f. *magnamque cadens leto addidit uno / invidiam Cannis*, 306f. *quem, soli si bella agitanda darentur, / aequares forsan Fabio* (lofty praise in the form of reserve).

[9] In 280 Shackleton Bailey's punctuation ((1959), 174f.) introduces a heavy stop at a point very rare in Silius; and the colloquialism looks suspicious. The line is most likely corrupt (*ac nunc* momentarily crosses the mind, *nunc* meaning 'now this has happened', and *ac* having been adjusted to fit *hinc*).

[10] *parva* naturally converts Virg. *Aen.* iv. 654, with a certain boldness; *parvus* frequently relates to standing in society, and *Aen.* xii. 648f. reinforce this undertone.

What more remains, now my life is done, save to show the blind commons that Paullus knows how to die?

Here *Paullum* is grandly and alliteratively opposed to the morally and socially inferior plebs, who had mistreated him in the past (and had elected Varro, who has fled). Paullus' need to confute them gives his proud words a less boastful appearance; even the expression *scire mori*, 'knows how to die', though highly impressive, has in this context an air of simplicity and restraint. But the self-conscious magnificence once more shines superbly through. So too does the noble generality of the attitude to death. *acta ... vita*, 'now my life is done', and *quid superest*, 'what remains', are here splendidly succeeded by a supremely positive act, seen in terms of universal validity. Both in magnificence and in generality Silius goes far beyond Livy: *(nuntia) privatim Q. Fabio L. Aemilium praeceptorum eius memorem et vixisse adhuc et mori*, 'tell Quintus Fabius privately that Lucius Aemilius has remembered his counsel both in his life hitherto and in his death' (xxii. 49. 10).[11]

For all the philosophical ring of *scire mori*, 'know how to die', Paullus does not meet his long-deferred end in physically passive endurance, like Tacitus' Seneca, or in self-contemplation. The lines quoted are taken up in the active *nec Paullus inultum quod superest de luce sinit* (p. 291). Paullus acts with the instincts and ambitions of the warrior.

Less straightforward in its effect is the treatment of Aeson's death at the end of **Valerius'** first book. Certainly this shows little of the complicating wit which we would have found had Seneca or Lucan handled the scene, and which we find in other exploitations of death by Valerius.[12] Yet Valerius' ingenuity here distances as well as heightening; and he treats reality with a boldness that makes the episode astonishing and strange, and transforms the impact of death.

Valerius found in one line of tradition (not in Apollonius) the data that when Pelias, Jason's enemy and uncle, wished to slay

[11] Plutarch creates a slightly more statuesque version than Livy's, *Fab.* 16. 8. None of these accounts should make us depreciate any of the others. On the general topic of self-praise cf. Plut. *Laud. Ips.* (539a–547f).

[12] So vi. 279–316, taking up 123–8 (the passage has links with ours); 414–6; and so even in the intense and moving death of Cyzicus, e.g. iii. 241f. For that episode see Burck (1981c); on ours, Strand (1972), 73–81; Vessey (1973), 245–8 (237–58 on necromancy and witchcraft in earlier poetry; cf. further e.g. Headlam (1902), adding Aesch. fr. 273a Radt); Perutelli (1982); Franchet d'Esperey (1988).

Jason's parents, they slew themselves; that Jason's father Aeson did so by drinking bull's blood; that Pelias also killed Jason's young brother.[13] These data he cleverly combines with other matters related to death, most particularly with chthonic ritual. The broad design of the passage is this (730–850). After we have seen Pelias moving towards his action, we see Jason's mother engaging in a chthonic rite, with her husband Aeson present; she summons up the ghost of Aeson's father, who tells them of Jason's future and theirs (730–51). The rite is interrupted when they hear Pelias' force arrive; Aeson resolves on suicide (752–73), and returns to ritual. In this second religious portion, Aeson takes command; he sacrifices a bull to the forces of the underworld, and prays and curses Pelias; he and his wife Alcimede drink the blood (774–817; drinking blood 815–17). They are interrupted a second time, as Pelias' men appear; the men find the couple dying, and slay their young son (818–21, 823–6). The pair are conducted to Elysium, and learn of the torments awaiting Pelias (827–50).

This design is elegant and, as we shall see, expressive; its content and proportions are unexpected. The death itself occupies only a few lines; the chthonic rites with their attendant speeches occupy a large and unlooked-for space. These parts take their origin genetically from the simple datum of the bull's blood; one pleasure of reading the passage is to find ourselves moving towards this datum and to enjoy the exuberant and ingenious invention which has sprung from it.

It is Alcimede who initiates and conducts the first part of the ritual, out of anxiety for Jason; Aeson leads the second, where noble death is embraced. We recall the scene of Jason's departure; there Alcimede had lamented, and Aeson, her hierarchical superior, had accepted the departure with cheerful and rousing heroism (315–49). The division of roles thus proves significant; but at the start of the first part we are to relish the poet's wry yet sympathetic depiction of Aeson: he is as anxious as his wife, conceals this, but is very willing to be led, *facilem tamen* (733 f.). More startling here is the sudden transformation of Alcimede into a witch: *saevoque vocat grandaeva tumultu / Thessalis exanimes atavos*, 'the agèd Thessalian woman calls forth their dead ancestors with savage noise' (736 f.). *Thessalis*, 'Thessalian woman', can only have

---

[13] Diod. iv. 50. 1–3; Apollod. i. 9. 27. Probably in both the incident occurs when Jason's voyage has ended, not, as in Valerius, when it has just begun.

been inserted to suggest its frequent connotations of 'witch', and to show how the poet is ingeniously and surprisingly exploiting the familiar tradition of Thessalian magic. This element of ingenuity ensures a corresponding element of detached delight.[14]

The world of the dead intrudes still more dramatically with the speech of Aeson's father, Cretheus. The direct communication of living and dead seems to reduce the interval between these states which we might expect to find crucial in a scene of suicide. The content of the speech has a splendid elevation in its strange setting. Grandly and weirdly, at the end, the dead father urges his living son to commit suicide.

> quin rapis hinc animam et famulos citus effugis artus?
> i, meus es ... (749 f.)

Snatch your spirit hence, flee swiftly the servile body. Come, you are my son ...

Philosophical hierarchy is succeeded by paternal warmth and pride (for an agèd son). The powerfully simple utterance *meus es*, 'you are my son', furnishes both a challenge and the promise of Elysium.[15]

The interruption suddenly gives an urgent sense of time, and of space: we now locate the couple in a grove within their house as the men of Pelias approach. Aeson and the action start ascending afresh to heroic status. He is compared to a lion even in his hesitation (757–61); then Alcimede herself changes and rises to accept death with him, if need be (762–6). What Aeson now ponders is only the means of death. He thinks at first of taking arms, old and unwarlike as he now is (759 f.); but the echoes here of Virgil's Priam only set the true glory of Aeson's act of suicide against Priam's pathetic endeavours to fight.[16] Aeson's valorous pride stresses the continuity in his family and in himself, which he will grandly sustain.

---

[14] For Thessaly and magic see e.g. Luc. vi. 434 ff.; Plin. *NH* xxx. 6 f.; Stat. *Theb.* iii. 140–6; Sch. Eur. *Alc.* 1128 (and Goethe, *Faust* 6977 f.!). On Alcimede cf. n. 18 below.

[15] Compare the simplicity of Pind. *Nem.* 10. 80; the words have naturally a different force there.

[16] With 759 f. *ferrumne capessat / imbelle atque aevi senior gestamina primi* cf. Virg. *Aen.* ii. 544 *senior, telumque imbelle,* 509–11, 518 *iuvenalibus armis.* In 756 f. Delz (1976), 99 f., makes Alcimede the subject of *circumspicit* too; but although this requires no real pause, the verb itself is more suitable to Aeson. Thus Aeson begins with fear. On the place of the action see Strand (1972), 73, cf. Winterbottom on [Quint.] *Decl. Min.* 298. 14; note especially *per moenia* 753 and *subitisque pavens* 756.

(circumspicit) quae fata capessat
digna satis: magnos obitus natumque domumque
et genus Aeolium pugnataque poscere bella.   (768–70)

He looked about to see what death he could find that would be sufficient
in worth: a great death was demanded by his son [Jason], his house, the
line of Aeolus, and the wars he himself had fought.

digna satis, 'sufficient in worth', comes at the start of the line with
fine surprise, in this pressing situation. The series of subject nouns
has a resounding richness. But then by a pathetic turn Valerius
adds that Aeson wishes to teach his little boy 'a mighty spirit',
ingentes animos, so that he can remember in the future his father's
death (771–3). This family continuity will be broken: Aeson will see
that son killed.

The ritual takes on in its second part a new and more grandiose
significance, to encounter not the dead but death. None the less,
the poet does not diminish its bizarre and distancing element.[17]
He gains a witty pleasure from his bull: with an incongruous and
pleasing shift in perspective we see the poor bull itself

impatiensque loci visaque exterritus umbra.   (778)

unable to endure the place and terrified at the sight of Cretheus' ghost.

Agreeably fortuitous, and agreeably sinister, is the notion that
Alcimede had left the bull there for her witch's purposes, *gentis de
more nefandae*, 'after the fashion of that wicked race'.[18]
Aeson's speech raises us, like Cretheus' before, to a grander
level. Again the mighty tradition of his race appears as he calls on
his ancestors, and as he addresses more pathetically, strangely,
and paradoxically his father, who is still present. His father, he
declares, was raised from the dead only to see the death of his son
and to suffer the forgotten woes of the living, *ut nostra videres /
funera et oblitos superum paterere dolores* (791f.). Aeson's curse on his
brother Pelias, which causes and looks forward in detail to Pelias'
future, patently recalls Dido's curse on Aeneas (Virg. *Aen.* iv.
607–29); the very conception of magic in the face of death has

---

[17] Whether we see *sacra novat* (774) as meaning 'alter' or 'renew' does not greatly matter;
the idea of continuation is plain (note 778, 791).
[18] Given the locale, *Thessalis* must here be Alcimede: *servaverat*, etc., could hardly suit
another enchantress. This in turn confirms that *Thessalis* in 737 is Alcimede too, which *sacra
...ferebat* (730) in any case suggests. In the vivid description of the bull *sordidus* is deliberately disagreeable; for *ferrugine* cf. Edgeworth (1978).

already brought her to mind. But Aeson's curse conveys a more pointed and elaborate meditation on the plot, and dialectic on death.

He prays that Pelias will live long and not be able to commit suicide like him.

> mors sera viam temptataque claudat
> effugia. (803 f.)

May death come late and close off the path to his attempts at escape!

The life that he wishes on Pelias, one of constant fear, will be a fate far worse than his own noble death. We do not have here the same sharpness of expression in reversing life and death that we find, say, in Seneca or Lucan; but the underlying ingenuity of thought is there, and Aeson's paradoxical triumph is made gloatingly apparent (cf. 806f.).[19] The ethical point on death is obvious, and is reinforced by what follows. When Pelias does die, his death is to be the reverse of Aeson's *magnos obitus*, 'great death', his *fata ... digna satis*, 'death sufficient in worth' (769). Pelias' is to be an inglorious end, *indecoresque obitus* (810); he is not to be thought worthy, *dignatus*, even of dying by the sword of Aeson's son (*non ... aut nati precor ille mei dignatus ut umquam / ense cadat*, 810f.: the collocation of pronouns is expressive). Valerius plainly intimates through Aeson's words the death that Pelias will in fact undergo, to be mistakenly slain and cut up by his own daughters (812–14); he presents it, not with Ovidian cleverness of language, but with evident enjoyment of its monstrous novelty.[20]

> tum vobis siquod inausum
> arcanumque nefas et adhuc incognita leti
> sors superest ... (807–9)

If you [the Furies, etc.] have some crime left not yet dared and kept secret, some form of death still unknown ...

---

[19] Cf. e.g. Sen. *Med.* 19f., in the opening curse, *num peius aliquid* (than death for Jason)? ... / *vivat*, or the perverted clemency which refuses death at Luc. ii. 511–25 (cf. Sil. vii. 72). Compare in Valerius himself iv. 381–3. In treating the life that awaits Pelias, and its length, Valerius derives advantage from his chronology.

[20] For Ovid's play on the event see *Met.* vii. 335–42. In 810 Baehrens's *annis*, besides avoiding the tautology, gives a much better range of things to set against the actual death; the disjunction *aut* makes a reference back to 800 and 803 undesirable. *annis* will connect with *fallaci ... senectae* (809).

superest, 'have left', is pleasingly chosen. The enjoyment is characteristic of the period; here it is brought into an intricate and significant treatment which purposefully manifests the victory of glorious death, and yet also offers a passage complicated in tone and diverse in colour.

The death of Jason's parents itself is made an exciting moment. They drink the bull's blood *avide*, 'greedily' (817): the poet makes their desire for noble death extreme. And then: *fit fragor; inrumpunt foribus*, 'there is a noise; Pelias' men burst in at the doors'.[21] The victory in the nick of time may be contrasted with Messalina's fate in Tacitus (pp. 262 f.); the elemental excitement of the brevity and asyndetic abruptness may be contrasted with the historian's syntax. It is actually a triumph for 'the old people' that they are 'already in the midst of death', *in media iam morte senes* (820). The impact of that triumph is only a little complicated by the revolting consequences of their impressive mode of death: they are *undanti revomentes veste cruorem*, 'vomiting back the bull's blood, with their garments overflowing' (821). More powerfully, the triumph is soured by the killing of their little son.

> primoque rudem sub limine rerum
> te, puer, et visa pallentem morte parentum
> diripiunt adduntque tuis. procul horruit Aeson
> excedens, memoremque tulit sub manibus umbram.[22]

(823–6)

You, child, ignorant and on the mere threshold of life, pale at the sight of your parents' death, they tear apart, and add you to your own. Aeson, at a distance, shook with horror as he departed; his shade did not forget as he bore it to the world of the dead.

The opening phrase contrasts the child pathetically with the *senes*, the 'old people' (820). The poet's address gives a special directness of emotion, while the close of the first sentence gives a grim

---

[21] *foribus* Heinsius: *sonitus* LV, -*u* S (by conjecture, the stemma suggests). After *fit fragor*, *sonitu* is ineffectually weak (contrast Virg. *Aen.* ii. 466). Watt (1984), 164, prefers *senibus*, but the repetition he remarks in 820 seems uninviting. For confusion of *b* and *t* cf. iii. 150.

[22] *manibus* Weichert: *nubibus* codd. Despite Strand (1972), 11 f., the context does not give enough support to take *nubibus* in an extended sense as 'darkness'. *sub* is fairly common in relation to the underworld, e.g. Hor. *Odes* iii. 11. 29. In 825 *procul* is perhaps a little surprising. As to 821, for the ablative absolute in -*i* see Neue–Wagener (1892–1905) ii. 100. On the impressiveness of the mode of death in itself cf. Cic. *Brut.* 43.

elegance to the savage extinction of Jason's family.[23] The effect
on Aeson is made clear; but so also is his purpose of revenge.

The bulk and weight of prophecy and curse have already made
the defeat of Pelias almost overshadow the brief and terrible
moment of death. Immediately after it Valerius moves on to describe the way to the Elysian Fields. Death is not allowed to form a
close, even to the episode. We do not have, as sometimes, an
allusive brevity, in which the after-life supplies as it were a final
major cadence. Nor do we have even a break between books, as
when Lucan prevents Pompey's death from forming an absolute
ending by starting the book after it with his ascent to a higher
world. The death of Aeson and Alcimede is promptly redeemed
and obliterated; the ghastly moment yields to perpetual light and
song. Death now joins Aeson to his race in actuality as in deed: he
and his wife are reunited with his father. The punishments in
store for Pelias are starkly touched on near the close (848f.); the
punishments of this world do not suffice the author's sternness. So
yet another aspect of death affirms the thought, and overcomes
the darkness, of what precedes.

The whole passage in a way is vigorously simple; in a way its
richness surprises and absorbs. The moment of heroic death is in
part the centre and climax of a significant structure; the proportions of the passage also show, conversely, how the moral value of
the suicide outweighs its physical anguish. Simultaneously, however, they incorporate the stark horror of the death into a whole
that is complex in its impact and audacious in its manifold
unreality.

Statius' treatment of death in the *Thebaid* displays, and is
meant to display, the range and inventiveness of his art. Yet
modification of grandeur, or play with greatness, are generally
present and important, in very different ways and degrees. They
are particularly evident in the deaths of the Argive champions
and of the brothers which form the backbone of the second half.
Several of these deaths have been discussed already. We may add
the death of Parthenopaeus, whose boyishness ceases to surmount
the limits of hierarchy, and both pleases and moves us (ix. 855–62,
878f., *al.*); contrasted with this is the death of the imposing Hippomedon. In his battle with the river he finds himself losing 'the

---

[23] The ghastly *diripiunt* reminds us of what will be done to Pelias, *diripiat* 813 (even there
more extreme than in Ovid).

opportunity for a mighty death', *magnae copia mortis* (ix. 491, cf. 506–10); he is rescued thence at the behest of Juno, but promptly meets an end which Statius' account makes more conspicuous for its bizarreness than for its grandeur (ix. 526–39). The death we shall consider now, that of Maeon at the start of Book iii, is much less central to the structure than these, and, in accordance with our purpose, is more straightforward in its greatness.[24] This greatness appears partly through the bold directness and vigour of the poet's language and conception, partly through his close and clever handling of the situation. And yet his ingenuity and wit also produce a restrained but a recurring and purposeful complication of the sublimity; this complication delicately but unmistakably colours the whole passage. It springs much more than in the Valerius from the author's verbal brilliance, and feels an intimate and indispensable part of his very style. By contrast with Valerius' episode, the handling of physical reality in this passage is (for Statius) austerely simple.

The seer Maeon has alone been spared out of the fifty men sent by the tyrant Eteocles to ambush the Argives' emissary Tydeus. He speaks to Eteocles with dauntless defiance, and kills himself (53–113).[25] The episode preoccupies itself with the character's and the poet's evaluation of life and death in particular circumstances. Maeon's first speech to Eteocles (59–77) in schematic outline states that all save he have been slain (59–63), that his survival is not blameworthy (63–9), that Eteocles has acted disastrously (69–77). But it is so devised that his own self and his attitudes to death and life dominate and direct it—specific attitudes, bound to his situation and strongly joined to action.

His opening announcement, in a dramatic gesture, presents the killing of the others by focusing on himself. He imports into this announcement, in a conspicuous position, his own regret at remaining alive.

---

[24] On the episode see Vessey (1973), 107–16; Ahl (1986), 2830–2; on Parthenopaeus' death see Dewar (1991), pp. xxiv–xxvii, xxxiv–xxxvii; on Hippomedon's, Klinnert (1970), 100–18; Juhnke (1972), 24–44; on both, Vessey (1973), 294–303; more generally, Schetter (1960), 237–51. With regard to Hippomedon's lot, one might perhaps bear in mind Palinurus (Virg. *Aen.* vi. 337–62).

[25] Our principal evidence for the story is the brief statement in Homer that Tydeus spared Maeon alone, heeding the gods' omens (*Il.* iv. 397 f.). Maeon's being a seer probably derives from that passage (cf. Kirk on 394 f.)

> hanc tibi de tanto donat ferus agmine Tydeus
> infelicem animam. (59 f.)

From so great a force fierce Tydeus allows you to have this one unhappy life.

His regret he develops in the second section. Paradoxical inversions of life and death are common in the period; here the particular situation is exploited both to intensify the paradox of the misfortune (he alone is spared from death), and to adumbrate feeling that is individual and vivid. Not to have died in arms with his comrades Maeon in his extreme sense of martial honour regards as inglorious. He speaks, in a line that forms a climax, of *crudelem veniam atque inhonorae munera lucis*, 'this cruel act of mercy, the gift of dishonoured life' (66); the elegant paradox that begins the line is succeeded by a bitterer phrase. Yet he is also moved by intense grief for the comrades slain (42–5, 51f., cf. 63f.). More distinctively still, his professional knowledge of fate gives his misfortune, for him, a heavy and grandiose weight. With no mere idle rhetoric he asseverates that the gods and the Fates have 'snatched away his death', *eripuere necem* (69). This closing phrase runs forcefully and ingeniously counter to ordinary language, where we might expect life as the object, or death as the subject.[26]

When Maeon turns to rebuke Eteocles, his transition converts the words that are to come into a heroic precipitation of death: his rebuke will mean that he cannot escape alive.

> iamque ut mihi prodiga vitae
> pectora et extremam nihil horrescentia mortem
> aspicias: ... (69–71)

And now, so you may see I have a spirit extravagant in expending life and not fearful at all of death, the last of things ...

In this stylish movement, the speaker affects to stand back from the coming utterance as he turns that utterance into a glorious act; his very control, coolness, and address make the valour and

---

[26] Cf. e.g. Cic. *Leg.* i. 41; *CLE* 56. 6. Still more elaborate is Luc. vi. 724f. The special significance of fate is prepared by ii. 692f., and marked out by iii. 64f. and 68; so too *iratus fatis* 41. For Maeon's attitude to his survival cf. 41 *tristis morte negata* and ii. 691, 695f.; the poet's *vita ... inerti* chiefly suggests not his but Maeon's lavish feeling. Note Hdt. vii. 232 (and the whole passage); that tale was told to illuminate Sparta and Thermopylae. ii. 695 and iii. 63–6 imply that Maeon's sense of dishonour is not confined to fears that he will be falsely thought a coward.

pride exciting. Exciting too are the implicit generality in *prodiga vitae*, 'extravagant in expending life', and the neat and scornful use of his audience the king.[27]

The following assault in words offers us the stark and magnificent primary colours of virtue defying tyranny and its power to kill, of the moral and political hierarchies at their most extreme and absolute conflict.[28] It closes thus:

> te series orbarum excisa domorum
> planctibus adsiduis, te diro horrore volantes
> quinquaginta animae circum noctesque diesque
> assilient, neque enim ipse moror.   (74–7)

You will be assailed with constant laments by the long line of bereft homes that you have destroyed, you will be assailed by fifty spirits flying around you with ghastly terror day and night: fifty, for I myself make no delay.

The exalted energy of the prophecy animatedly makes Eteocles into the powerless individual; the *te*s impress us alike by their stylistic elevation and by their unflinching directness of encounter. The emphasis on *quinquaginta*, 'fifty', lies at first (not without ingenuity) on its appalling size. In the final clause the emphasis moves startlingly to its precision: fifty, not forty-nine, for Maeon will shortly join them. This declaration is linked to a sudden descent in grandeur, and to an obtrusive cleverness. The casual manner to some degree enhances the heroism, but simultaneously the splendour is complicated somewhat, and contained. The speaker's greatness and the poet's conspicuous modification of greatness meet in a deliberately arresting and intriguing compound.

Maeon slays himself: his action asserts his freedom from death and from the tyrant's power not only mentally but physically. Like Aeson he thwarts the tyrant's will by anticipation, and

---

[27] On *prodiga* see Nisbet and Hubbard on Hor. *Odes* i. 12. 38. *extremam ... mortem*, though possibly derived by Statius from Virg. *Aen.* ii. 447 and xi. 848, seems here somewhat dubious; *extremam* should not mean 'the cruellest', in view of what is to happen and of 83 f. If there is corruption, *mortem* is probably the word to change.

[28] The theme had long existed, and had acquired rich associations of thought and history; here a contemporary political interpretation appears highly unlikely. Soph. *Ant.* 441–525 presents (in essence) an early example, Hor. *Epist.* i. 16. 72–9 an Augustan one; the Horace suggests the characteristic elements that philosophy imports. Sil. vii. 20–73 offers a forceful instance in poetry under Domitian. Sen. *Tranq.* 14. 3, Epict. i. 2. 21, etc., effectively illustrate the clash of hierarchies and values.

creates his own fine death. Unlike Valerius, Statius produces a
starkly simple mode of death, and a narrative surprising for its
sense not of extension but of rapidity. In a forcefully direct tableau
Maeon stands with drawn sword as Eteocles' henchmen prepare
to act. He makes a second speech (83–7), asserting his own power
to die as he wishes; in doing so he looks now at the glowering
tyrant, whose will he eludes, now at the sword, which will free him
(81–3): *trucis ora tyranni*, 'the face of the cruel tyrant' is set both
against *magnanimus vates*, 'the great-spirited seer', and against the
curt elided disyllable *ferrum*, 'sword'.[29] Maeon's swiftness has been
suggested, ambiguously, in the close of his first speech (*neque enim
ipse moror*, 'I myself make no delay'); it appears thrillingly when the
men who act for Eteocles prepare, *sed iam nudaverat ensem /
magnanimus vates*, 'but the great-spirited seer had already drawn
his sword'. It appears much more strangely when Statius displaces
the death-blow. He here boldly diverges from epic norms, in the
opposite direction from Silius. We expect, especially after the
tableau, that the speech will be followed by a precise description
of the act. Instead, it breaks off in mid-sentence; we learn that in
the course of that short speech the blow has already taken place.

> 'te superis fratrique—'. et iam media orsa loquentis
> absciderat plenum capulo latus.   (87f.)

'You to the gods and your brother—'. And already his words were
broken off, in mid-utterance, because his chest was filled with the sword,
hilt and all.

The audacity of the technique is intensified by the very violent
action implied in the resulting state. The expressive device has
been pushed to an extreme where visible mannerism lightly complicates its expressive impact.

The second speech itself exhilarates by its defiant and joyful
assurance. The defiance is at first splendidly direct and taunting:
numquam tibi sanguinis huius / ius erit, 'you will never have power or
right over this blood' (82f.); Statius then draws it compressedly
into the network of his themes. The joy too is no generalized love
of death, but is tied to the situation: *vado equidem exultans*, 'I go

---

[29] The contrast with *ferrum* 80 of *ensem* 81 and *ferrum* 83 is not accidental: others act for
Eteocles, Maeon performs for himself his violence on himself. *proturbare* 81 is in any case
problematic; the expected 'drive away' (cf. Snijder ad loc.) is intolerably weak for the
context and the parenthesis.

rejoicing', is followed by the specific *ereptaque fata / insequor*, 'I
pursue the death snatched from me'. Joy appears in more open
paradox after the death. Maeon's loved ones

> servantem vultus et torvum in morte peracta,
> non longum reducem laetati, in tecta ferebant. (94 f.)

bore him back to the house. He kept his expression and remained grim
even in a death that was now completed; they were happy that he had
not returned for long.

The first line has a sombre majesty of content which the ponderous rhythm reinforces; it grandly and darkly displays the physical
firmness that Maeon maintained in death. The phrase *non longum
reducem laetati*, 'they were happy that he had not returned for long',
brings in more disengaging tones. It assuredly suggests the desir-
ability of his death and the brutality of Eteocles (whom Maeon
had already clashed with, ii. 694). But the peculiarity of such
feelings appearing in the devoted, and the neatness with which
Homer's story has been undone, produce a slight irritation and
impurity in the greatness. This again serves somewhat to distance
and contain at a point of close.

The dying itself, by contrast with the decisive action, is presented as an extended process. The agonies of the hero are vividly
conveyed. Statius closes with a faintly distancing strangeness and
symmetry. From the drastic conception of the man 'doubled, by
effort, on to the mighty blow', *ingentem nisu duplicatus in ictum*, we
pass to

> extremisque animae singultibus errans
> alternus nunc ore venit, nunc vulnere sanguis. (90 f.)

The blood wandered in the final convulsions of breath, and came in
alternation now from his mouth, now from his wound.

The sweeping torrent of sublimity in the episode, and the
gentle current of modification, run through the poet's final
outburst. The exclamation does not break into the run of the
episode, though it breaks up the larger narration. The poet's
lavish emotion here principally confirms emotion in us. The
soaring admiration he displays for his fiction is supported and
grounded by his broad and generalizing praise for the assertion of
freedom in death:

> qui comminus ausus
> vadere contemptor regi, quaque ampla veniret
> libertas sancire viam.[30]   (100-2)

you who dared go close to a hostile king and scorn him, and to consecrate the path by which freedom can come in full.

The poet praises the prophet, whose death will make the oracles fall silent; his imagination develops the thought with an intriguing and distancing autonomy. At the close of his sentence on this theme he says that the prophetess at Delphi *gaudebit tacito populos suspendere Phoebo*, 'will delight to hold the world in suspense through Apollo's silence' (107).[31] The unlooked-for emotions please, and remove us a little from involvement in the poet's exclamation. The whole passage closes, not in exalted sublimity, but in a narrative touch which charms and slightly distances us in its ingenious fantasy. We had learned before the outburst that Eteocles had forbidden burial (96–8); now we are told that Maeon's body is miraculously spared the standard violation from beasts and birds. This happens in part through the *tristis volucrum reverentia*, the 'sad reverence of the birds'. The tyrant is thwarted once more, but with an alluringly clever use of the augur's profession.[32]

With our passage from **Seneca** we come a step further in regard to complication. The last act of the *Troades* depicts through the speeches of a messenger the deaths of Astyanax and Polyxena, inflicted by the Greeks.[33] In this scene we see features familiar in

---

[30] *contemptor* Müller: *-um* codd.; *regi* Madvig: *-is (-es)* codd. This combination offers a makeshift but conceivable text, which 'to go at close quarters in order to despise kings' does not. Statius can use agent nouns adjectivally or in apposition without a genitive, even when they are not from intransitive verbs (here the object is evident from the context): cf. e.g. iv. 369, and note the predicative i. 712.

[31] Something of the effect will stand whatever the text and point of *gaudebit* (Markland for *audebit*). But *audebit* is hard to justify (the oracles can hardly be supposed to make obscure prophecies independently of Apollo); I doubt if we are given enough of a lead to see relief in *gaudebit* (Housman (1972), 1202), and suspect it denotes a more malevolent and, alas, self-explanatory pleasure.

[32] *nemus* if sound no doubt makes a related point. For the protection of bodies by gods, which might have been expected here, see Juhnke (1972), 79. It might just enter the mind to begin a new sentence after *Ogygiis*, and refer *valent* to this world. Otherwise the transition to *durant* is very harsh (we should at the least have required *sed* rather than *-que*). The extreme *Ogygiis* seems more acceptable in this position than coupled to the obvious, and even weakly obvious, clause that would follow. *sontis* would still make a connection with the previous sentence. But I am far from sure about this suggestion.

[33] On the episode see Lawall (1981–2), and also Owen (1970); we are not concerned here with the issue of posthumous survival in the play. In general on death in the tragedies see Regenbogen (1961).

prose explored much further, brought to an extreme, and modified with strident ingenuity. So the opposition of the individual to others present, of his calmness to their tears, we have seen often in prose; Seneca here greatly develops the motif. First there is the crowd. With the poet's particularity and extravagance, Seneca sharply crystallizes and lavishly expands the frequent idea of death as a spectacle. Through his crowds he provides a background of physical immensity and spiritual inferiority for his isolated and heroic protagonists. The first narrative, on Astyanax, stresses the visual and spatial aspect, depicting with vivacious particularity and wit the Greek crowd filling the area, with spectators at every high point of vantage (1068–87). The second narrative, on Polyxena, takes this up: the whole shore is filled (1135f.), the physical features of the place recall a theatre (1123–5).[34] But this second narrative dwells rather on the minds of the crowd: Seneca presents colourfully their diversity of feeling (1126–9); and he now includes Trojans as well as Greeks (1129–31). Both accounts direct our evaluation through the crowd's reactions. In both all present are moved because the one dying is unmoved. *non flet e turba omnium / qui fletur*, 'the only one in all that multitude who did not weep was the one who was wept for' (1099f., cf. 1159f.): the phrase ingeniously joins Astyanax to the gigantic crowd only to separate him from them. In the second account, both peoples, and all that diverse crowd, become united in their response of admiration and grief ('both' 1136f., 1160; 'all' 1146, 1153). 'All' (*omnium, omnes*) has a strong, and different, force in the two narratives.

Yet the summit of the heroes' virtue is displayed by the reaction of their chief enemies. Astyanax and Polyxena overcome the extremes of impassive cunning and of active cruelty, Ulysses and Pyrrhus; in each narrative the name of the enemy comes as a climax and is felt as an extreme. The rest of the play, and the versification and expression, give the moment in each case an ingenious brilliance which lightly separates us from a full involvement. This is evident with the second instance:

---

[34] The connection with spectators is apparent at *Virg. Aen.* v. 286–90; here it is suggested by collocation (the *litus* includes the *vallis*), but not spelt out. Contrast Plin. *Ep.* v. 6. 7. The element of the crowd is derived particularly from the narrative of Polyxena's death at Eur. *Hec.* 518–582. The tower (1068–77) is a potent and multiple image, visually and symbolically; some aspects of its significance are drawn out by Jakobi (1987), 38f.

> tam fortis animus omnium mentes ferit,
> novumque monstrum est Pyrrhus ad caedem piger. (1153 f.)

The minds of all were powerfully struck by so valiant a spirit; an unheard-of prodigy appeared, a Pyrrhus sluggish to kill.

omnium, 'all', is itself significant, but leads into the more significant *Pyrrhus*. *piger*, 'sluggish', forcefully alliterating, has here an unexalted quality which clashes paradoxically with *monstrum*, 'prodigy'; this keeps us from a straightforward response.[35] In 1099 f. *moverat vulgum ac duces / ipsumque Ulixem*, 'he stirred the crowd, the commanders, Ulysses himself', the name after enjambment carries immense force thanks to the role of Ulysses earlier and the earlier use of his name (568 f., 614).

The form of the whole scene presents us with two more reactions: those of Astyanax' and Polyxena's mothers, Andromache and Hecuba. An outburst from Andromache follows the first narration; one from Hecuba follows the second. The place of lament in this scene is greatly reduced in comparison with Seneca's main sources, Euripides and Ovid, and with the general practice of Greek tragedy. The emphasis is thrown strongly on to narration, and in the light of the narration the mothers' comments themselves are partly to be considered. The mothers see only the pathos of the young deaths, where the narrative has shown us both pathos and heroism. The messenger had offered us both, in a balanced couplet:

> mactata virgo est, missus e muris puer;
> sed uterque letum mente generosa tulit. (1063 f.)

The girl has been sacrificed, the boy cast from the walls; but each endured death with noble spirit.

Hecuba takes up this couplet with lines that stress only the atrocity; bitterly addressing the Greeks she says:

> concidit virgo ac puer:
> bellum peractum est. (1167 f.)

A girl and a boy have died: now the war is [truly] finished.

Andromache, not heeding the bold leap of Astyanax to his death, dwells only on the Greeks' barbarity to a child (1104–9). The mothers' response in part guides our own; it underlines the pathos

---

[35] Against this passage one sets particularly 308–10.

of the event, and excites our vehement pity for the mothers. Yet we should also be conscious of its limitations.

The passage with Andromache goes on to treat even the pathos and horror of the death with a brilliant and exhilarating wit. The messenger describes abundantly the appalling destruction of the body once like Hector's (1113); now Astyanax lies an unsightly body, *iacet / deforme corpus* (1116 f.). Andromache comments only *sic quoque est similis patri*, 'in this too he is like his father' (dragged by Achilles). The underlying thought expresses her misery and her outlook; but we must be chiefly struck by the sudden, dry brevity of form, and the stunning ingenuity. The phrase turns round the sense of *similis*, 'like', which is expected here, that of family resemblance, and so affirms what seemed to have been denied, that he remains like his father.[36] At the highest points of emotion, as of greatness, the poet most deliberately modifies straightforward power with cleverness that complicates and withdraws.

Both the boy and the maiden press beyond the limits of hierarchy in the courage of their deaths. The theme is one we have seen in prose (pp. 271 ff., 282 ff.). Seneca's poetic treatment, removed from actual events or direct didacticism, is more elaborate in its effect than any in prose, and tonally more complex; the description is also more concrete, and yet remoter from familiar reality. Seneca takes the courage of his two figures to drastic and somewhat distancing extremes; yet he also explores the complexities of their status subtly and richly, and savours the contrast as well as the likeness between them. Astyanax, usually a helpless young child, has before this scene given us a momentary hint of his courage (503–6); he has spoken, however, only in childish fear, begging his *mother* to have pity (*miserere, mater*, 732) as he clings to her bosom and doom awaits. In deliberate and striking contrast, Seneca now presents a boy who transcends boyhood in his freedom from fear.[37] The handling of the verse exhibits the collision and interaction of transcendence and pathos.

---

[36] The line takes up and reverses 464 (cf. 464–8). The end of the *Phaedra* should be compared, not only for the destruction of the body, but for its more startling and drastic undoing of pathos in wit (1110–14, 1246–74). Seneca cannot there be unconscious of his impact.

[37] Seneca will also be exploiting a familiar licence in the presentation of children's ages (Kassel (1954), 54 f.). It would hardly seem plausible to ascribe the change to Andromache's speech 793–812 (no rousing oration), nor to its conceptions about death. With Astyanax'

                                     sublimi gradu
                incedit Ithacus parvulum dextra trahens
                Priami nepotem; nec gradu segni puer
                ad alta pergit moenia.   (1088–91)

With tall step Ulysses came on, leading Priam's little grandson by the
hand; and the boy proceeded with no reluctant step to the high walls.

In the first clause the contrast of size engenders only pathos. It is
Ulysses who acts; the gesture grimly distorts a tender and parental
action; the diminutive *parvulum*, 'little', appeals simply to our
pity.[38] Yet the next clause unexpectedly makes Astyanax into a
determined agent too. The parallelism with *gradu*, 'step', makes
the change obvious; yet the lack of a 'but' and the litotes give a
classic and understated nobility. *puer*, 'boy', is expressively placed
at the end of the line between the valorous bearing and the fatal
action; it displays with force how he excels his status. The resumption of the passage in 1097 f. presents the point still more
strongly: *sic ille dextra prensus hostili puer / ferox superbit*, 'so that boy
held by an enemy's hand showed ferocity and pride'. The first line
suggests a terrifying situation, and ends expressively in *puer*, 'boy';
but the start of the next line confounds the natural suggestion of
the language.

Polyxena surpasses the categories too, still more than Astyanax;
but we are made to taste the intrinsic differences between maiden
and boy. Astyanax looks all about him, *vultus huc et huc acres tulit /
intrepidus animo*, 'he cast his courageous eyes all about, dauntless in
spirit' (1092 f.); Polyxena, by contrast, walking in procession, 'kept
her eyes cast modestly down', *deiectos gerit / vultus pudore* (1137 f.).
There is indeed an implicit opposition between Polyxena's calm
and the terror of the spectators (1136 f., cf. 1130); but the emphasis
falls, unexpectedly, on her chaste observation of maidenly dec-
orum. Yet Polyxena's fierce heroism is still more strongly presented than Astyanax': she, who comes second, is the more
complicated, paradoxical, and extreme of the two figures. The

utterance one contrasts his silence at Eur. *Tro.* 749–51, and Polyxena's silence at Sen. *Tro.*
945–8. Compare and contrast Stat. *Theb.* ix. 350 (with Dewar's note). With 503–6 cf. Stat.
Ach. i. 271–7.

[38] *trahens* (better not translated 'dragging') distorts Virg. *Aen.* ii. 457. For *sublimi* cf. *celso*,
celsa at *Ag.* 587, 717. On *nec gradu segni* one should remember in general how much more
significant and expressive manners of walking were for Greeks and Romans than for the
modern English (or [Dem.] 25. 52 would have reformed me long ago).

face which displayed such virginal modesty shows a vigorous harshness as she meets the death-blow, *truci vultu ferox*, 'fierce and savage in expression' (1152): *truci*, 'savage', goes beyond the language used of Astyanax. Her courage is still more impressively conveyed; with the words quoted above on Astyanax' step we may compare

audax virago non tulit retro gradum.   (1151)

The bold heroine did not move her step back.

The negative statement has in its context a superb greatness; the term *virago*, 'heroine, heroic *virgo*', turns as it were her status itself into grandeur.[39] The form of a complete line in 1151 gives a particular simplicity and harmony to the utterance in comparison with 1090f. Astyanax was *intrepidus*, 'dauntless', in spirit (1093); Polyxena's spirit is described with more open heightening as *tam fortis animus*, 'so brave a spirit' (1153). This itself takes up a phrase more penetrating in implication than those used of Astyanax, *animus fortis et leto obvius*, 'a brave spirit, pressing forward to meet death' (1146). The phrase has none of the homeliness of the ending to *Naturales Quaestiones* vi (p. 286); and transferred from active suicide to an attitude it searchingly suggests a valour of the mind.

We see the richness of Seneca's treatment more fully in considering the similes that are applied to both. Astyanax has earlier been compared to a fearful calf pressing against its mother as the lion approaches (793–9). Now with a significant shift he is likened to the young of a fierce animal (presumably a lion):

qualis ingentis ferae
parvus tenerque fetus et nondum potens
saevire dente iam tamen tollit minas
morsusque inanes temptat atque animis tumet ...   (1093–6)

As the small and weak offspring of a mighty beast, not yet able to do violence with its teeth, already acts to threaten, tries biting, uselessly, and in its spirit swells with fury ...

There follow the lines already cited: *sic ille dextra prensus hostili puer / ferox superbit*, 'so that boy held by an enemy's hand showed ferocity and pride'. Seneca's use of this simile resembles Silius' use of his on the tigress (p. 291); Seneca's has more charm, and he

---

[39] Cf. Tarrant on *Ag.* 668, Skutsch on Enn. *Ann.* 220.

gains a still more complex effect from the device of simile, one of the richest and most open in poetry's rich and open language. The simile in itself evokes a certain pathetic and endearing futility: this effect is especially carried through by *inanes*, 'uselessly'. The first half of the last line makes the mental pride in the second half seem not quite grandiose; this is unlike *intrepidus animo*, 'dauntless in spirit' (1093), from which the simile takes its cue. In the application of the simile a more heroic spirit is seen than in the simile itself, and a more imposing dignity. We sense the divergence, while still feeling the pathos involved in Astyanax' courage. The reaction of the Greeks, admiring tears, brings out this pathos, sublimer than that in the simile and more closely linked with greatness.[40]

Polyxena is beautifully and startlingly compared to the sun (1140–2): her eyes, like its light, are loveliest at setting. This comparison forms part of an intricate pair of sentences (1136–48). The reactions of the spectators to Polyxena are used to create a complex reaction in us: *mirantur ac miserantur*, 'they admire and pity' (1148), elegantly summarizes, but the compound is produced by beauty, youth, misfortune, and above all courage. The beauty of her eyes introduces an especially subtle and devious source of pity. It paradoxically defeats her efforts to conceal it; the idea of its increasing with the approach of death lends it a grandiose significance, and divorces it lyrically from accustomed reality. The comparison with the sun, presented in its astronomical context, gives further grandeur to the beauty, but also a warm and sensuous loveliness: *ut esse Phoebi dulcius lumen solet / iam iam cadentis*, 'as the sun's light is wont to be sweeter when it is on the point of setting'. The preceding lines have made us expect simply 'brighter'; *dulcius*, 'sweeter', surprises and attracts.[41] Through the interaction of imagery and drama the poet creates a particularly involved and subtle treatment of his young heroes' status.

The moments of death offer not intricacy but extremity; the extremity is of a kind that deliberately somewhat distances our reaction. This is again particularly obvious with Polyxena.

---

[40] Statius likes to explore the minds and actions of young lions, in the pleasing complications of greatness that they offer: *Theb.* viii. 572–6, ix. 739–43, xii. 356–8. Note too the beast similes at *Thy.* 707–11, 732–6, *Ag.* 892–6; no doubt Seneca's manner here is an influence on Statius.

[41] Cf. Fantham's note. In 1143–8 I should accept Zwierlein's admirable deletions.

nec tamen moriens adhuc
deponit animos: cecidit, ut Achilli gravem
factura terram, prona et irato impetu.   (1157–9)

Not even as she died did she lay down her strength of spirit. To make the
earth heavy for Achilles, she fell urging forward with an angry force.

Polyxena is being slain as a bride at the tomb of the still
enamoured Achilles; the force of her fall she intends to increase
the weight of the earth on him, whereas kindred usually prayed
for the earth to rest lightly on the deceased. Like Astyanax' death,
but more ingeniously, Polyxena's is converted by her conduct into
an action. The opening clause of anticipation leads us to expect a
superb display of courage. Yet the poet's thought is oblique; the
action combines, in a strange and arresting fancy, fierce ingenuity
from Polyxena with an almost bizarre exploitation of close physicality. Her extreme continuance of hostilities cannot in the circumstances strike us as simply grandiose in its impact. One should
note here particularly how the clause of purpose delays and so
stresses *prona et irato impetu*, 'urging forward and with an angry
force', where the language strikingly infuses and combines the
physical with the mental. We are far from the concern with
decorous chastity which Euripides' and Ovid's Polyxenas exhibit
in their falls (*Hec.* 568–70, *Met.* xiii. 479f.); Seneca pushes
greatness quite differently to a strange and pleasing climax.[42]

Astyanax is not hurled from the tower; while the Greeks are
conducting a perverted religious ceremony which is to culminate
in his death

sponte desiluit sua
in media Priami regna.   (1102f.)

He leapt down of his own will into the midst of Priam's kingdom.

It is interesting to compare the leap into the chasm at *NQ* vi. 32. 4
(p. 285f.). The distancing ingenuity is here marked out less, and is
treated less abruptly in rhythm: here *desiluit*, 'he leapt down', is

---

[42] It is interesting to note the distasteful anticlimax found in the Euripides by Hermogenes, *Inv.* iv. 12 p. 204 Rabe; Ovid naturally relishes the sexual piquancy. It is notable
that *pronus* should be given such a connotation of intent in regard to a dying person falling;
contrast πρηνής at Quint. Smyrn. xiv. 316 (his whole account of the death, 257–321, is
worth comparing with Seneca's for its utterly different handling of Polyxena). For the
ingenious hostility in falling cf. Stat. *Theb.* x. 778f. (Menoeceus); Polyxena's anger is not of
course caused by resentment at her lot (cf. 945–8).

supported by *sponte sua*, 'of his own will', and we close not with *desiluit* but with the proud assertion of his lineage, which itself ennobles his action.[43] Yet the place in *NQ* vi suggests the possibility of some distancing here; this passage itself confirms it. The Greeks' ceremony is boldly interrupted and robbed of its dignity; we must enjoy the resource and audacity with which Astyanax wrests the situation and Seneca (in all likelihood) wrests the myth. The whole action is introduced with a mere *ac*, 'and', which enhances the disruptive surprise by affecting to reduce it. Greatness is again forced, though less stridently, to a spectacular yet agreeable extreme. This whole masterly episode shows the richness of language and physical intensity with which poetry can handle magnificent scenes of death, but also the strangeness, the extravagance, the wit which makes its force so intricate and aesthetically challenging.

Lucan, who in handling death deploys grotesque ingenuity with unmatched vigour and invention, never allows his treatment to display only a simple splendour. Even with the great suicide of Vulteius and his comrades (iv. 474–581) the profuse moral and intellectual paradoxes of the narrative complicate radically the effect that had been produced by Vulteius' largely magnificent oration. Conspicuous too is Lucan's boldness and unpredictability in using narrative: an obvious example is the contrast between the gruesomely lingering physical detail of the sea-battle in Book iii and the ostentatious abandonment of individualized, epic narrative at the battle of Pharsalia (vii. 617–46). Both tonal complication and narrative audacity are prominent in Lucan's treatment in Book viii of the death of Pompey, stabbed and beheaded off the coast of Egypt. It is the most important, and the most overwhelming, death in the unfinished poem.[44]

We shall consider first the outbursts of the poet, which in their

[43] I feel doubtful whether the half-line embodies at any rate Seneca's final intention; *Phoen.* 319 and the parallel of Virgil are scarcely encouraging. (Soph. *Phil.* 785–805 or *OT* 1468–75 would not have suggested a precedent.) Otherwise Tarrant on *Thy.* 100, Zwierlein on *Phaedr.* 605.

[44] On this episode see, among other treatments, Schnepf (1970); Holgado Redondo (1978); Johnson (1987), 79–81; and on death in Lucan generally Metger (1957); Rutz (1960). Lucan's recitation at his death of a death from his own poem (Tac. *Ann.* xv. 70. 1), assuming it to be historical, admits of various interpretations; it certainly does not establish the straightforward seriousness of his treatments of death, and the passage itself (Luc. iii. 635 (642?)–46) makes that unlikely. One might best see defiance of the suppressor of his poetry, and a certain magnificent frivolity (cf. Suet. *Poet.* 31. 31–4 Rostagni).

treatment appear so distinctive a feature of Lucan, in comparison with other epic, and with history. History itself, on such a theme, is ready enough for expatiation: so Dio declaims eloquently on Pompey's death once it has occurred (xlii. 5. 1–6), and in the midst of it comments morally on the consequences for the killers and for Egypt (3. 4).[45] But the readiness and especially the passion of Lucan's entries give his account a very different quality. And yet the effect of these entries is not at all so chaotic or so straight-forwardly emotive as might be thought. In the treatment of Pompey's death emotion, narration, and provoking mannerism possess a very involved relationship; this complexity is seen at a height in the poet's interventions.

The passages of prolonged author's comment are carefully planned. From the preparations of the Egyptians to the beheading of Pompey, Lucan has only two. At the beginning he deplores (viii. 542–60) Egypt's involvement in the killing of Pompey; he particularly assails the 'boy' king Ptolemy. At 599–610 he deplores the participation of the Roman Septimius.[46] Immediately after the decapitation itself the narrative blends with comment (674–91), until Lucan launches into a harangue and lament on the treatment of Pompey's body (692–711). This ends the part on the killing. The lengthy treatment of Pompey's burial by a follower contains a brief address from Lucan to the follower near the end of the narrative (781–6), and after the narrative a very long and fine declamation on the epitaph, tomb, and burial (793–872); this forms the peroration of the book. The whole account thus culminates in the author's lyricism; so does the account of the killing itself (536–711), to which we must here confine ourselves. But the poet carefully allows to the killing what seems, at least on the surface, a sequence of narrative that can involve us in its movement. The intrusions of the poet do not here simply destroy the narrative momentum. The two earlier attacks by the poet separate and reinforce divisions of the narrative: both are

[45] Compare with the former passage App. *BC* ii. 363, and also Vell. ii. 53. 3; the contrast with Pompey's past is naturally a commonplace, cf. e.g. Cic. *Div.* ii. 22, Man. iv. 50–6. Interesting too in Dio is the historian's assertion of incredulity on the contemplation of flight to Parthia, 2. 5 f.: this intrusion is quite unlike the poet's manner.

[46] As we shall see, these two outbursts are very clearly formed as a pair; it of course makes no difference to this that the first also provides in its second part the author's reply to the speech of his character Pothinus in the preceding debate (cf. 550 f. with 528, 552 *audes* with 530, 558 f. with 518 f.).

typically followed by resumptive *iams*, 'now, already' (560; 610, 612), which hold in the outburst and mark the opening of a new paragraph. The placing of the first attack demarcates and highlights the arrival of Pompey on the scene. The second separates Pompey's fateful decision to enter the boat where he is killed from the actual killing itself. This division in some ways even intensifies our concentration on the moment of stabbing itself, which the poet so fills with significance. These two passages themselves to some degree heighten our emotion over the event: to some extent, we enter into the poet's lavish outrage. Yet the form and the passages themselves also serve decidedly to distance us.

The poet has neatly divided his narrative, in accord with these passages: the Egyptians, led by Achillas, stab Pompey, and Septimius decapitates him.[47] Lucan's two protests, first that Egyptians not Romans are to kill Pompey, and then that a Roman is to decapitate him, are so presented that we sense and are meant to sense the poet on the verge of self-contradiction, in his wild passion and restless ingenuity. The expression itself is full of extreme and intriguing paradox, with little pathos. The virtual contradiction between the passages is stressed when Lucan laments that a 'civil crime' (Septimius') should occur even in Egypt (*facinus civile*, 604). He had begged, 'civil wars, at least keep faith to this degree', and let Romans do the deed: *hanc certe servate fidem, civilia bella* (547). In the latter phrase itself the wish, the 'at least', and the address are full of paradox and strangeness. Differently linked are the indignant question to Ptolemy, with its lingering verb, *quid viscera nostra / scrutaris gladio?*, 'Why do you delve in our Roman innards with your sword?' (556f.), and the remark on Septimius which trumps it:

> Pellaeusque puer gladio tibi colla recidit
> Magne, tuo.   (607f.)

The Macedonian boy cut your head off, Pompey, with your own sword.

The first line in itself appears to ascribe the violence to the inert Ptolemy's own hand, with a still more daring precision than in 556f.; but the remainder heightens the enormity by bringing in,

---

[47] In Plutarch and Appian Septimius stabs Pompey first, others follow, including in Plutarch Achillas; Egyptians decapitate him (*Pomp.* 79. 4, 80. 2, *BC* ii. 359, 361). Dio is vague. Seneca presents Achillas alone as the slayer, doubtless for rhetorical point (*Marc.* 20. 4, *Brev.* 13. 7; cf. Cic. *Tusc.* i. 86 *servorum ferrum*). Lucan's arrangement is probably his own. It is

with the last disyllable, Pompey's own former soldier. *tuo* itself, 'your own', on the surface strengthens the enormity, but with brilliant neatness and surprise. Our chief reactions here are not wrath and horror.[48]

The climactic outburst at the end of the narrative of killing has a very different character. The rhetoric possesses a superb *élan* and power which excite us in themselves, and it is made the bearer of a momentous pathos. And yet Lucan determinedly limits and holds in, by instants of an unelevated wit, the flowing sublimity of his utterance; he does not here undo the sublimity, but lightly contains it. A large and magnificent period sets the Ptolemies and their pyramids against Pompey's headless corpse floating in the sea: ingenuity and indignity here subserve tragic grandeur.[49] But Lucan adds the short complaint

> adeone molesta
> totum cura fuit socero servare cadaver?   (699f.)

Was it such a troublesome thing to keep the whole corpse for Caesar?

The deliberate weakness of language, sarcasm of tone, and obliquity of thought bring us abruptly down. Lucan goes on to treat nobly of Pompey's unmixed good and then unmixed evil fortune; he closes:

> pulsatur harenis,
> carpitur in scopulis hausto per vulnera fluctu,
> ludibrium pelagi; nullaque manente figura
> una nota est Magno capitis iactura revulsi.   (708–11)

He is struck by the sands, torn into on the rocks; water floods his wounds; he is the plaything of the sea. His own form is all lost, and Pompey's only distinguishing feature is the loss of his severed head.

---

notable how much less dramatically Lucan uses the actual contact of Septimius and Pompey before the killing than do Plutarch and Appian (79. 1; ii. 359): this suits the purposes of his design.

[48] The exploitation of the proverb (Housman ad loc.; Otto (1890), 154) makes *tuo* the more elegant, and adds an acid colloquialism; but it is only the starting point of the wit.

[49] Add to Mayer's note Hornblower (1982), 253 (though Tarn remained wrong about *indigna*). Only if Housman approached Man. iv. 53 rightly would Lucan's point be anticipated; but that is very uncertain. Cf. Shackleton Bailey (1956), 84. Shackleton Bailey's own conjecture on the Manilius, in essence attractive, in the form he gives it seems too unclear (an *ex* would be needed for comprehension).

Through its position in the passage the first half of the extract has a grim and sombre power. This is slightly modified by the characteristic relish in the macabre, but reaffirmed by the expressive *ludibrium pelagi*, 'the plaything of the sea'. The last line, however, while affecting to reach an extreme of degradation, plays so ingeniously with the horror that we smile and are moved away.[50]

It is clear enough that these interventions of the poet are not in fact undisciplined interruptions; it is clear too that their purpose is not simply to arouse unmixed emotion in us. They are complicated in themselves, and they make the whole passage more complex, particularly when we consider their disposition. The last substantial intervention seeks a much more powerful emotional impact than the first two; it follows, and in part contrasts with, the part of the narrative that stands furthest from straightforwardness. The first two are set in, and partly distance us from, the part of the narrative that stands nearest to straightforwardness. The narrative proper, it will be seen, shows both complexity and calculated shape. Though rarely quite uncomplicated, it moves onward to a climax of immense power and depth as Pompey endures the Egyptian swords; from that point the complications and strangeness increase. The proportions and manner of narration become strange sooner, when we arrive at the stabbing itself; this strangeness too increases. Lucan's aims are both to express and to provoke; the latter aim comes much further to the fore after the climax. Lucan's art, as ever, is highly deliberate; both the movement of rising power and the movement of gathering complication are true to his aesthetic purposes and the character of his artistry.

The first main section of narrative (560–98), which tells of Pompey's decision to enter the Egyptian boat, essentially prepares for and builds up towards the second. It moves at first (560–7) with a prose-like simplicity and factuality (and a couple of abusive adjectives). Pompey's decision, variously treated in the historical writers, is ennobled by Lucan:

---

[50] The effect is made particularly ingenious and bizarre by *nota*. This word, used of something possessed by which one is recognized as oneself, we would rather have expected to refer to features of the face; the very impossibility of such features here makes Pompey recognizable. In relation to severed heads themselves note ii. 167; Curt. viii. 3. 13 (cf. Luc. ix. 1033–7). In this usage *nota* is normally plural, and *una nota*, especially of so gross an aspect, sounds stranger than *nulla nota* (cf. Liv. xxxix. 53. 3).

> sed cedit fatis classemque relinquere iussus
> obsequitur, letumque iuvat praeferre timori. (575 f.)

He yielded to fate; told to leave his fleet, he obeyed. It pleased him to prefer death to fear.

The resignation to fate conveys a large wisdom (deplorable as fate is in Lucan); the seeming slavery to the king has an appearance of ignobility, marked out by the enjambment. Both are transcended by the final clause, which turns the acceptance into a positive act of spiritual greatness and even freedom. But at present spiritual themes are only lightly touched.[51]

The narrative suddenly rises into dramatic force, and into a passion and fullness quite unlike prose, when Pompey's wife enters it. Cornelia, fearing Pompey's murder, actually seeks to go into the boat with him: Lucan seeks a more extravagant drama than history offered. The two make contrasted speeches; Pompey's is calm, Cornelia's exceedingly agitated. Pompey's coolness reaches a chilling and ghastly close: *in hac cervice tyranni / explorate fidem*, 'test the trustworthiness of a king by the example of my neck' (581 f.). That he should command his wife and son so to 'test', not say he will do so himself (cf. 141 f.), has an especially icy effect. Cornelia's frenzy expresses itself in wild accusation, and drastic but elegant paradox.[52] Pompey in his action has renounced fear; Cornelia in 'stunned fear', *attonitoque metu*, can neither look away nor watch Pompey, *nec quoquam avertere visus / nec Magnum spectare potest* (591 f.). Here paradox, the theme of the spectator, and poetic closeness in handling the moment produce an impressive union of power and psychological penetration. We have in this passage in part the contrast of a male and a female ethos, in part the familiar contrast between the person who is to die and others. But the contrast is subtle (Cornelia's passion is courageous, devoted, and valid), and it takes up explicitly themes and scenes long important in the poem. In particular we look back in form and matter to the scenes of their previous parting (v. 722–98) and of their first meet-

---

[51] Lucan utilizes but avoids Pompey's overt if stylish acceptance of slavery in the quotation from Sophocles (fr. 873 Radt) which appears in the historical accounts. It is interesting to see the stories of philosophers who reverse this unacceptable quotation (*SVF* i. 219; Diog. Laert. ii. 82).

[52] The close in particular shows ingenuity of a decidedly distancing sort. In Plutarch she at this point laments his death in advance (προαποθρηνοῦσαν, *Pomp.* 78. 7); Lucan here deliberately restrains himself.

ing after Pharsalia (viii. 40–107). And yet the contrast of husband
and wife, significant and animated as it is, serves above all to
prepare for the more powerful confrontation of their speeches in
the scene of death itself.

The first section of the account of the killing reduces emphasis
on the actual stabbing, which appears in a subordinate clause
(619 f.): this subordination is both mannerist and expressive.
What matters more than that action is Pompey's conquest of it.
His covering of his head, seen as it were from without in Dio and
Plutarch, in Lucan is intensely imagined from within: we feel
Pompey's physical and mental apprehension, and his victorious
effort to prevail morally through his physical bearing. So:

> tum lumina pressit
> continuitque animam, ne quas effundere voces
> vellet et aeternam fletu corrumpere famam.   (615–17)

He closed his eyes and held in his breath, lest he should come to pour
out any utterance or spoil by weeping his everlasting fame.

The actions, briefly stated, potently evoke Pompey's anticipation; but the sentence culminates in the primacy of his great
purpose and enduring fame. *aeternam ... famam*, 'everlasting
fame', gains much force from its position; the strong alliteration
fletus ... famam, 'weeping ... fame', scornfully sets the low act of
weeping against the supremacy of glory.

More important even than Pompey's action is the mental
soliloquy which Lucan gives him as he is being killed. The technique springs from epic convention, but is here especially bold
and especially purposeful. Pompey's mind is what counts: his
control over his mind is what Lucan dwells on after the speech
(635 f.). In and through his mind Pompey can convert, and truly,
a sordid and horrible event into a glorious triumph; the speech
presents this mighty raising. The poet sets *orbe*, 'world', and
ratem, 'boat', together at the beginning of a line (624): the whole
world, in future ages, is contemplating this little boat. Our own
act of reading is to confirm this poignant perspective. Through
his endurance of evil in this moment Pompey will win the vastest
glory. Not that Pompey himself deploys a grandiloquent pride,
even in the fashion of Paullus: only the earnest imperative and
noble brevity of *nunc consule famae*, 'now have regard to your
fame' (624). With superb defiance Pompey pronounces himself

immune from physical circumstance and from the power of heaven:

> spargant lacerentque licebit,
> sum tamen, o superi, felix, nullique potestas
> hoc auferre deo. (629–31)

Even if they rend and scatter my body, yet I am fortunate, O gods, and no divinity has the power to take that away.

The supporting argument is elaborate and strained (his continuous good fortune cannot now be changed; the fate of his corpse does not affect it); but the present verb 'am', at such a moment, and the proud address to the gods, convey the magnificence and imperviousness of the great man in death.[53] The closing thought of the speech deviously transfigures the appalling circumstance of having his loved ones see him die: he must avoid showing pain, not to save them distress, but to guarantee their admiration and so their posthumous love. The obliquity and unexpectedness of this close very slightly remove us from the essential grandeur of the speech; but its broad sublimity of impact should not be mistaken.

Lucan, who has already been pronouncedly 'imperfective', now begins to protract his narrative startlingly. Pompey is still not dead; but Lucan brings in Cornelia again, and has her deliver a speech. It is interesting to compare here Tacitus' interruption of Seneca's death with his account of Paulina (pp. 266 f.). Tacitus achieves a distance that enhances his historian's detachment, and the ultimate force of his account. Lucan too creates a sense of miserable prolongation for Pompey's death, but with a greater sense of physical bizarreness and artistic mannerism. It is a poet's distance that he achieves, in the complication of tone. We may also compare generally Silius' handling of Paullus' death, protracted both in actual time and by the poet's design of his narrative (pp. 289 ff.). Silius' purposes are more straighforwardly heroic; Lucan aims at modification. Lucan is more daringly unrealistic, but his unreality will create not grandeur, like Silius', but a complicating extreme of physical nastiness.

Cornelia's speech again contrasts with Pompey's, the more so because his soliloquy is not actually spoken, whereas she 'fills the air with pitiable utterance', *miserandis aethera complet / vocibus*

---

[53] Compare perhaps with the present tense Epic. 1. 118 Arrighetti (and Sen. *Ep.* 66. 18, etc.); *SVF* iii. 586.

(639f.). The contrast between the speeches again highlights Pompey's control; but it also complicates the emotional force of the narrative.[54] After a few lines of ingenious self-accusation, Cornelia's substantial speech (639–61) is entirely concerned with her own wish to die now. The extravagance and cleverness of the writing is of such a kind as to keep us from a full engagement in what might have been a piercingly tragic lamentation. Thus when she urges Pompey's assassin to kill her first, she begins by playing gorily on the word *viscera* (both 'innards' and the dearest thing to a person): *nescis, crudelis, ubi ipsa / viscera sint Magni*, 'cruel man that you are, you do not know where Pompey's actual innards are' (644f.).[55] She proceeds to:

> poenas non morte minores
> pendat et ante meum videat caput. (645f.)

Let him suffer a penalty no less than his death and see my head first.

She is so devoted to her husband that she wishes to die before him; but this devotion breathtakingly expresses itself in a cunning suggestion to his killer how he might torture him more painfully. Of course this suggestion is a means to attain her ends, but the extraordinary disguise for love, and its very craftiness, remove us far from a simple involvement. The anticipation of the plot in *caput*, 'head', makes the effect still odder. We had not been thus distanced even when Cornelia had earlier (88f.) shown her devotion to the defeated Pompey by wishing she had married his rival (for she brings bad luck to her husbands). In that earlier scene Cornelia had, in my view, moved us more than Pompey; now, after Pompey's great rise through the course of the book, that position is reversed.[56]

The final section of narrative, particularly run through with emotive comment, is also particularly complex in its effect. Pompey's actual death is hideously deferred: he has still not quite died

[54] Cornelia's speech, and the situation, are effectively used at Sil. vi. 497–520. The close there at 516–18 is strikingly brilliant and distancing.

[55] *viscera* is more boldly used here than in the standard application to children. For the connection of the two senses here note the comparisons of hurting what one loves to assailing one's own innards at Liv. xxviii. 32. 4, Curt. vi. 9. 19; cf. also Luc. vii. 579.

[56] That scene is a complicated one; Pompey's speech is illuminated by Ov. *Trist.* iv. 3. 71–84, but his own behaviour at the start of the book contrives to alienate us in some measure here. The whole book displays essentially a grand ascent in Pompey from the nadir of the opening; the hopes in the middle for a practical and military recovery form an intermediate stage between prostration and spiritual victory.

when his head has been cut off and is being put on a stake. And beyond this, the poet treats the line of physical narrative audaciously. The moment of death itself is left unstated; this is made the more curious by the incidental description of the near-final stages in Pompey's impossibly extended decease (682 f.). The decapitation is first narrated in a startling subordinate clause, from a strange perspective: Pompey kept his majesty in death, say those who saw his severed head (663–7). The historian's concern with evidence (seen at Otho's death, p. 258) is here used to jolt; the poet is also confronting degradation and sustained dignity.[57] The primary facts of death and decapitation are thus handled with conspicuous indirectness. On the other hand, the physicality of all that befalls Pompey's head is treated with a wilfully nasty gusto: the poet is conveying the humiliation and the suffering, but is also enjoying himself. So on the decapitation itself:

> spirantiaque occupat ora
> collaque in obliquo ponit languentia transtro.
> tunc nervos venasque secat nodosaque frangit
> ossa diu: nondum artis erat caput ense rotare.   (670–3)

He seized the breathing face and placed the expiring neck sideways on a bench of the boat. Then he cut the sinews and veins and broke the knotty bones for a long while—it was not yet an art to roll a head off with a sword.

The detail of the bench gives a brilliant and sordid practicality to the action: only poetry would give such detail, but the detail is demeaning. From Pompey's continuing unexpectedly alive (the first two lines) the grizzly deeds in the last two lines gain a real ghastliness. But Lucan has such obvious pleasure in delaying the short, crucial, and improbably horrid *diu*, 'for a long while', that it is hard to be simply shocked. One's reaction is confirmed when in the last clause we are abruptly transported to see the historical 'working' behind Lucan's invention, and to witness an agile moral tilt against his own time too.[58]

[57] Francken's (and Shackleton Bailey's) *placatamque* for the unlikely *iratamque* (665) does not fit the emphasis on maintaining the general appearance of the living Pompey (and the motif itself is unwelcome). Conjectures that carry through *sacrae* and *venerabile* seem preferable.

[58] On the change from axe to sword in executions see Mayer ad loc.; as to the date cf. Mommsen (1899), 917 f., 924. The embalment of the head with which Lucan ends is presumably his own adroit application of ethnographical lore; the poet takes pleasure, for all his indignation, in recounting the bizarre details drily and accurately. Cf. Lloyd (1976), 354, 357.

   The head itself is made the focus of Pompey's grandeur, of
pathos, horror, and grotesqueness. This accumulation upon a
single object serves expressive purposes; but it also emphasizes the
multiplicity of tone, and creates strange effects. The first part of
the sentence describing how Pompey's head was fixed on a pole
moves significantly but giddily between the head placed on a pole,
still gasping in life, and the head which (not the man who) urged
Rome to war (681–5). The continuity and intricacy of syntax
already adds a somewhat disconcerting element to the pathos.
The latter part of the sentence provides a burst of lyricism (684–6,
taking up 676–8); the final clause brings this to a climax, but in the
most surprising imagery and language.

hac facie Fortuna tibi Romana placebas.   (686)

Wearing this face, Fortune of Rome, you were pleased with yourself.

Our reaction must be distanced and complicated by the superim-
position of heads, Fortune's and Pompey's, and by the intrusion of
unelevated self-satisfaction and feminine vanity along with the
elevated Fortune of Rome.[59]

   This last section (663–91) of Lucan's narrative attains a particularly weird and elaborate mixture in its treatment of death. Certainly Lucan wishes Pompey's apparent fortunes to reach a low
point before their slow resuscitation. (He will later receive burial,
but in a wretched fashion; this will be turned to good by the poet's
cleverness; his soul will mount to the heaven of the virtuous.) But
the complexity cannot be explained entirely in expressive terms.
Lucan seeks to move us, but also to repel, distance, and entertain.
As we have seen, the complications, evident in some degree
throughout, grow more so after the stabbing, first with Cornelia's
speech, and then still more with this elaborate passage of narrative. The death is allowed to make a powerful impact, and to
convey its rich significance; but even at this supreme moment, the
art of Lucan would not desire us to rest in uncluttered magnificence or unbroken simplicity.

---

[59] The ablative is formally open, with the possible sense 'because of', cf. Mart. iii. 55. 4,
iv. 59. 5; but we inevitably ascribe the face to Fortune too, and connect *placeo* with physical
appearance: cf. e.g. Ov. *Am.* iii. 4. 27; *Met.* xiii. 862. *Fortuna . . . Romana* (not the same as
Fortune): cf. e.g. Liv. vii. 34. 6, Tac. *Hist.* iii. 46. 3. Less strange than 684f. . . . *suffixum caput
est quo numquam bella iubente / pax fuit* is Brutt. Nig. fr. 2 Peter *inter duas manus positum in rostris
caput conspectum est, quo totiens auditum erat loco*; the connection with the physical head is easier
there.

It is from the cavalcade of scenes itself that the reader of the last two chapters should derive some direct sense of the literature and its different genres and authors. In summary of them we can only mention schematically some of the interconnected aspects that we have observed. Despite our stress on especially elevated episodes, we have in the poetry seen Seneca and Lucan in particular complicating and modifying a direct and grandiose effect, as well as achieving an exciting nobility: so central is this element of complication to the high poetry, above all that of Seneca, Lucan, and Statius. The element has also been apparent in Seneca's prose, which stands much closer to the poetry than does the prose of other writers. This proximity has been evident too in the handling of physical reality. Most of the authors have used physical detail to ennoble and to intensify; but some of the poetry, and Seneca's prose, has also used it with strange, bizarre, or even sordid effect to distance our responses. But we must notice also more varied features in the handling of physical reality: the closeness, vividness, and force seen in much of the poetry, the fantasy in Valerius, the wild improbability in Lucan especially, the poignancy of unelevated or everyday detail in Tacitus. Especially characteristic of Seneca's prose in this and other respects was the vigorous oscillation between different levels of grandeur or lowness; this was still more important than a felt complexity of impact and response. We may add to these features the evocation in the Lucan and at one moment in the Seneca of intimate experience, half physical half mental, from the viewpoint of the dying. Here we depart from a certain externality of perspective which has generally been evident in these scenes.

Generalizing moral implication was present in all these episodes, but was mostly contained and confined by their strong particularity. Seneca's philosophical prose naturally offered a quite different angle of vision. In Quintilian's personal prologue and in Pliny's letter, narrative and moral concerns stood in notable relations. Narrative we have seen boldly and expressively handled in the poetry, and also in Tacitus; the handling in the poetry is more obtrusive, and that in the epic stands out against the background of generic convention. So do the author's interventions in Lucan and Statius, which both enhance and modify our emotional reaction.

Moral greatness and aesthetic sublimity have worn different

literary guises; each genre, and author, has used its and his different manners to achieve resounding utterance. The characters have mostly displayed a self-conscious and self-contemplating grandeur, though the expression, and the relation to concern for other people, have been diversely handled. Extremity has been generally present, but poetry and Seneca's prose have carried it to lavish degrees, and often with startling effect, especially in Lucan and in Seneca's tragedy. Seneca's treatment of Marcellinus handled extremity in a different fashion, strangely but not strenuously. Poetry and Seneca's prose, particularly, often feel and present noble behaviour and noble attitudes towards death and life as steeped in paradox—and not the less noble for that. Tacitus' Otho surprises too, but the paradox is less explicit. We have felt generally the vigour and firmness of the authors' ethic, and commonly their moral lavishness; we have felt their potent sense of greatness and achievement amid external failure. These are all highly characteristic of the period: the deepest elements in the literature are closely bound to the rest.

We have sampled in the book only a limited number of episodes and moments, and considered only a few (though important) aspects of this literature. But something of the quality and life of its art and the interest of the literary period may perhaps have come through to some readers. Readers might even be tempted to consider whether the period as a whole may not merit a still more central place than at present in the mental conception of Latin literature which many of us ordinary classicists, students and scholars, would appear to entertain. So much can be lost from one's total understanding and enjoyment of Latin literature if one allows this period, save for particular works, too slight a position. Many, for example, enjoy in Virgil and Propertius the daring and subtle exploitation of the possibilities of Latin; fewer fully realize the pleasures of expression to be had from the epics of Statius. Many have read the poem of Lucretius; fewer its great Stoic, prose, Imperial counterpart the *Naturales Quaestiones* of Seneca. Even for one's knowledge of the genre, one would not want to be well acquainted with only two of the Attic tragedians; but many know well only half (or less) of Latin epic. Rebuke or censure would be inappropriate and absurd; if this book has aroused in any reader a little curiosity for exploration, my wishes have been abundantly fulfilled.

BIBLIOGRAPHY

Commentaries and editions are not listed here, save when they have been referred to above by page number rather than by the place in the ancient author.

ABEL, K. (1965), 'Senecas De brevitate vitae: Datum und Zielsetzung', *Gymnasium* 72, 308–27.

—— (1967), *Bauformen in Senecas Dialogen. Fünf Strukturanalysen: dial. 6, 11, 12, 1 und 2* (Heidelberg).

—— (1985), 'Seneca. Leben und Leistung', *ANRW* ii. 32. 2, 653–775.

ADAMIETZ, J. (1972), *Untersuchungen zu Juvenal* (*Hermes* Einzelschriften 26; Wiesbaden).

—— (1976), *Zur Komposition der Argonautika des Valerius Flaccus* (Zetemata 67; Munich).

—— (1986a), 'Quintilians "Institutio oratoria"', *ANRW* ii. 32. 4, 2226–71.

—— (1986b), 'Juvenal', in J. Adamietz (ed.), *Die römische Satire* (Darmstadt), 231–307.

AHL, F. M. (1976), *Lucan: An Introduction* (Ithaca, NY, and London).

—— (1986), 'Statius' "Thebaid": A Reconsideration', *ANRW* ii. 32. 5, 2803–912.

—— DAVIS, M. A., and POMEROY, A. (1986), 'Silius Italicus', *ANRW* ii. 32. 4, 2492–561.

AHLHEID, F. (1983), *Quintilian: The Preface to Book VIII and Comparable Passages in the Institutio Oratoria* (Amsterdam).

ALBERTINI, E. (1923), *La Composition dans les ouvrages philosophiques de Sénèque* (Bibliothèque des Écoles Françaises d'Athènes et de Rome, 27; Paris).

ALBRECHT, M. VON (1964), *Silius Italicus. Freiheit und Gebundenheit römischer Epik* (Amsterdam).

—— (1970), 'Der Dichter Lucan und die epische Tradition', in *Lucain* (Entr. Hardt 15; Geneva), 269–301.

ALEXANDER, W. H. (1952), 'The Tacitean 'Non Liquet' on Seneca', *Univ. Cal. Publ. Class. Phil.* 14. 8.

ANDERSON, W. S. (1982a (orig. 1960)), 'Part versus Whole in Persius' Fifth Satire', *Essays on Roman Satire* (Princeton), 153–68.

—— (1982b (orig. 1957)), 'Studies in Book I of Juvenal', ibid. 197–254.

—— (1982c (orig. 1956)), 'Juvenal 6: A Problem in Structure', ibid. 255–76.

—— (1982d (orig. 1964)), 'Anger in Juvenal and Seneca', ibid. 293–61.

ANDRÉ, J.-M. (1983), 'Sénèque théologien: L'Évolution de sa pensée jusqu'au "De superstitione"', *Helmantica* 34, 55–71.

ANLIKER, K. (1960), *Prologe und Aktenteilung in Senecas Tragödien* (Noctes Romanae 9; Bern and Stuttgart).

ARICÒ, G. (1972), *Ricerche staziane* (Palermo).

—— (1986), 'L'Achilleide di Stazio: Tradizione letteraria e invenzione narrativa', *ANRW* ii. 32. 5, 2925–64.

ARMISEN-MARCHETTI, M. (1989), *Sapientiae Facies. Étude sur les images de Sénèque* (Paris).

—— (1990), 'Pline le Jeune et le sublime', *REL* 68, 88–98.

ASHBY, T. (1935), *The Aqueducts of Ancient Rome* (Oxford).

ASMIS, E. (1990), 'The Poetic Theory of the Stoic "Aristo"', *Apeiron* 23, 147–201.

AβFAHL, G. (1932), *Vergleich und Metapher bei Quintilian* (Tübinger Beiträge zur Altertumswissenschaft 15; Stuttgart).

ATHERTON, C. (1988), 'Hand over Fist: The Failure of Stoic Rhetoric', *CQ* NS 38, 392–427.

AUSTIN, R. G. (1948), *Quintiliani Institutionis Oratoriae Liber XII* (Oxford).

AX, W. (1990), 'Die Geschichtsschreibung bei Quintilian' in W. Ax (ed.), *Memoria Rerum veterum. Festschrift für Carl Joachim Classen* (Palingenesia 32; Stuttgart), 133–68.

AXELSON, B. (1933), *Seneca-Studien. Kritische Bemerkungen zu Senecas Naturales Quaestiones* (Lunds Universitets Årsskrift NF Avd. 1, Bd. 29, Nr. 3; Lund).

—— (1939), *Neue Seneca-Studien. Textkritische Beiträge zu Senecas epistulae morales* (Lunds Universitets Årsskrift NF Avd. 1, Bd. 36, Nr. 1; Lund).

BADSTÜBNER, E. (1901), *Beiträge zur Erklärung und Kritik der philosophischen Schriften Senecas* (Progr. Hamburg).

BARNES, T. D. (1986), 'The Significance of Tacitus' *Dialogus de oratoribus*', *HSCP* 225–44.

BARWICK, K. (1959), *Martial und die zeitgenössische Rhetorik* (BSAW Phil.-hist. Kl. 104. 1).

BASSET, E. L. (1955), 'Regulus and the Serpent in the *Punica*', *CP* 50, 1–20.

BAUMERT, J. (1989), 'Identifikation und Distanz: Eine Erprobung satirischer Kategorien bei Juvenal', *ANRW* ii. 33. 1, 734–69.

BAUZÀ, H. F. (1981), 'El tema de la edad de oro en *Fedra* de Séneca', *Dioniso* 52, 55–66.

BEAZLEY, J. D. (1947), 'The Rosi Krater', *JHS* 67, 1–9.

BECK, R. (1979), 'Eumolpus *Poeta*, Eumolpus *Fabulator*: A Study of Characterization in the *Satyricon*', *Phoenix* 33, 239–53.

BELLANDI, F. (1988), *Persio: Dai 'verba togae' al solipsismo stilistico* (Bologna).

BENZ, E. (1929), *Das Todesproblem in der stoischen Philosophie* (Tübingen Beiträge zur Altertumswissenschaft 7; Stuttgart).

BESSLICH, S. (1974), 'Anrede an das Buch: Gedanken zu einem Topos in der römischen Dichtung', in A. Swierk (ed.), *Beiträge zur Geschichte des Buches und seiner Funktion in der Gesellschaft. Festschrift für Hans Widmann* (Stuttgart).

BILLANOVICH, G., and MONTI, C. M. (1979), 'Una nuova fonte per la storia della scuola di grammatica e retorica nell'Italia del Trecento', *Italia Medioevale e Umanistica* 22, 367–412.

BILLERBECK, M. (1986), 'Stoizismus in der römischen Epik neronischer und flavischer Zeit', *ANRW* ii. 32. 5, 3116–51.

BLÜMNER, H. (1919), 'Die Schilderung des Sterbens in der römischen Dichtung', *NJbb* 43, 244–72.

BÖLTE, F. (1914), 'Hyampolis', *RE* ix. 1, 17–22.

BOISSIER, G. (1903), *Tacite* (Paris).

BONDS, W. S. (1985), 'Two Combats in the *Thebaid*', *TAPA* 115, 225–35.

BONNER, S. F. (1949), *Roman Declamation in the Late Republic and Early Empire* (Liverpool).

—— (1966), 'Lucan and the Declamation Schools', *AJP* 97, 257–89.

BÖRNER, J. (1911), *De Quintiliani institutionis oratoriae dispositione (pars prior)* (diss. Leipzig).

BOSWORTH, A. B. (1988), *From Arrian to Alexander: Studies in Historical Interpretation* (Oxford).

BOWERSOCK, G. (1990), 'The Pontificate of Augustus', in K. A. Raaflaub and M. Toher (edd.), *Between Republic and Empire: Interpretations of Augustus and his Principate* (Berkeley, Los Angeles, and Oxford), 380–94.

BOYLE, A. J. (1985), 'In Nature's Bonds: A Study of Seneca's "Phaedra"', *ANRW* ii. 32. 2, 1284–347.

BRAMBLE, J. C. (1974), *Persius and the Programmatic Satire* (Cambridge).

—— (1982*a*), 'Lucan', in E. J. Kenney and W. V. Clausen (edd.), *Cambridge History of Classical Literature*, ii. *Latin Literature* (Cambridge), 533–57.

—— (1982*b*), 'Martial and Juvenal', ibid. 597–623.

BRAUND, S. H. (1988), *Beyond Anger: A Study of Juvenal's Third Book of Satires* (Cambridge).

BREMMER, J. N., and HORSFALL, N. M. (1987), *Roman Myth and Mythography* (*BICS* Supp. 52).

BRIGHT, D. F. (1980), *Elaborate Disarray: The Nature of Statius' Silvae* (Beiträge zur Kl. Philol. 108; Meisenheim am Glan).

BRINK, C. (1989), 'Quintilian's *De Causis Corruptae Eloquentiae* and Tacitus' *Dialogus de Oratoribus*', *CQ* NS 39, 472–503.

BROECKER, H. (1954), *Animadversiones ad Plutarchi libellum περὶ εὐθυμίας* (diss. Bonn).

BROWN, R. D. (1987), *Lucretius on Love and Sex: A Commentary on De Rerum Natura IV, 1030–1287 with Prolegomena, Text, and Translation* (Columbia Studies in the Classical Tradition 15; Leiden).

330 *Bibliography*

BRUÈRE, R. T. (1958), '*Color Ovidianus* in Silius *Punica* 1–7', in N. Herescu (ed.), *Ovidiana: Recherches sur Ovide* (Paris), 475–99.

—— (1959), '"Color Ovidianus" in Silius "Punica" 8–17', *CP* 54, 228–45.

BÜCHNER, K. (1978 (orig. 1970)), 'Aufbau und Sinn von Senecas Schrift über die Clementia', *Studien zur römischen Literatur IX* (Wiesbaden), 190–211.

BÜHLER, W. (1964), *Beiträge zur Erklärung der Schrift vom Erhabenen* (Göttingen).

BURCK, E. (1961 (orig. 1953)), 'Die Schicksalsauffassung des Tacitus und Statius', *Vom Menschenbild in der römischen Literatur. Ausgewählte Schriften* (Heidelberg), 305–17.

—— (1971), *Vom römischen Manierismus. Von der Dichtung der frühen römischen Kaiserzeit* (Darmstadt).

—— (1979), ed., *Das römische Epos* (Darmstadt).

—— (1981*a*), 'Epische Bestattungsszenen. Ein literaturhistorischer Vergleich', *Vom Menschenbild in der römischen Literatur. Ausgewählte Schriften, Zweiter Teil* (Heidelberg), 429–87.

—— (1981*b* (orig. 1978)), 'Unwetterszenen bei den flavischen Epikern', ibid. 488–521.

—— (1981*c* (orig. 1971)), 'Kampf und Tod des Cyzicus bei Valerius Flaccus', ibid. 537–57.

—— (1984*a*), *Silius Italicus. Hannibal in Capua und die Rückoberung der Stadt durch die Römer* (AAWM 1984. 13).

—— (1984*b*), *Historische und epische Tradition bei Silius Italicus* (Zetemata 80; Munich).

BURNIKEL, W. (1980), *Untersuchungen zur Struktur des Witzepigramms bei Lukillios und Martial* (Palingenesia 15; Stuttgart).

—— (1990), 'Zur Bedeutung der Mündlichkeit im Martials Epigrammenbüchern I–XII', in G. Vogt-Spira (ed.), *Strukturen der Mündlichkeit in der römischen Literatur* (Tübingen), 221–34.

BUSCH, G. (1961), 'Fortunae resistere in der Moral des Philosophen Seneca', *AuA* 10, 131–54.

BÜTLER, H.-P. (1970), *Die geistige Welt des jüngeren Plinius. Studien zur Thematik seiner Briefe* (Bibl. der klass. Altertumswissenschaften NF, 2. Reihe, Bd. 38; Heidelberg).

CADUFF, G. A. (1986), *Antike Sintflutsagen* (Hypomnemata 82; Göttingen).

CAIRNS, F. (1989), *Virgil's Augustan Epic* (Cambridge).

CALBOLI, G. (1987), 'Iperbole', *Enciclopedia Virgiliana* (Rome), iii. 11–13.

CAMERON, A. (1967) 'Tacitus and the Date of Curiatius Maternus' Death', *CR* NS 17, 258–61.

CAMPBELL, J. B. (1984), *The Emperor and the Roman Army 31 BC–AD 325 (Oxford)*.

CANCIK, H. (1965), *Untersuchungen zur lyrischen Kunst des P. Papinius Statius* (Spudasmata 13; Hildesheim).

CANTER, H. V. (1925), 'Rhetorical Elements in the Tragedies of Seneca', *University of Illinois Studies in Language and Literature* 10. 1, 1–185.

CARPENTER, T. H. (1986), *Dionysiac Imagery in Archaic Greek Art: Its Development in Black-Figure Vase Painting* (Oxford).

CARRARA, P. (1986), 'Stazio e i *primordia* di Tebe: Poetica e polemica nel prologo della Tebaide', *Prometheus* 12, 146–58.

CASAUBON I. (1647), *Auli Persi Flacci Satirarum Liber*³, ed. M. Casaubon (London).

CHAUMARTIN, F.-R. (1985), *Le De Beneficiis de Sénèque, sa signification philosophique, politique et sociale* (Lille).

CICHORIUS, C. (1922), *Römische Studien* (Leipzig).

CITRONI, M. (1969), 'La teoria lessinghiana dell'epigramma e le interpretazioni moderne di Marziale', *Maia* 21, 215–43.

CLAIRMONT, CHR. (1951), *Das Parisurteil in der antiken Kunst* (Zurich).

CLASSEN, C. J. (1965), 'Der Aufbau des zwölften Buches der Institutio oratoria Quintilians', *MH* 22, 181–90.

—— (1985), 'Martial', *Gymnasium* 92, 329–49.

—— (1988), 'Satire—the Elusive Genre', *SO* 63, 95–121.

COCKLE, W. E. H. (1987), *Euripides, Hypsipyle: Text and Annotation Based on a Re-examination of the Papyri* (Testi e Commenti 7; Rome).

COLEMAN, K. M. (1988), *Statius, Silvae IV*, edited with an English translation and Commentary (Oxford).

COLISH, M. L. (1990) *The Stoic Tradition from Antiquity to the Early Middle Ages*, i. *Stoicism in Classical Latin Literature*² (Leiden).

CONTE, G. B. (1985), *Memoria dei poeti e sistema letterario: Catullo, Virgilio, Ovidio, Lucano* (Turin).

COURTNEY, E. (1962), 'Parody and Literary Allusion in Menippean Satire', *Philologus* 106, 86–100.

—— (1980), *A Commentary on the Satires of Juvenal* (London).

COVA, P. V. (1966), *La critica letteraria di Plinio il Giovane* (Brescia).

CURRIE, H. MacL. (1966), 'The Younger Seneca's Style: Some Observations', *BICS* 13, 76–87.

DALZELL, A. (1955), 'C. Asinius Pollio and the Early History of Public Recitations at Rome', *Hermathena* 86, 20–8.

DAMS, P. (1970), *Dichtungskritik bei nachaugusteischer Dichtung* (diss. Marburg).

D'ARMS, J. H. (1981), *Commerce and Social Standing in Ancient Rome* (Harvard).

DE DECKER, J. (1913), *Juvenalis declamans. Étude sur la rhétorique déclamatoire dans les Satires de Juvénal* (Gand).

DE LACY, P. (1948), 'Stoic Views of Poetry', *AJP* 69, 241–71.

DEIPSER, B. (1881), *De P. Papinio Statio Vergilii et Ovidii imitatore* (diss. Strasburg).

DELZ, J. (1976), review of Courtney's text of Valerius, *Museum Africum* 5, 96–100.

DELZ, J. (1983), 'Apollo Musagetes in der "Thebais" des Statius', *Hermes* III, 381–4.

DEVELIN, R. (1983), 'Tacitus and Techniques of Insidious Suggestion', *Antichthon* 17, 64–95.

DEWAR, M. J. (1991), *Statius*, Thebaid IX, edited with an English translation and commentary (Oxford).

DICK, B. F. (1967), '*Fatum* and *Fortuna* in Lucan's *Bellum Civile*', *CP* 62, 235–42.

DILKE, O. A. W. (1963), '"Magnus Achilles" and Statian Baroque', *Latomus* 22, 498–503.

DILLON, J. (1977), *The Middle Platonists: A Study of Platonism 80 BC to AD 220* (London).

DINGEL, J. (1974), *Seneca und die Dichtung* (Heidelberg).

—— (1988), *Scholastica Materia: Untersuchungen zu den declamationes minores und der institutio oratoria Quintilians* (Berlin and New York).

DIONIGI, I. (1983), *Lucio Anneo Seneca, De Otio (dial. VIII). Testo e apparato critico, con introduzione, versione e commento* (Brescia).

DÖRING, K. (1979), *Exemplum Socratis. Studien zur Sokratesnachwirkung in der kynischen-stoischen Popularphilosophie der frühen Kaiserzeit und im frühen Christentum* (*Hermes* Einzelschriften 42; Wiesbaden).

DOSSON, S. (1887), *Étude sur Quinte Curce. Sa vie et son œuvre* (Paris).

DRAGONA-MONACHOU, M. (1976), *The Stoic Arguments for the Existence and Providence of the Gods* (Athens).

DUE, O. S. (1962), 'An Essay on Lucan', *C&M* 23, 68–113.

DÜRR, K. (1940), 'Seneca bei Tacitus', *Gymnasium* 51, 42–61.

DURRY, M. (1938), *Pline le Jeune, Panégyrique de Trajan* (Paris).

DYSON, S. L. (1970), 'The Portrait of Seneca in Tacitus', *Arethusa* 3, 71–84.

ECKARDT, L. (1936), *Exkurse und Ekphraseis bei Lucan* (diss. Heidelberg).

EDGEWORTH, R. J. (1978), 'What Color is "*ferrugineus*"?', *Glotta* 56, 297–305.

—— (1990), 'The Eloquent Ghost: Absyrtus in Seneca's *Medea*', *C&M* 41, 151–61.

EDMUNDS, L. (1972), 'Juvenal's Thirteenth Satire', *RhM* NF 115, 59–73.

EGERMANN, F. (1972 (orig. 1940)), 'Seneca als Dichterphilosoph', in E. Lefèvre (ed.), *Senecas Tragödien* (WdF 310; Darmstadt), 33–57.

EHLERS, W. (1948), 'Triumphus', *RE* vii A, 493–511.

EIGLER, U. (1988), *Monologische Redeformen bei Valerius Flaccus* (Beiträge zur Kl. Philol. 187; Frankfurt am Main).

ENDT, J. (1905), 'Der Gebrauch der Apostrophe bei den lateinischen Epikern', *WS* 27, 106–29.

ERREN, M. (1970), 'Zierlicher Schauder—Das Gefällige am Grauen der Thebais des Statius', in W. Wimmel (ed.), *Forschungen zur römischen Literatur. Festschrift für Karl Büchner* (Wiesbaden), i. 88–95.

FABBRI, R. (1978/9), 'La pagina "senecana" di Tacito (*Ann.* 15, 60–65)', *Atti del Ist. Veneto* 137, 409–27.

FAIRWEATHER, J. (1981), *Seneca the Elder* (Cambridge).

FANTHAM, E. (1982), *Seneca's* Troades: *A Literary Introduction with Text, Translation, and Commentary* (Princeton).

FEENEY, D. C. (1991), *The Gods in Epic: Poets and Critics of the Classical Tradition* (Oxford).

FITCH, J. G. (1987), *Seneca's Hercules Furens: A Critical Text with Introduction and Commentary* (Cornell Studies in Class. Phil. 45; Ithaca, NY, and London).

FLINTOFF, T. E. S. (1982), 'Food for Thought: Some Imagery in Persius Satire 2', *Hermes* 110, 341–54.

—— (1990), 'Juvenal's Fourth *Satire*', *PLILS* 6, 121–37.

FOWLER, D. P. (1990), 'Deviant Focalization in Virgil's *Aeneid*', *PCPS* NS 36, 42–63.

FRAENKEL, ED. (1964 (orig. 1932)), 'Selbstmordwege', *Kleine Beiträge zur klassischen Philologie* (Rome), i. 465–7.

FRANCHET D'ESPEREY, S. (1988), 'Une étrange descente aux enfers: Le Suicide d'Éson et Alcimédé (Valerius Flaccus, *Arg.* I 730–851)', in D. Porte and J.-P. Néraudau (edd.), *Hommages à Henri Le Bonniec. Res sacrae* (Coll. *Latomus* 201; Brussels), 193–27.

FREDERICKS, S. C. (1971), 'Rhetoric and Morality in Juvenal's Eighth [Seventh *codd.*] Satire', *TAPA* 102, 111–32.

—— (1979), 'Irony of Overstatement in the Satires of Juvenal', *ICS* 4, 178–91.

FREDERIKSEN, M. (1984), *Campania*, ed. N. Purcell.

FREISE, H. (1989), 'Die Bedeutung der Epikur-Zitate in den Schriften Senecas', *Gymnasium* 96, 532–55.

FRIEDLÄNDER, L. (1920), *Darstellungen aus der Sittengeschichte Roms*[9] (Leipzig).

FRIEDRICH, H. (1963), 'Über die Silvae des Statius (inbesondere v, 4, Somnus) und die Frage des literarischen Manierismus', in H. Meier (ed.), *Wort und Text. Festschrift für Fritz Schalk* (Frankfurt am Main), 34–56.

FRIEDRICH, W.-H. (1933), *Untersuchungen zu Senecas dramatischer Technik* (diss. Freiburg).

—— (1938), 'Cato, Caesar und Fortuna bei Lucan', *Hermes* 73, 391–423.

—— (1954), 'Caesar und sein Glück', in *Thesaurismata. Festschrift für Ida Kapp* (Munich), 1–24, 165.

—— (1956), 'Episches Unwetter', in *Festschrift für B. Snell* (Munich), 77–87.

—— (1972 (orig. 1967)), 'Die Raserei des Hercules', in E. Lefèvre (ed.), *Senecas Tragödien* (WdF 310; Darmstadt), 142–8.

FUGIER, H. (1963), *Recherches sur l'expression du sacré dans la langue latine* (Paris).

FUHRMANN, M. (1960), 'Das Vierkaiserjahr bei Tacitus. Über den Aufbau der Historien Buch I–III', *Philologus* 104, 250–78.

—— (1968), 'Die Funktion grausiger und ekelhafter Motive in der lateinischen Dichtung', in H. R. Jauß (ed.), *Die nicht mehr schönen Künste* (Munich), 23–66.

FUNAIOLI, G. (1914), 'Recitationes', *RE* i A, 435–46.

GALINSKY, K. G. (1972), *The Herakles Theme* (Oxford).

—— (1989), 'Was Ovid a Silver Latin Poet?', *ICS* 14, 69–88.

GAMBERINI, F. (1983), *Stylistic Theory and Practice in the Younger Pliny* (Altertumswissenschaftliche Texte und Studien II; Hildesheim, Zurich, and New York).

GEIGER, J. (1979), 'Munatius Rufus and Thrasea Paetus on Cato the Younger', *Athenaeum* NS 57, 48–72.

GELZER, T. (1970), 'Quintilians Urteil über Seneca', *MH* 27 (1970), 212–23.

GEORGE, P. A. (1966), 'Style and Character in the Satyricon', *Arion* 5, 336–58.

GÉRARD, J. (1972), *Juvénal et la réalité contemporaine* (Paris).

GERCKE, A. (1885), 'Chrysippea', *Jb. f. cl. Philol.* Supp. 14, 689–781.

GIANCOTTI, F. (1963), *Ricerche sulla tradizione manoscritta delle Sentenze di Publilio Siro* (Messina).

GIGANTE, M. (1979), *Catalogo dei papiri ercolanesi* (Naples).

—— (1983), *Ricerche Filodemee*[2] (Naples).

GILL, C. (1983), 'The Question of Character-Development: Plutarch and Tacitus', *CQ* NS 38, 469–87.

GINSBURG, J. (1981), *Tradition and Theme in the Annals of Tacitus* (Salem).

GNILKA, CHR. (1973), 'Trauer und Trost in Plinius' Briefen', *SO* 49, 105–25.

GOAR, R. J. (1987), *The Legend of Cato Uticensis from the First Century B.C. to the Fifth Century A.D.* (Coll. Latomus 197; Brussels).

GÖRLER, W. (1976), 'Caesars Rubikon-Übergang in der Darstellung Lucans', in H. Görgemanns and E. A. Schmidt (edd.), *Studien zum antiken Epos* (Beiträge zur Kl. Philol. 72; Meisenheim am Glan).

—— (1979), 'Kaltblütiges Schnarchen. Zum literarischen Hintergrund der Vesuv-Briefe des jüngeren Plinius', in G. W. Bowersock *et al.* (edd.), *Arktouros: Hellenic Studies Presented to Bernard M. W. Knox* (Berlin and New York), 427–33.

GÖTTING, M. (1969), *Hypsipyle in der Thebais des Statius* (diss. Tübingen).

GOODYEAR, F. R. D. (1968), 'Development of Language and Style in the *Annals* of Tacitus', *JRS* 58, 22–31.

—— (1970), *Tacitus* (*G&R* Surveys 4; Oxford).

—— (1972 and 1981), *The Annals of Tacitus, Books 1–6, Edited with a Commentary*, i. Annals 1. 1–54, ii. Annals 1. 55–81 and Annals 2 *(Cambridge)*.

GRAF, F. (1929), *Untersuchungen über die Komposition der Annalen des Tacitus* (diss. Bern).

GRANSDEN, K. W. (1984), *Virgil's Iliad: An Essay on Epic Narrative* (Cambridge).

GRAßL, H. (1973), *Untersuchungen zum Vierkaiserjahr 68/69 n. Chr. Ein Beitrag zur Ideologie und Sozialstruktur des frühen Prinzipats* (diss. Graz).

GRIFFIN, J. (1978), 'The Divine Audience and the Religion of the *Iliad*', *CQ* ns 28, 1–22.

GRIFFIN, M. (1976), *Seneca: A Philosopher in Politics* (Oxford).

—— (1984), *Nero: The End of a Dynasty* (London).

—— (1986), 'Philosophy, Cato, and Roman Suicide', *G&R* 2nd ser. 33, 64–77, 192–202.

GRIFFITH, J. G. (1969), 'Juvenal, Statius, and the Flavian Establishment', *G&R* 2nd ser. 16, 134–50.

—— (1970), 'The Ending of Juvenal's First Satire and Lucilius, Book XXX', *Hermes* 98, 56–70.

GRIMAL, P. (1949–50), 'La Composition dans les "dialogues" de Sénèque. I: Le *De constantia sapientis*', *REA* 51, 246–61, 'II: Le *De Providentia*', 52, 238–57.

—— (1960), 'Le Plan du *De Brevitate Vitae*', in *Studi in onore di Luigi Castiglioni* (Florence), i. 409–19.

—— (1970), 'Le Poète et l'histoire', in *Lucain* (Entr. Hardt 15; Geneva), 51–117.

—— (1977), *La Guerre civile de Pétrone dans ses rapports avec la Pharsale*[2] (Paris).

GRISÉ, Y. (1982), *Le Suicide dans la Rome antique* (Paris).

GROSS, N. (1989), *Senecas Naturales Quaestiones: Komposition, Naturphilosophische Aussagen und ihre Quellen* (Palingenesia 27; Stuttgart).

GUIDO, G. (1976), *Petronio Arbitro, Dal 'Satyricon': Il 'Bellum Civile'. Testo, traduzione e commento* (Bologna).

GUILLEMIN, A.-M. (1929), *Pline et la vie littéraire de son temps* (Paris).

—— (1952–4), 'Sénèque directeur d'âmes. I: L'Idéal', *REL* 30, 202–19, 'II: Son activité pratique', 31, 215–34, 'III: Les Théories littéraires', 32, 250–74.

HADOT, I. (1969), *Seneca und die griechisch-römische Tradition der Seelenleitung* (Berlin).

HAGEDORN, D. (1964), *Zur Ideenlehre des Hermogenes* (Hypomnemata 8; Göttingen).

HÅKANSON, L. (1979), 'Problems of Textual Criticism and Interpretation in Lucan's *De Bello Civili*', *PCPS* ns 25, 26–51.

HALM, E. (1933), *Die Exkurse in den Annalen des Tacitus* (diss. Munich).

HAMMOND, N. G. L., and GRIFFITH, G. T. (1979), *A History of Macedonia*, ii. *550–336 B.C.* (Oxford).

HARDIE, A. (1983), *Statius and the Silvae: Poets, Patrons and Epideixis in the Graeco-Roman World* (Liverpool).

—— (1990), 'Juvenal and the Condition of Letters: The Seventh Satire', *PLILS* 6, 145–209.

HARDIE, P. R. (1986), *Virgil's* Aeneid: Cosmos *and* Imperium (Oxford).

HARMAND, R. (1898), *De Valerio Flacco Apollonii Rhodii imitatore* (Nancy).

HARTMANN, A. (1912), *Aufbau und Erfindung der siebenten Satire Juvenals* (Basle).

HASLAM, M. W., EL-MAGHRABI, H., and THOMAS, J. D. (1990), *The Oxyrhynchus Papyri*, lvii (London).

HÄUßLER, R. (1965), *Tacitus und das historische Bewußtsein* (Heidelberg).

—— (1969), 'Zum Umfang und Aufbau des Dialogus de oratoribus', *Philologus* 113, 24–67.

—— (1978), *Das historiche Epos von Lucan bis Silius und seine Theorie. Studien zum historischen Epos der Antike*, ii. *Geschichtliche Epik nach Vergil* (Heidelberg).

HEADLAM, W. (1902), 'Ghost-Raising, Magic, and the Underworld', *CR* 16, 52–61.

HEATH, M. (1989), *Unity in Greek Poetics* (Oxford).

HECK, E. (1970), 'Scipio am Scheideweg', *WS* NF 9, 156–80.

HEILMANN, W. (1967), 'Zur Komposition der vierten Satire und des ersten Satirenbuches Juvenals', *RhM* NF 110, 358–70.

—— (1989), '"Goldene Zeit" und geschichtliche Zeit im Dialogus de oratoribus. Zur Geschichtsauffassung des Tacitus', *Gymnasium* 96, 385–405.

HEINZ, K. (1948), *Das Bild Kaiser Neros bei Seneca, Tacitus, Sueton und Cassius Dio (Historisch-philologische Synopsis)* (diss. Bern).

HELDMANN, K. (1974), *Untersuchungen zu den Tragödien Senecas* (*Hermes* Einzelschriften 31; Wiesbaden).

—— (1982), *Antike Theorien über Entwicklung und Verfall der Redekunst*, (Zetemata 77; Munich).

HELMBOLD, W. C. (1951), 'The Structure of Juvenal I', *Univ. Cal. Publ. Class. Phil.* 14. 2

—— and O' NEIL, E. N. (1956), 'The Structure of Juvenal IV', *AJP* 77, 68–73.

—— —— (1959), 'The Form and Purpose of Juvenal's Seventh Satire', *CP* 54, 100–8.

HENRICHS, A. (1968), 'Vespasian's Visit to Alexandria', *ZPE* 3, 51–80.

HENRY, D., and WALKER, B. (1965), 'The Futility of Action: A Study of Seneca's *Hercules Furens*', *CP* 60, 11–22.

—— (1966), 'Phantasmagoria and Idyll: An Element of Seneca's *Phaedra*', *G&R* 2nd ser. 13, 223–9.

HERINGTON, C. J. (1966), 'Senecan Tragedy', *Arion* 5, 422–71.

HEUBNER, H. (1963–82), *P. Cornelius Tacitus. Die Historien. Kommentar* (Heidelberg).

HINE, H. M. (1980), 'The Manuscript Tradition of Seneca's *Naturales Quaestiones*', *CQ* NS 30, 183–217.

—— (1981), 'The Structure of Seneca's Thyestes', *PLLS* 3, 259–75.

—— (1984), 'The Date of the Campanian Earthquake, A.D. 62 or A.D. 63, or Both?', *AC* 53, 266–9.

HIRSCHBERG, TH. (1989), *Senecas Phoinissen: Einleitung und Kommentar* (Untersuchungen zur antiken Literatur und Geschichte 31; Berlin and New York).

HIRZEL, R. (1895), *Der Dialog. Ein literarhistorischer Versuch* (Leipzig).

—— (1908), 'Der Selbstmord', *Archiv für Religionswissenschaft* 11, 75–104, 243–84, 417–76.

HOLFORD-STREVENS, L. A. (1988), *Aulus Gellius* (London).

HOLGADO REDONDO, A. (1978), 'Encabalgamiento y pathos. La "muerte de Pompeyo" en la "Farsalia" (VIII, 536–711)', *Cuad. de Fil. Clás.* xv, 251–60.

HOLMES, N. P. (1990), 'A Commentary on the Tenth Book of Lucan' (Oxford D. Phil. thesis, unpublished).

HOLTSMARK, E. B. (1972–3), 'The Bath of Claudius Etruscus', *CJ* 68, 216–20.

HOLZBERG, N. (1988), *Martial* (Heidelberg).

HORNBLOWER, S. (1982), *Mausolus* (Oxford).

HOUSMAN, A. E. (1972 (orig. 1933)), 'Notes on the Thebais of Statius [I]', *Classical Papers* (Cambridge), iii. 1197–213.

HÜBNER, U. (1975), 'Studien zur Pointentechnik in Lucans Pharsalia', *Hermes* 103, 200–11.

HUNZIKER, R. (1896), *Die Figur der Hyperbel in den Gedichten Vergils* (diss. Berlin).

HUTCHINSON, G. O. (1988), 'Juvenal, Satire, and the Real World', *Omnibus* 15, 20–22.

INNES, D. C., and WINTERBOTTOM, M. (1988), *Sopatros the Rhetor: Studies in the Text of the Διαίρεσις Ζητημάτων* (*BICS* Supp. 48).

INWOOD, B (1985), *Ethics and Human Action in Early Stoicism* (Oxford).

JAKOBI, R. (1988), *Der Einfluß Ovids auf den Tragiker Seneca* (Untersuchungen zur antiken Literatur und Geschichte 28; Berlin and New York).

JAL, P. (1962), 'Les Dieux et les guerres civiles dans la Rome de la fin de la République', *REL* 40, 170–200.

JENKYNS, R. H. A. (1982), *Three Classical Poets: Sappho, Catullus and Juvenal* (London).

JOCELYN, H. D. (1971), 'Urbs Augurio Augusto Condita: Ennius ap. Cic. *Div.* I. 107 (= *Ann.* 77–96 V²)', *PCPS* NS 17, 44–74.

JOHNSON, W. R. (1987), *Momentary Monsters: Lucan and his Heroes* (New York).

JONES, C. P. (1986), 'Suetonius in the Probus of Giorgio Valla', *HSCP* 90, 245–51.

JONES, F. (1989), 'Juvenal, *Satire* VII', in *Studies in Latin Literature and Roman History* 5 (Coll. *Latomus* 206; Brussels), 444–64.

JONG, I. J. F. DE (1987), *Narrators and Focalizers: The Presentation of the Story in the Iliad* (Amsterdam).

JUHNKE, H. (1972), *Homerisches in römischer Epik flavischer Zeit. Untersuchungen zu Szenennachbildungen und Strukturentsprechungen in Statius' Thebais und Achilleis und in Silius' Punica* (Zetemata 53; Munich).

KAJANTO (1957), *God and Fate in Livy* (Turku).

KASSEL, R. (1954), *Quomodo quibus locis apud veteres scriptores Graecos infantes atque parvuli pueri inducantur describantur commemorentur* (Meisenheim am Glan).

KEITZEL, E. (1987), 'Otho's Exhortations in Tacitus' *Histories*', *G&R* 2nd ser. 34, 73–82.

KENNEDY, G. (1989), *The Cambridge History of Literary Criticism*, i. *Classical Criticism* (Cambridge).

KENNEY, E. J. (1962), 'The First Satire of Juvenal', *PCPS* NS 8, 29–40.

KER, A. (1967), 'Siliana', *PCPS* NS 13, 14–31.

KIDD, I. G. (1988), *Posidonius*, ii. *The Commentary* (Cambridge).

—— (1989), 'Posidonius as Philosopher-Historian', in J. Barnes and M. Griffin (edd.), *Philosophia Togata: Essays on Philosophy and Roman Society* (Oxford), 38–50.

KILPATRICK, R. S. (1973), 'Juvenal's "Patchwork" Satires: 4 and 7', *YCS* 23, 229–41.

KIßEL, W. (1978), 'Petrons Kritik der Rhetorik (Sat. 1–5)', *RhM* NF 122, 311–28.

—— (1979), *Das Geschichtsbild des Silius Italicus* (Studien zur Kl. Philol. 2; Frankfurt am Main).

KLINGNER, F. (1964 (orig. 1940)), 'Die Geschichte Kaiser Othos bei Tacitus' in *Studien zur griechischen und römischen Literatur* (Zurich and Stuttgart), 605–24.

KLINNERT, TH. C. (1970), *Capaneus-Hippomedon. Interpretationen zur Heldendarstellung in der Thebais des P. Papinius Statius* (diss. Heidelberg).

KORZENIEWSKI, D. (1978), 'Der Satirenprolog des Persius', *RhM* NF 122, 329–49.

KOSTER, S. (1970), *Antike Epos-Theorien* (Palingenesia 5; Stuttgart).

—— (1979), 'Liebe und Krieg in der Achilleis des Statius', *WJbb* NF 5, 189–208.

KÖSTERMANN, E. (1934), *Untersuchungen zu den Dialogschriften Senecas* (SBPA Phil.-hist. Kl. 1934. 22.

KÖSTLIN, H. (1889), 'Zur Erklärung und Kritik des Valerius Flaccus', *Philologus* 8, 647–73.

KROLL, W. (1924), *Studien zum Verständnis der römischen Literatur* (Stuttgart).

KRÖNER, H. O. (1968), 'Zu den künstlerischen Absichten des Valerius Flaccus. Die Darstellung des Faustkampfes zwischen Amycus und Pollux (Val. Fl. 4, 252–314)', *Hermes* 96, 733–54.

KROYMANN, J. (1969 (orig. 1952)), 'Fatum, Fors und Verwandtes im Geschichtsdenken des Tacitus', in V. Pöschl (ed.), *Tacitus* (WdF 97; Darmstadt), 130–60.

KRUMBHOLZ, G. (1955), 'Der Erzählungsstil in der Thebais des Statius', *Glotta* 34, 93–129, 231–60.

KUEPPERS, J. (1986), *Tantarum causas irarum. Untersuchungen zur einleitenden Bücherdyade der Punica des Silius Italicus* (Untersuchungen zur antiken Literatur und Geschichte 23; Berlin and New York).

KURFESS, A. (1955), 'C. Valerius Flaccus Setinus Balbus', *RE* viii A, 9–15.

KYTZLER, B. (1986), 'Zum Aufbau der statianischen "Thebais". Pius Coroebus, Theb. I 557–692', *ANRW* ii. 32. 5, 2913–24.

LAMER, H. (1924), 'Lectica', *RE* xii. 1, 1089 f.

LAPIDGE, M. (1979), 'Lucan's Imagery of Cosmic Dissolution', *Hermes* 107, 344–70.

LAUDIZI, G. (1989), *Silio Italico. Il passato tra mito e restaurazione etica* (Galatina).

LAUSBERG, M. (1985), 'Lucan und Homer', *ANRW* ii. 32. 3, 1565–672.

—— (1990), 'Epos und Lehrgedicht. Ein Gattungsvergleich am Beispiel von Lucans Schlangenkatalog', *WJbb* NF 16, 173–203.

LAVERY, G. B. (1987), 'The *Adversarius* in Seneca's *De Beneficiis*', *Mnemosyne* 4th ser. 40, 97–106.

LAWALL, G. (1981–2), 'Death and Perspective in Seneca's *Troades*', *CJ* 77, 244–52.

LAZENBY, J. F. (1978), *Hannibal's War: A Military History of the Second Punic War* (Warminster).

LEBEK, W. D. (1976), *Lucans Pharsalia. Dichtungsstruktur und Zeitbezug* (Hypomnemata 44; Göttingen).

—— (1987), 'Die drei Ehrenbogen für Germanicus: Tab. Siar. frg. I 9–34; CIL VI 31199a 2–17', *ZPE* 67, 129–48.

—— (1988), 'Die circensischen Ehrungen für Germanicus und das Referat des Tacitus im Lichte von Tab. Siar. frg. II col. c 2–11', *ZPE* 73, 249–74.

LE BONNIEC (1968), 'Lucain et la religion', in *Lucain* (Entr. Hardt 15; Geneva), 159–200.

LEEMAN, A. D. (1963), *Orationis Ratio: The Stylistic Theories and Practice of the Roman Orators* (Amsterdam).

—— (1971), 'Das Todeserlebnis im Denken Senecas', *Gymnasium* 78, 322–333.

LEFÈVRE, E. (1970), 'Die Bedeutung des Paradoxen in der römischen Literatur der Kaiserzeit', *Poetica* 3, 59–82.

LEGRAS, L. (1905), *Étude sur la Thébaïde de Stace* (Paris).

Leo, F. (1878), *L. Annaei Senecae Tragoediae*, i. *De Senecae Tragoediis Observationes criticae* (Berlin).

—— (1960 (orig. 1897)), review of Langen's edn. of VF, *Ausgewählte kleine Schriften* (Rome), 223–48.

Lepper, F., and Frere, S. (1988), *Trajan's Column: A New Edition of the Cichorius Plates* (Gloucester).

Levick, B. (1976), *Tiberius the Politician* (London).

—— (1990), *Claudius* (London).

Levy, Fr. (1927/8), 'Der Weltuntergang in Senecas naturales quaestiones', *Philologus* 83, 459–66.

Lewis, C. S. (1936), *The Allegory of Love: A Study in Medieval Tradition* (Oxford).

Liebermann, W.-L. (1974), *Studien zu Senecas Tragödien* (Beiträge zur Kl. Philol. 39; Meisenheim am Glan).

Liebeschuetz, J. H. W. G. (1979), *Continuity and Change in Roman Religion* (Oxford).

Lloyd, A. B. (1976), *Herodotus Book II: Commentary 1–98* (Leiden).

Lloyd, G. E. R. (1983), *Science, Folklore and Ideology: Studies in the Life Sciences in Ancient Greece* (Cambridge).

Lloyd-Jones, H. (1990a (orig. 1972)), 'Pindar fr. 169', *Greek Epic, Lyric, and Tragedy* (Oxford), 154–65.

—— (1990b (orig. 1967)), 'Heracles at Eleusis', ibid. 167–87.

—— and Wilson, N. G. (1990), *Sophoclea: Studies in the Text of Sophocles* (Oxford).

Long, A. A. (1982), 'Body and Soul in Stoicism', *Phronesis* 27, 34–57.

López Kindler, A. (1966), 'Problemas de composición y estructura en el *De Clementia* de Seneca', *Emérita* 34, 39–60.

Lorenz, G. (1968), *Vergleichende Interpretationen zu Silius und Statius* (diss. Kiel).

Luce, T. (1989), 'Ancient Views of the Causes of Bias in Historical Writing', *CP* 84, 16–31.

Luipold, H.-A. (1970), *Die Bruder-Gleichnisse in der Thebais des Statius* (diss. Tübingen).

Lüthje, E. (1971), *Gehalt und Aufriss der Argonautica des Valerius Flaccus* (diss. Kiel).

McDevitt, A. S. (1968), 'The Structure of Juvenal's Eleventh *Satire*', *G&R* 2nd ser. 15, 173–9.

McFarland, W. N., Pough, F. H., Cade, T. J., and Heiser, J. B. (1985), *Vertebrate Life*² (New York).

MacMullen, R. (1981), *Paganism in the Roman Empire* (New Haven and London).

Madvig, J. N. (1873), *Adversaria critica ad scriptores Graecos et Latinos*, ii. *Emendationes Latinae* (Copenhagen).

Maltby, R. (1991), *A Lexicon of Ancient Latin Etymologies* (Leeds).

MANZO, A. (1988), *L'adynaton poetico-retorico e le sue implicazioni dottrinali* (Genoa).

MARTI, B. M. (1968), 'La Structure de la *Pharsale*', in *Lucain* (Entr. Hardt 15; Geneva), 3–50.

—— (1975), 'Lucan's Narrative Techniques', *Par. del Pass.* 30, 74–90.

MARTIN, R. H. (1981), *Tacitus* (London).

—— (1990), 'Structure and Interpretation in the "Annals" of Tacitus', *ANRW* ii. 33. 2, 1500–81.

—— and WOODMAN, A. J. (1989), *Tacitus, Annals Book IV* (Cambridge).

MARTINDALE, C. A. (1976), 'Paradox, Hyperbole and Literary Novelty in Lucan's *De Bello Civili*', *BICS* 23, 45–54.

—— (1981), 'Lucan's Hercules: Padding or Paradigm? A Note on De Bello Civili 4. 589–660', *SO* 56, 71–80.

MARTYN, J. R. C. (1979), 'Juvenal's Wit', *Gräzer Beiträge* 8, 219–38.

MARX, F. A. (1937–8), 'Tacitus und die Literatur der exitus illustrium virorum', *Phil.* 92, 83–103.

MASON, H. A. (1963 (orig. 1962)), 'Is Juvenal a Classic?', in J. P. Sullivan (ed.), *Critical Essays on Roman Literature: Satire* (London), 93–176.

MAURACH, G. (1970), *Der Bau von Senecas Epistulae morales* (Bibl. der Altertumswissenschaften NF, 2. Reihe, Bd. 30; Heidelberg).

—— (1991), *Seneca. Leben und Werke* (Darmstadt).

MAZZOLI, G. (1970), *Seneca e la poesia* (Milan).

MEHMEL, F. (1934), *Valerius Flaccus* (diss. Hamburg).

MEIGGS, R. (1982), *Trees and Timber in the Ancient Mediterranean World* (Oxford).

MEISE, E. (1969), *Untersuchungen zur Geschichte der Julischen-Claudischen Dynastie* (Munich).

MELTZER, G. (1988), 'Dark Wit and Black Humor in Seneca's *Thyestes*', *TAPA* 118, 309–30.

MERKLIN, H. (1988), 'Probleme des "Dialogus de oratoribus"', *AuA* 34, 170–89.

METGER, W. (1957), *Kampf und Tod in Lucans Pharsalia* (diss. Kiel).

MEYER, H. (1842), *Oratorum Romanorum Fragmenta ab Appio inde Caeco et M. Porcio Catone usque ad Q. Aurelium Symmachum*[2] (Zurich).

MICHEL, A. (1962) *Le 'Dialogue des orateurs' et la philosophie de Cicéron* (Études et commentaires 44; Paris).

—— (1969), 'Rhétorique, tragédie, philosophie: Sénèque et le sublime', *Giorn. It. di Fil.* 21, 245–57.

MICHLER, W. (1914), *De P. Papinio Statio M. Annaei Lucani imitatore* (diss. Breslau).

MOISY, S. VON (1971), *Untersuchungen zur Erzählweise in Statius' Thebais* (diss. Bonn).

MOLES, J. (1990), 'The Kingship Orations of Dio Chrysostom', *PILLS* 6, 296–376.

MOMIGLIANO, A. (1990), *The Classical Foundations of Modern Historiography* (Berkeley, Los Angeles, and Oxford).

MOMMSEN, TH. (1887), *Römisches Staatsrecht*[3] (Leipzig).

—— (1899), *Römisches Strafrecht* (Leipzig).

MONTEIL, P. (1964), *Beau et laid en latin. Étude de vocabulaire* (Études et commentaires 54; Paris).

MORFORD, M. P. O. (1967*a*), *The Poet Lucan: Studies in Rhetorical Epic* (Oxford).

—— (1967*b*), 'The Purpose of Lucan's Ninth Book', *Latomus* 26, 123–9.

—— (1973), 'Juvenal's Thirteenth Satire', *AJP* 94, 26–36.

—— (1977), 'Juvenal's Fifth Satire', *AJP* 98, 219–45.

—— (1990), 'Tacitus' Historical Methods in the Neronian Books of the "Annals"', *ANRW* ii. 33. 2, 1582–626.

MORTURAUX, B. (1973), *Recherches sur le "De clementia" de Sénèque* (Coll. *Latomus* 128; Brussels).

MOTTO, A. L. (1955*a*), 'Seneca on Theology', *CJ* 50, 181f.

—— (1955*b*), 'Seneca on Death and Immortality', *CJ* 50, 187–9.

—— (1970), *Seneca Sourcebook: Guide to the Thought of Lucius Annaeus Seneca* (Amsterdam).

—— and CLARK, J. R. (1970), '*Epistle* 56: Seneca's Ironic Art', *CP* 65, 102–5.

—— —— (1973), 'Dramatic Art and Irony in Seneca *De Providentia*', *AC* 42, 28–35.

MUELLER-GOLDINGEN, CHR. (1985), *Untersuchungen zu den Phönissen des Euripides* (Palingenesia 22; Stuttgart).

MUTH, R. (1976), 'Martials Spiel mit dem ludus poeticus', in A. Morpurgo Davies and W. Mied (edd.), *Studies in Greek, Italic, and Indo-European Linguistics, Offered to Leonard R. Palmer* (Innsbruck), 199–207.

NARDUCCI, E. (1979), *La provvidenza crudele. Lucano e la distruzione dei miti augustei* (Pisa).

NESSELRATH, H.-G. (1984), review of Macleod, text of Lucian, *Gnomon* 56, 577–610.

—— (1985), *Lukians Parasitendialog. Untersuchungen und Kommentar* (Untersuchungen zur antiken Literatur und Geschichte 22; Berlin and New York).

—— (1986), 'Zu den Quellen des Silius Italicus', *Hermes* 114, 203–30.

NEUE, E., and WAGENER, C. (1892–1905), *Formenlehre der lateinischen Sprache*[3] (Lepizig).

NEWMYER, S. T. (1979), *The Silvae of Statius: Structure and Theme* (*Mnemosyne* Supp. 53; Leiden).

NIEMANN, K.-H. (1975), *Die Darstellung der römischen Niederlagen in den Punica des Silius Italicus* (diss. Bonn).

NISBET, R. G. M. (1963), 'Persius', in J. P. Sullivan (ed.), *Critical Essays on Roman Literature: Satire* (London), 39–71.

—— (1978), 'Felicitas at Surrentum (Statius, Silvae II. 2)', JRS 68, 1–11.

—— (1982–4), 'Sacrilege in Egypt (Lucan IX 150–61)', Acta Antiqua 30, 309–17.

—— (1987), 'The Oak and the Axe: Symbolism in Seneca, Hercules Oetaeus 1618 ff.', in M. Whitby et al. (edd.), Homo Viator: Essays for John Bramble (Bristol and Oak Park).

NORDEN, E. (1915), Die Antike Kunstprosa, i³ (Leipzig).

OLTRAMARE, A. (1926), Les Origines de la diatribe romaine (thesis, Geneva).

O'NEIL, E. N. (1960), 'The Structure of Juvenal's Fourteenth Satire', CP 55, 251–5.

ÖNNERFORS, A. (1956), 'Pliniana', in Plinii Maioris Naturalium Historiarum studia grammatica semantica critica (Uppsala Universitets Årsskrift 1956. 6).

OTTO, A. (1890), Die Sprichwörter und sprichwörtlichen Redensarten der Römer (Leipzig).

OWEN, W. H. (1970), 'Time and Event in Seneca's Troades', WS NF 4, 118–37.

PARSONS, P. J. (1971), 'A Greek Satyricon?', BICS 18, 53–68.

PATILLON, M. (1988), La Théorie du discours chez Hermogène le rhéteur. Essai sur les structures linguistiques de la rhétorique ancienne (Paris).

PAUKSTADT, R. (1876), De Martiale Catulli imitatore (diss. Halle).

PECCHIURA, P. (1965), La figura di Catone Uticense nella letteratura latina (Turin).

PELLING, C. B. R. (1990), 'Truth and Fiction in Plutarch's Lives', in D. A. Russell (ed.), Antonine Literature (Oxford), 19–52.

PERTSCH, E. (1911), De Valerio Martiale Graecorum poetarum imitatore (diss. Berlin).

PERUTELLI, A. (1982), 'Pluralità di modelli e discontinuità narrativa: L'episodio della morte di Esone in Valerio Flacco (1, 747 sgg.)', Mat. e Disc. 7, 123–40.

PETER, H. (1901), Der Brief in der römischen Literatur (ASAW 47, Phil.-Hist. Kl. 20. 3).

—— (1906–14), Historicorum Romanorum Reliquiae² (Leipzig).

PETRONE, G. (1981), 'Il disagio della forma: la tragedia negata di Seneca', Dioniso 52, 357–67.

PIACENTINI, U. (1963), Osservazioni sulla tecnica epica di Lucano (Deutsche Akademie der Wissenschaften zu Berlin, Sekt. Altertumswissenschaft, 39; Berlin).

PIPPIDI, D. M. (1944), Autour de Tibère (Bucharest).

PLASS, P. (1988), Wit and the Writing of History: The Rhetoric of Historiography in Imperial Rome (Madison).

POWELL, J. G. F. (1988), Cicero, Cato Maior De Senectute, Edited with Introduction and Commentary (Cambridge).

PRATT, N. T. (1983), *Seneca's Drama* (Chapel Hill).

'R.M.' (1829), 'On the Epic Poetry of the Romans', *Cl. Journal* 39, 341–5; 40, 14–25.

RAABE, H. (1974), *Plurima mortis imago. Vergleichende Interpretationen zur Bildersprache Vergils* (Zetemata 59; Munich).

RAWSON, E. (1985), *Intellectual Life in the Late Roman Republic* (London).

—— (1991 (orig. 1978)), 'The Introduction of Logical Organization in Roman Prose Literature', *Roman Culture and Society: Collected Papers* (Oxford), 324–51.

REEVE, M. D. (1984), 'The Addressee of the *Laus Pisonis*', *ICS* 9. 1, 42–8.

REGENBOGEN, O. (1961 (orig. 1930)), 'Schmerz und Tod in den Tragödien Senecas', *Kleine Schriften* (Munich), 409–62.

REICHEL, M. (1990), 'Retardationstechniken in der Ilias', in W. Kullmann and M. Reichel (edd.), *Der Übergang von der Mündlichkeit zur Literatur bei den Griechen* (Tübingen), 125–51.

REITZ, C. (1985), 'Hellenistische Züge in Statius' Thebais', *WJbb* NF II, 129–34.

RICHARDS, W. J. (1964), *Gebed by Seneca, die Stoïsyn. 'n Godsdienshistoriese studie met verwysing na aanrakingspunte in die Voorsocratici* (diss. Utrecht).

RIPOSATI, B. (1983), 'La concezione religiosa di Tacito', in *Letterature comparate. Problemi e metodi. Studi in onore di Ettore Paratore* (Bologna), ii. 699–706.

RIST, J. M. (1969), *Stoic Philosophy* (Cambridge).

ROCHEBLAVE, S. (1890), *De M. Fabio Quintiliano L. Annaei Senecæ judice* (diss. Paris).

ROLLAND, E. (1906), *De l'influence de Sénèque le père et des rhéteurs sur Sénèque le philosophe* (Gand).

ROMANO, A. C. (1979), *Irony in Juvenal* (Altertumswissenschaftliche Texte und Studien 7; Hildesheim and New York).

ROSENMEYER, T. G. (1989), *Senecan Drama and Stoic Cosmology* (Berkeley, Los Angeles, and London).

ROSNER-SIEGEL, J. A. (1983), 'The Oak and the Lightning: Lucan, *Bellum Civile* I. 135–157', *Athenaeum* NS 61, 165–77.

RUDD, N. J. (1976), *Lines of Enquiry: Studies in Latin Poetry* (Cambridge).

—— (1986), *Themes in Roman Satire* (London).

RUSSELL, D. A. F. M., (1964), '*Longinus*', *On the Sublime*, edited with introduction and commentary (Oxford).

—— (1974), 'Seneca's Letters to Lucilius', in C. D. N. Costa (ed.), *Seneca* (London), 70–95.

—— (1981a), *Criticism in Antiquity* (London).

—— (1981b), 'Longinus Revisited', *Mnemosyne* 4th ser. 34, 72–86.

—— (1989), *The Place of Poetry in Ancient Literature: A Valedictory Lecture* (Oxford).

RUTHERFORD, R. B. (1989), *The Meditations of Marcus Aurelius: A Study* (Oxford).

RUTZ, W. (1960), 'Amor mortis bei Lucan', *Hermes* 88, 462–75.

—— (1970 (orig. 1950)), 'Studien zur Kompositionskunst und zur epischen Technik Lucans', in W. Rutz (ed.), *Lucan* (WdF 225; Darmstadt), 160–216.

RYBERG, I. S. (1942), 'Tacitus' Art of Innuendo', *TAPA* 73, 383–404.

SALEMME, C. (1976) *Marziale e la "poetica" degli oggetti* (Naples).

SCARPAT, G. (1977), *Il pensiero religioso di Seneca e l'ambiente ebraico e cristiano* (Brescia).

SCHENDEL, H. (1908), *Quibus auctoribus L. Annaeus Seneca in rebus patriis usus sit* (diss. Greifswald).

SCHENKEVELD, D. M. (1964), *Studies in Demetrius* On Style (Amsterdam).

SCHETTER, W. (1960), *Untersuchungen zur epischen Kunst des Statius* (Klassisch-Philologische Studien 20; Wiesbaden).

—— (1972 (orig. 1965)) 'Zum Aufbau von Senecas Troerinnen', in E. Lefèvre (ed.), *Senecas Tragödien* (WdF 310; Darmstadt), 230–71.

—— (1978), *Das römische Epos* (Athenaion Studientexte 4; Wiesbaden).

SCHIROLI, M. G. CAVALCA (1981), *Lucio Anneo Seneca, De Tranquillitate Animi* (Bologna).

SCHMID, W. (1906), 'Bericht über die Literatur aus den Jahren 1901–1904 zur zweiten Sophistik', *Burs. Jahresber.* 129, 220–99.

SCHNEIDER, B. (1983), 'Die Stellung des zehnten Buches im Gesamtplan der Institutio oratoria des Quintilian', *WS* NF 17, 109–25.

SCHNEPF, H. (1970 (orig. 1953)), 'Untersuchungen zur Darstellungskunst Lucans im 8. Buch der Pharsalia', in W. Rutz (ed.), *Lucan* (WdF 235; Darmstadt), 380–406.

SCHOLZ, U. W. (1986), 'Persius', in J. Adamietz (ed.), *Die römische Satire* (Darmstadt), 179–230.

SCHÖNBERGER, J. K. (1951), 'Zum Stil des Petronius', *Glotta* 31, 20–8.

SCHÖNBERGER, O. (1965) 'Zum Weltbild der drei Epiker nach Lucan', *Helikon* 5, 123–45.

SCHREMPP, O. (1964), *Prophezeiung und Rückschau in Lucans "Bellum civile"* (diss. Zurich).

SCHUNCK, P. (1964), 'Studien zur Darstellung des Endes von Galba, Otho und Vitellius in den Historien von Tacitus', *SO* 39, 38–82.

SCOTT, I. G. (1927), 'The Grand Style in the Satires of Juvenal', *Smith College Classical Studies* 8.

SCOTT, W. T. (1968), *Religion and Philosophy in the History of Tacitus* (Papers and Monographs of the American Academy in Rome 22).

SEGAL, C. P. (1984), 'Senecan Baroque: The Death of Hippolytus in Seneca, Ovid, and Euripides', *TAPA* 114, 311–25.

—— (1986), *Language and Desire in Seneca's* Phaedra (Princeton).

SEIDENSTICKER, B. (1969), *Die Gesprächsverdichtung in den Tragödien Senecas* (Heidelberg).

SEIF, K. PH. (1973), *Die Claudiusbücher in den Annalen des Tacitus* (diss. Mainz).

SEILER, H. G. (1936), *Die Masse bei Tacitus* (Erlangen).

SEITZ, K. (1965), 'Der pathetische Erzählstil Lucans', *Hermes* 93, 205–32.

SERBAT, G. (1973), 'La Référence comme indice de distance dans l'énoncé de Pline l'Ancien', *RPh* 3ᵉ sér, 47, 38–49.

SETAIOLI, A. (1985), '*Seneca e lo stile*', *ANRW* ii. 32. 2, 776–858.

SHACKLETON BAILEY, D. R. (1952), 'Echoes of Propertius', *Mnemosyne* 4th ser. 5, 307–33.

—— (1956), 'Maniliana', *CQ* NS 6, 81–6.

—— (1959), 'Siliana', *CQ* NS 9, 173–80.

—— (1977), 'On Valerius Flaccus', *HSCP* 81, 199–215.

—— (1979), 'Notes on Seneca's *Quaestiones Naturales*', *CQ* NS 29, 448–56.

—— (1982), 'On Lucan', *PCPS* NS 28, 91–100.

SHARPLES, R. W. (1983), *Alexander of Aphrodisias On Fate: Text, Translation and Commentary* (London).

SHELTON, J.-A. (1978), *Seneca's Hercules Furens: Theme, Structure and Style* (Hypomnemata 50; Göttingen).

SHELTON, J. E. (1974–5), 'The Storm Scene in Valerius Flaccus', *CJ* 70. 2, 14–22.

SHERWIN-WHITE, A. N. (1969), 'Pliny, the Man and his Letters', *G&R* 2nd ser. 16, 76–99.

SHOCHAT, Y. (1981), 'Tacitus' Attitude to Otho', *Latomus* 40, 365–75.

SIEDSCHLAG, E. (1977), *Zur Form von Martials Epigrammen* (Berlin).

SLATER, N. W. (1990), *Reading Petronius* (Baltimore and London).

SMITH, W. S. (1989), 'Heroic Models for the Sordid Present: Juvenal's View of Tragedy', *ANRW* ii. 33. 1, 811–23.

STEGEMANN, W. (1913), *De Iuvenalis Dispositione* (diss. Leipzig).

STEIN, J. P. (1970), 'The Unity and Scope of Juvenal's Fourteenth Satire', *CP* 65, 34–6.

STEINMETZ, P. (1964), 'Gattungen und Epochen der griechischen Literatur in der Sicht Quintilians', *Hermes* 92, 454–66.

—— (1982), *Untersuchungen zur röm. Lit. des zweiten Jahrhunderts n. Chr. Geburt* (Palingenesia 16; Stuttgart).

STINTON, T. C. W. (1991 (orig. 1965)), 'Euripides and the Judgement of Paris', *Collected Papers on Greek Tragedy* (Oxford), 17–75.

STOSCH, GRÄFIN VON (1968), *Untersuchungen zu den Leichenspielen in der Thebais des P. Papinius Statius* (diss. Tübingen).

STRAND, J. (1972), *Notes on Valerius Flaccus' Argonautica* (Studia Graeca et Latina Gothoburgensia 31; Göteborg).

STRASBURGER, H. (1982 (orig. 1968)), 'Zur Sage von der Gründung Roms', *Studien zur Alten Geschichte* (Hildesheim and New York), ii. 1017–55.

STREIFINGER, J. (1892), *Der Stil des Satirikers Juvenalis* (Prog. Regensburg).

STUBE, H. (1933), *Die Verseinlagen im Petron* (*Philologus* Supp. 25. II; Leipzig).

SULLIVAN, J. P. (1968), *The* Satyricon *of Petronius: A Literary Study* (London).

SUMMERS, W. C. (1894), *A Study of the Argonautica of Valerius Flaccus* (Cambridge).

—— (1910), *Select Letters of Seneca* (London).

SUSSMANN, L. A. (1978), *The Elder Seneca* (*Mnemosyne* Supp. 51; Leiden).

SUTTON, D. F. (1986), *Seneca on the Stage* (*Mnemosyne* Supp. 96; Leiden).

SYME, R. (1939), *The Roman Revolution* (Oxford).

—— (1958), *Tacitus* (Oxford).

—— (1970), *Ten Studies in Tacitus* (Oxford).

—— (1979 (orig. 1968)), 'People in Pliny', *Roman Papers*, ii (Oxford), 649–723.

—— (1980), *Some Arval Brethren* (Oxford).

—— (1986), *The Augustan Aristocracy* (Oxford).

—— (1988*a* (orig. 1983)), 'Eight Consuls from Patavium', *Roman Papers*, iv (Oxford), 371–96.

—— (1988*b* (orig. 1985)), 'Correspondents of Pliny', *Roman Papers*, v (Oxford), 440–77.

SYNDIKUS, H. P. (1958), *Lucans Gedicht vom Bürgerkrieg (Untersuchungen zur epischen Technik und zu den Grundlagen des Werkes)* (diss. Munich).

SZELEST, H. (1972), 'Mythologie und ihre Rolle in den "Silvae" des Statius', *Eos* 60, 309–17.

—— (1986), 'Martial—eigentlicher Schöpfer und hervorragendster Vertreter des römischen Epigramms', *ANRW* ii. 32. 4, 2563–623.

TADIC-GILLOTEAUX, N. (1963), 'Sénèque en face au suicide', *AC* 32, 541–51.

TANDOI, V. (1965–6), 'Morituri verba Catonis', *Maia* 17, 315–39; 18, 20–41.

—— (1985), 'Per la comprensione del *De Bello Germanico* staziano muovendo dalla parodia di Giovenale', in V. Tandoi (ed.), *Disiecti membra poetae. Studi di poesia latina in frammenti* (Foggia), 223–4.

TARRANT, R. J. (1976, *Seneca: Agamemnon, Edited with a Commentary* (Cambridge).

—— (1985), *Seneca's Thyestes, Edited with Introduction and Commentary* (APA Textbook Series II; Atlanta).

THEILER, W. (1966 (orig. 1946)), 'Tacitus und die antike Schicksalslehre', *Forschungen zum Neuplatonismus* (Quellen und Studien zur Geschichte der Philosophie 10; Berlin), 46–103.

—— (1982), *Poseidonios. Die Fragmente* (Texte und Kommentare 10; Berlin and New York).

THOMAS, R. F. (1982), *Lands and Peoples in Roman Poetry: The Ethnographical Tradition* (*PCPS* Supp. 7).

THOMPSON, D. W. A. (1947), *A Glossary of Greek Fishes* (London).

TIGERSTEDT, E. N. (1965–78), *The Legend of Sparta in Classical Antiquity* (Uppsala).

TIMPANARO, S. (1978 (orig. 1951)), '*Atlas cum compare gibbo* (Marziale VI 77)', *Contributi di filologia e di storia della lingua latina* (Rome), 333–43.

TOSI, C. FACCHINI (1977), 'Giovenale (6, 634–644) di fronte a Persio (5, 1–20) sul tono *grandis* riguardo alla satira', *Prometheus* 3, 241–54.

TOWNEND, G. B. (1960), 'The Sources of the Greek in Suetonius', *Hermes* 88, 98–120.

——(1973), 'The Literary Substrata to Juvenal's Satires', *JRS* 63, 148–60.

TRAINA, A. (1974), *Lo stilo 'drammatico' del filosofo Seneca* (Bologna).

TRÄNKLE, H. (1990), *Appendix Tibulliana, herausgegeben und kommentiert* (Berlin and New York).

TRAUB, H. W. (1955), 'Pliny's Treatment of History in Epistolary Form', *TAPA* 86, 213–32.

TRESCH, J. (1965), *Die Nerobücher in den Annalen des Tacitus: Tradition und Leistung* (Heidelberg).

TREVES, P. (1970), 'Il giorno della morte di Seneca', in *Studia Florentina Alexandro Ronconi sexagenario oblata* (Rome), 507–24.

TRISOGLIO, F. (1973), *Opere di Plinio Cecilio Secondo* (Turin).

UHL, A. (1899), *Quaestiones criticae in L. Annaei Senecae Dialogos* (diss. Strasburg).

VAN DAM, H.-J. (1984), *P. Papinius Statius, Silvae Book II: A Commentary* (*Mnemosyne* Supp. 82; Leiden).

VEITH, G. (1920), *Der Feldzug von Dyrrachium zwischen Caesar und Pompejus* (Vienna).

VENINI, P. (1961), 'Studi sulla Tebaide di Stazio. La composizione', *RIL* 95, 55–88.

VERBRUGGHE, G. P. (1989). 'On the Meaning of *Annales*, on the Meaning of Annalist', *Philologus* 133, 192–330.

VERTRAETE, B. C. (1983), '*Originality and Mannerism in Statius' Use of Myth in the Silvae*', *AC* 52, 195–205.

VESSEY, D. W. T. C. (1972), 'Aspects of Statius' *Epithalamium*', *Mnemosyne* 4th ser. 25, 172–87.

——(1972–3), 'The Myth of Falernus in Silius, *Punica* 7', *CJ* 68, 240–6.

——(1973), *Statius and the Thebaid* (Cambridge).

——(1974), 'Silius Italicus on the Fall of Saguntum', *CP* 69, 28–36.

——(1982), 'Flavian Epic', in E. J. Kenney and W. V. Clausen (edd.), *Cambridge History of Classical Literature*, ii. *Latin Literature* (Cambridge), 558–96.

——(1983), '*Mediis discumbere in astris*: Statius, *Silvae*, IV, 2', *AC* 52, 206–20.

——(1986a), 'Transience Preserved: Style and Theme in Statius' 'Silvae', *ANRW* ii. 32. 5, 2794–802.

—— (1986*b*), '*Pierius menti calor incidit*: Statius' Epic Style', *ANRW* ii. 32. 5, 2965–3019.

VEYNE, P. (1990), 'La Providence stoïcienne intervient-elle dans l'Histoire?', *Latomus* 49, 553–74.

VINSON, M. P. (1989), 'Domitia Longina, Julia Titi and the Literary Tradition', *Historia* 38, 431–50.

VÖGLER, G. (1968), 'Das neunte Buch innerhalb der Pharsalia des Lucan und die Frage der Vollendung des Epos', *Philologus* 112, 222–68.

VOSS, B. R. (1963), *Der pointierte Stil des Tacitus*² (Orbis Antiquus 19, Münster).

WAIBLINGER, F. P. (1977), *Senecas Naturales Quaestiones. Griechische Wissenschaft und römische Form* (Zetemata 70; Munich).

WALKER, B. (1968), *The Annals of Tacitus: A Study in the Writing of History*³ (Manchester).

WALLACE-HADRILL, A. (1983), *Suetonius* (London).

—— (1990), 'Pliny the Elder and Man's Unnatural History', *G&R* 2nd ser. 37, 80–96.

WALSH, P. G. (1968), 'Eumolpus, the *Halosis Troiae* and the *De Bello Civili*', *CP* 63, 208–12.

WANKE, CHR. (1964), *Seneca Lucan Corneille. Studien zum Manierismus der römischen Kaiserzeit und der französischen Klassik* (Studia Romanica 6; Heidelberg).

WASZINK, J. H. (1963), 'Das Einleitungsgedicht des Persius', *WS* 76, 78–91.

WATT, W. S. (1984), 'Notes on Latin Epic Poetry', *BICS* 31, 153–70.

WEAVER, P. R. C. (1972), *Familia Caesaris: A Social Study of the Emperor's Freedmen and Slaves* (Cambridge).

WEBER (1895), *De Senecae philosophi dicendi genere Bioneo* (diss. Marburg).

WELLESLEY, K. (1971), 'A Major Crux in Tacitus: *Histories* II, 40', *JRS* 61, 28–51.

WEST, M. L. (1983), *The Orphic Poems* (Oxford).

WHITAKER, R. (1983), *Myth and Personal Experience in Roman Love-Elegy* (Hypomnemata 76; Göttingen).

WHITEHEAD, D. (1979), 'Tacitus and the Loaded Alternative', *Latomus* 38, 474–95.

WIESEN, D. S. (1973), 'Juvenal and the Intellectuals', *Hermes* 101, 464–83.

—— (1989), 'The Verbal Basis of Juvenal's Satiric Vision', *ANRW* ii. 33. 1, 708–33.

WILLE, G. (1983), *Der Aufbau der Werke des Tacitus* (Heuremata 9; Amsterdam).

WILLIAMS, G. (1978), *Change and Decline: Roman Literature in the Early Empire* (Berkeley, Los Angeles, and London).

350   *Bibliography*

WILSON, M. (1988), 'Seneca's Epistles to Lucilius: A Revaluation', in A. J. Boyle (ed.), *The Imperial Muse, Ramus Essays on Roman Literature of the Empire: To Juvenal through Ovid* (Victoria), 102–21.

WINKLER, M. M. (1983), *The Persona in Three Satires of Juvenal* (Altertumswissenschaftliche Texte und Studien 10; Munich).

WINTERBOTTOM, M. (1983), 'Quintilian and Declamation', in *Hommages à Jean Cousin* (Paris), 225–35.

—— (1984), *The Minor Declamations ascribed to Quintilian: Edited with Commentary* (Texte und Kommentare 13; Berlin and New York).

WIRTH, H. (1900), *De Vergili apud Senecam philosophum usu* (diss. Freiburg).

WISEMAN, T. P. (1979), *Clio's Cosmetics: Three Studies in Graeco-Roman Literature* (Leicester).

—— (1987), *Roman Studies Literary and Historical* (Liverpool).

WÖLFFIN, E. (1867), 'Ein verkannter gräcismus bei Tacitus', *Philologus* 24, 115–23.

WOLF, J. G. (1988), *Das Senatusconsultum Silianum und die Senatsrede des C. Cassius Longinus aus dem Jahre 61 n. Chr.* (SHAW 1988. 2).

WOOD, J. R. (1980), 'The Myth of Tages', *Latomus* 39, 325–44.

WOODMAN, A. (1988), *Rhetoric in Classical Historiography* (London and Sydney).

—— (1989), 'Tacitus' Obituary of Tiberius', *CQ* NS 39, 197–205.

WORTHEN, T. (1988), 'The Idea of "Sky" in Archaic Greek Poetry', *Glotta* 66, 1–19.

WRIGHT, J. R. G. (1974), 'Form and Content in the *Moral Essays*', in C. D. N. Costa (ed.), *Seneca* (London).

WUENSCH, M. (1930), *Lucan-Interpretationen* (diss. Kiel).

ZEITLIN, F. (1971a), 'Petronius as Paradox: Anarchy and Artistic Integrity', *TAPA* 102, 631–84.

—— (1971b), 'Romanus Petronius: A Study of the *Troiae Halosis* and the *Bellum Civile*', *Latomus* 30, 56–82.

ZIEGLER, K. (1952), 'Polybios', *RE* xxi. 2, 1440–1578.

ZWIERLEIN, O. (1966), *Die Rezitationsdramen Senecas. Mit einem kritisch-exegetischen Anhang* (Beiträge zur Kl. Philol. 20; Meisenheim am Glan).

—— (1977), 'Weiteres zum Seneca Tragicus (I)' *WJbb* NF 3, 149–77.

—— (1984a) *Prolegomena zu einer kritischen Ausgabe der Tragödien Senecas* (AAWM 1983. 3).

—— (1984b) *Senecas Hercules im Lichte kaiserzeitlicher und spätantiker Dichtung* (AAWM 1984. 6).

—— (1986), 'Lucans Caesar in Troja', *Hermes* 114, 460–78.

—— (1987), *Senecas Phaedra und ihre Vorbilder* (AAWM 1987. 5).

—— (1988), 'Statius, Lucan, Curtius Rufus und das hellenistiche Epos', *RhM* NF 131, 67–84.

I. INDEX OF PASSAGES DISCUSSED

II. GENERAL INDEX

'Seneca' normally refers to the prose works, 'Statius' to the epics, unless 'tragedies' or
'*Silvae*' is added.

a (exclamation) 75 n. 73
Alcaeus 8
Apollonius Rhodius 288 n. 1
    see also Valerius Flaccus
Appian:
    and Lucan 316 n. 47
    and Seneca 275
Aristotle on hyperbole III
author:
    and addressee 133 (Pliny); 18, 44,
        273 f. (Seneca); 95 f. (Statius,
        Silvae); etc.
    authority 103, 230 (Seneca); 56, 105
        (Tacitus); etc.
    in critics 22
    formal withdrawal of 10
        (dialogue-form), 21 (Petronius)
    and morality 91 f., 94
    obtrudes 64 (Seneca, tragedies); 74, 75
        (Statius); 83, 84, 86, 213, 264 f.,
        etc.; *see also* narrator
    relation to narrator 66 (Lucan)
    relation to speaker 34 (Juvenal)
    self-presentation 27 f. (Persius); 108 f.
        (Pliny); 42 (Quintilian); 79 (Elder
        Seneca); 75, 174 n. 47 (Statius);
        35–7, 135 (Statius, *Silvae*)
    intellectual 240 (Pliny); 40, 42–5
        (Seneca); 40, 50–6, 240 (Tacitus)
    self-critical 272 f. (Quintilian); 44 f.
        (Seneca)

bellus 25
bizarreness 35, 69, 168 f., etc. (Lucan);
    20 (Petronius); 64 f. (Seneca,
    tragedies); 71 f., 90, 119, 289, 291
    (Silius); 74, 301 (Statius); 297
    (Valerius)

Callimachus 23 f., 28 n. 53
Cato 165 f., 170 (Lucan); 48 f., 227,
    273–6 (Seneca)
Catullus, *see* Martial
characters, changing responses to 165–7,
    321 f. (Lucan); 173 f. (Statius)

Cicero:
    as glorious figure 96, 256 n. 1
    and Quintilian 9, 109
    and Seneca 44 n. 12
    and sublimity 14
    and Tacitus 57, 107
    used 96 (Martial)
Claudius 158, 263
close
    infringing 29, 32 (Juvenal)
    not climactic 174 n. 47 (Statius)
    with speech 159 f.
    surprises with 157 (Quintilian); 131
        (Seneca); etc.
    see also Seneca the Younger (prose and
        tragedies)
critics, ancient on hyperbole III–13,
    127 f.
    limitations on value 4 f., 39, 112 f.
Curtius Rufus 51 n. 27, 104 n. 54

death:
    after-life 300 (Lucan); 159, 273 n. 29,
        286 n. 51 (Seneca); 300 (Valerius)
    brings seriousness and grandeur to
        height 185, 256
    chthonic ritual 294
    fear of underworld 103 f.
    and freedom 138 n. 49 (Juvenal); 270
        (Pliny); 16, 138 n. 49, 275, 282 f.
        (Seneca); 306 (Statius); 268
        (Tacitus); cf. 319 n. 51
    generality and particularity in
        treatments of 294–7, 301, 305 f.,
        325
    and gods 228 (Seneca); 200 (Statius)
    heroic 154 f. (Seneca); Chs. 8 and 9;
        twisted 281
    ingenuity with 288 (epic); 289 (Silius);
        298 (Valerius)
    language of exploited 234 f. (Seneca)
    life as paradoxically undesirable 292,
        298, 302; as death 283
    means of suicide 138 n. 49, 228 n. 9

failure, nobility in 86 f., 166 (Lucan);
   163 n. 30 (Seneca, tragedies); 71 f.
   (Silius); 14 (poetry); Chs. 8 and 9
Fate 197, 200, 251, 302, 319
Fortune 19, 170, 247 n. 37, 251, 274 f.,
   324
freedom 19 (Seneca); 163 f. (Seneca,
   tragedies); 11 (Tacitus, *Dialogus*)
   see also death
Furies 31 (Juvenal); 64, 214 (Seneca,
   tragedies); 171, 176 (Statius)

Galba 52
genre:
   civil war in Lucan and Tacitus 132
   contrast of prose with verse expression
     277 f.
   contrast of Seneca and history 274
   death brings together 185, 256; 268
     (history, letters); 264 (history,
     philosophy)
   differences in treatment of dead 61
     n. 43
   differences in handling of author 61 f.,
     268 f., 271
   can be related to life 10 f., 18,
     240 f.
   and relations of wit 78, 79 f.
     (differences felt); 96 f. (epigram,
     epic); 97 (Martial, Silius); 98,
     100 f. (satire, epic); 101 (Seneca,
     'high' poetry); 129 (Seneca,
     Ovid); 107 (Tacitus' history,
     Dialogus); 107 (Tacitus, Pliny)
   seen in single author 133 (Pliny);
     62 f., 127, 130, 187 (Seneca,
     prose and verse); 36 f., 95
     (Statius, epics and *Silvae*); 107,
     268 (Tacitus); cf. 240 n. 26 (Livy,
     Posidonius)
   epic and elegy 35, 205 f.
   epic and history (style) 299
   epic and *Silvae* 134
   excursion treated differently in poetry
     and prose 149; 165 (Lucan)
   falling beneath 8 f., 39
   gods differentiate genres 184 f., 222 f.,
     239 f., 240 f., 247 n. 37
   hierarchy of 8, 10, 16 f., 18, 23 f., 29,
     34–6, 38, 79, 80
   history and declamation 58 n. 38
     and oratory 12, 107, 241
   relation to poetry 6

letters and history 13
Lucan and genre 66 f., 250 f., 314 f.
   and history 21, 68, 113, 323
   play with prose manner 168
   luxury in different genres 33
     (Juvenal); 85 f. (Lucan); 98
     (Persius); 46, 60, 229, 231
     (Seneca); 75 (Statius); 59–61
     (Tacitus)
   oratory and poetry 14 f.
   philosophy and history 60
   'play' and genre 24 (Martial); 15
     (Pliny); 36 (Statius, *Silvae*); cf.
     nugae 28 (Persius)
   play on genre 29 f. (Juvenal); 20 f.
     (Petronius); 12–14 (Pliny); 11
     (Tacitus, *Dialogus*)
   related manners with different relation
     to truth 239 (poetry, Seneca)
   rivalry between genres 5, 10, 15 f.,
     and Ch. 1 *passim*; 48 (Seneca,
     history); 129 (Seneca, Ovid)
   satire and epic 27, 29, 30 f., 75, 181,
     288 n. 1
     and tragedy 28, 29 f.
   and statements on genre 5, 10, 15, 20,
     etc.
   storms in different genres 130, 142
   see also prose *and under individual genres*
gods (God):
   allegorical? 177 n. 52, 187, 189 f., 209
   amours 187, 198 f.
   anger of 201 (epic); 247, 249 (Tacitus)
     with 251 (Lucan); 259 (Tacitus)
   aquatic 37, 202 n. 4
   dark visions of 63, 208–16 (Seneca,
     tragedies); 196–8 (Statius); 247 f.
     (Tacitus); toyed with 226 f.
     (Seneca)
   divine society 190, 192, 198, 200, 211,
     213
   divinity of emperors 254 (Lucan); 108,
     133 f. (Pliny); 134–6 (Statius,
     Silvae)
   gate of heaven 213 n. 45
   impiety 118
   and men 72 (Silius); 224–39 (Seneca);
     207–21 (mythological poetry)
   metonymy 197 (Statius); 194 f.
     (Valerius)
   how personal in Seneca 223, 228,
     232 f., 237
   personification toyed with 216 f.

Lucan (*cont.*)

Pompey 35, 86 f., 165–7, 315–24
Quintilian on 9
and reality 66–9
and Seneca 49 n. 25, 251
and Seneca, tragedies 252
and Silius 321
and Statius 170
Statius, *Silvae*, on 35 f.
and Stoicism 67, 251
structure in 164–70, 300, 314–24, 319 f.
and Tacitus 321
wit in 85–8
see also genre, reality
Lucilius 29
Lucretius 40 n. 2, 200, 326
lyric, Greek 8

Manilius, date of 82 n. 8
nature of wit 81 f.
Mars 211 (Seneca, tragedies); 196–201 (Statius); 191–5 (Valerius)
Martial:
art in 24 f.
bulk of poem not merely 'waiting' 139, 141
and Catullus 23, 24 n. 42, 26, 140
confrontation 24–7
down-to-earth persona 25–7, 97
extravagance in 139–41
genre in 23–7
Greek models 24, 25
imagination in 140 f.
importance of published book 147
and Juvenal 32
noble death in 256 n. 1, 257 n. 3
and Silius 23
supposed moral purpose 24
varied handling of elegiac couplet 139 f.
wit in 96 f.
Medea 30 (Juvenal); 63–5 (Seneca, tragedies); 70 f. (Valerius)

names as extremes 64, 293, 307 f.
third-person use 49, 275 (Seneca); 212 f. (Seneca, tragedies); 202 f., 293 f. (Silius); 260 (Tacitus); 119, 193 (Valerius)
in address 215 (Seneca, tragedies)
narrative, *see* death: narrations of death

narrator, outbursts from 66, 68 f., 73, 115 f., 165, 166 f., 251–4, 314–18 (Lucan); 66, 314 f. (Lucan and others); 71 f. (Silius); 73, 75 f., 305 f. (Statius); 69 f. (Valerius)
design in 314 f. (Lucan)
rarer in Valerius 69
see also Lucan, Silius
Nero:
in Epictetus 158 n. 20
and Lucan 66, 314 n. 44
in Pliny the Elder 109
in Tacitus 58, 59 f., 106 n. 56, 157–9, 246–9, 265–8

oratory, *see* genre
Otho 59, 257–61
Ovid:
alleged indiscipline 9, 81
and declamation 78, 148
disruption in 37 n. 71
in Martial 24
Ovidian play 68 (Lucan); 64 (Seneca, tragedies); 199 (Statius)
play with own work 24 n. 42
Quintilian on 9
relation to this 'high' poetry 62
Seneca the Elder on 81
Seneca on 129, 187
and structure 148, 179
used 288 (epic); 33 n. 63 (Juvenal); 252 (Lucan); 23 n. 41, 24 n. 42 (Martial); 27 n. 51 (Persius); 236 n. 22 (Seneca); 126 n. 30 (Seneca, tragedies and prose); 308, 313 (Seneca, tragedies); 72 (Silius); 121–3, 174 n. 47, 179, 198 n. 13, 218 n. 53 (Statius); 35 (Statius, *Silvae*)
and Valerius 298; 300 n. 23
wit 81, 129

pathos 66, 68, 317, 324 (Lucan); 270 (Pliny); 271–3 (Quintilian); 311 f. (Seneca, tragedies); 289 n. 2, 292 (Silius); 73, 121, 123, 178 (Statius); 53 (Tacitus); 297, 299 (Valerius)
and heroism 308 f., 312 (Seneca, tragedies)
modified 291 (Silius)
Persius:
comedy in 27 f.
Cornutus 28